STAR PROJECT

CHIRO 치로

1

BAEK HYE-KYOUNG

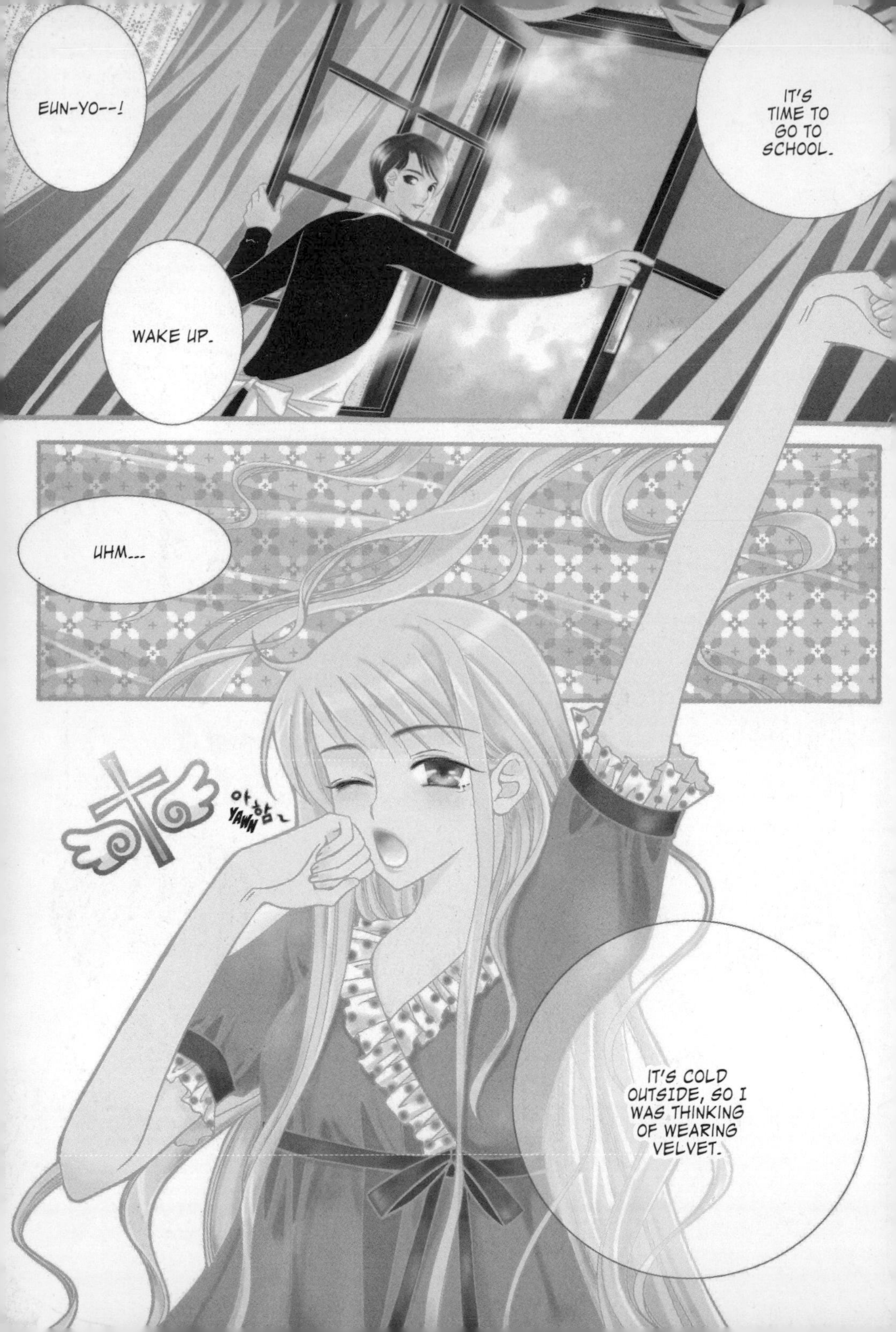
EUN-YO--!
WAKE UP.
IT'S TIME TO GO TO SCHOOL.
UHM...
아함~
YAWN
IT'S COLD OUTSIDE, SO I WAS THINKING OF WEARING VELVET.

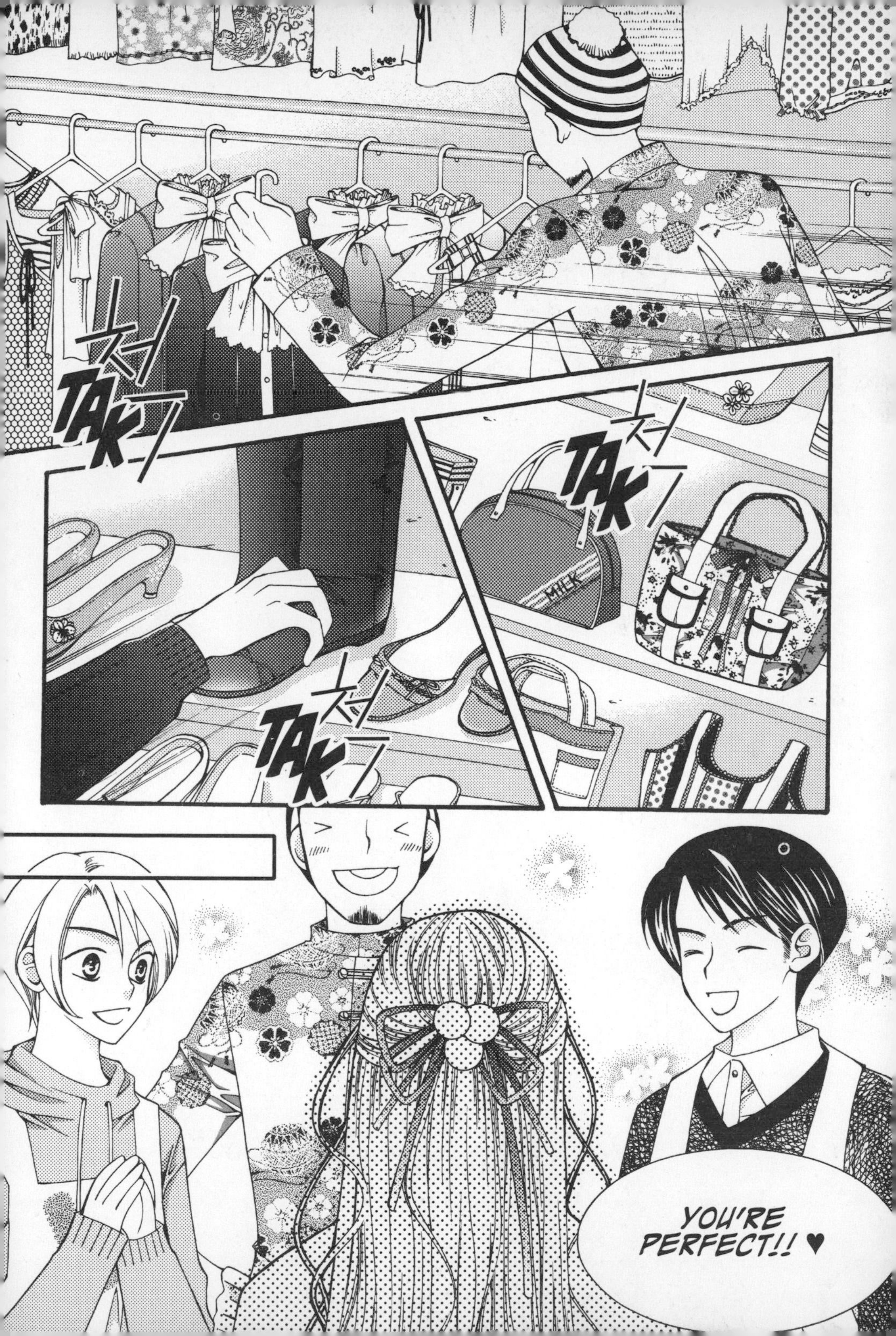
TAK
TAK
TAK
YOU'RE PERFECT!! ♥

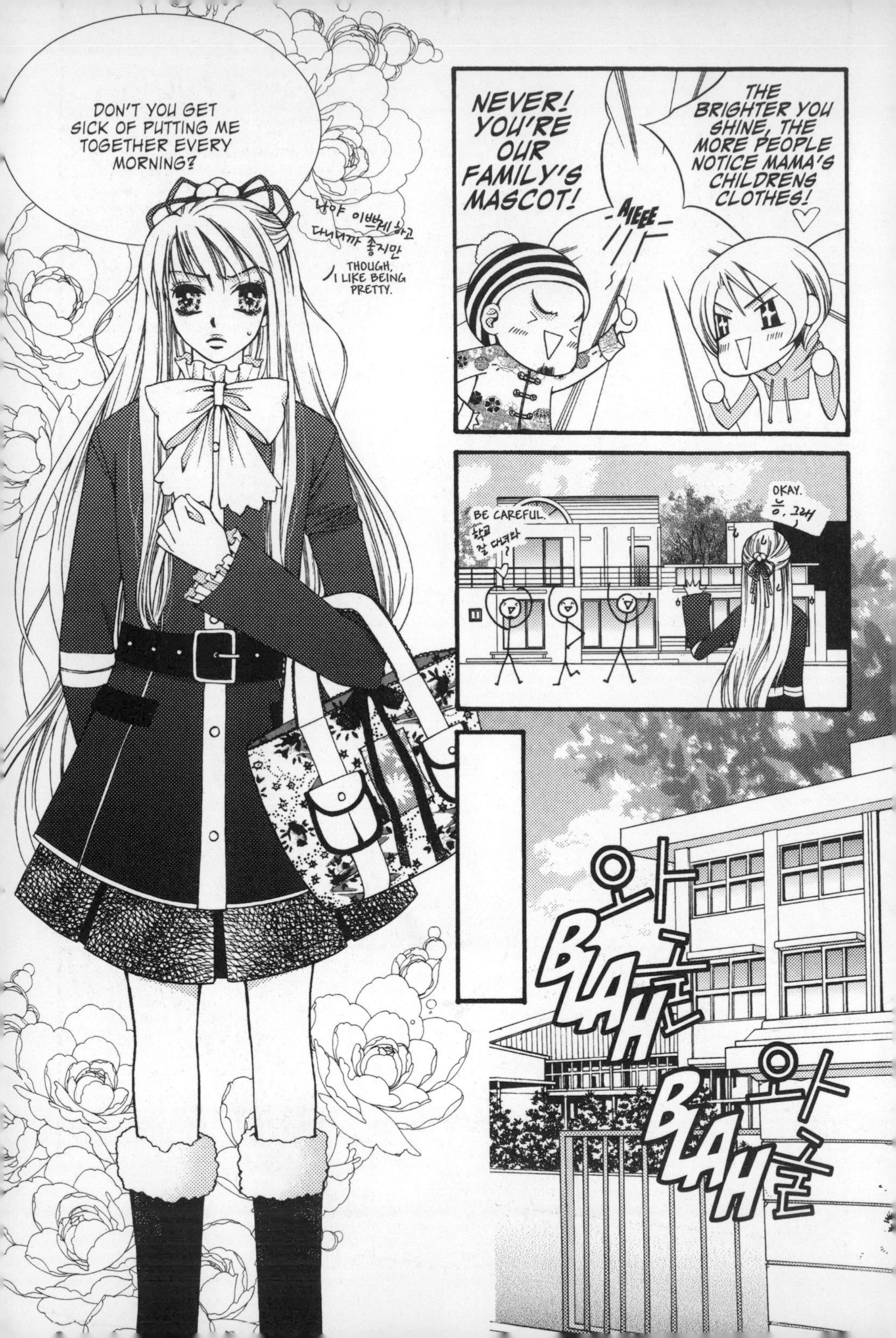
DON'T YOU GET SICK OF PUTTING ME TOGETHER EVERY MORNING?
나야 이쁘게 하고 다니니까 좋지만
THOUGH, I LIKE BEING PRETTY.
NEVER! YOU'RE OUR FAMILY'S MASCOT!
-AIEEE-
THE BRIGHTER YOU SHINE, THE MORE PEOPLE NOTICE MAMA'S CHILDRENS CLOTHES!
BE CAREFUL.
학교 잘 다녀라~
OKAY.
응, 그래
BLAH 와글
BLAH 와글

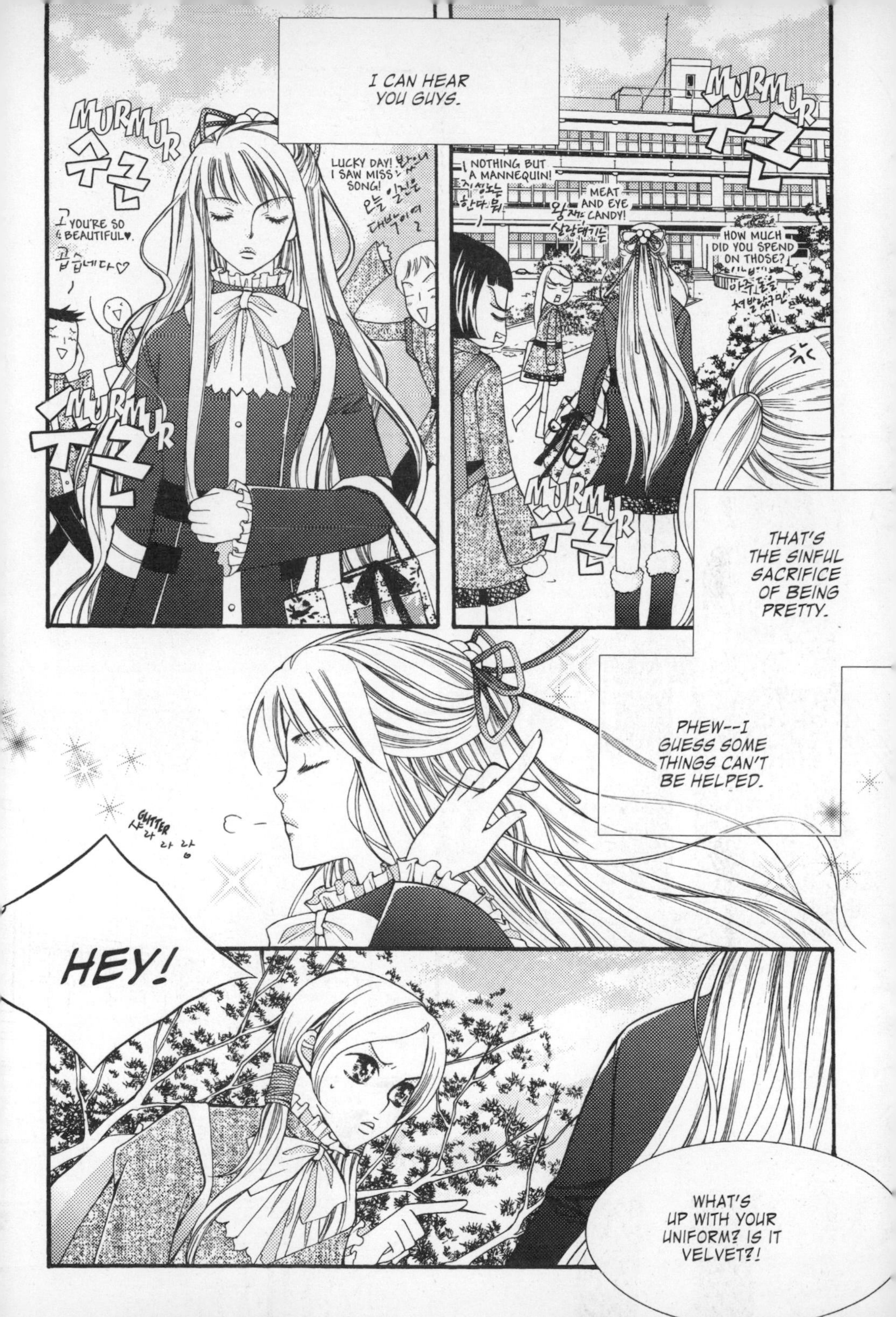

I CAN HEAR YOU GUYS.
MURMUR
YOU'RE SO BEAUTIFUL♥.
LUCKY DAY! I SAW MISS SONG!
MURMUR
MURMUR
I NOTHING BUT A MANNEQUIN!
MEAT AND EYE CANDY!
HOW MUCH DID YOU SPEND ON THOSE?
MURMUR
THAT'S THE SINFUL SACRIFICE OF BEING PRETTY.
PHEW--I GUESS SOME THINGS CAN'T BE HELPED.
GLITTER
HEY!
WHAT'S UP WITH YOUR UNIFORM? IS IT VELVET?!

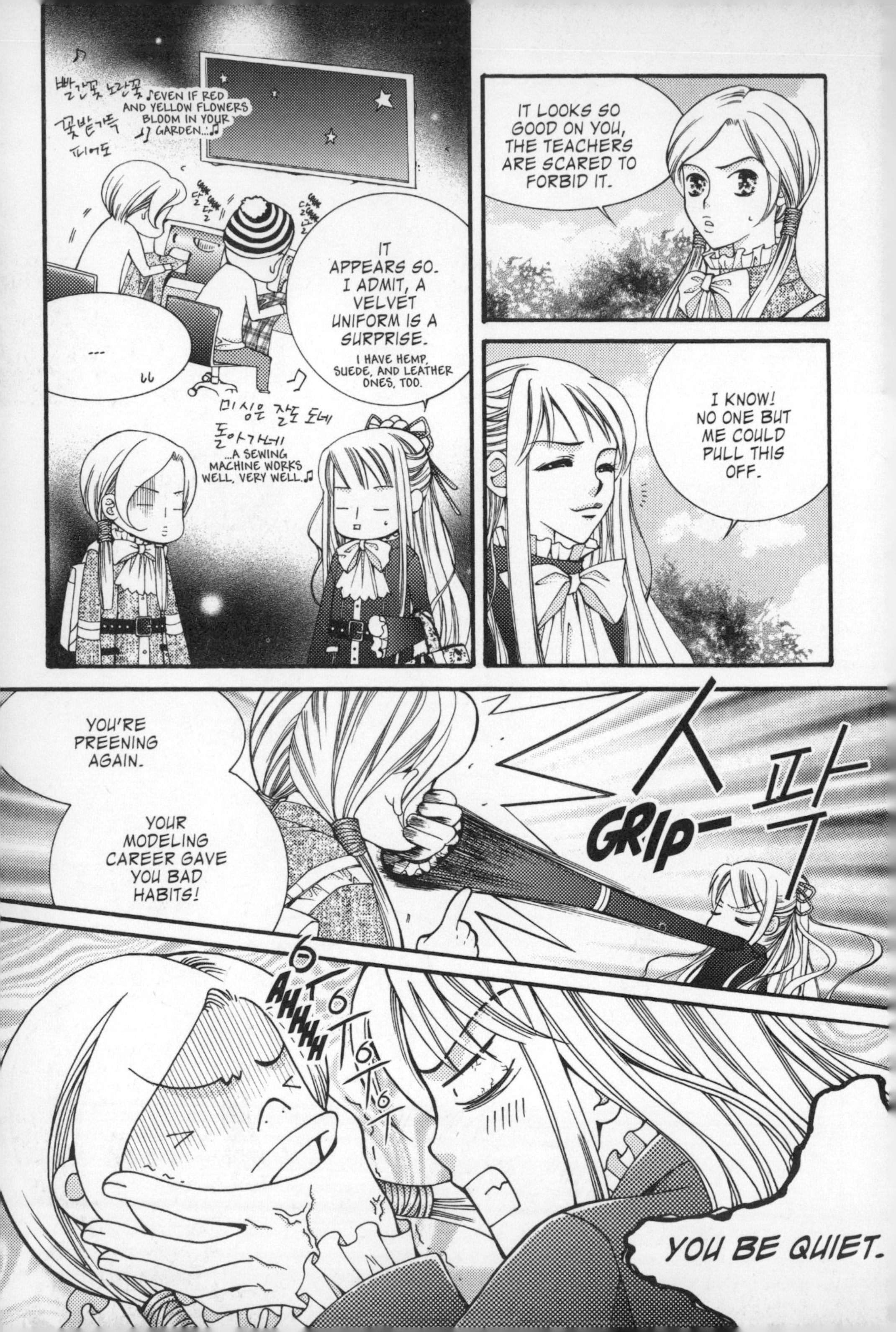
빨간꽃 노란꽃 꽃밭가득 피어도
♪EVEN IF RED AND YELLOW FLOWERS BLOOM IN YOUR GARDEN...♪
...
IT APPEARS SO. I ADMIT, A VELVET UNIFORM IS A SURPRISE.
I HAVE HEMP, SUEDE, AND LEATHER ONES, TOO.
미싱은 잘도 도네 돌아가네
...A SEWING MACHINE WORKS WELL, VERY WELL.♪
IT LOOKS SO GOOD ON YOU, THE TEACHERS ARE SCARED TO FORBID IT.
I KNOW! NO ONE BUT ME COULD PULL THIS OFF.
YOU'RE PREENING AGAIN.
YOUR MODELING CAREER GAVE YOU BAD HABITS!
GRIP—
AHHHH
YOU BE QUIET.

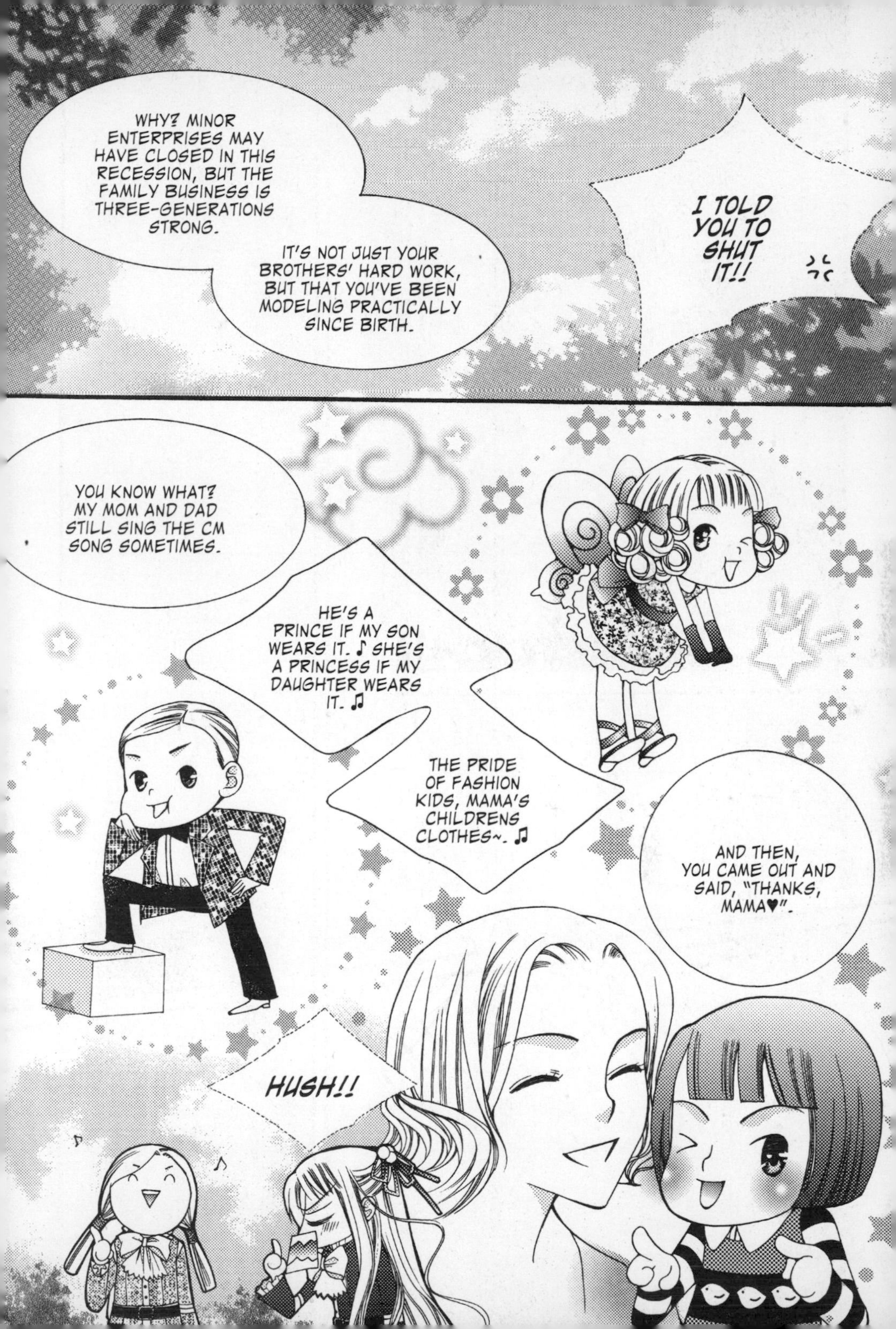
WHY? MINOR ENTERPRISES MAY HAVE CLOSED IN THIS RECESSION, BUT THE FAMILY BUSINESS IS THREE-GENERATIONS STRONG.
IT'S NOT JUST YOUR BROTHERS' HARD WORK, BUT THAT YOU'VE BEEN MODELING PRACTICALLY SINCE BIRTH.
I TOLD YOU TO SHUT IT!!
YOU KNOW WHAT? MY MOM AND DAD STILL SING THE CM SONG SOMETIMES.
HE'S A PRINCE IF MY SON WEARS IT. ♪ SHE'S A PRINCESS IF MY DAUGHTER WEARS IT. ♫
THE PRIDE OF FASHION KIDS, MAMA'S CHILDRENS CLOTHES~. ♫
AND THEN, YOU CAME OUT AND SAID, "THANKS, MAMA♥".
HUSH!!

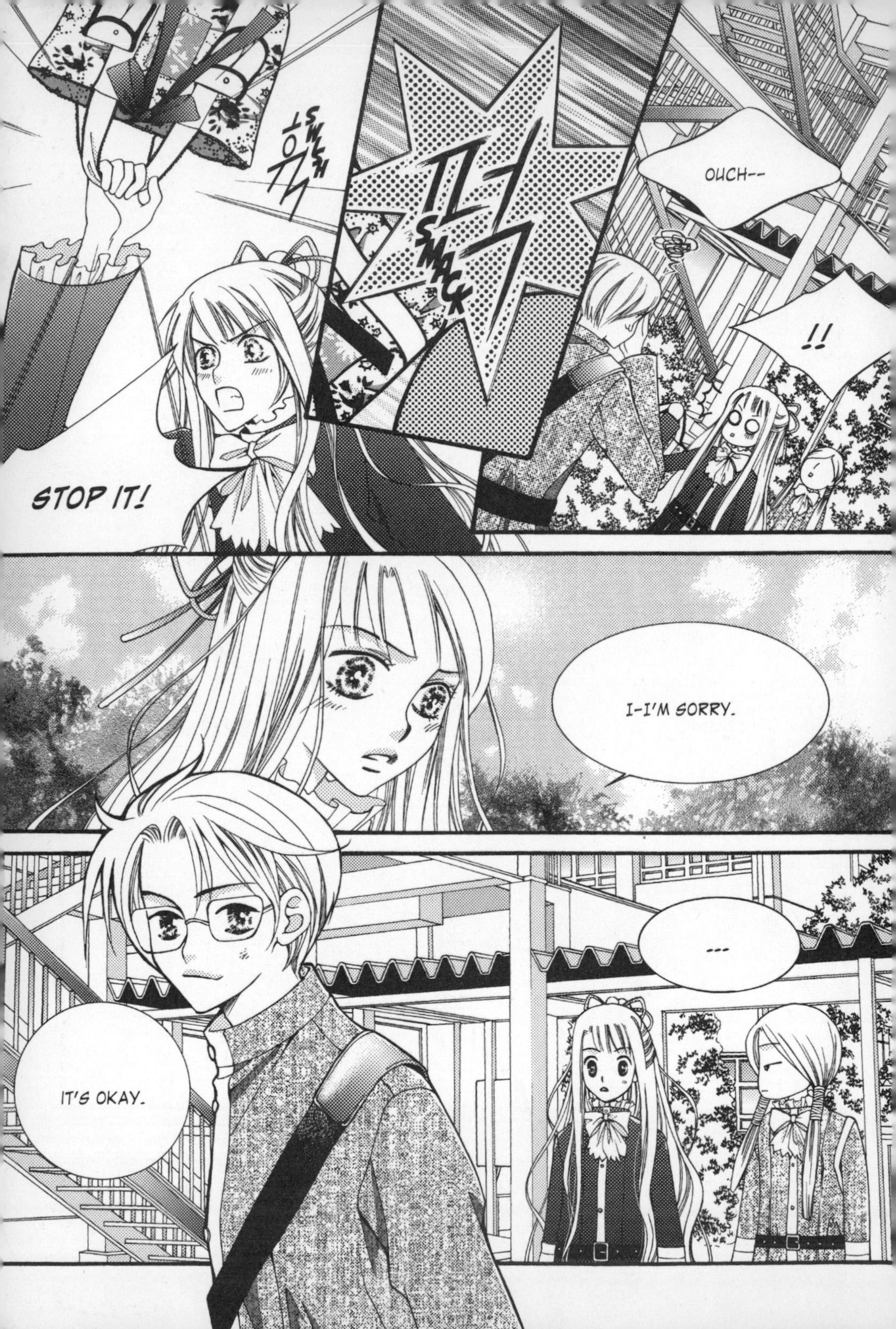
SWISH
STOP IT!
SMACK
OUCH--
!!
I-I'M SORRY.
IT'S OKAY.
...

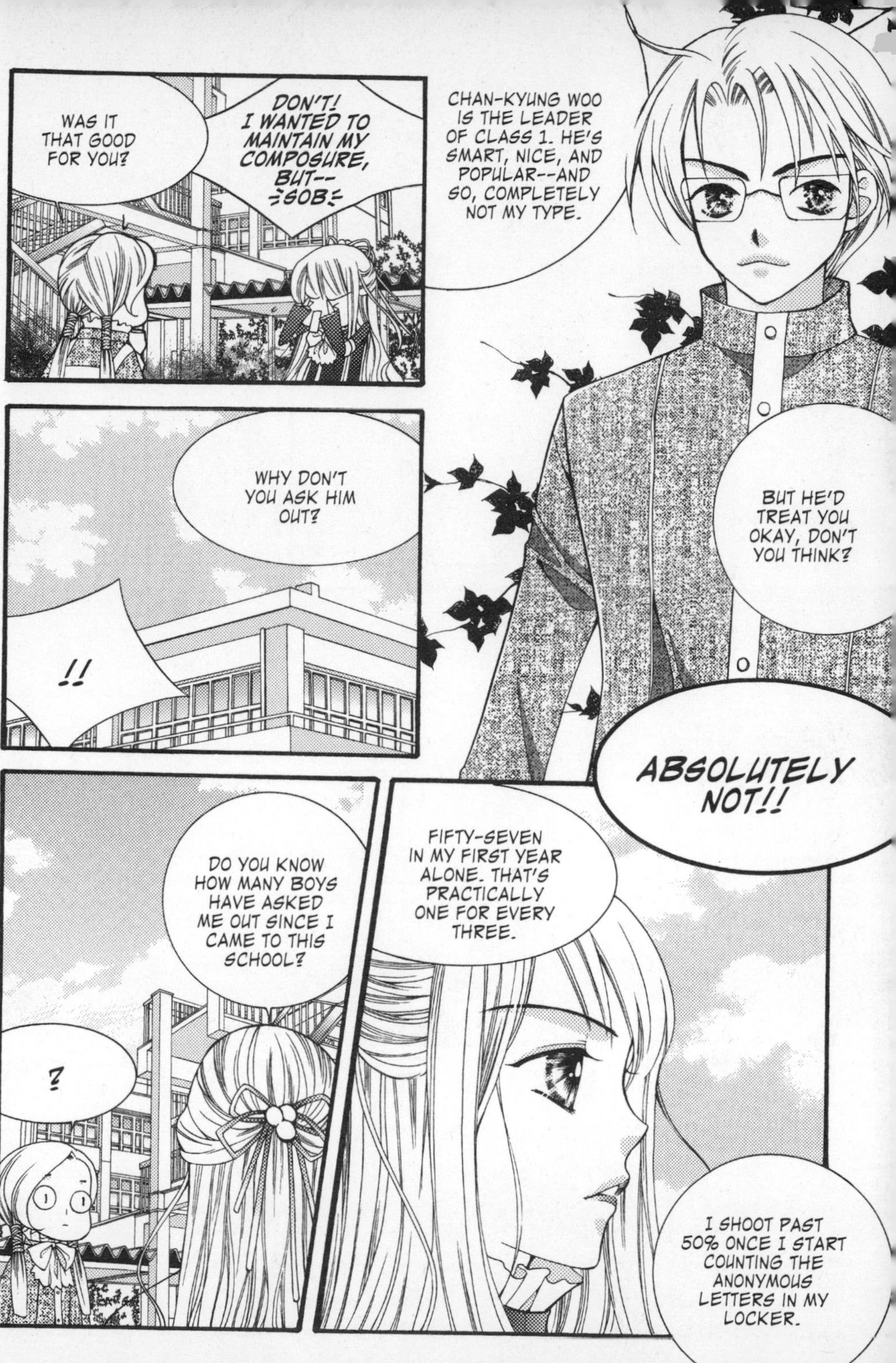
WAS IT THAT GOOD FOR YOU?
DON'T! I WANTED TO MAINTAIN MY COMPOSURE, BUT-- SOB
WHY DON'T YOU ASK HIM OUT?
!!
CHAN-KYUNG WOO IS THE LEADER OF CLASS 1. HE'S SMART, NICE, AND POPULAR--AND SO, COMPLETELY NOT MY TYPE.
BUT HE'D TREAT YOU OKAY, DON'T YOU THINK?
ABSOLUTELY NOT!!
DO YOU KNOW HOW MANY BOYS HAVE ASKED ME OUT SINCE I CAME TO THIS SCHOOL?
?
FIFTY-SEVEN IN MY FIRST YEAR ALONE. THAT'S PRACTICALLY ONE FOR EVERY THREE.
I SHOOT PAST 50% ONCE I START COUNTING THE ANONYMOUS LETTERS IN MY LOCKER.

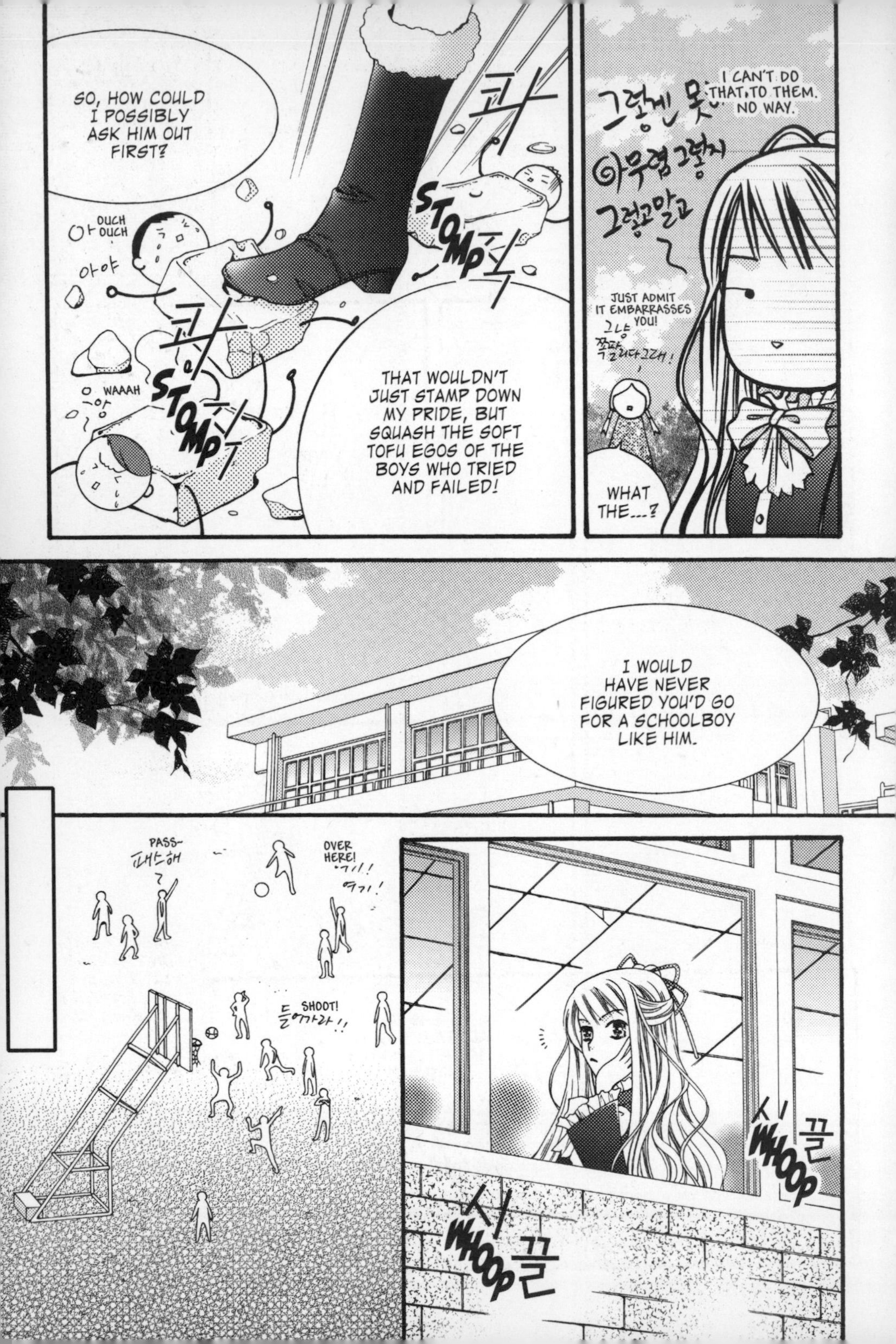

SO, HOW COULD I POSSIBLY ASK HIM OUT FIRST?
OUCH OUCH
아야
STOMP
STOMP
WAAAH
THAT WOULDN'T JUST STAMP DOWN MY PRIDE, BUT SQUASH THE SOFT TOFU EGOS OF THE BOYS WHO TRIED AND FAILED!
I CAN'T DO THAT TO THEM. NO WAY.
JUST ADMIT IT EMBARRASSES YOU!
WHAT THE...?
I WOULD HAVE NEVER FIGURED YOU'D GO FOR A SCHOOLBOY LIKE HIM.
PASS-
패스해
OVER HERE!
여기!
SHOOT!
들어가라!!
WHOOP
WHOOP

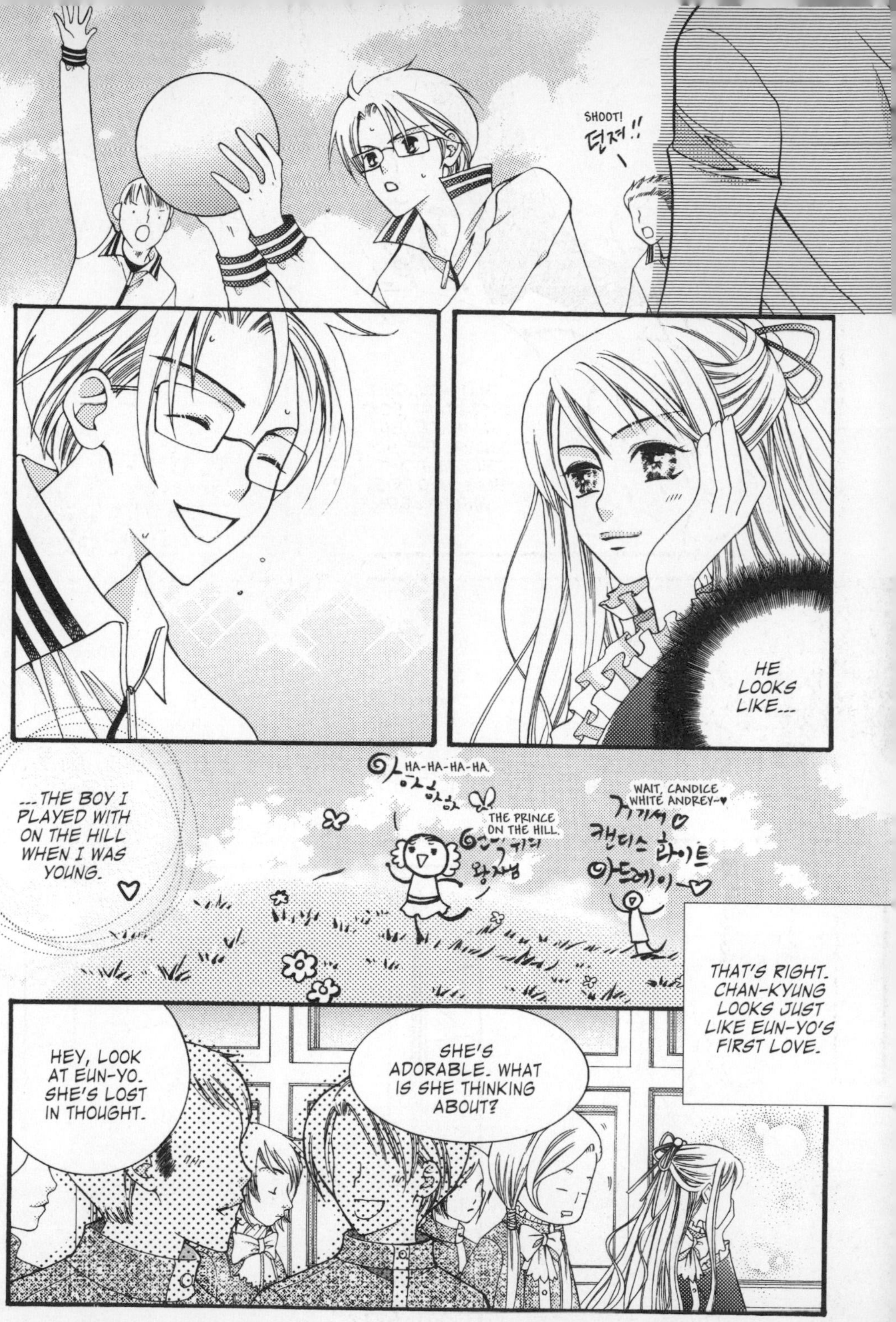
SHOOT!
던져!!
HE LOOKS LIKE...
...THE BOY I PLAYED WITH ON THE HILL WHEN I WAS YOUNG. ♥
HA-HA-HA-HA.
THE PRINCE ON THE HILL.
WAIT, CANDICE WHITE ANDREY~♥
THAT'S RIGHT. CHAN-KYUNG LOOKS JUST LIKE EUN-YO'S FIRST LOVE.
HEY, LOOK AT EUN-YO. SHE'S LOST IN THOUGHT.
SHE'S ADORABLE. WHAT IS SHE THINKING ABOUT?

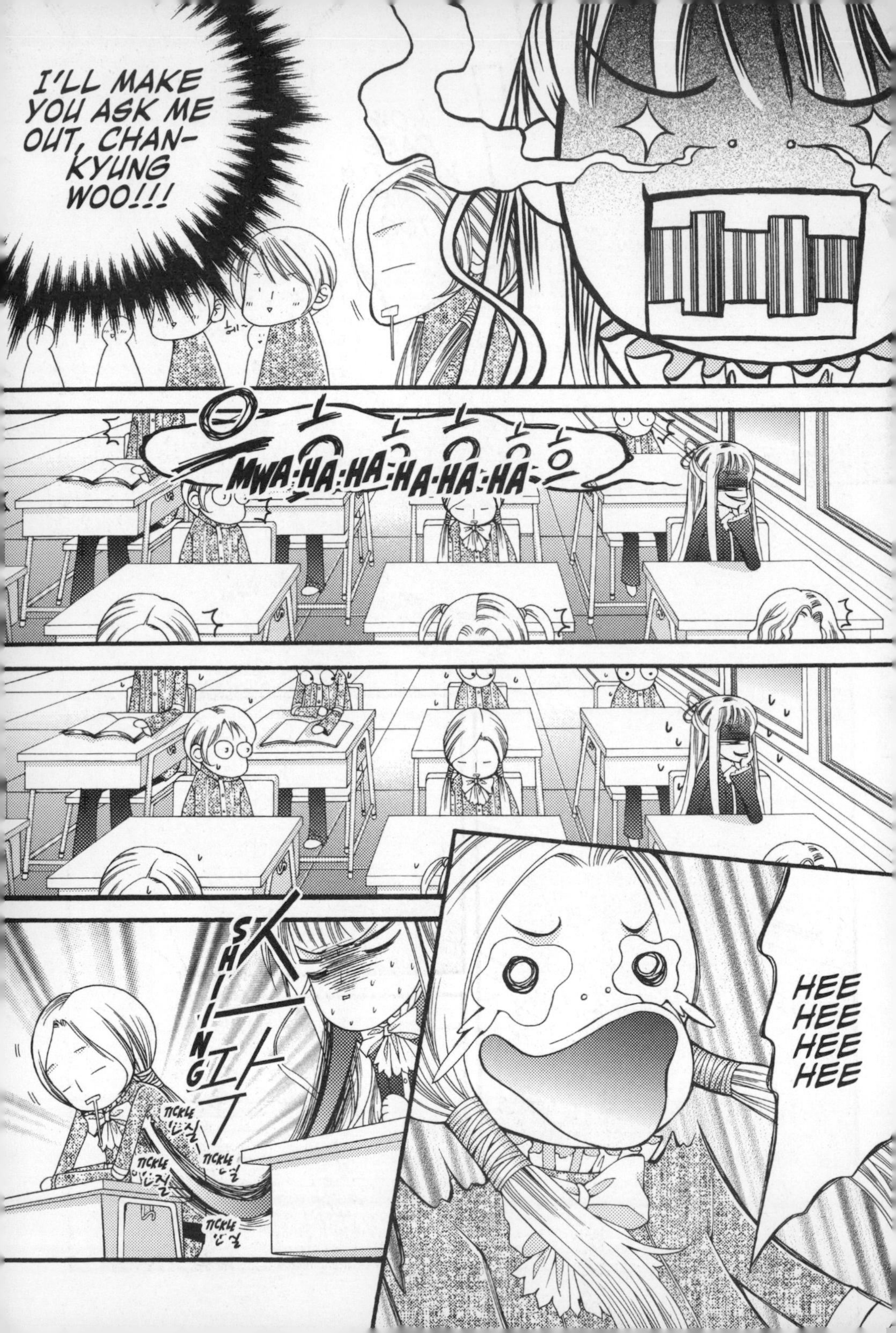

I'LL MAKE YOU ASK ME OUT, CHAN-KYUNG WOO!!!
MWA-HA-HA-HA-HA-HA
SHIING
TICKLE
TICKLE
TICKLE
TICKLE
HEE HEE HEE HEE

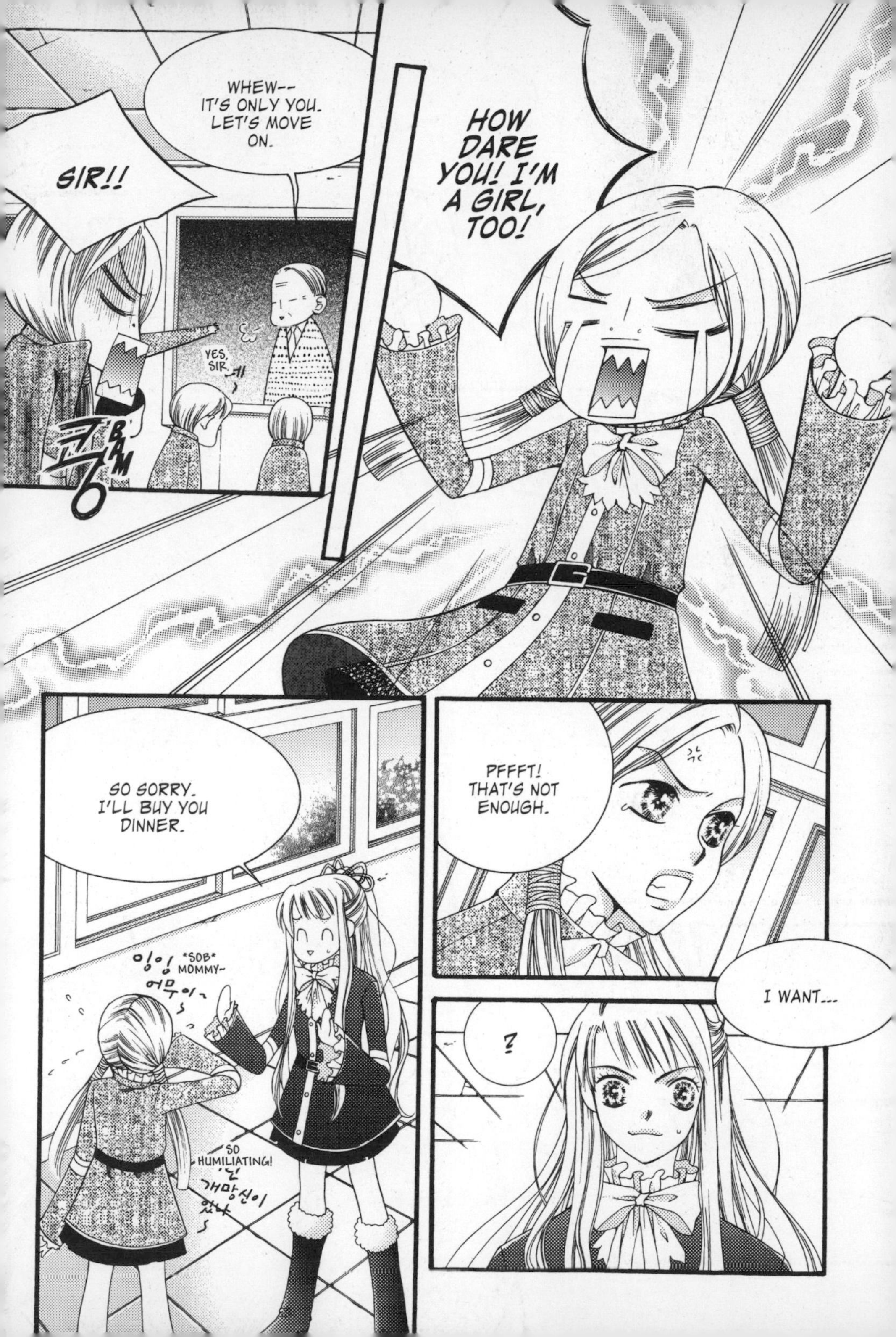
WHEW-- IT'S ONLY YOU. LET'S MOVE ON.
SIR!!
YES, SIR.
BAM
HOW DARE YOU! I'M A GIRL, TOO!
SO SORRY. I'LL BUY YOU DINNER.
SOB MOMMY~
SO HUMILIATING!
PFFFT! THAT'S NOT ENOUGH.
I WANT...
?

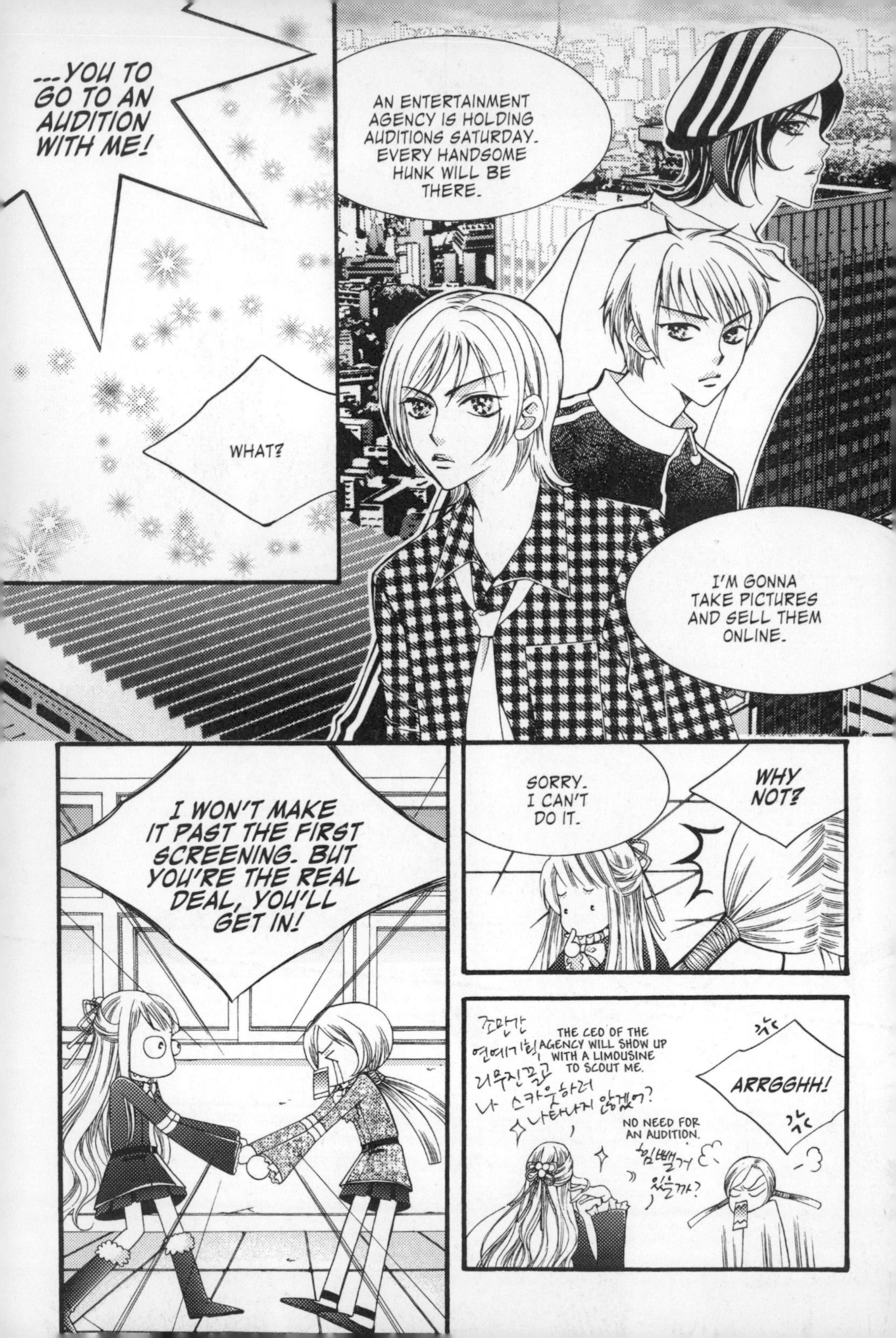

...YOU TO GO TO AN AUDITION WITH ME!
WHAT?
AN ENTERTAINMENT AGENCY IS HOLDING AUDITIONS SATURDAY. EVERY HANDSOME HUNK WILL BE THERE.
I'M GONNA TAKE PICTURES AND SELL THEM ONLINE.
I WON'T MAKE IT PAST THE FIRST SCREENING. BUT YOU'RE THE REAL DEAL, YOU'LL GET IN!
SORRY. I CAN'T DO IT.
WHY NOT?
조만간 연예기획, 리무진끌고 나 스카웃하러 나타나지 않겠어?
THE CEO OF THE AGENCY WILL SHOW UP WITH A LIMOUSINE TO SCOUT ME.
ARRGGHH!
NO NEED FOR AN AUDITION.
힘뺄거 있을까?

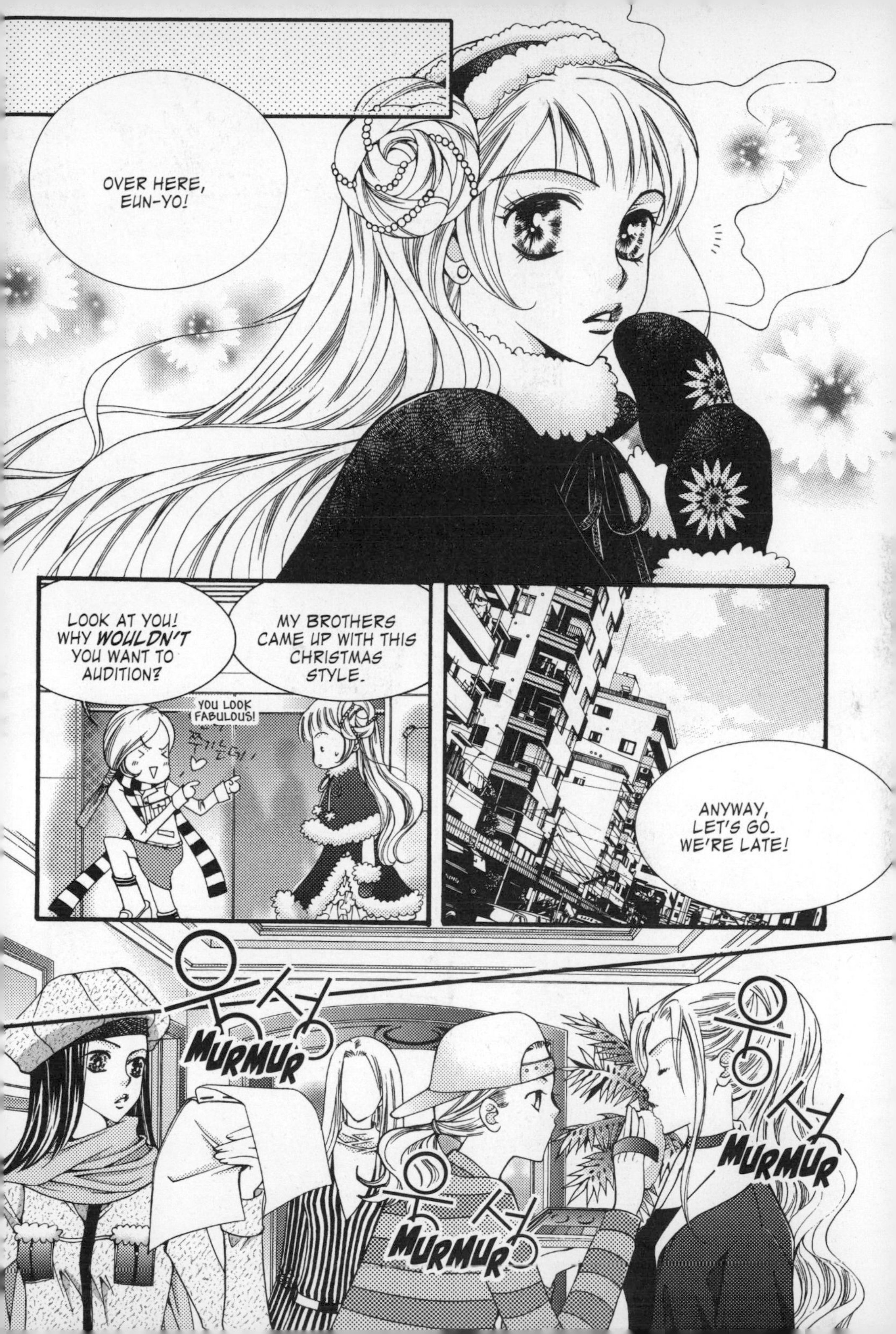
OVER HERE, EUN-YO!
LOOK AT YOU! WHY WOULDN'T YOU WANT TO AUDITION?
MY BROTHERS CAME UP WITH THIS CHRISTMAS STYLE.
YOU LOOK FABULOUS!
ANYWAY, LET'S GO. WE'RE LATE!
MURMUR
MURMUR
MURMUR

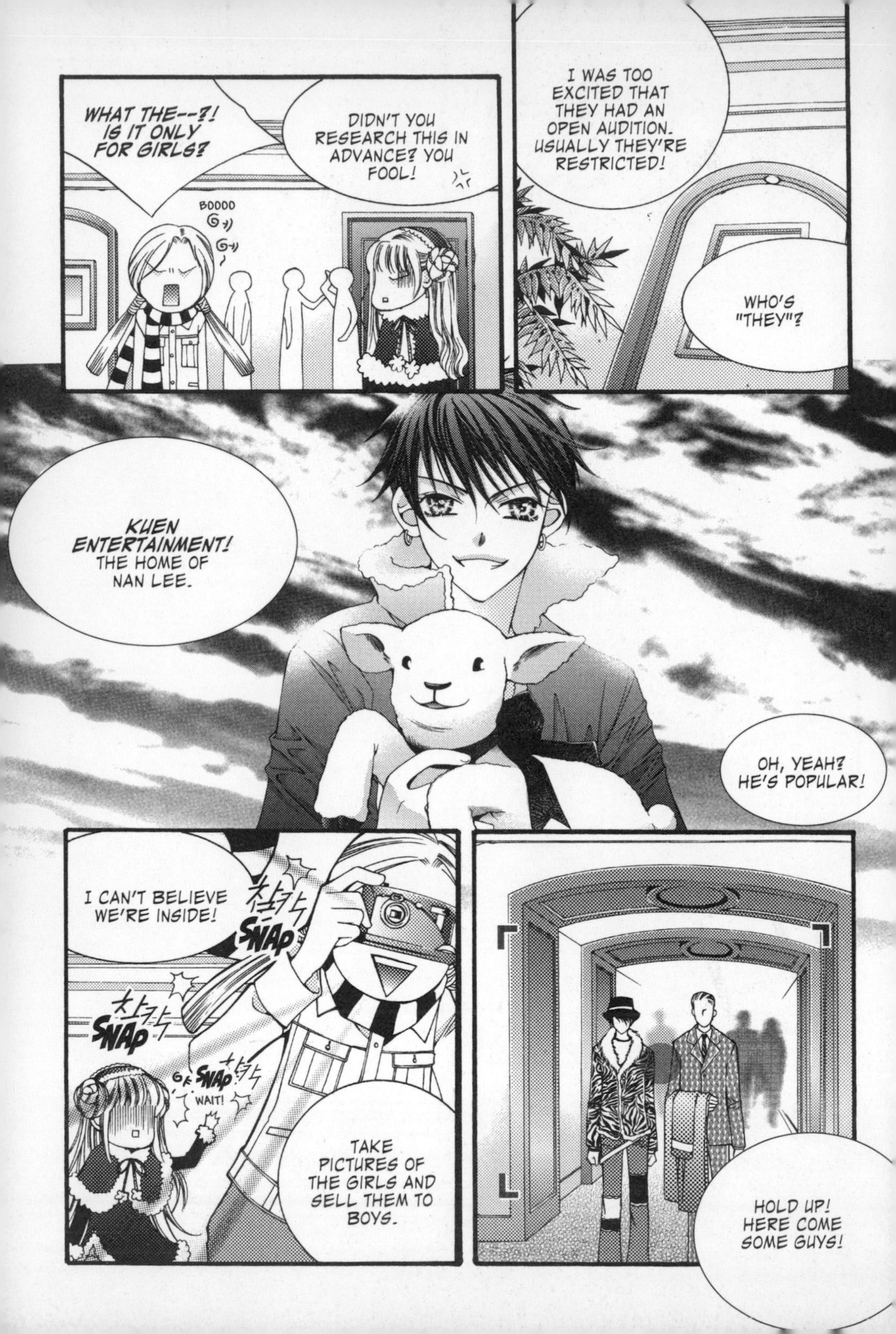
WHAT THE--?! IS IT ONLY FOR GIRLS?
DIDN'T YOU RESEARCH THIS IN ADVANCE? YOU FOOL!
BOOOO
I WAS TOO EXCITED THAT THEY HAD AN OPEN AUDITION. USUALLY THEY'RE RESTRICTED!
WHO'S "THEY"?
KUEN ENTERTAINMENT! THE HOME OF NAN LEE.
OH, YEAH? HE'S POPULAR!
I CAN'T BELIEVE WE'RE INSIDE!
SNAP
SNAP
SNAP
WAIT!
TAKE PICTURES OF THE GIRLS AND SELL THEM TO BOYS.
HOLD UP! HERE COME SOME GUYS!

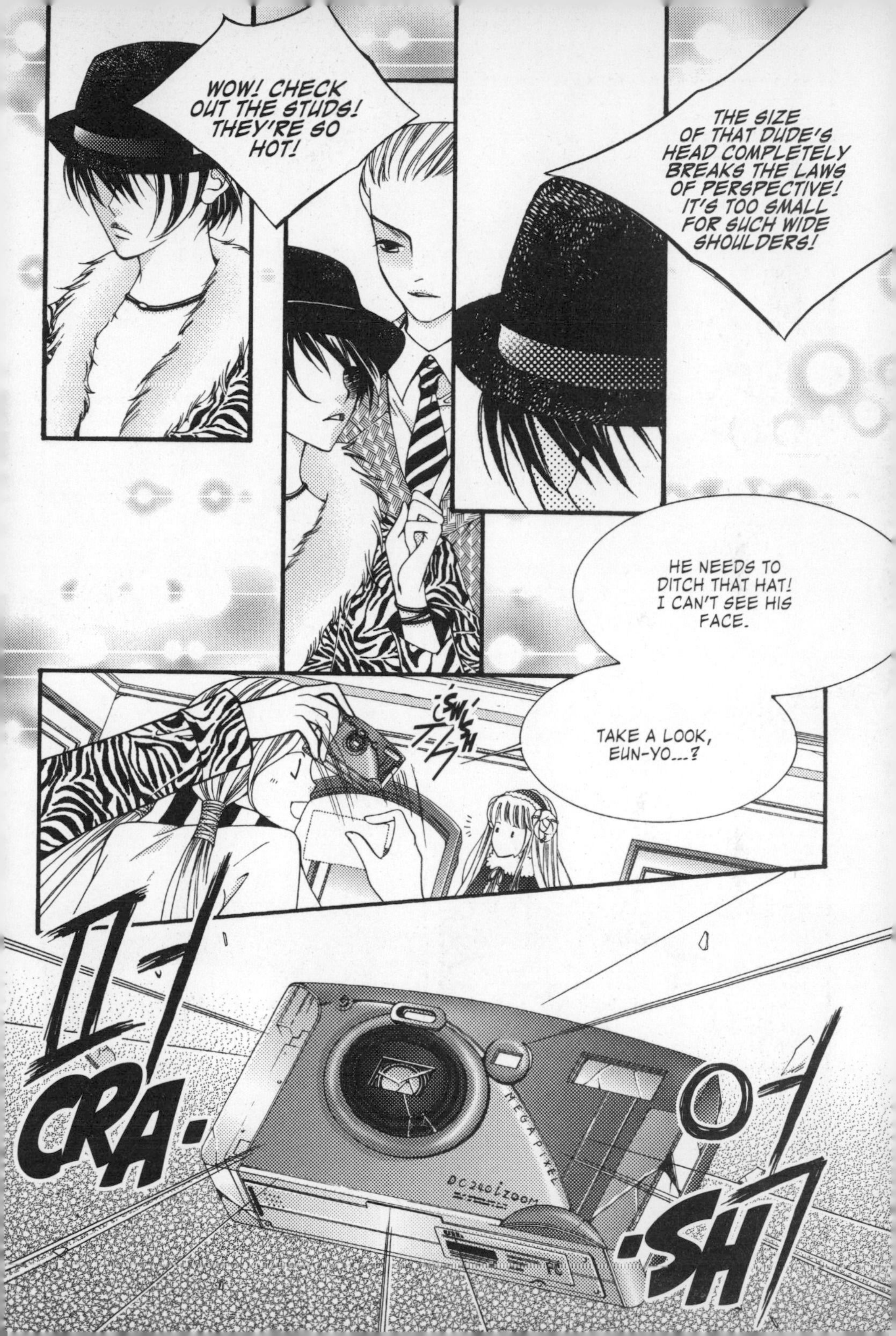
WOW! CHECK OUT THE STUDS! THEY'RE SO HOT!
THE SIZE OF THAT DUDE'S HEAD COMPLETELY BREAKS THE LAWS OF PERSPECTIVE! IT'S TOO SMALL FOR SUCH WIDE SHOULDERS!
HE NEEDS TO DITCH THAT HAT! I CAN'T SEE HIS FACE.
SWISH
TAKE A LOOK, EUN-YO...?
CRA-
-SH

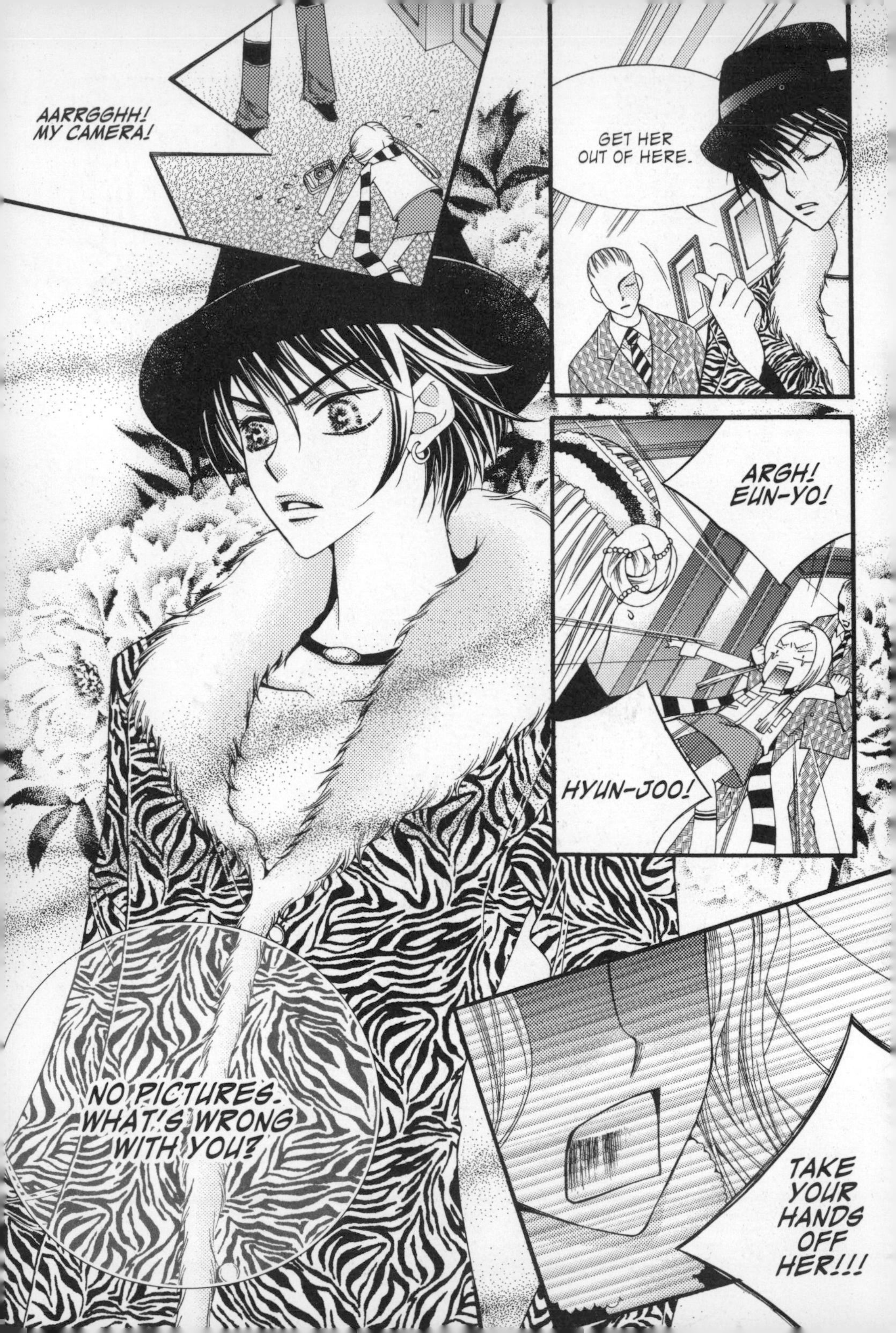
AARRGGHH! MY CAMERA!
NO PICTURES. WHAT'S WRONG WITH YOU?
GET HER OUT OF HERE.
ARGH! EUN-YO!
HYUN-JOO!
TAKE YOUR HANDS OFF HER!!!

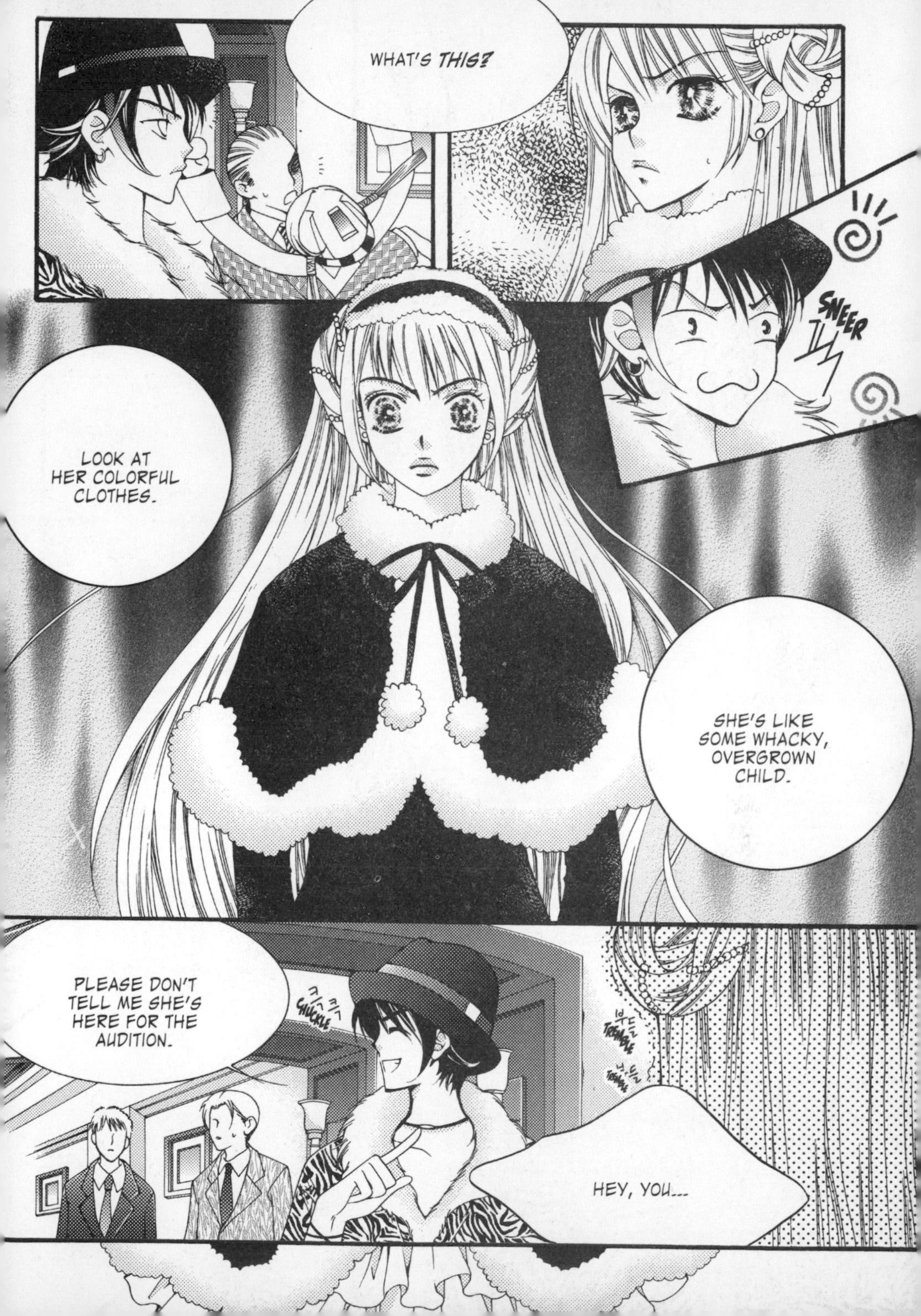
WHAT'S THIS?
SNEER
LOOK AT HER COLORFUL CLOTHES.
SHE'S LIKE SOME WHACKY, OVERGROWN CHILD.
PLEASE DON'T TELL ME SHE'S HERE FOR THE AUDITION.
CHUCKLE
TREMBLE
TREMBLE
HEY, YOU...

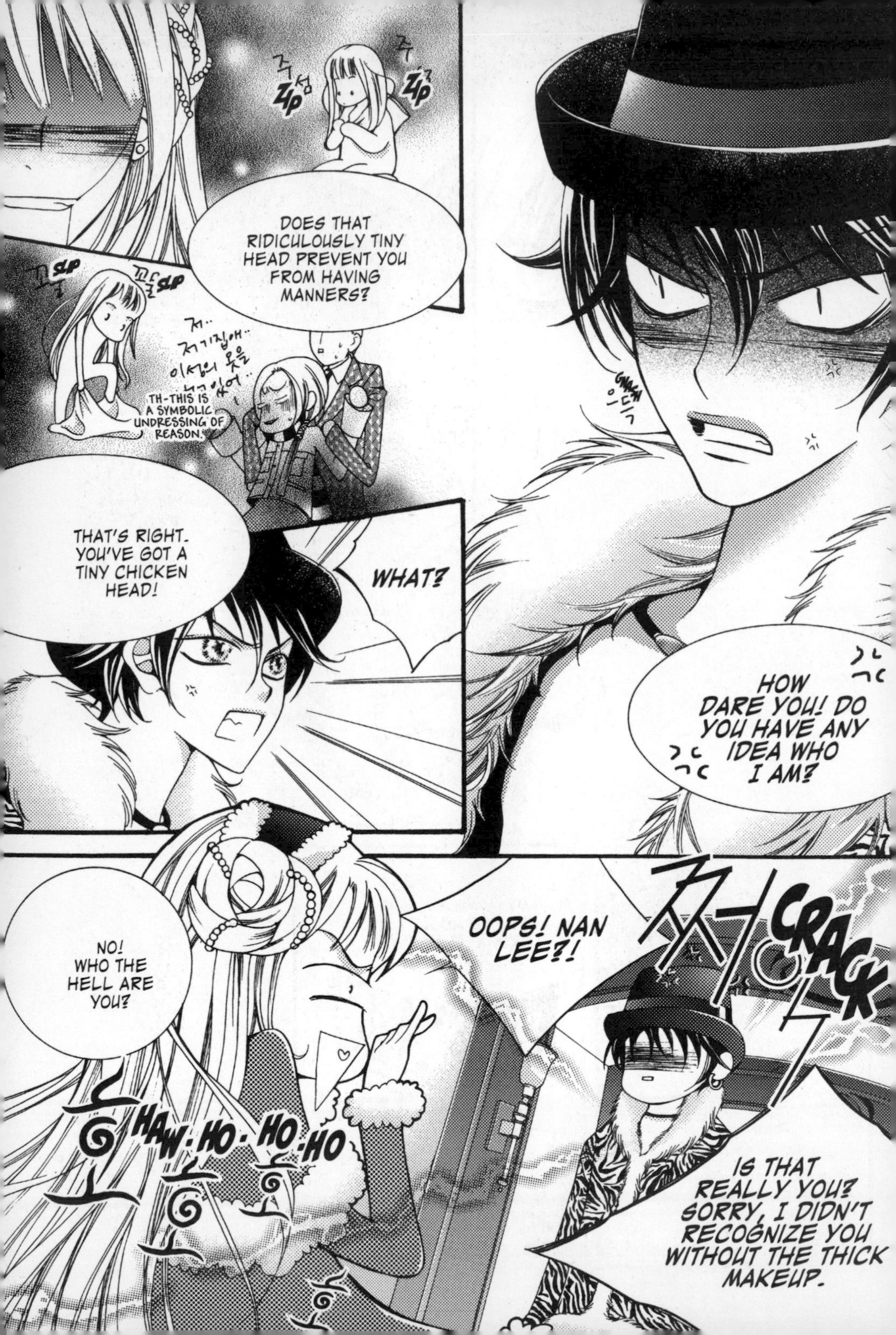

ZIP
ZIP
DOES THAT RIDICULOUSLY TINY HEAD PREVENT YOU FROM HAVING MANNERS?
SLIP
SLIP
저.. 저기집애.. 이성의 옷을
TH-THIS IS A SYMBOLIC UNDRESSING OF REASON.
THAT'S RIGHT. YOU'VE GOT A TINY CHICKEN HEAD!
WHAT?
GNASH
HOW DARE YOU! DO YOU HAVE ANY IDEA WHO I AM?
NO! WHO THE HELL ARE YOU?
HAW-HO-HO-HO
OOPS! NAN LEE?!
CRACK
IS THAT REALLY YOU? SORRY, I DIDN'T RECOGNIZE YOU WITHOUT THE THICK MAKEUP.

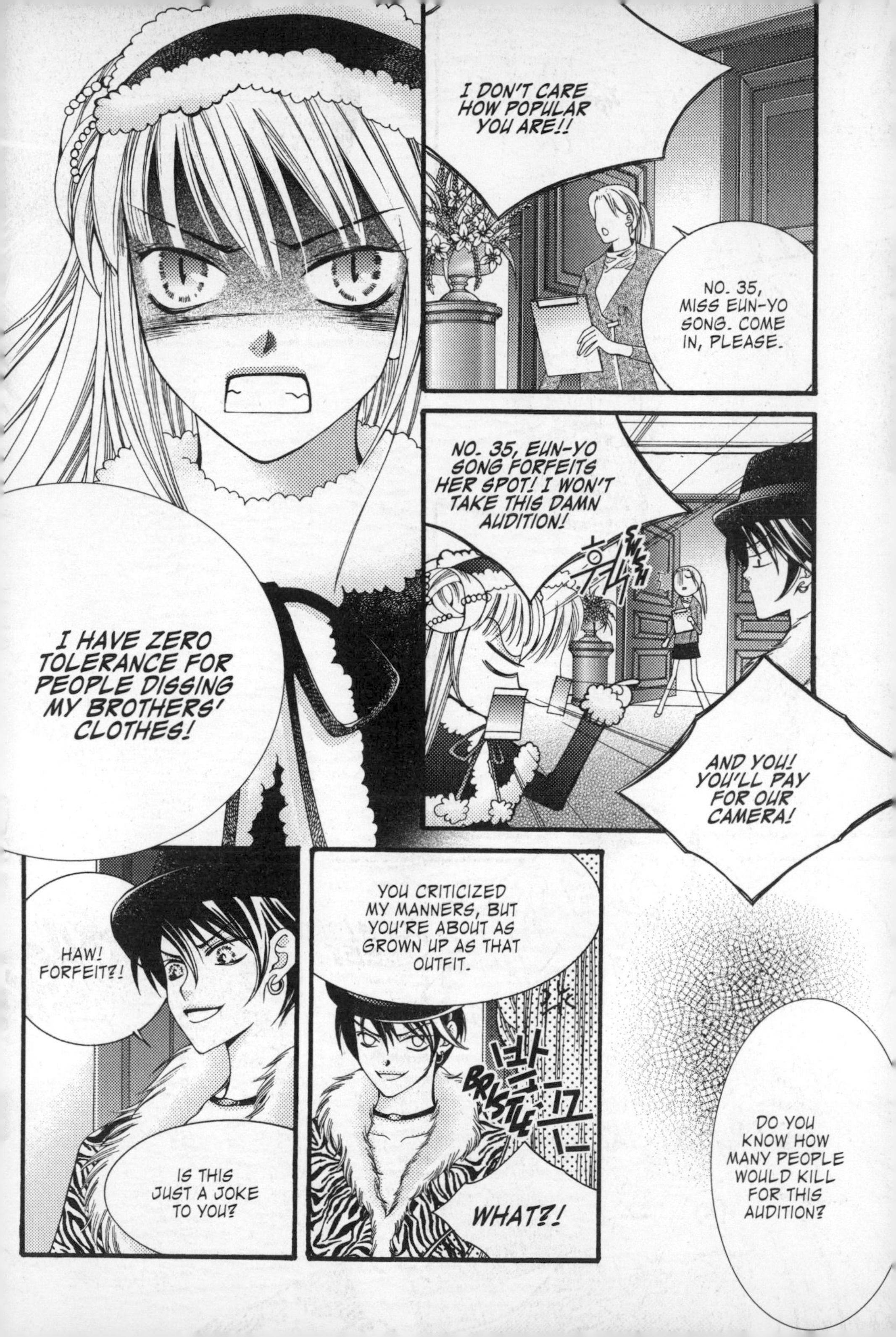
I HAVE ZERO TOLERANCE FOR PEOPLE DISSING MY BROTHERS' CLOTHES!
I DON'T CARE HOW POPULAR YOU ARE!!
NO. 35, MISS EUN-YO SONG. COME IN, PLEASE.
NO. 35, EUN-YO SONG FORFEITS HER SPOT! I WON'T TAKE THIS DAMN AUDITION!
SWISH
AND YOU! YOU'LL PAY FOR OUR CAMERA!
HAW! FORFEIT?!
IS THIS JUST A JOKE TO YOU?
YOU CRITICIZED MY MANNERS, BUT YOU'RE ABOUT AS GROWN UP AS THAT OUTFIT.
BRISTLE
WHAT?!
DO YOU KNOW HOW MANY PEOPLE WOULD KILL FOR THIS AUDITION?

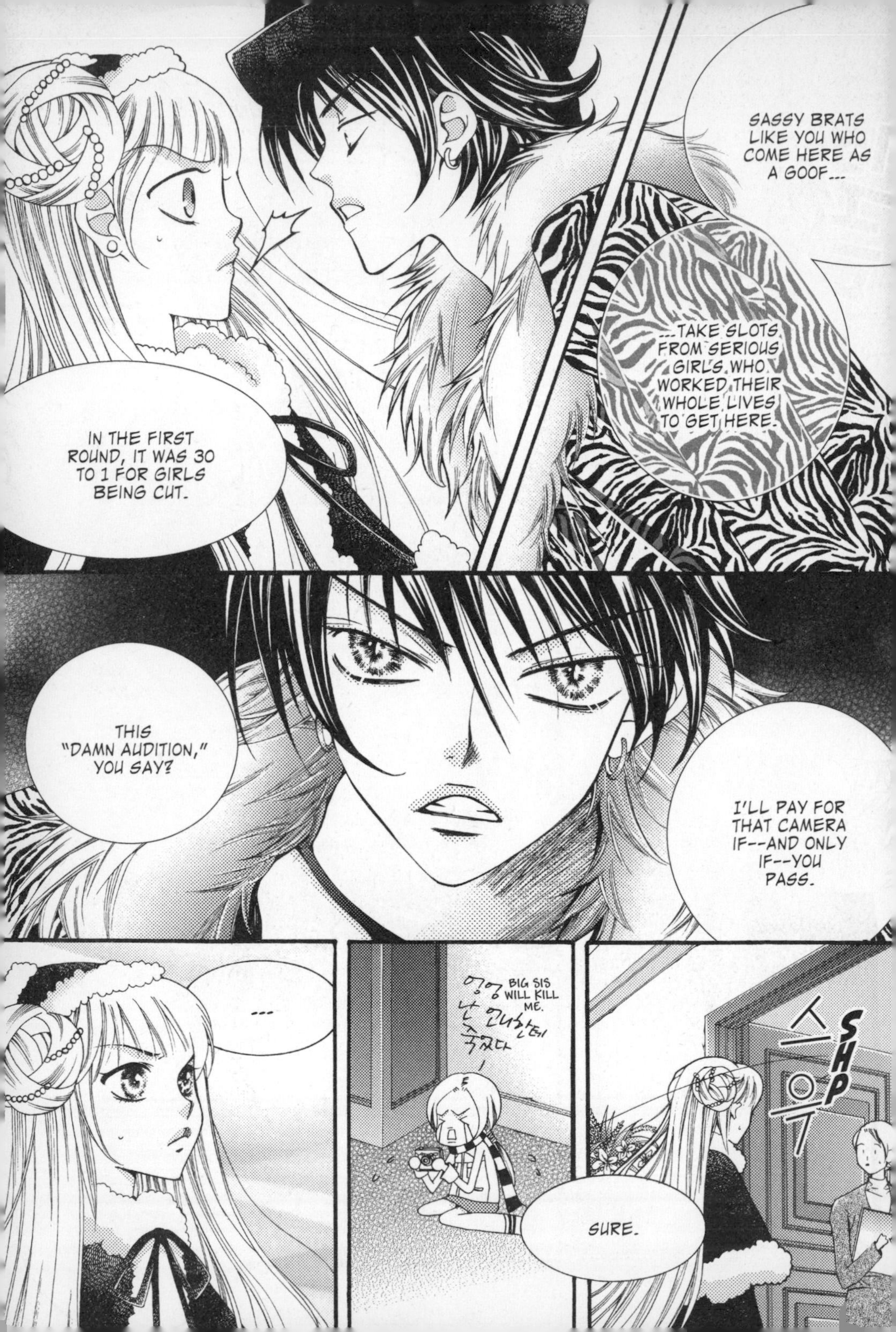
IN THE FIRST ROUND, IT WAS 30 TO 1 FOR GIRLS BEING CUT.
SASSY BRATS LIKE YOU WHO COME HERE AS A GOOF...
...TAKE SLOTS FROM SERIOUS GIRLS WHO WORKED THEIR WHOLE LIVES TO GET HERE.
THIS "DAMN AUDITION," YOU SAY?
I'LL PAY FOR THAT CAMERA IF--AND ONLY IF--YOU PASS.
...
BIG SIS WILL KILL ME.
SHP
SURE.

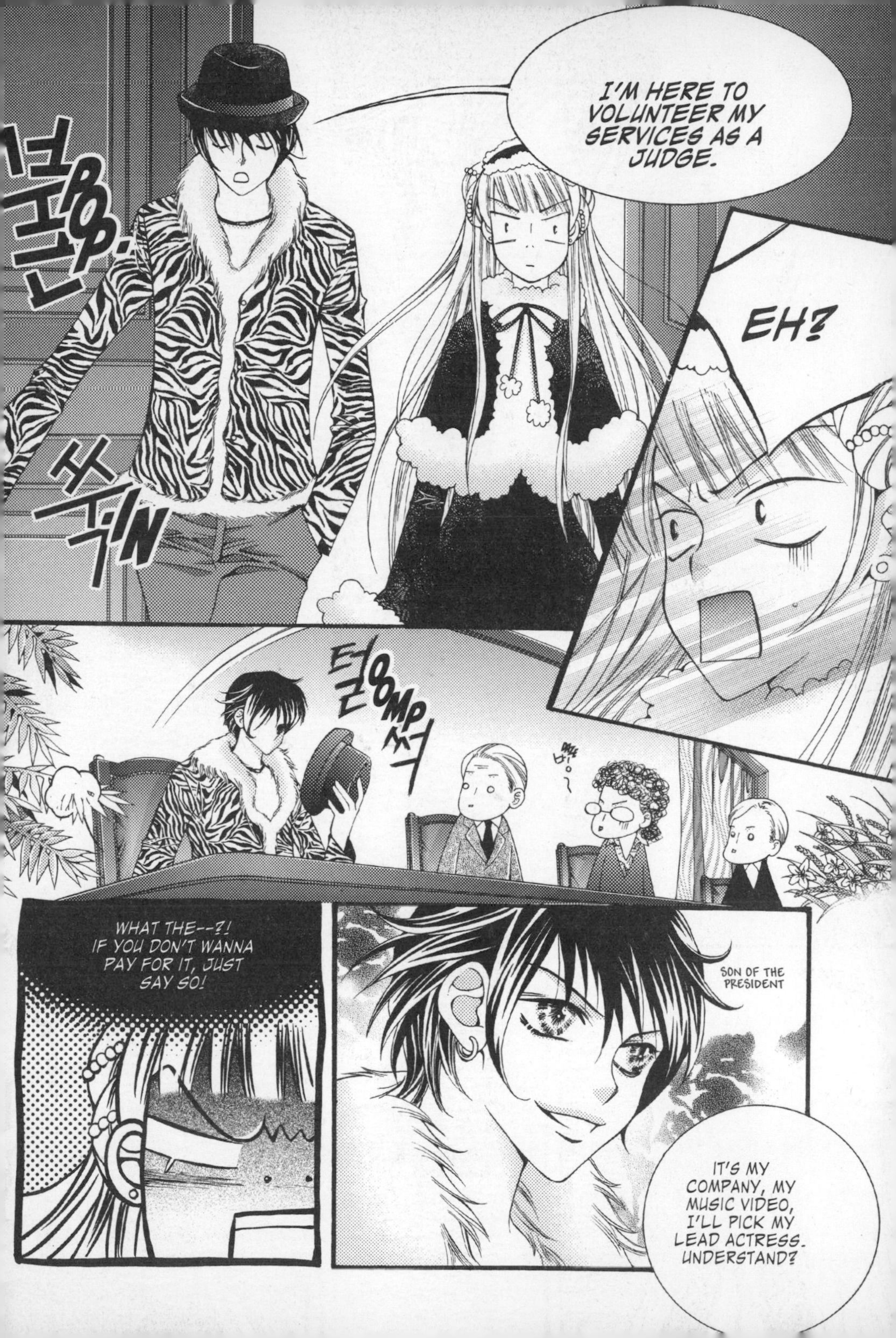

POP.
I'M HERE TO VOLUNTEER MY SERVICES AS A JUDGE.
EH?
OOMP
WHAT THE--?! IF YOU DON'T WANNA PAY FOR IT, JUST SAY SO!
SON OF THE PRESIDENT
IT'S MY COMPANY, MY MUSIC VIDEO, I'LL PICK MY LEAD ACTRESS. UNDERSTAND?

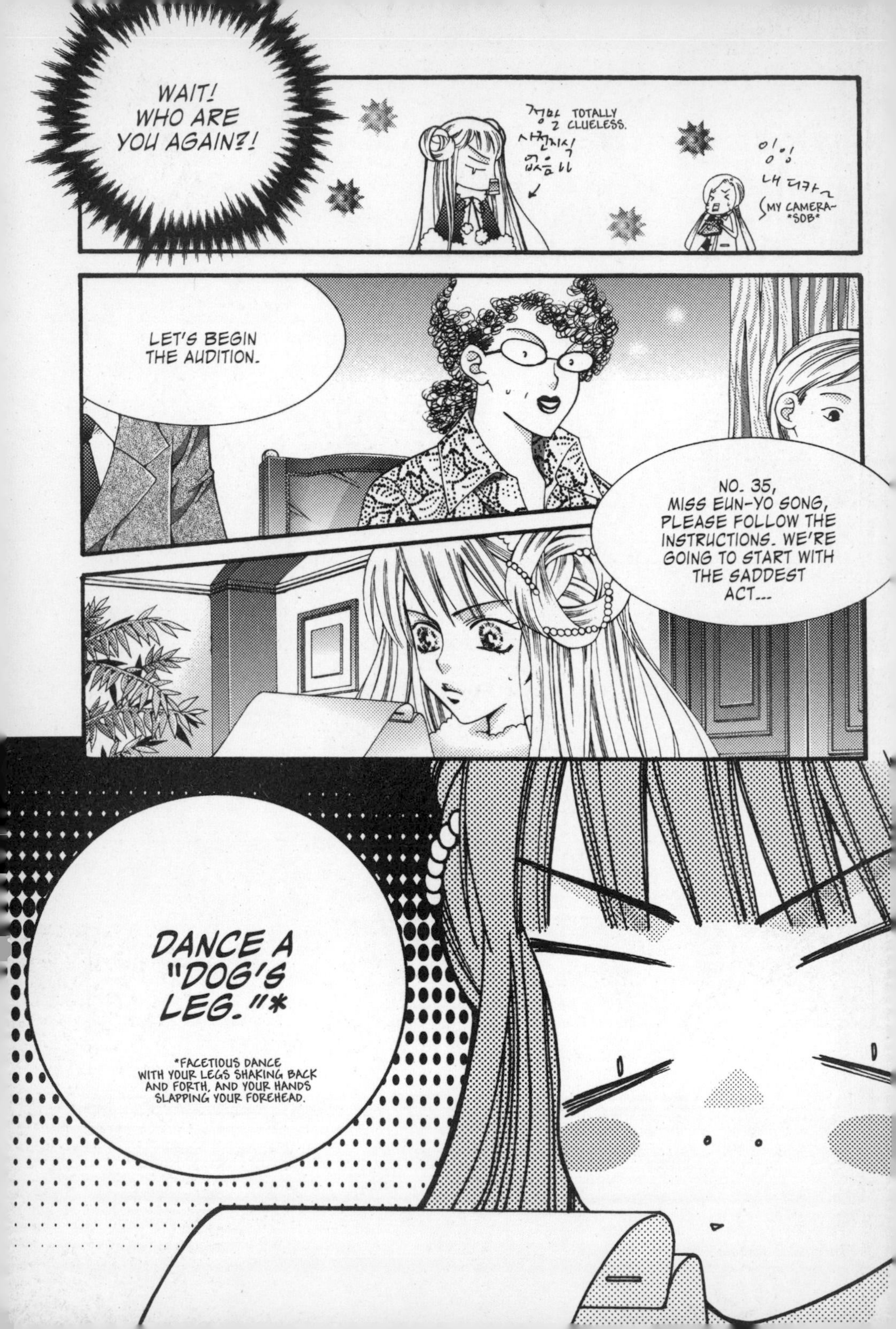
WAIT! WHO ARE YOU AGAIN?!
정말 사전지식 없음..
TOTALLY CLUELESS.
잉잉 내 디카ㅡ
MY CAMERA- *SOB*
LET'S BEGIN THE AUDITION.
NO. 35, MISS EUN-YO SONG, PLEASE FOLLOW THE INSTRUCTIONS. WE'RE GOING TO START WITH THE SADDEST ACT...
DANCE A "DOG'S LEG."*
*FACETIOUS DANCE WITH YOUR LEGS SHAKING BACK AND FORTH, AND YOUR HANDS SLAPPING YOUR FOREHEAD.

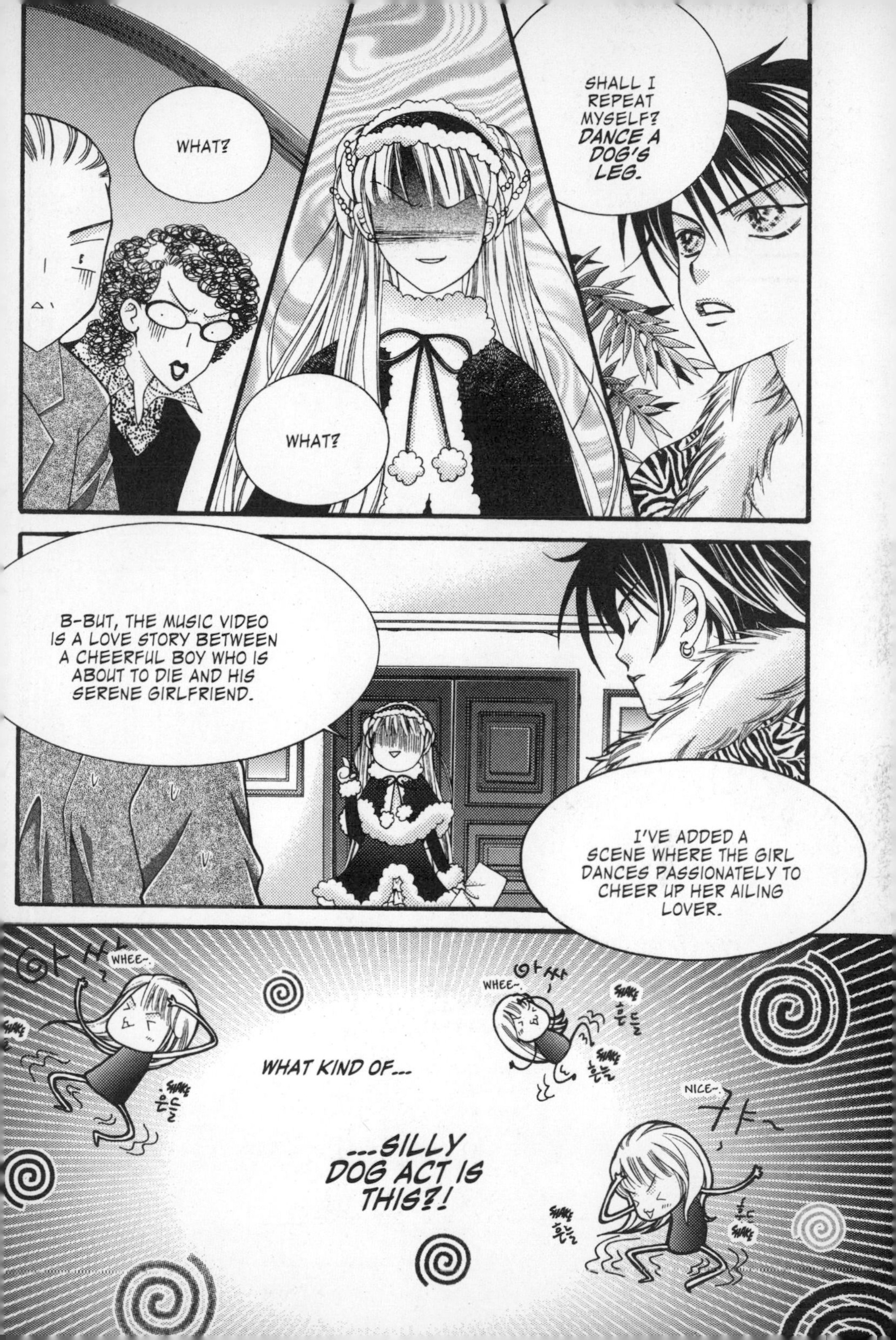
WHAT?
WHAT?
SHALL I REPEAT MYSELF? DANCE A DOG'S LEG.
B-BUT, THE MUSIC VIDEO IS A LOVE STORY BETWEEN A CHEERFUL BOY WHO IS ABOUT TO DIE AND HIS SERENE GIRLFRIEND.
I'VE ADDED A SCENE WHERE THE GIRL DANCES PASSIONATELY TO CHEER UP HER AILING LOVER.
WHEE~.
SHAKE
SHAKE
WHAT KIND OF---
WHEE~.
SHAKE
SHAKE
NICE~.
---SILLY DOG ACT IS THIS?!
SHAKE
SHAKE

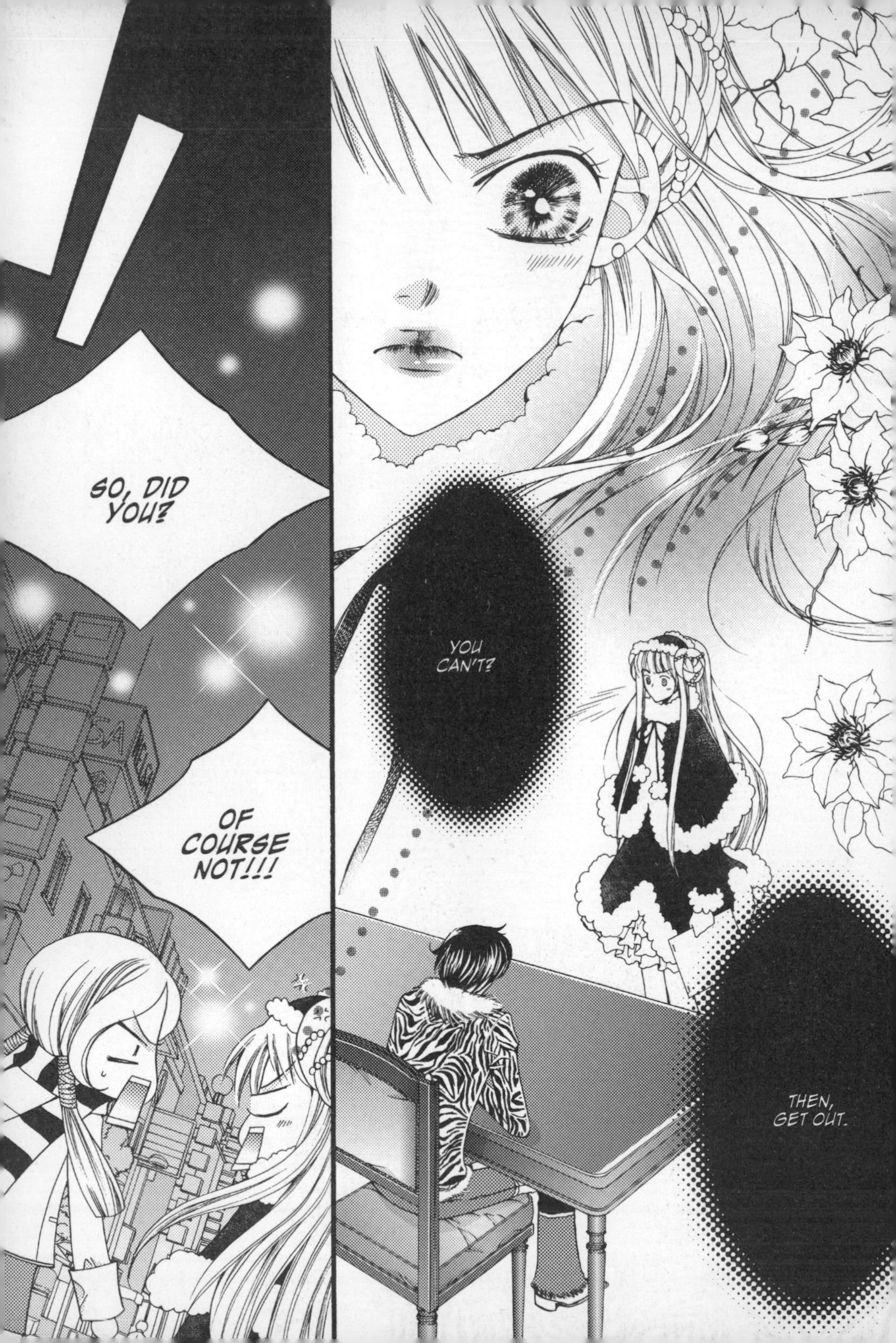
SO, DID YOU?
OF COURSE NOT!!!
YOU CAN'T?
THEN, GET OUT.

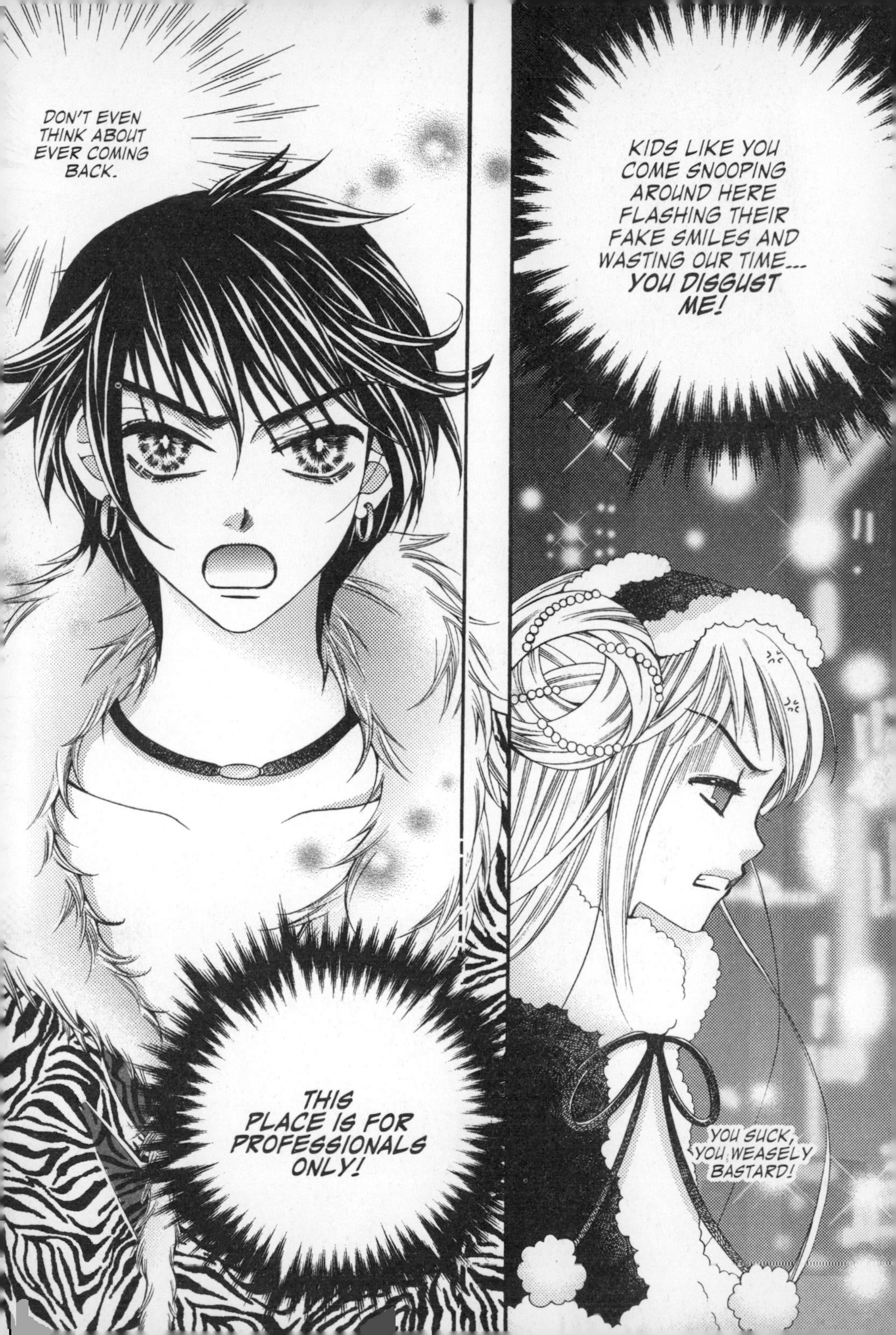
DON'T EVEN THINK ABOUT EVER COMING BACK.
THIS PLACE IS FOR PROFESSIONALS ONLY!
KIDS LIKE YOU COME SNOOPING AROUND HERE FLASHING THEIR FAKE SMILES AND WASTING OUR TIME... YOU DISGUST ME!
YOU SUCK, YOU WEASELY BASTARD!

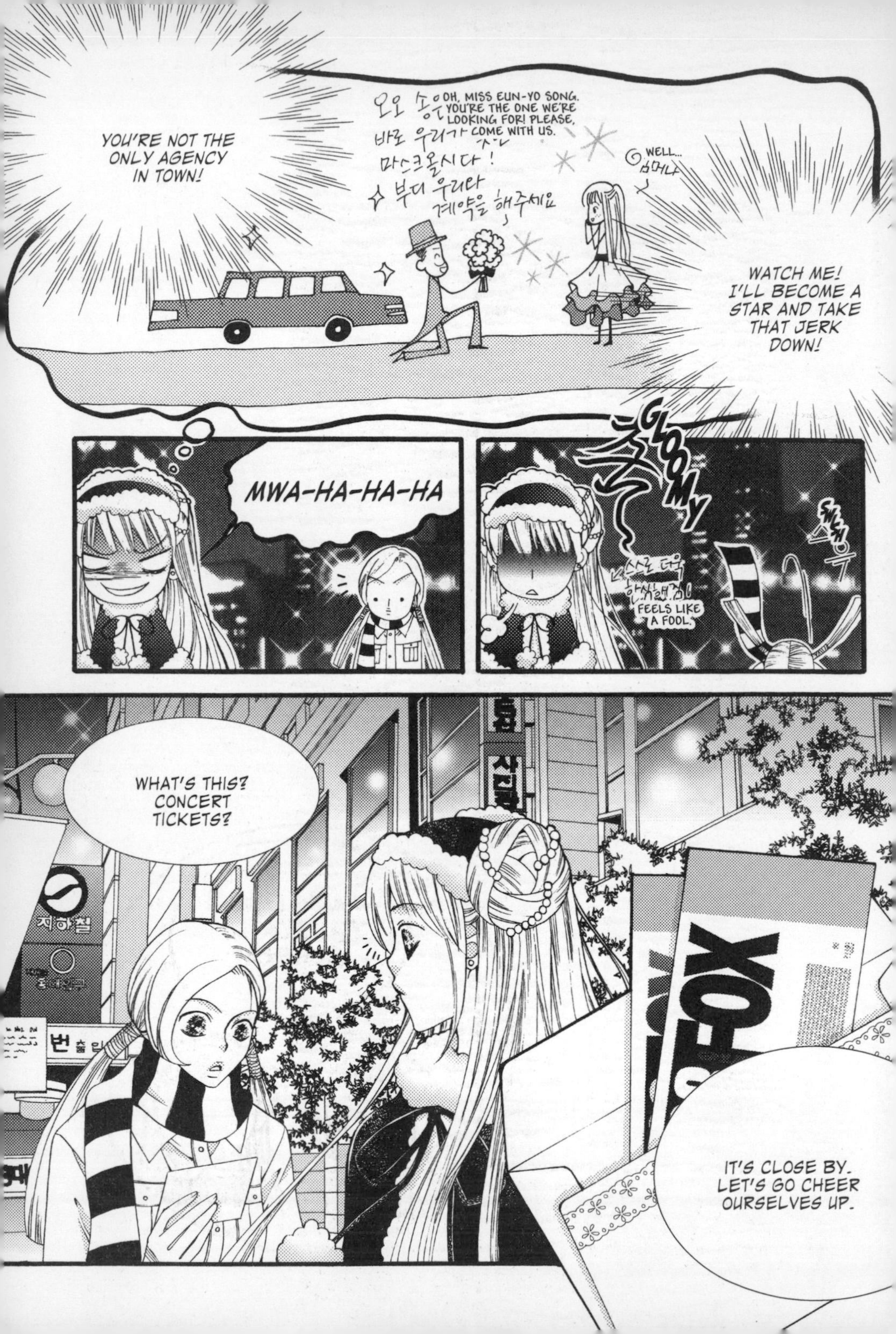

YOU'RE NOT THE ONLY AGENCY IN TOWN!
OH, MISS EUN-YO SONG. YOU'RE THE ONE WE'RE LOOKING FOR! PLEASE, COME WITH US.
WELL...
WATCH ME! I'LL BECOME A STAR AND TAKE THAT JERK DOWN!
MWA-HA-HA-HA
GLOOMY
FEELS LIKE A FOOL.
SWISH
WHAT'S THIS? CONCERT TICKETS?
IT'S CLOSE BY. LET'S GO CHEER OURSELVES UP.

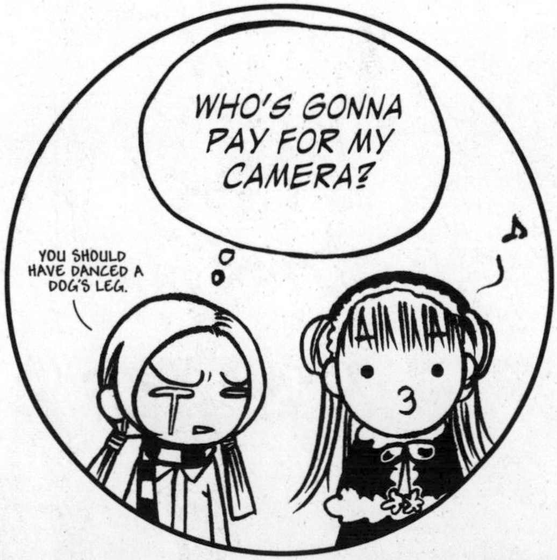
WHO'S GONNA PAY FOR MY CAMERA?
YOU SHOULD HAVE DANCED A DOG'S LEG.

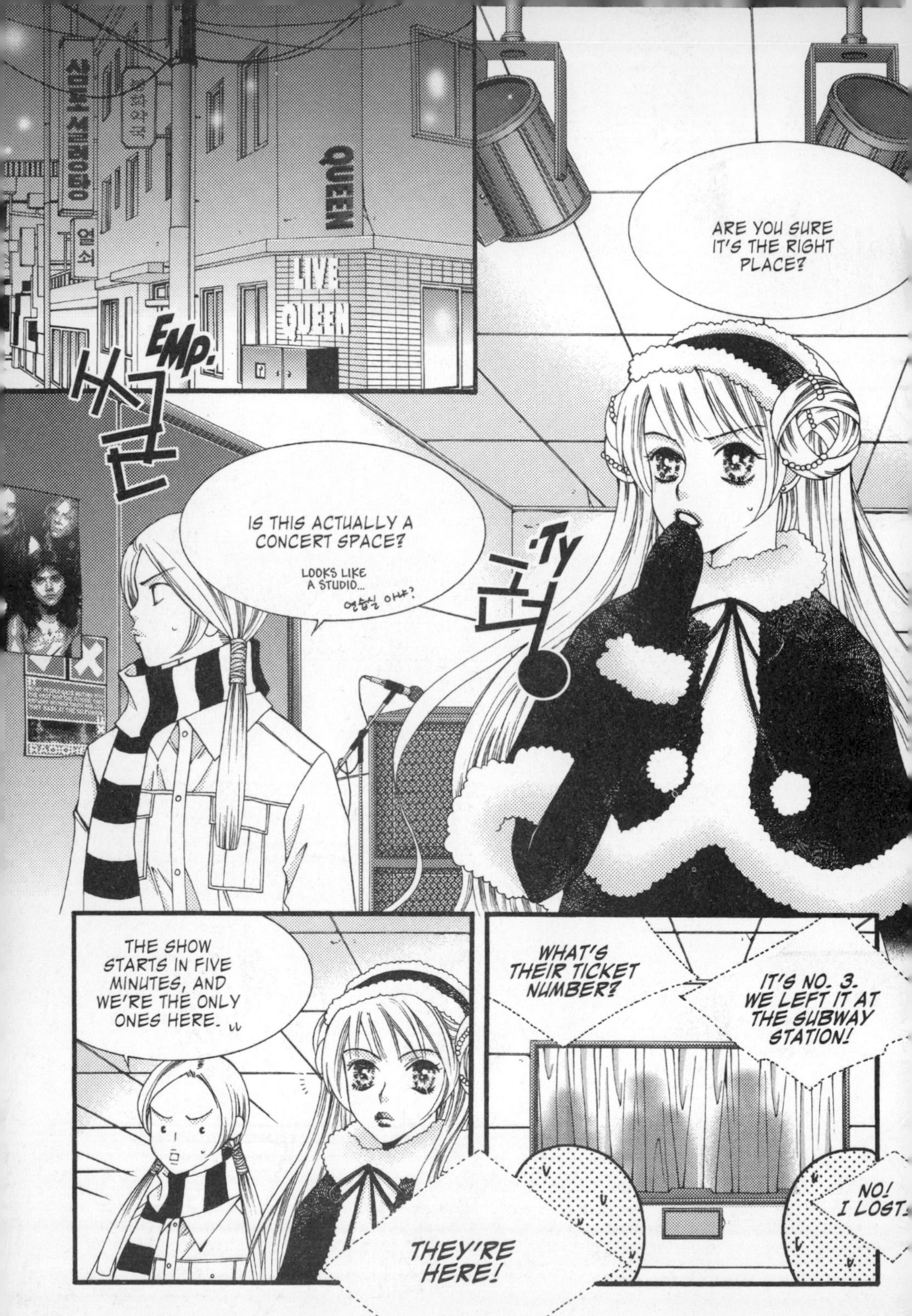
QUEEN
LIVE QUEEN
EMP.
ARE YOU SURE IT'S THE RIGHT PLACE?
IS THIS ACTUALLY A CONCERT SPACE?
LOOKS LIKE A STUDIO...
연습실 아냐?
'TY
THE SHOW STARTS IN FIVE MINUTES, AND WE'RE THE ONLY ONES HERE.
THEY'RE HERE!
WHAT'S THEIR TICKET NUMBER?
IT'S NO. 3. WE LEFT IT AT THE SUBWAY STATION!
NO! I LOST.

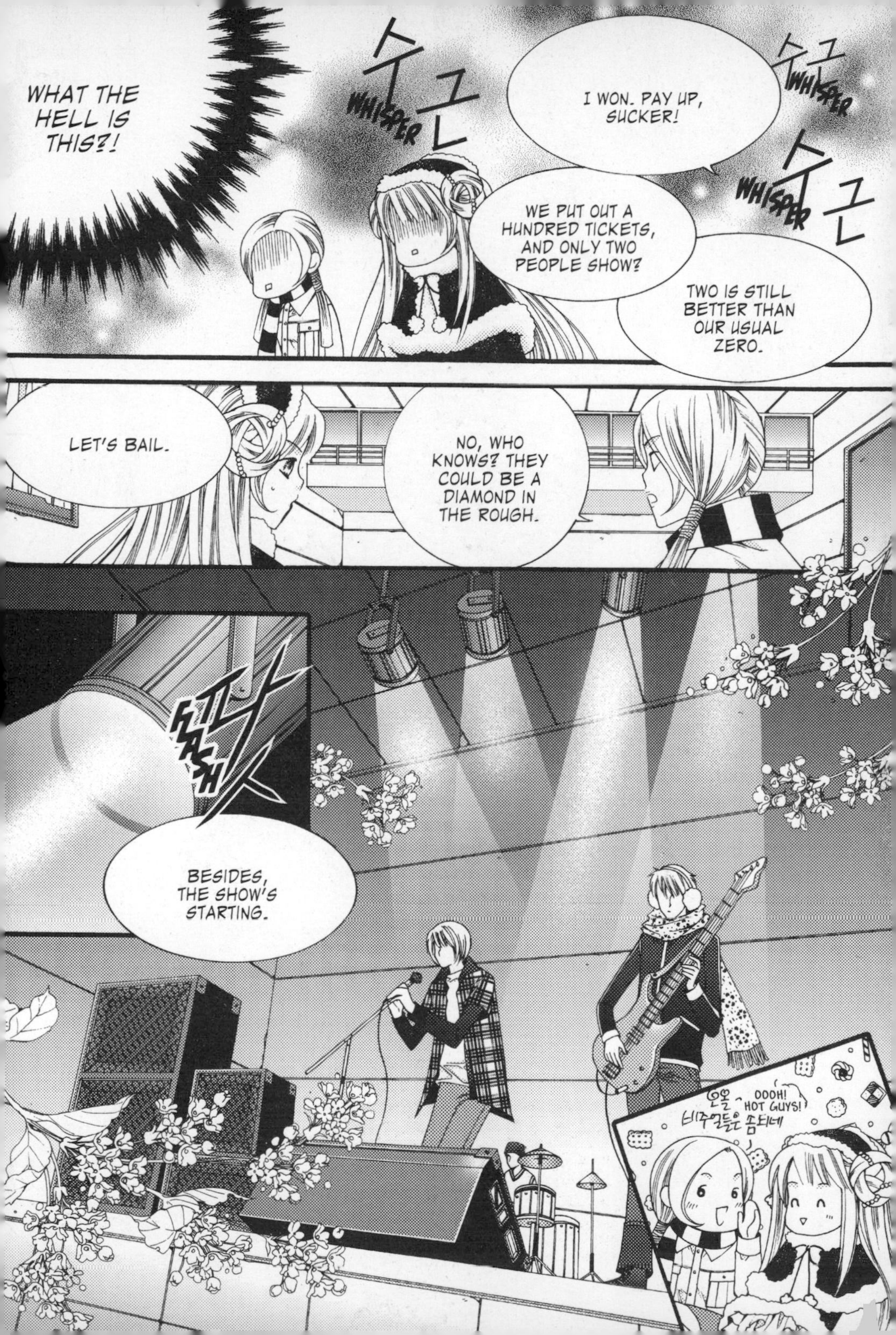
WHAT THE HELL IS THIS?!
WHISPER
I WON. PAY UP, SUCKER!
WHISPER
WE PUT OUT A HUNDRED TICKETS, AND ONLY TWO PEOPLE SHOW?
WHISPER
TWO IS STILL BETTER THAN OUR USUAL ZERO.
LET'S BAIL.
NO, WHO KNOWS? THEY COULD BE A DIAMOND IN THE ROUGH.
FLASH
BESIDES, THE SHOW'S STARTING.
오올~ 비주얼들은 좀 되네
OOOH! HOT GUYS!

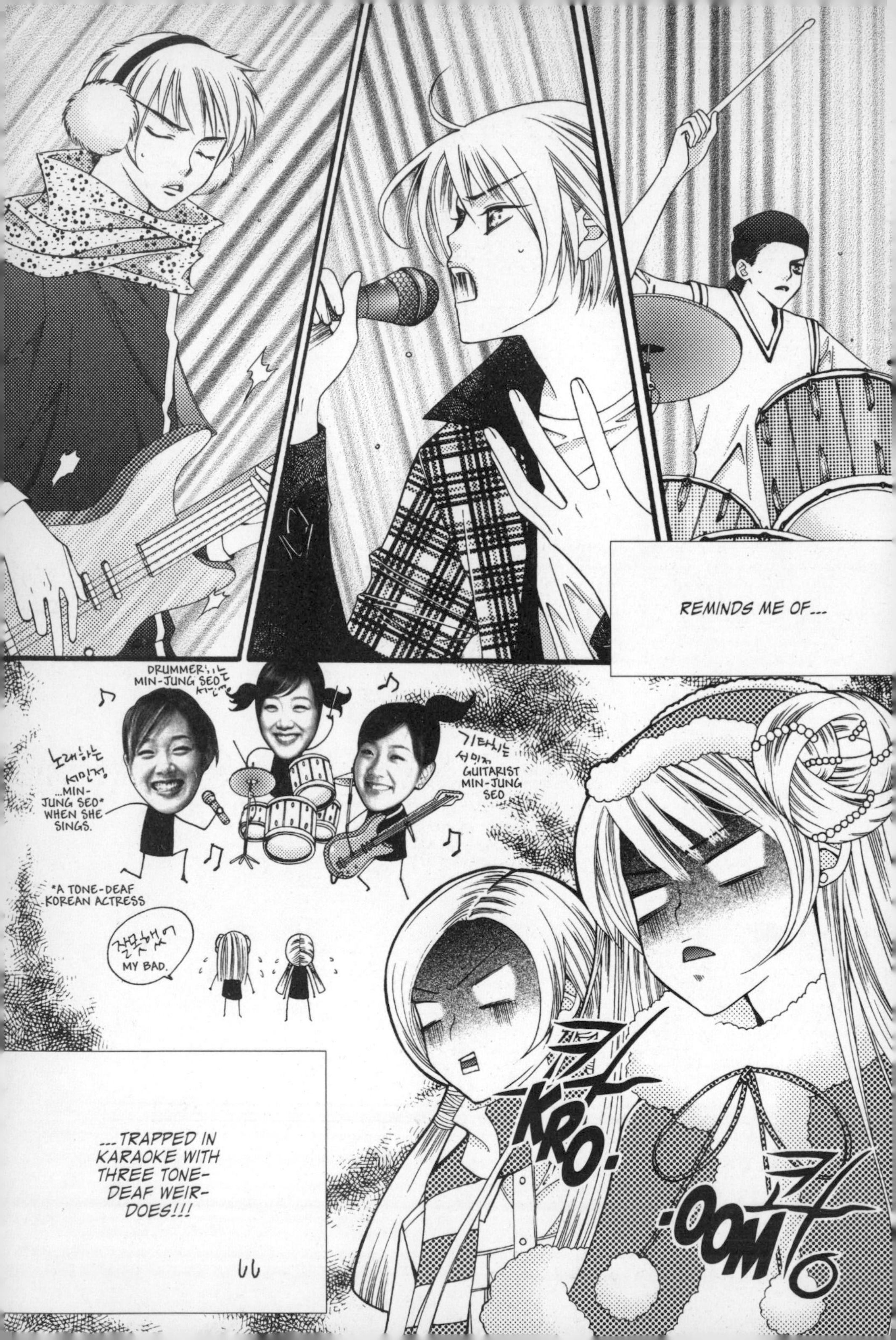
REMINDS ME OF...
DRUMMER
MIN-JUNG SEO
노래하는 서민정
...MIN-JUNG SEO* WHEN SHE SINGS.
기타치는 서민정
GUITARIST MIN-JUNG SEO
*A TONE-DEAF KOREAN ACTRESS
잘못했어
MY BAD.
...TRAPPED IN KARAOKE WITH THREE TONE-DEAF WEIR-DOES!!!
KRO-
-OOM!

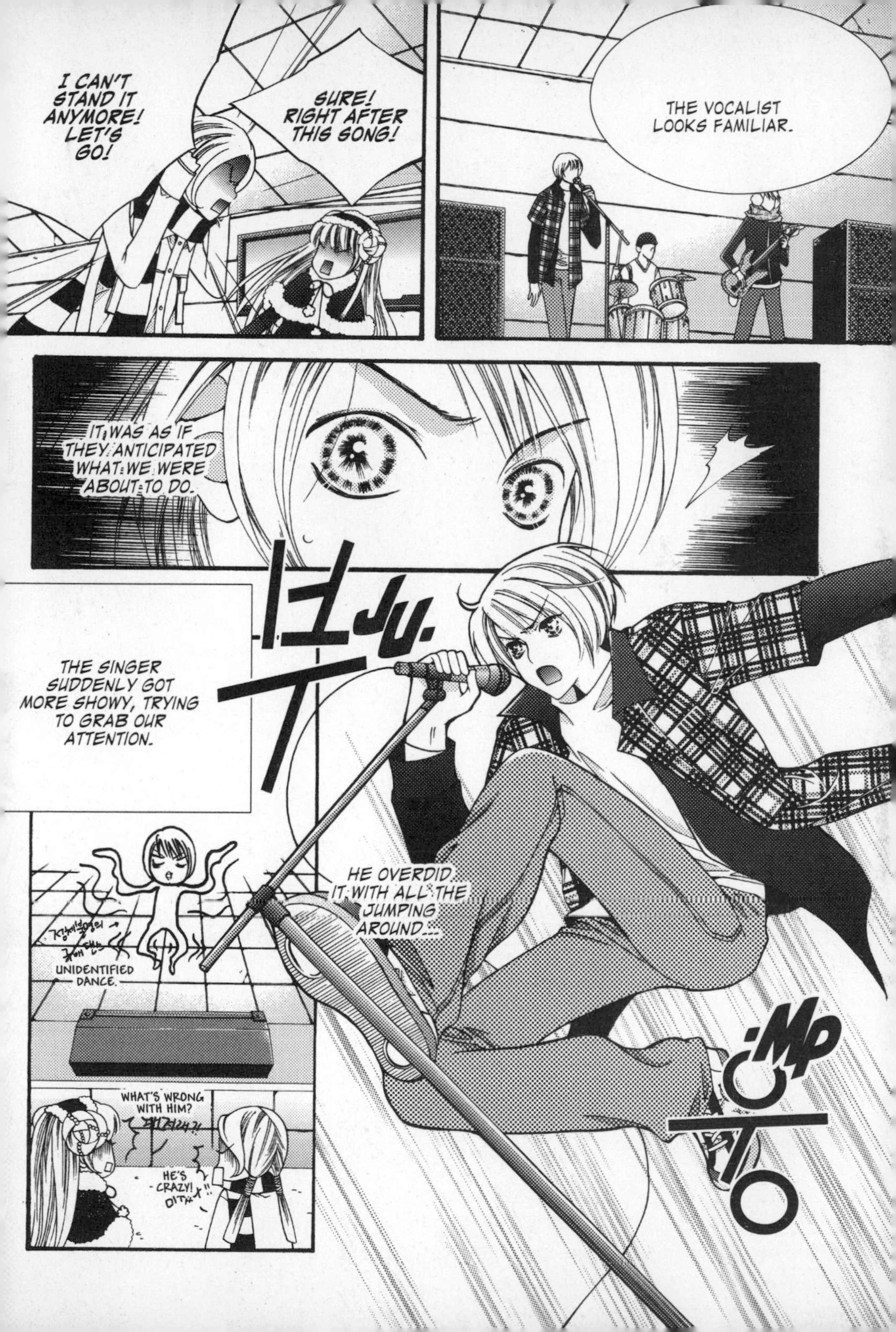
I CAN'T STAND IT ANYMORE! LET'S GO!
SURE! RIGHT AFTER THIS SONG!
THE VOCALIST LOOKS FAMILIAR.
IT WAS AS IF THEY ANTICIPATED WHAT WE WERE ABOUT TO DO.
THE SINGER SUDDENLY GOT MORE SHOWY, TRYING TO GRAB OUR ATTENTION.
UNIDENTIFIED DANCE.
WHAT'S WRONG WITH HIM?
HE'S CRAZY!
HE OVERDID IT WITH ALL THE JUMPING AROUND...

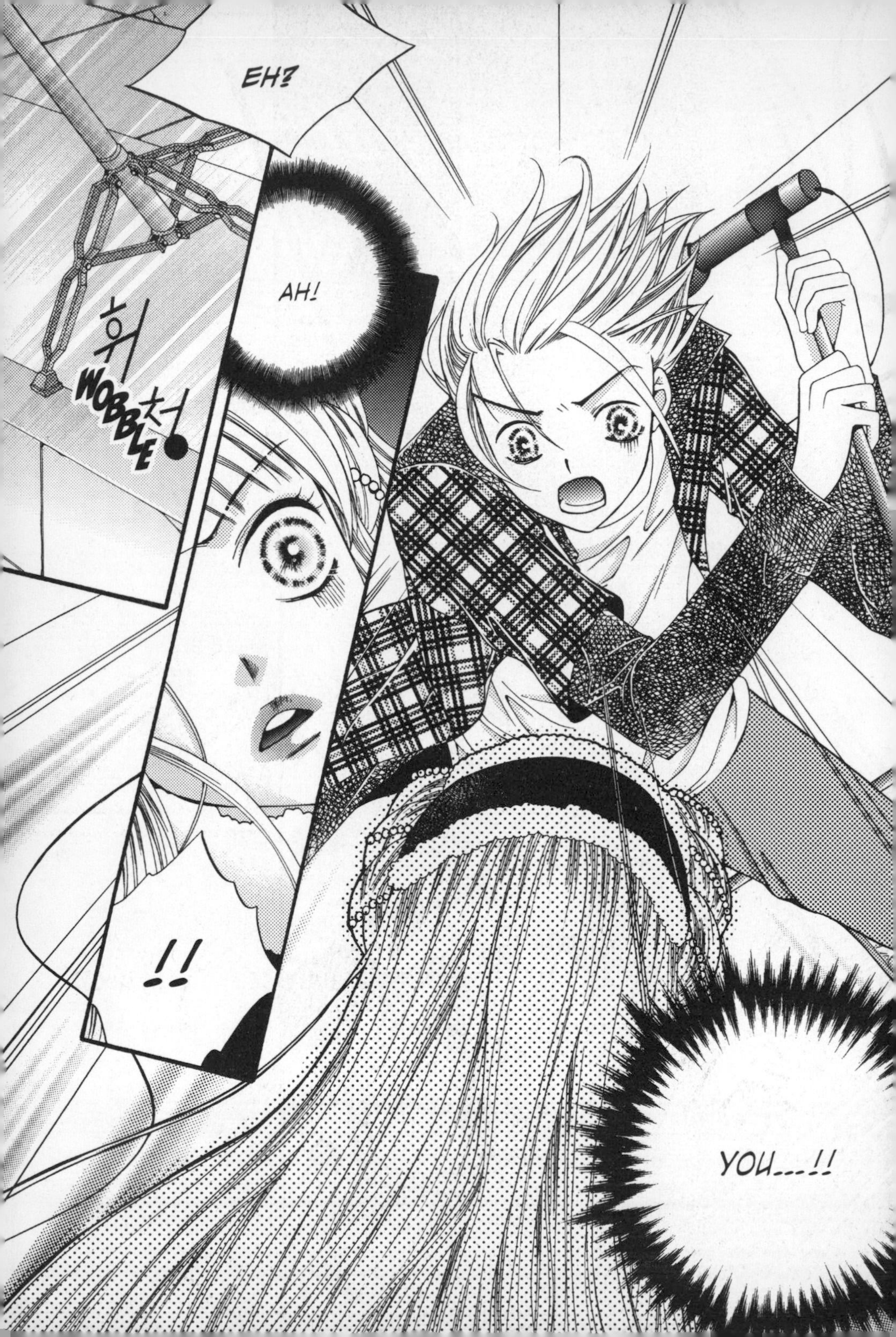
EH?
휘청
WOBBLE
AH!
!!
YOU...!!

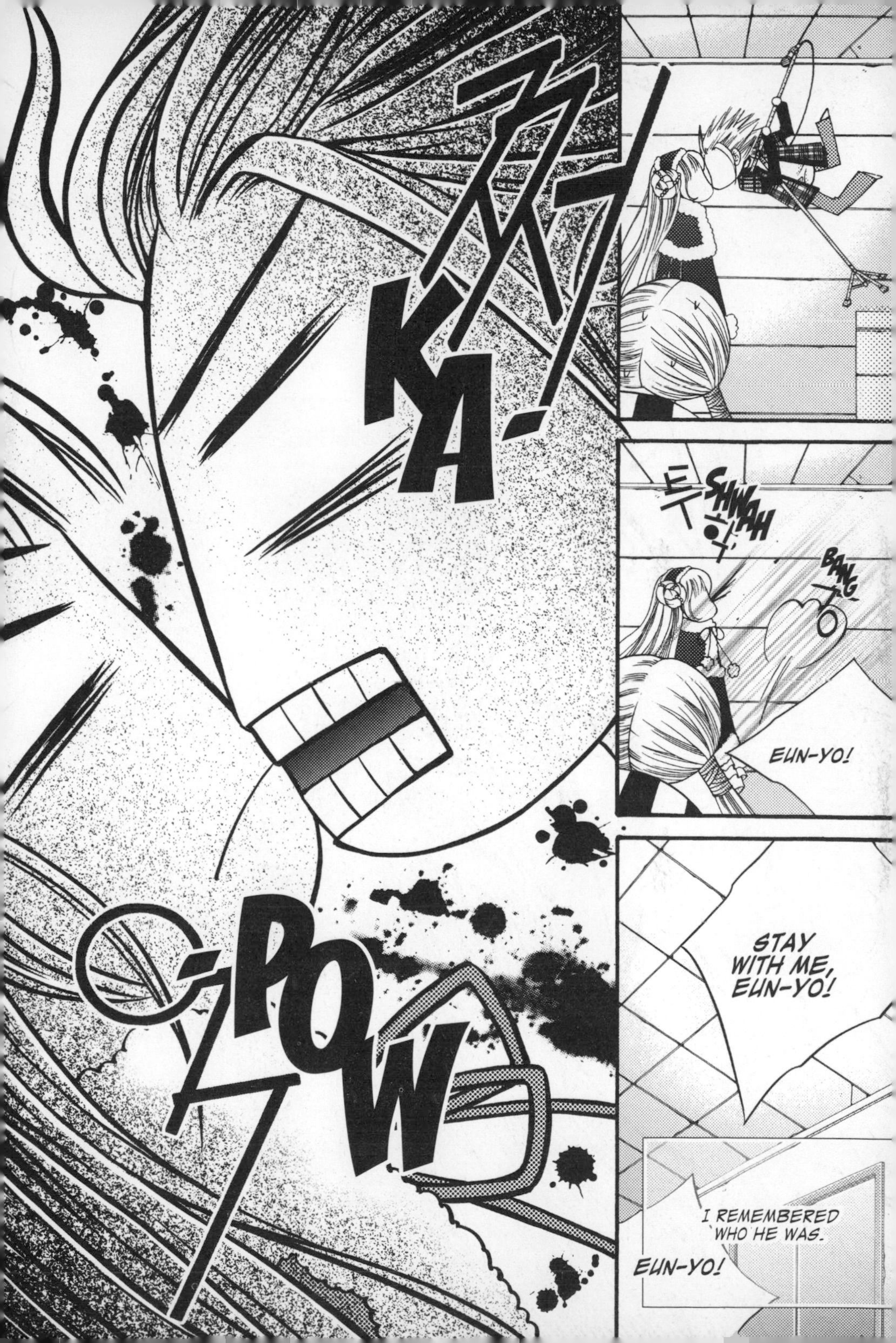
KA-
POW
SHWAAH
BANG
EUN-YO!
STAY WITH ME, EUN-YO!
I REMEMBERED WHO HE WAS.
EUN-YO!

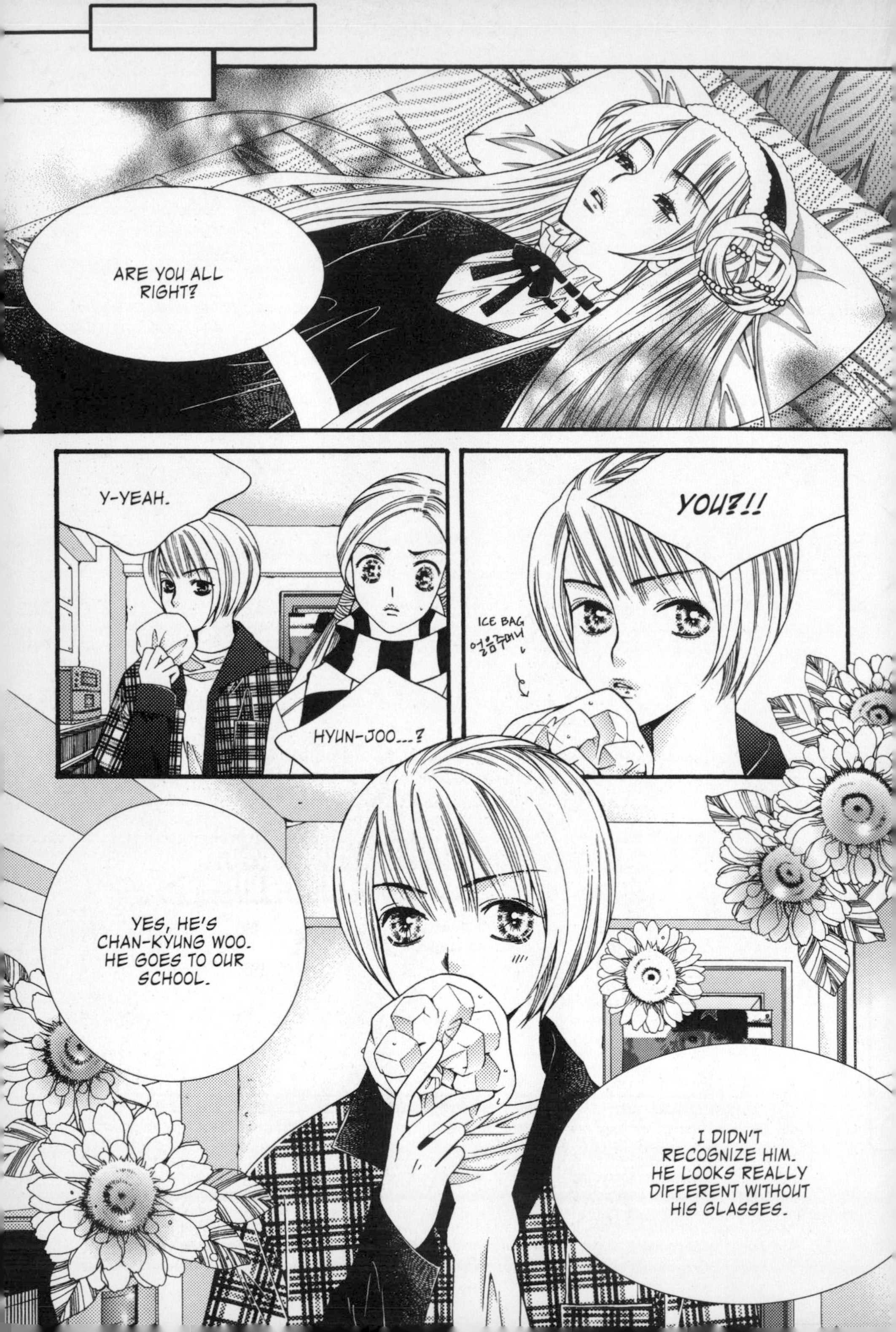
ARE YOU ALL RIGHT?
Y-YEAH.
HYUN-JOO...?
YOU?!!
ICE BAG
얼음주머니
YES, HE'S CHAN-KYUNG WOO. HE GOES TO OUR SCHOOL.
I DIDN'T RECOGNIZE HIM. HE LOOKS REALLY DIFFERENT WITHOUT HIS GLASSES.

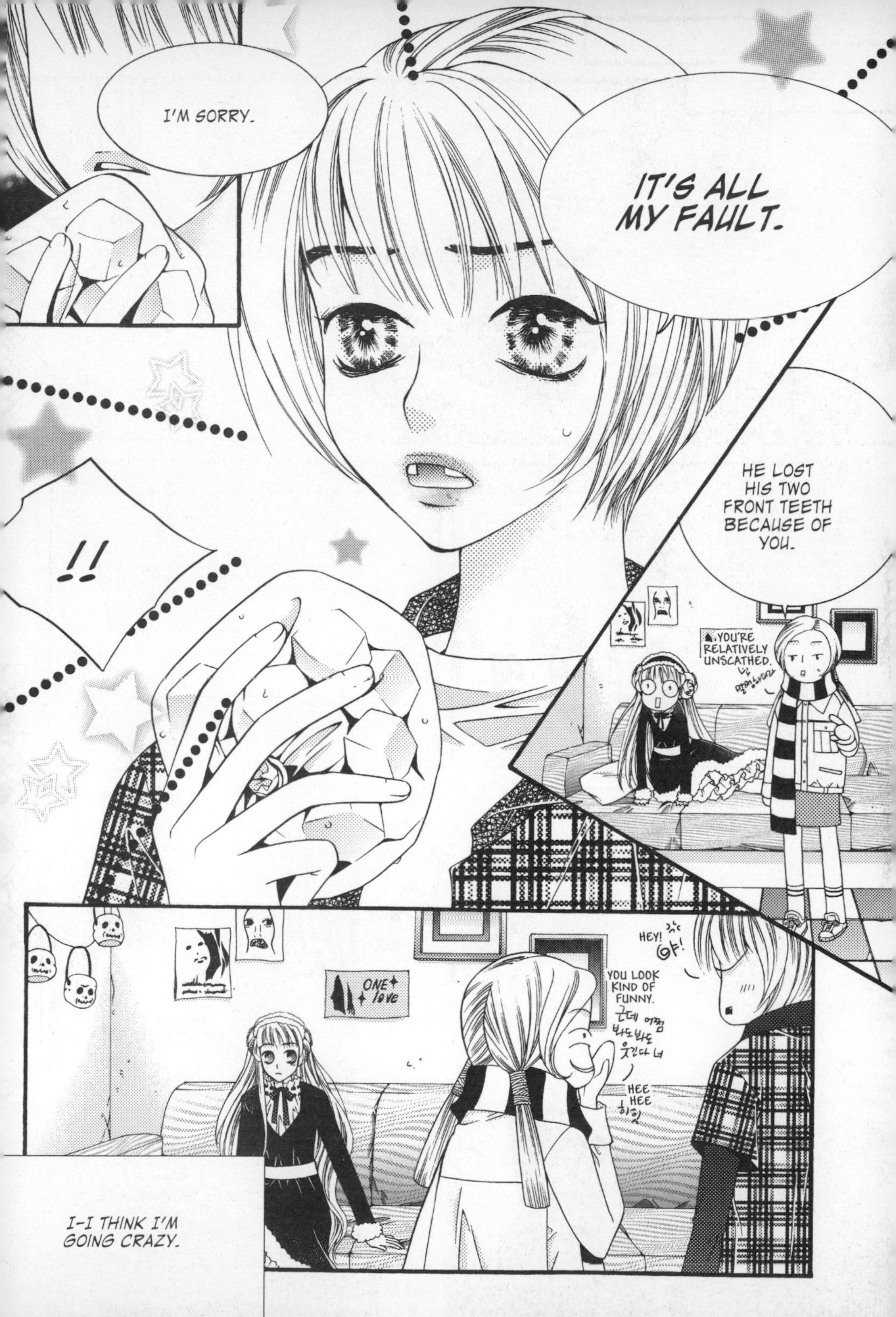
I'M SORRY.
IT'S ALL MY FAULT.
!!
HE LOST HIS TWO FRONT TEETH BECAUSE OF YOU.
YOU'RE RELATIVELY UNSCATHED.
HEY!
야!
YOU LOOK KIND OF FUNNY.
근데 어쩜 봐도봐도 웃긴다 너
HEE HEE
히힛
I-I THINK I'M GOING CRAZY.

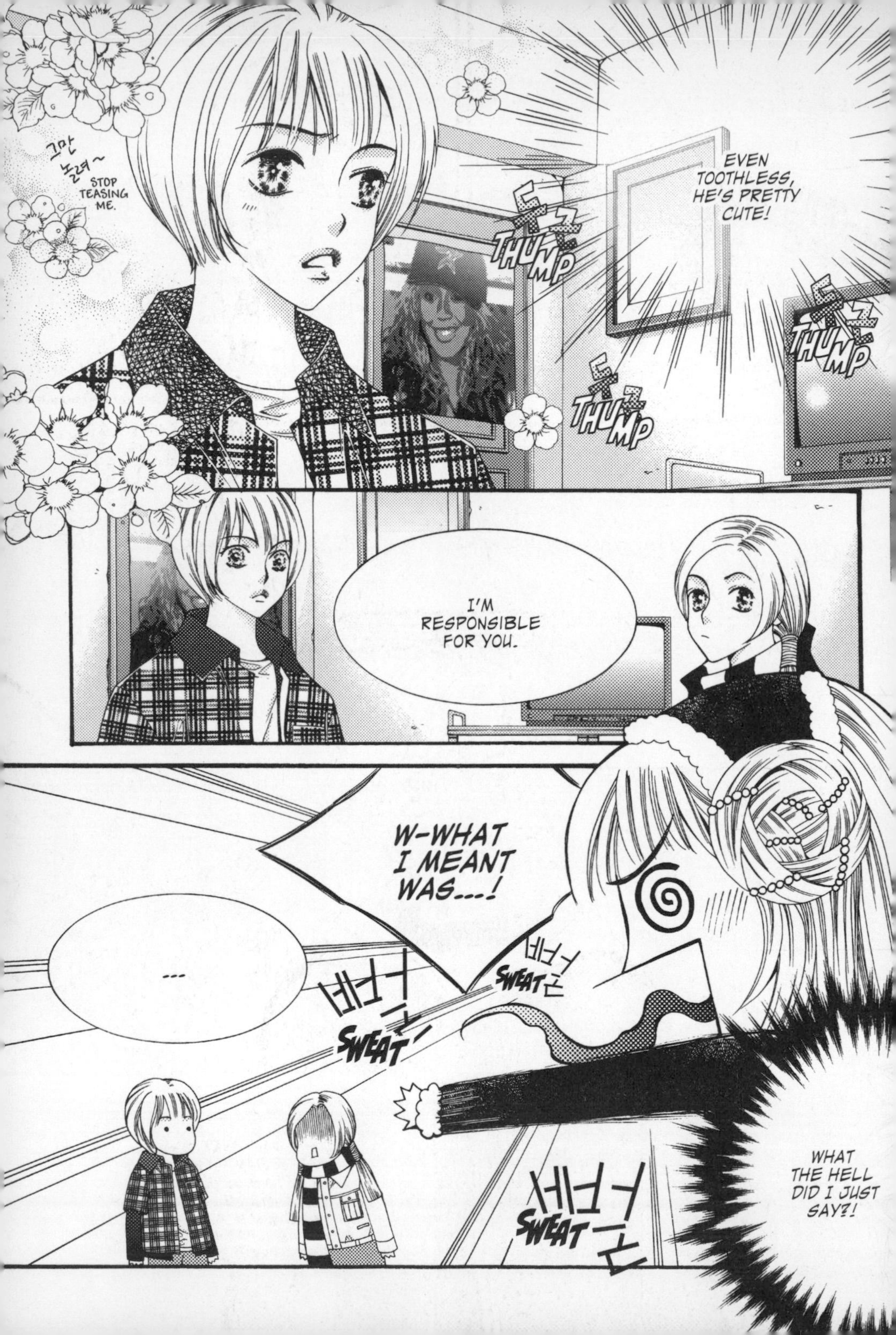
그만 놀려~
STOP TEASING ME.
THUMP
EVEN TOOTHLESS, HE'S PRETTY CUTE!
THUMP
THUMP
I'M RESPONSIBLE FOR YOU.
W-WHAT I MEANT WAS...!
...
SWEAT
SWEAT
SWEAT
WHAT THE HELL DID I JUST SAY?!

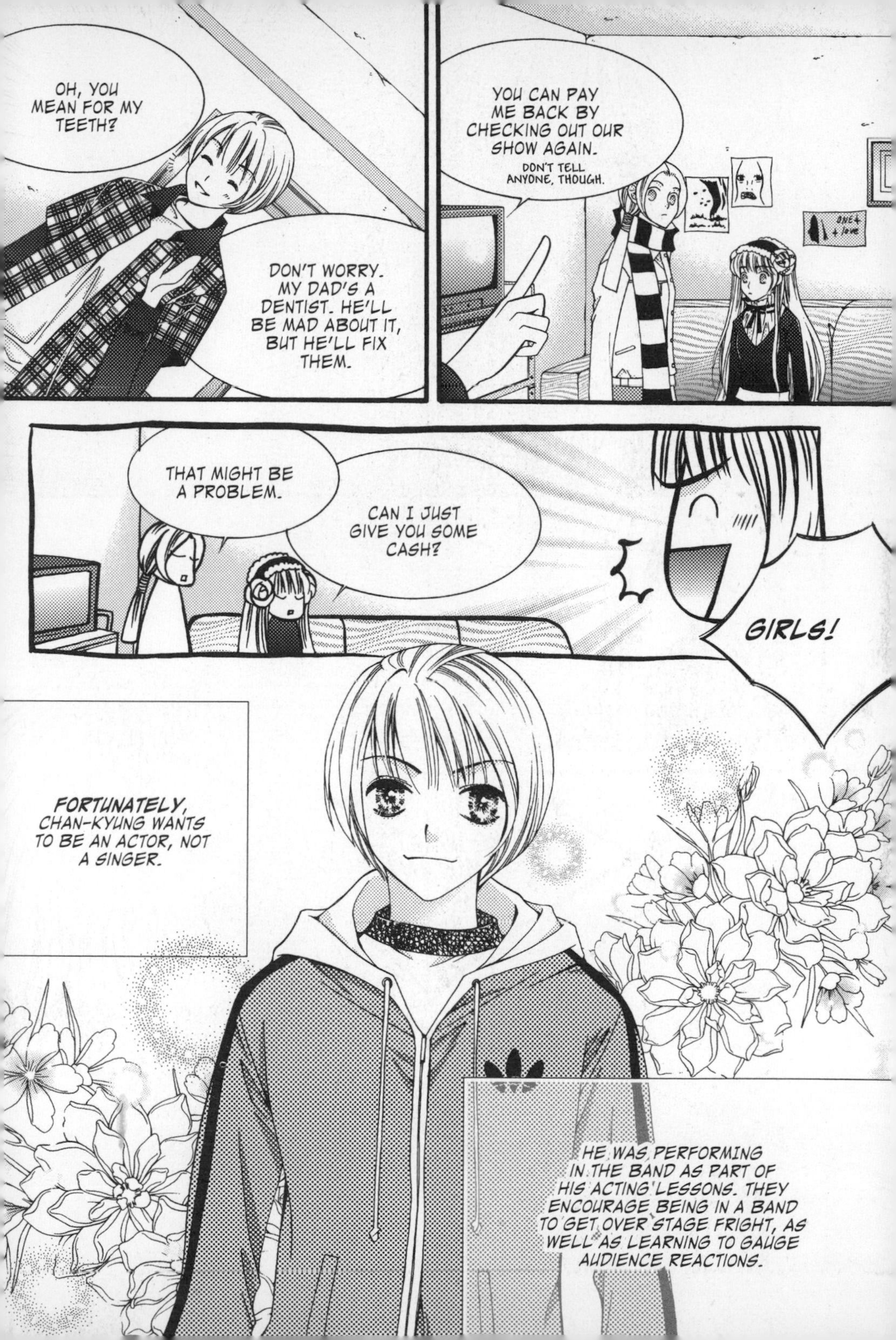
OH, YOU MEAN FOR MY TEETH?
DON'T WORRY. MY DAD'S A DENTIST. HE'LL BE MAD ABOUT IT, BUT HE'LL FIX THEM.
YOU CAN PAY ME BACK BY CHECKING OUT OUR SHOW AGAIN.
DON'T TELL ANYONE, THOUGH.
THAT MIGHT BE A PROBLEM.
CAN I JUST GIVE YOU SOME CASH?
GIRLS!
FORTUNATELY, CHAN-KYUNG WANTS TO BE AN ACTOR, NOT A SINGER.
HE WAS PERFORMING IN THE BAND AS PART OF HIS ACTING LESSONS. THEY ENCOURAGE BEING IN A BAND TO GET OVER STAGE FRIGHT, AS WELL AS LEARNING TO GAUGE AUDIENCE REACTIONS.

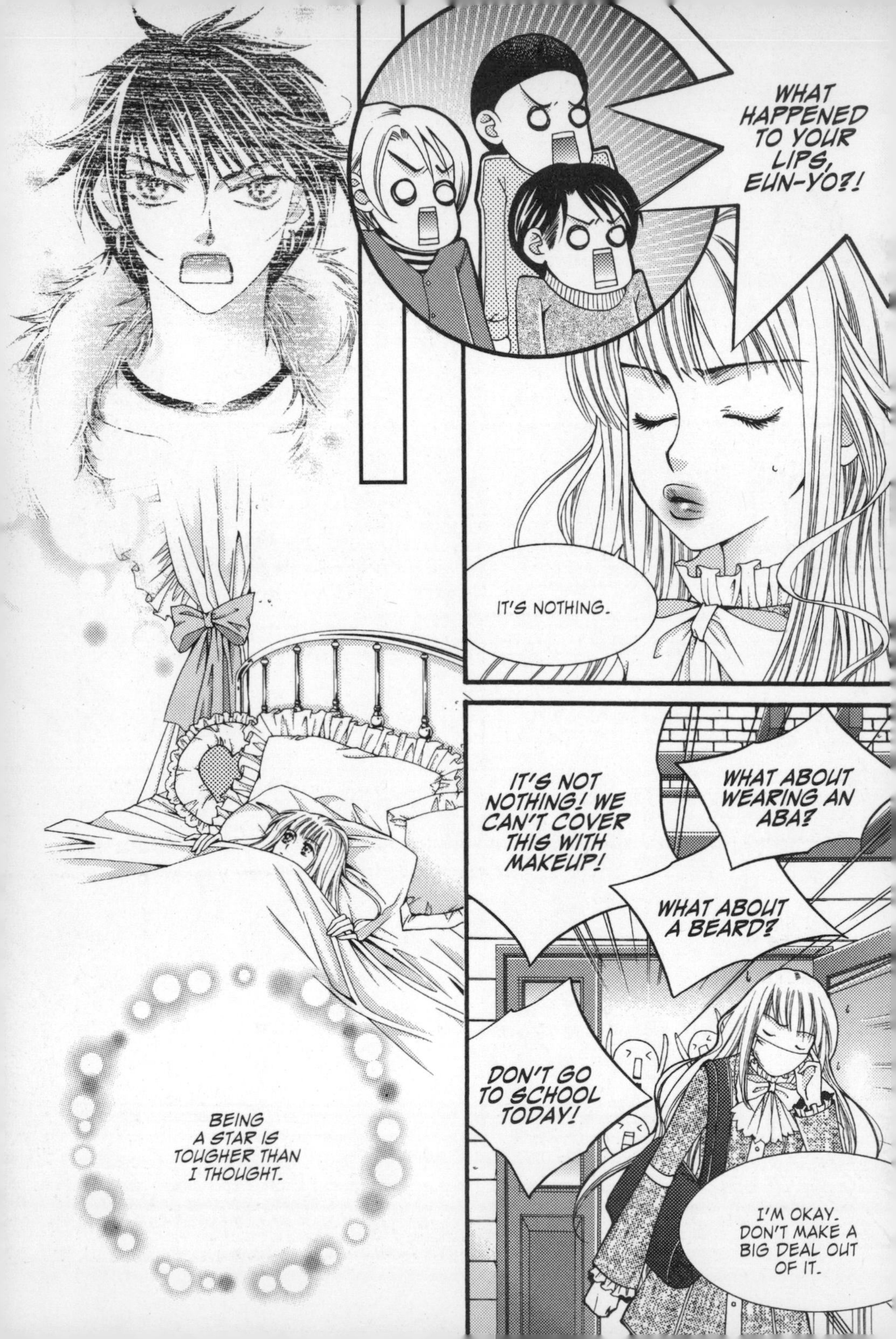
BEING A STAR IS TOUGHER THAN I THOUGHT.
WHAT HAPPENED TO YOUR LIPS, EUN-YO?!
IT'S NOTHING.
IT'S NOT NOTHING! WE CAN'T COVER THIS WITH MAKEUP!
WHAT ABOUT WEARING AN ABA?
WHAT ABOUT A BEARD?
DON'T GO TO SCHOOL TODAY!
I'M OKAY. DON'T MAKE A BIG DEAL OUT OF IT.

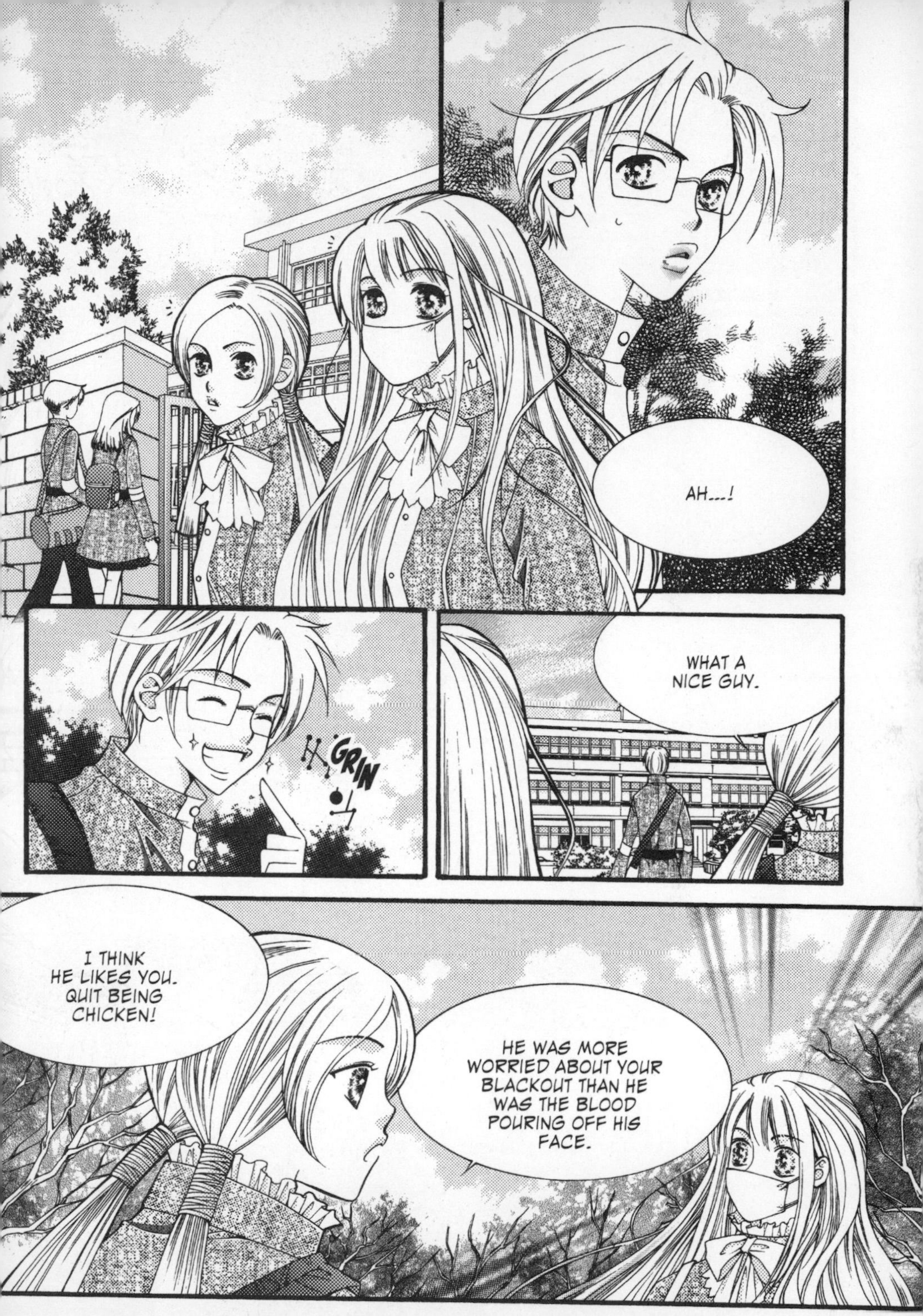
AH...!
GRIN
WHAT A NICE GUY.
I THINK HE LIKES YOU. QUIT BEING CHICKEN!
HE WAS MORE WORRIED ABOUT YOUR BLACKOUT THAN HE WAS THE BLOOD POURING OFF HIS FACE.

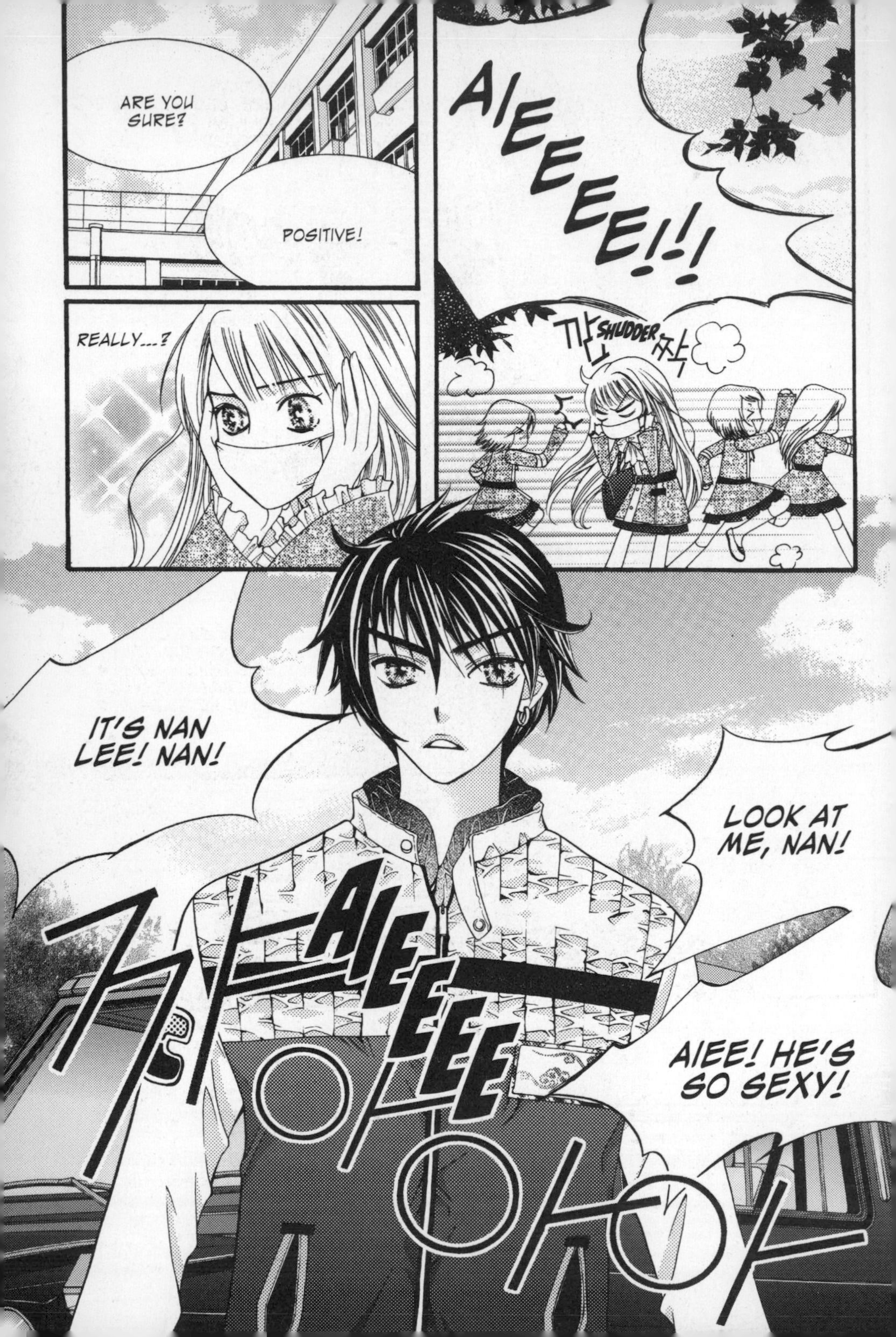
ARE YOU SURE?
POSITIVE!
REALLY...?
AIEEEEE!!!
SHUDDER
IT'S NAN LEE! NAN!
LOOK AT ME, NAN!
AIEEE
AIEE! HE'S SO SEXY!

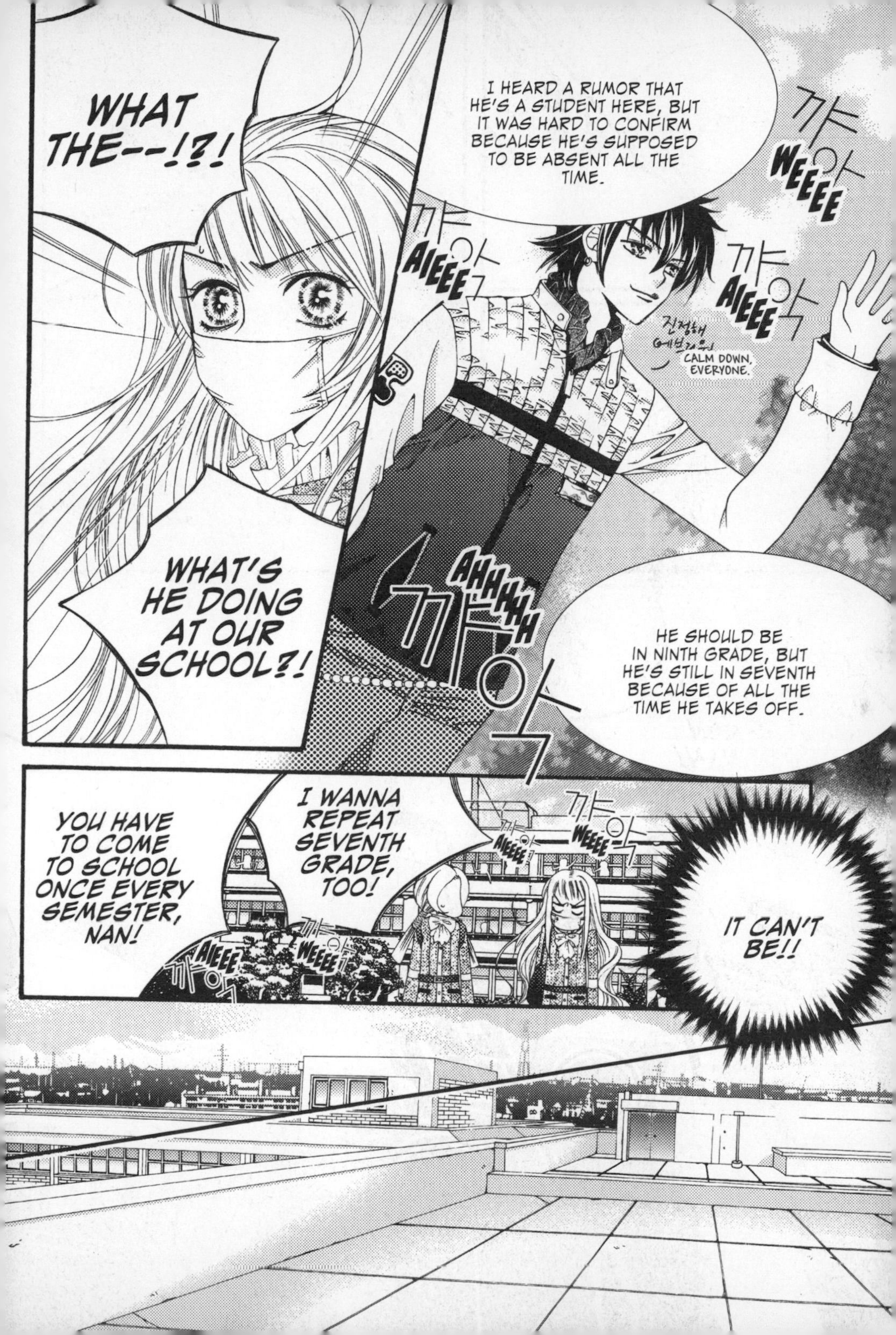
WHAT THE--!?!
WHAT'S HE DOING AT OUR SCHOOL?!
I HEARD A RUMOR THAT HE'S A STUDENT HERE, BUT IT WAS HARD TO CONFIRM BECAUSE HE'S SUPPOSED TO BE ABSENT ALL THE TIME.
WEEEE
AIEEE
AIEEE
CALM DOWN, EVERYONE.
AHHHHHH
HE SHOULD BE IN NINTH GRADE, BUT HE'S STILL IN SEVENTH BECAUSE OF ALL THE TIME HE TAKES OFF.
YOU HAVE TO COME TO SCHOOL ONCE EVERY SEMESTER, NAN!
I WANNA REPEAT SEVENTH GRADE, TOO!
AIEEE
WEEEE
AIEEE
WEEEE
IT CAN'T BE!!

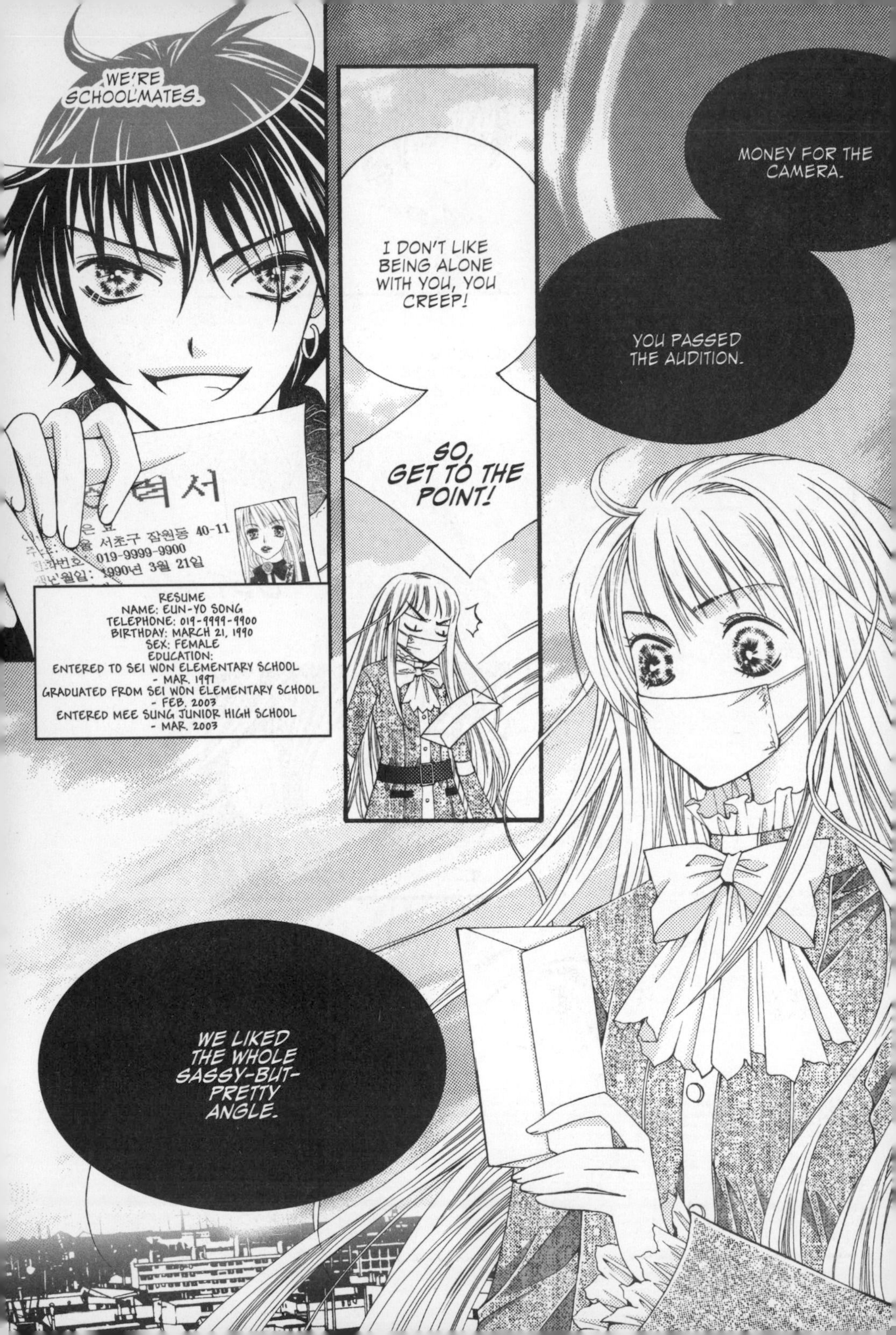
WE'RE SCHOOLMATES.
서초구 잠원동 40-11
019-9999-9900
1990년 3월 21일
RESUME
NAME: EUN-YO SONG
TELEPHONE: 019-9999-9900
BIRTHDAY: MARCH 21, 1990
SEX: FEMALE
EDUCATION:
ENTERED TO SEI WON ELEMENTARY SCHOOL - MAR. 1997
GRADUATED FROM SEI WON ELEMENTARY SCHOOL - FEB. 2003
ENTERED MEE SUNG JUNIOR HIGH SCHOOL - MAR. 2003
I DON'T LIKE BEING ALONE WITH YOU, YOU CREEP!
SO, GET TO THE POINT!
MONEY FOR THE CAMERA.
YOU PASSED THE AUDITION.
WE LIKED THE WHOLE SASSY-BUT-PRETTY ANGLE.

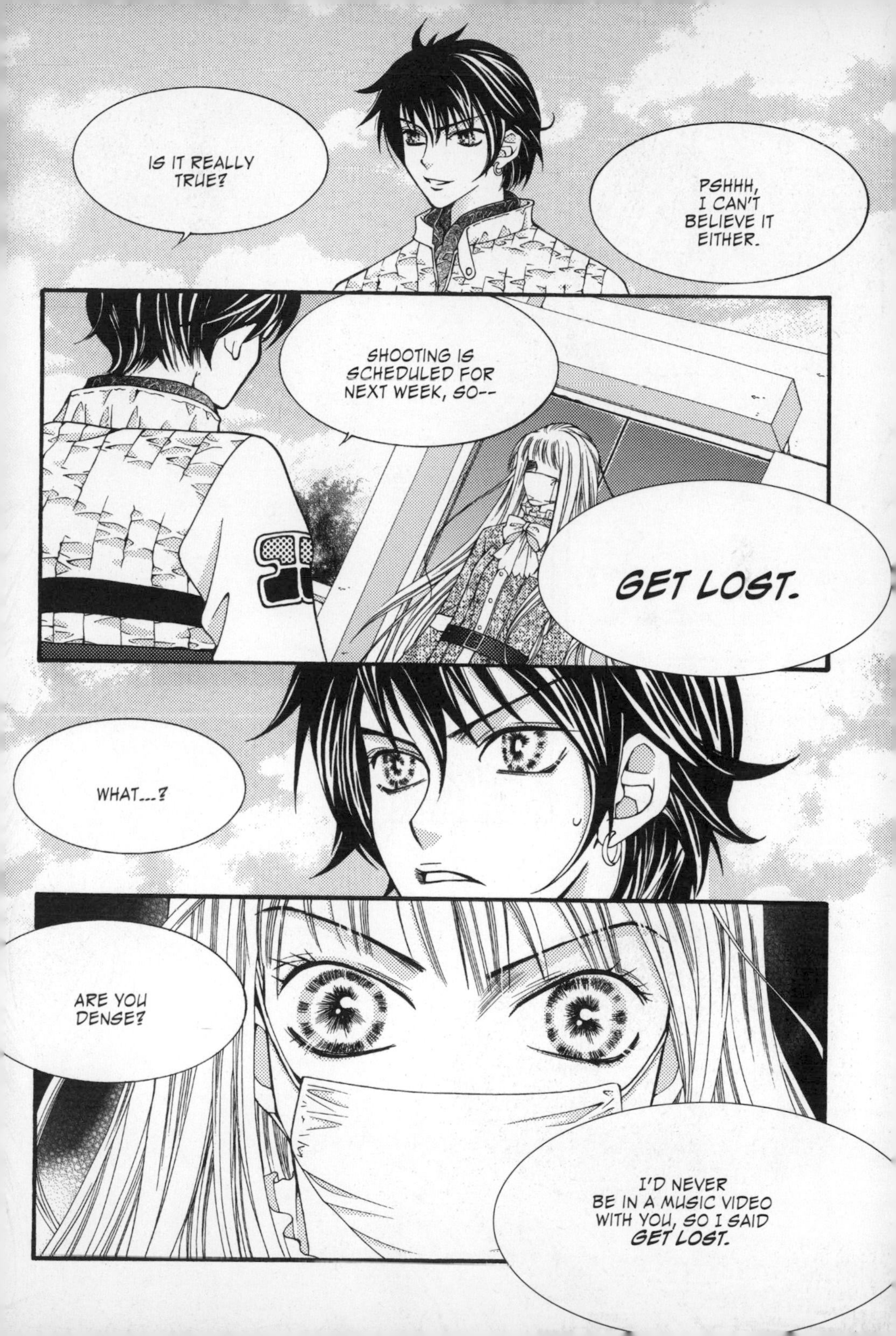
IS IT REALLY TRUE?
PSHHH, I CAN'T BELIEVE IT EITHER.
SHOOTING IS SCHEDULED FOR NEXT WEEK, SO--
GET LOST.
WHAT...?
ARE YOU DENSE?
I'D NEVER BE IN A MUSIC VIDEO WITH YOU, SO I SAID *GET LOST*.

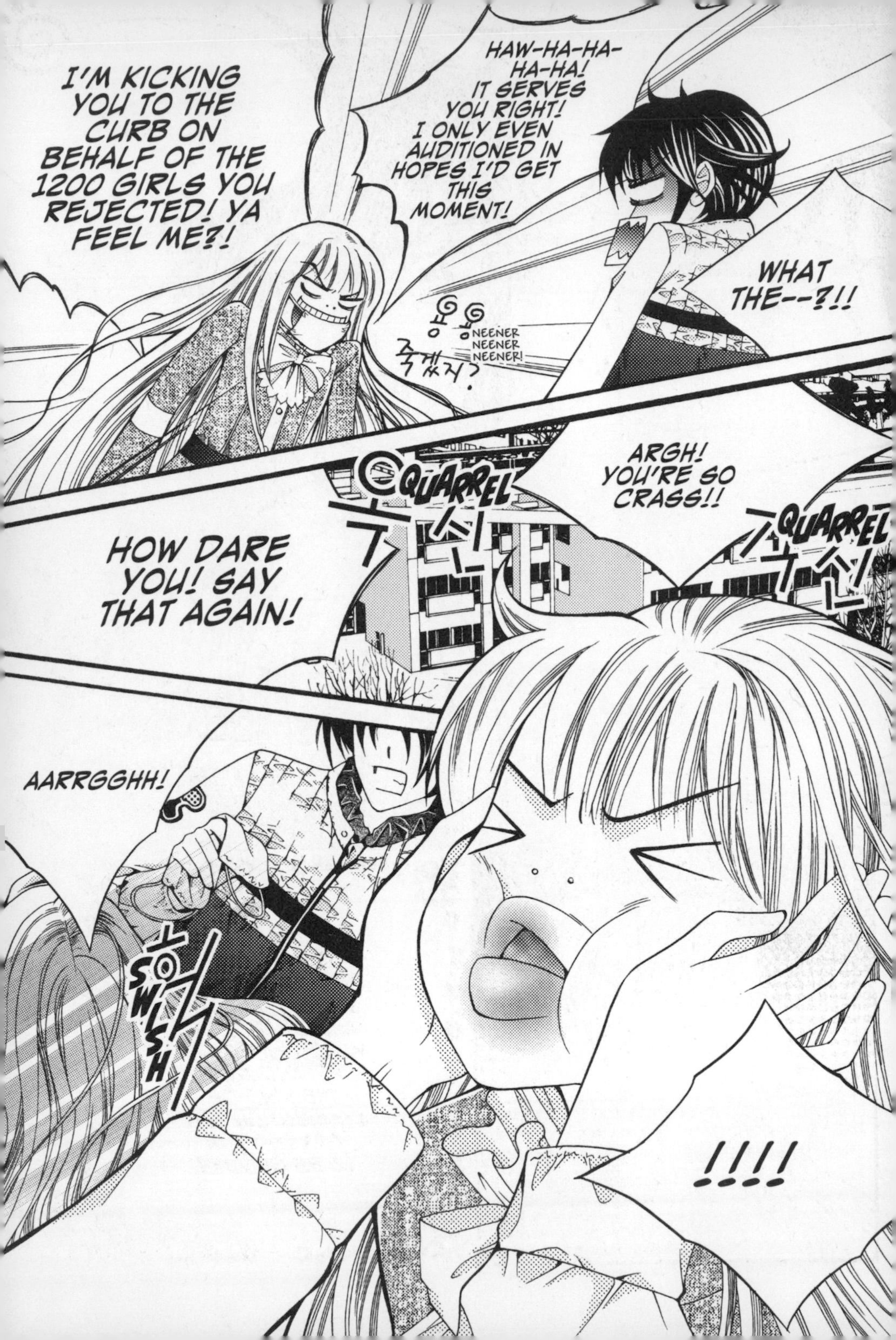
I'M KICKING YOU TO THE CURB ON BEHALF OF THE 1200 GIRLS YOU REJECTED! YA FEEL ME?!
HAW-HA-HA-HA-HA! IT SERVES YOU RIGHT! I ONLY EVEN AUDITIONED IN HOPES I'D GET THIS MOMENT!
용용 죽겠지?
NEENER NEENER NEENER!
WHAT THE--?!!
HOW DARE YOU! SAY THAT AGAIN!
QUARREL
ARGH! YOU'RE SO CRASS!!
QUARREL
AARRGGHH!
SWISH
!!!!

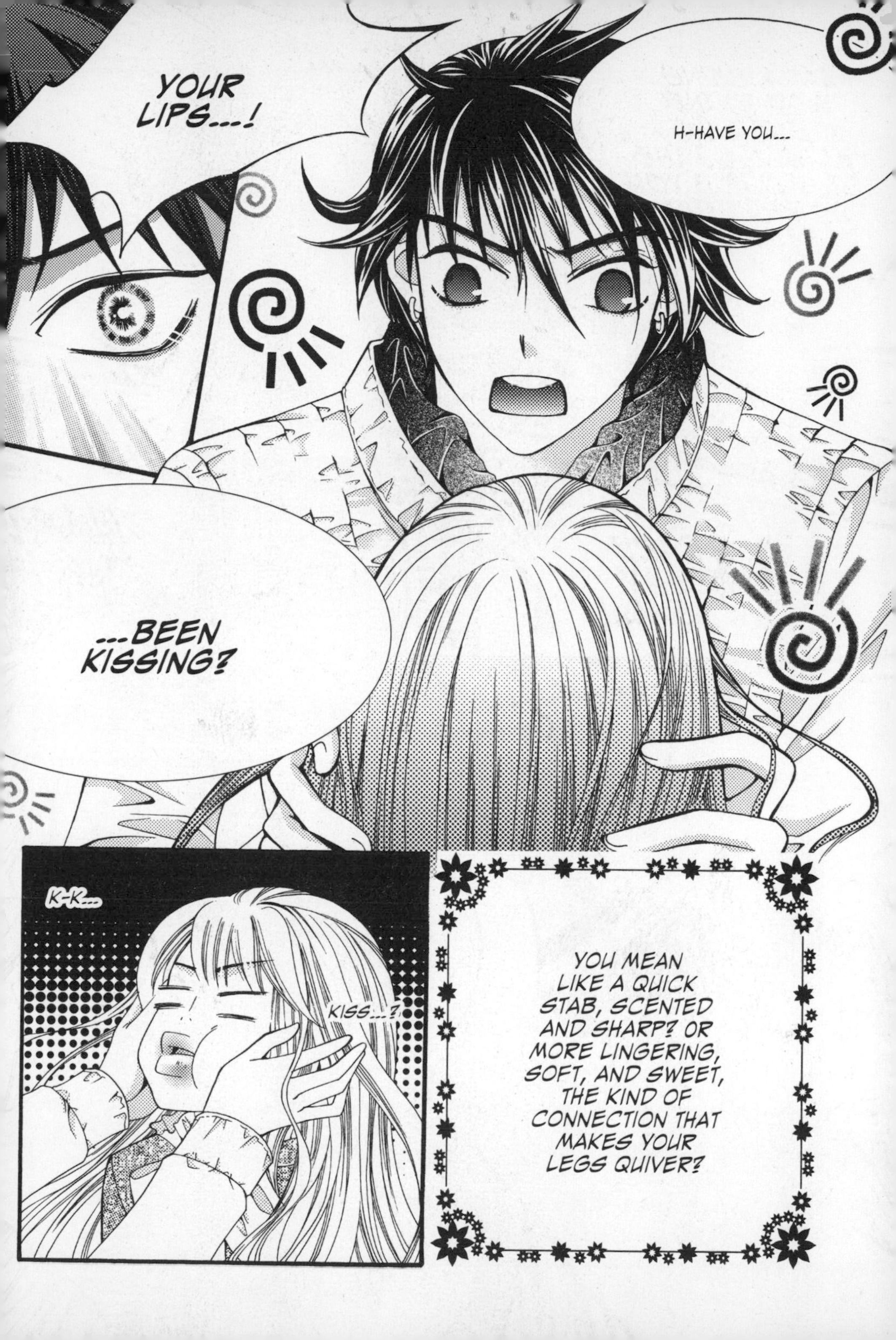
YOUR LIPS...!
H-HAVE YOU...
...BEEN KISSING?
K-K...
KISS...?
YOU MEAN LIKE A QUICK STAB, SCENTED AND SHARP? OR MORE LINGERING, SOFT, AND SWEET, THE KIND OF CONNECTION THAT MAKES YOUR LEGS QUIVER?

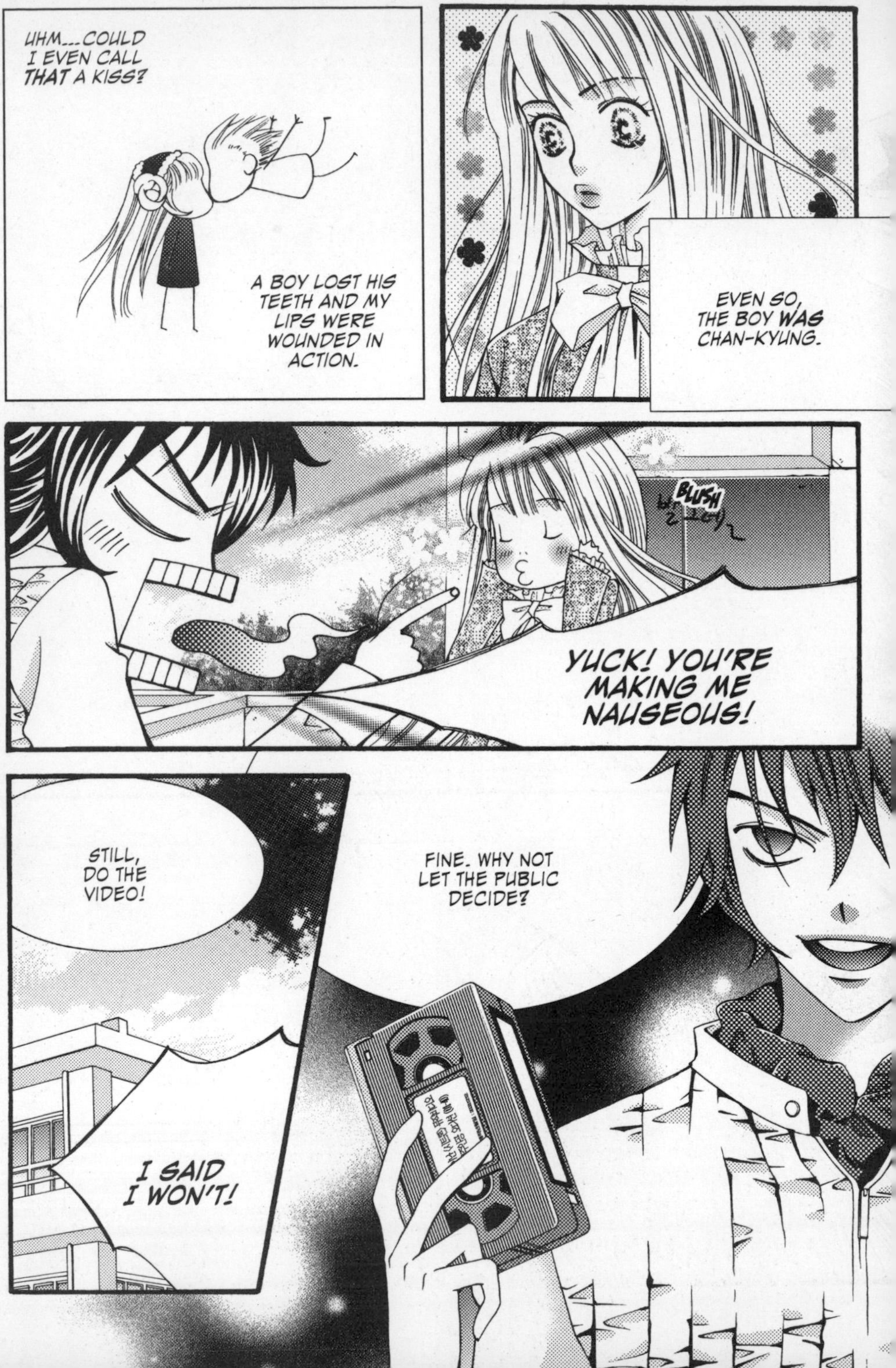
UHM...COULD I EVEN CALL THAT A KISS?
A BOY LOST HIS TEETH AND MY LIPS WERE WOUNDED IN ACTION.
EVEN SO, THE BOY WAS CHAN-KYUNG.
BLUSH
YUCK! YOU'RE MAKING ME NAUSEOUS!
STILL, DO THE VIDEO!
FINE. WHY NOT LET THE PUBLIC DECIDE?
I SAID I WON'T!

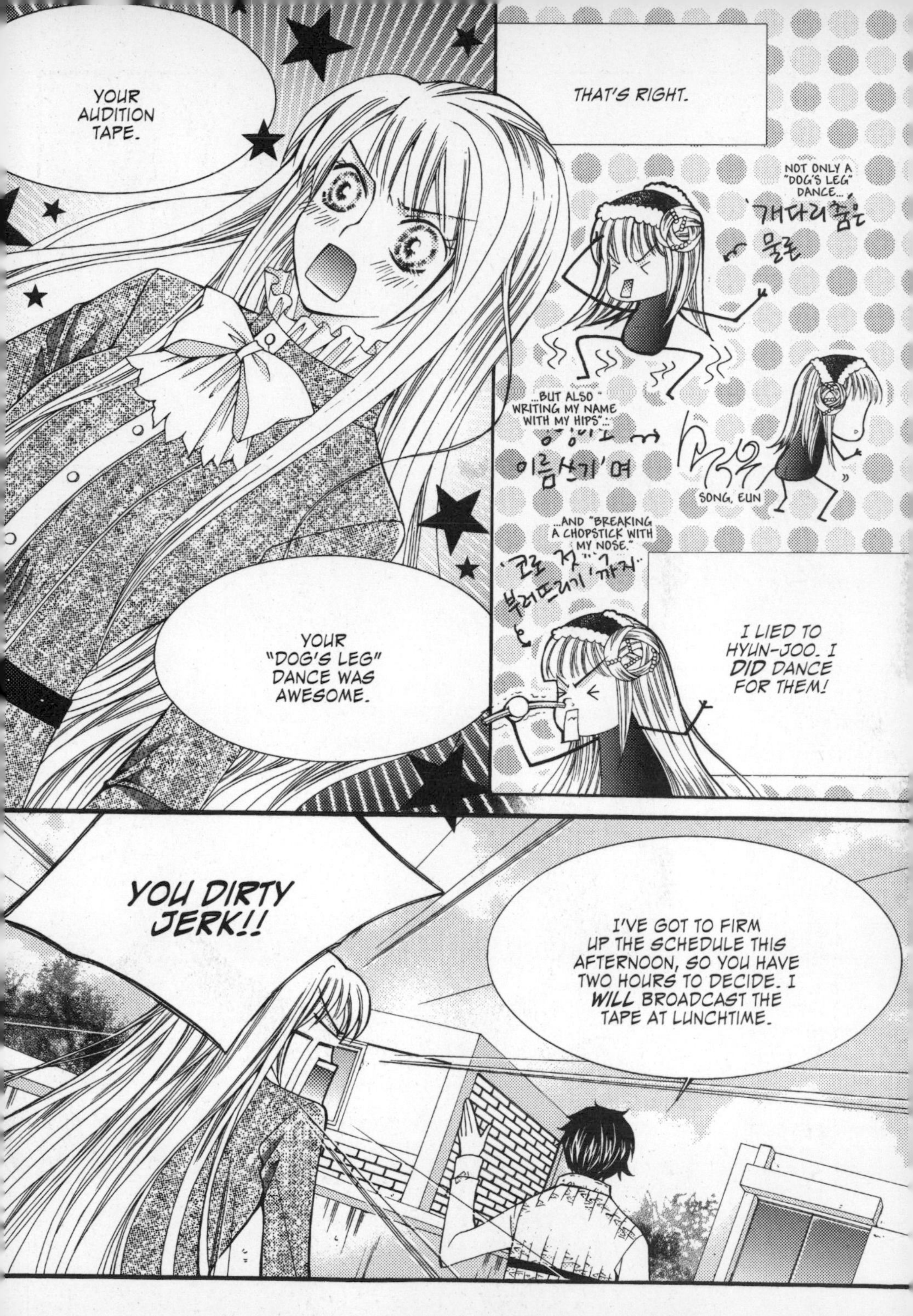
YOUR AUDITION TAPE.
YOUR "DOG'S LEG" DANCE WAS AWESOME.
THAT'S RIGHT.
NOT ONLY A "DOG'S LEG" DANCE...
개다리춤은
물론
...BUT ALSO "WRITING MY NAME WITH MY HIPS"...
이름쓰기'며
SONG, EUN
...AND "BREAKING A CHOPSTICK WITH MY NOSE."
I LIED TO HYUN-JOO. I DID DANCE FOR THEM!
YOU DIRTY JERK!!
I'VE GOT TO FIRM UP THE SCHEDULE THIS AFTERNOON, SO YOU HAVE TWO HOURS TO DECIDE. I WILL BROADCAST THE TAPE AT LUNCHTIME.

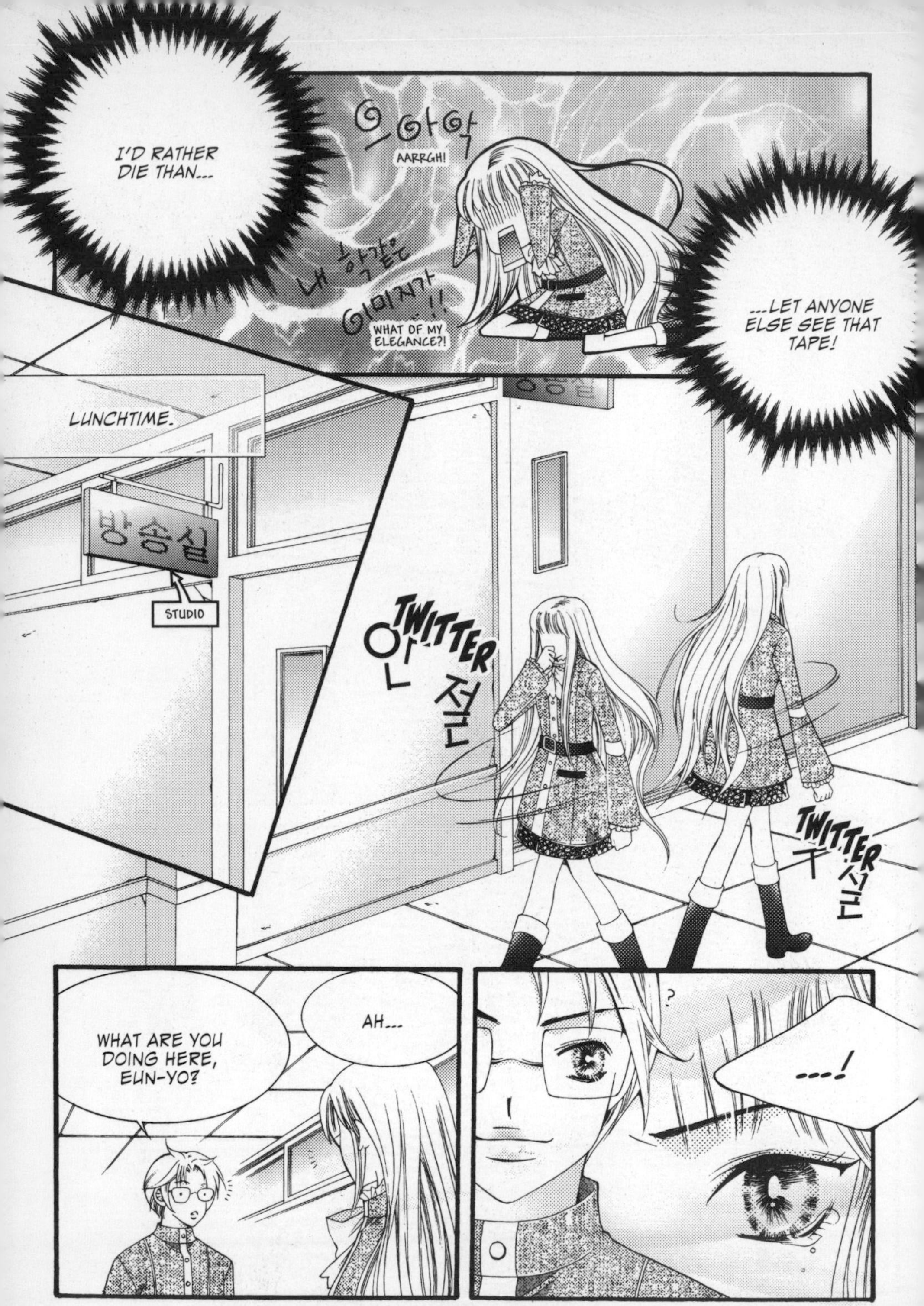
I'D RATHER DIE THAN...
으아악
AARRGH!
WHAT OF MY ELEGANCE?!
...LET ANYONE ELSE SEE THAT TAPE!
LUNCHTIME.
방송실
STUDIO
TWITTER
TWITTER
WHAT ARE YOU DOING HERE, EUN-YO?
AH...
?
...!

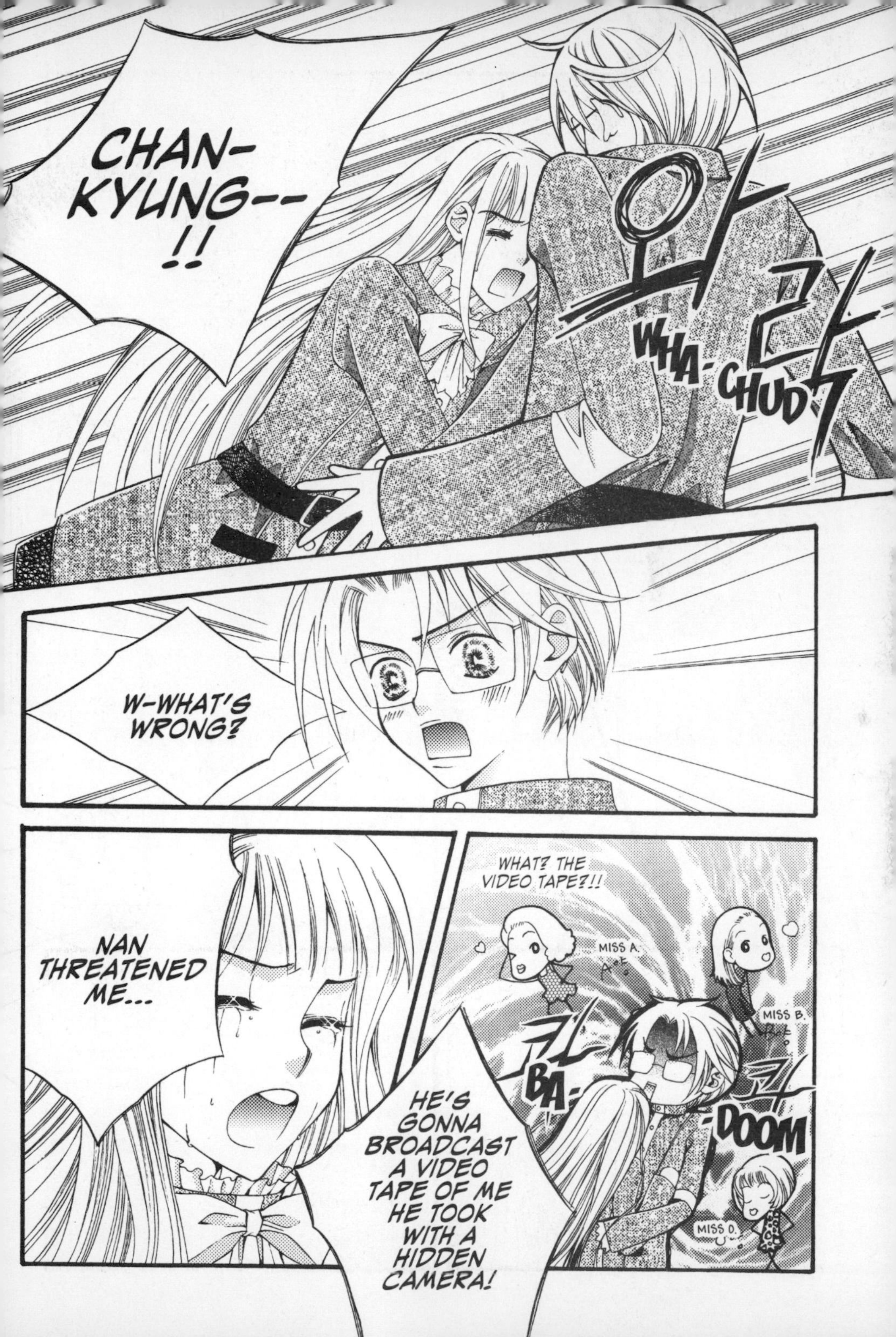
CHAN-KYUNG--!!
와락
WHA-CHUD
W-WHAT'S WRONG?
NAN THREATENED ME...
HE'S GONNA BROADCAST A VIDEO TAPE OF ME HE TOOK WITH A HIDDEN CAMERA!
WHAT? THE VIDEO TAPE?!!
MISS A.
MISS B.
BA-
-DOOM
MISS D.

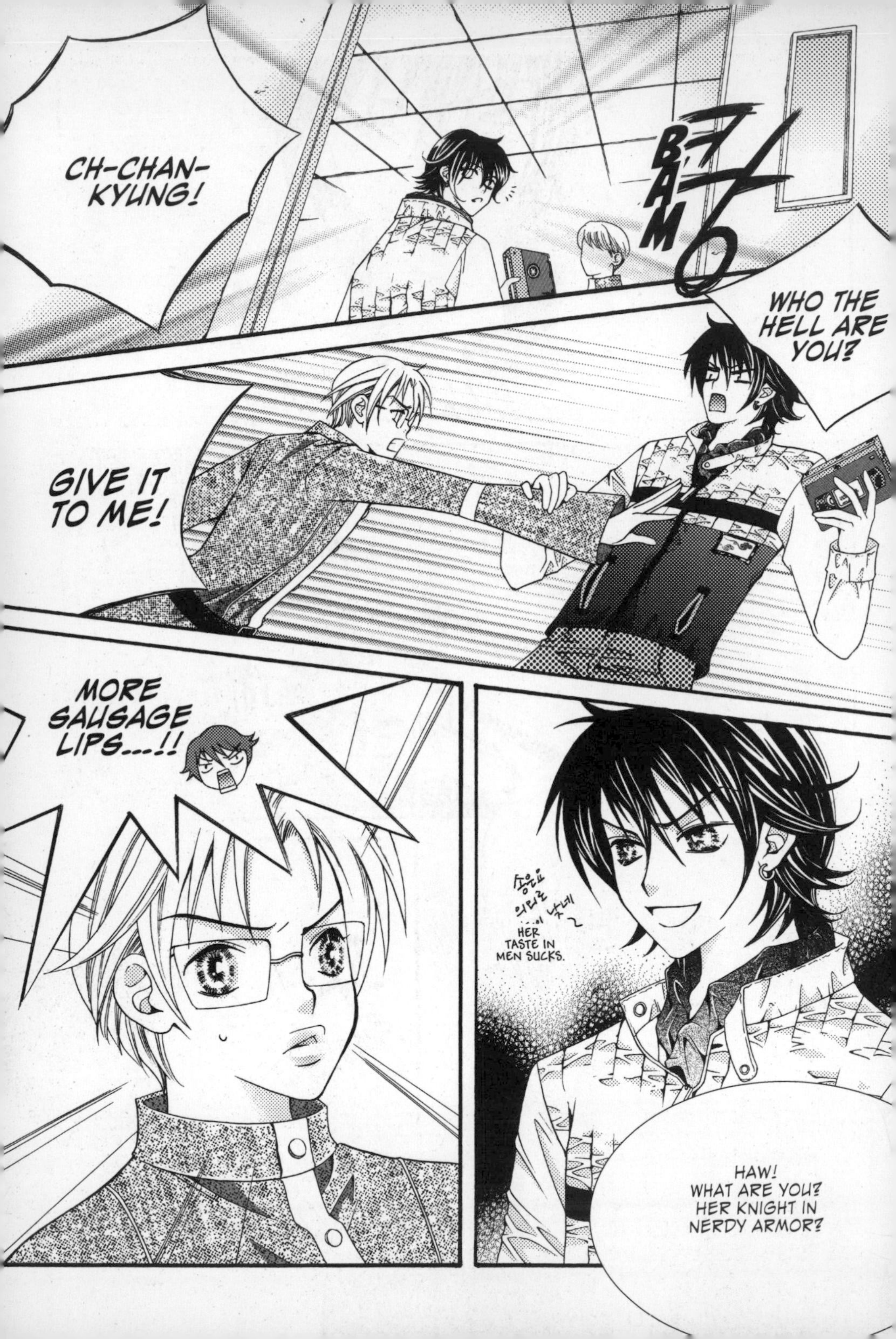
CH-CHAN-KYUNG!
BAM
GIVE IT TO ME!
WHO THE HELL ARE YOU?
MORE SAUSAGE LIPS...!!
HER TASTE IN MEN SUCKS.
HAW! WHAT ARE YOU? HER KNIGHT IN NERDY ARMOR?

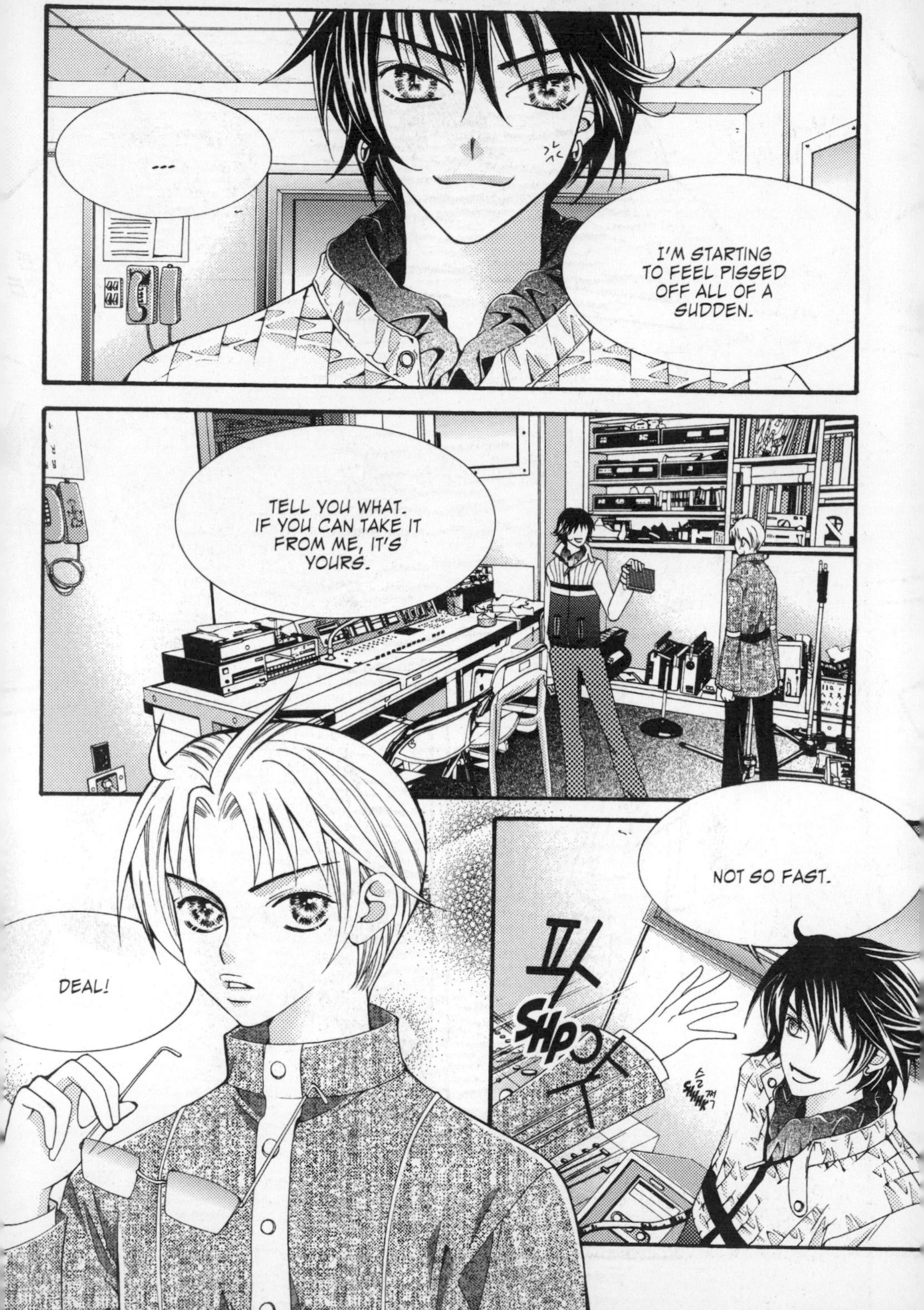
...
I'M STARTING TO FEEL PISSED OFF ALL OF A SUDDEN.
TELL YOU WHAT. IF YOU CAN TAKE IT FROM ME, IT'S YOURS.
DEAL!
NOT SO FAST.
SHP
SHWNK

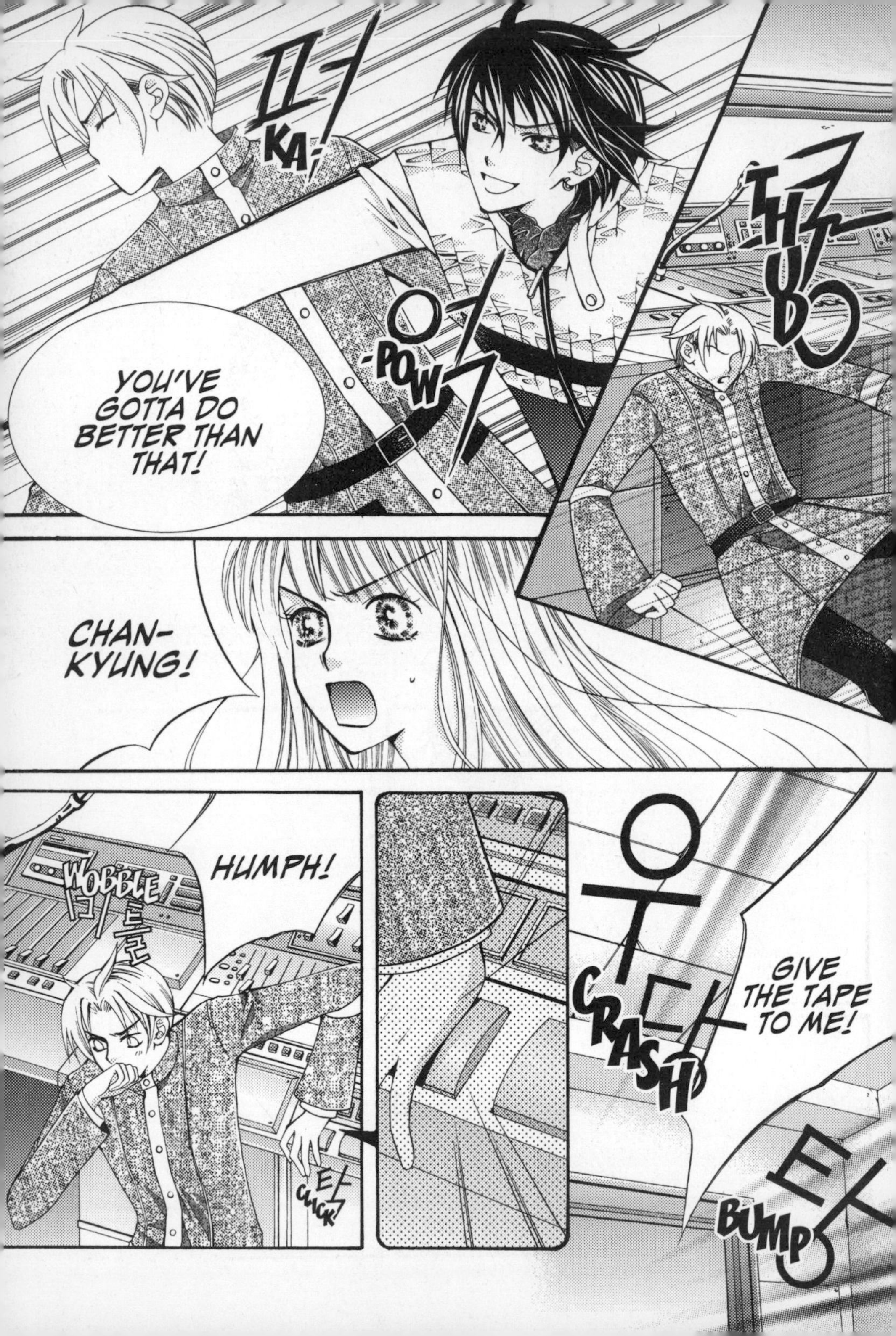
KA!
YOU'VE GOTTA DO BETTER THAN THAT!
POW
THUD
CHAN-KYUNG!
WOBBLE
HUMPH!
CLICK
CRASH
GIVE THE TAPE TO ME!
BUMP

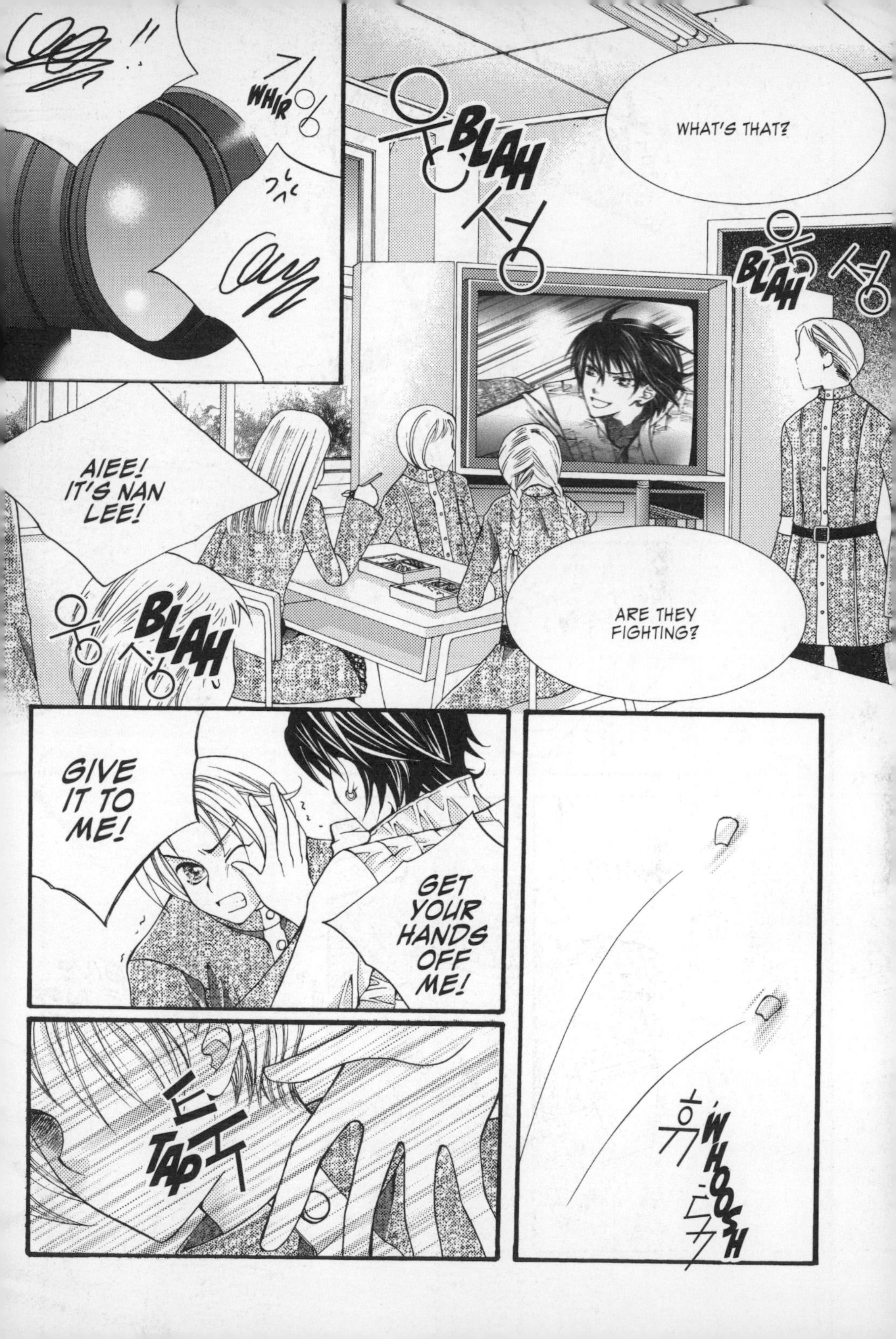
WHIR
BLAH
WHAT'S THAT?
BLAH
AIEE! IT'S NAN LEE!
BLAH
ARE THEY FIGHTING?
GIVE IT TO ME!
GET YOUR HANDS OFF ME!
TAP
WHOOSH

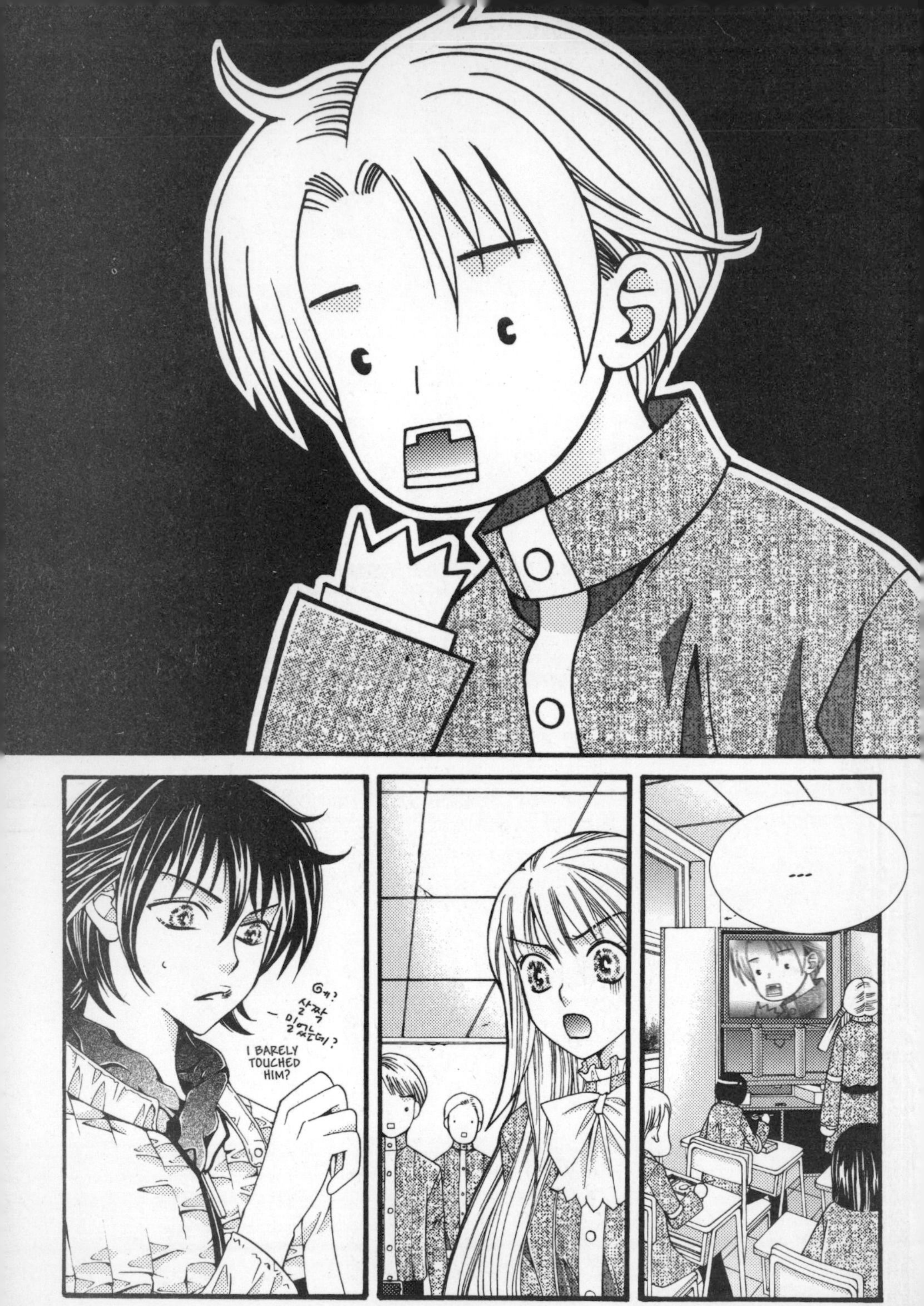
어? 살짝 밀었는데?
I BARELY TOUCHED HIM?
...

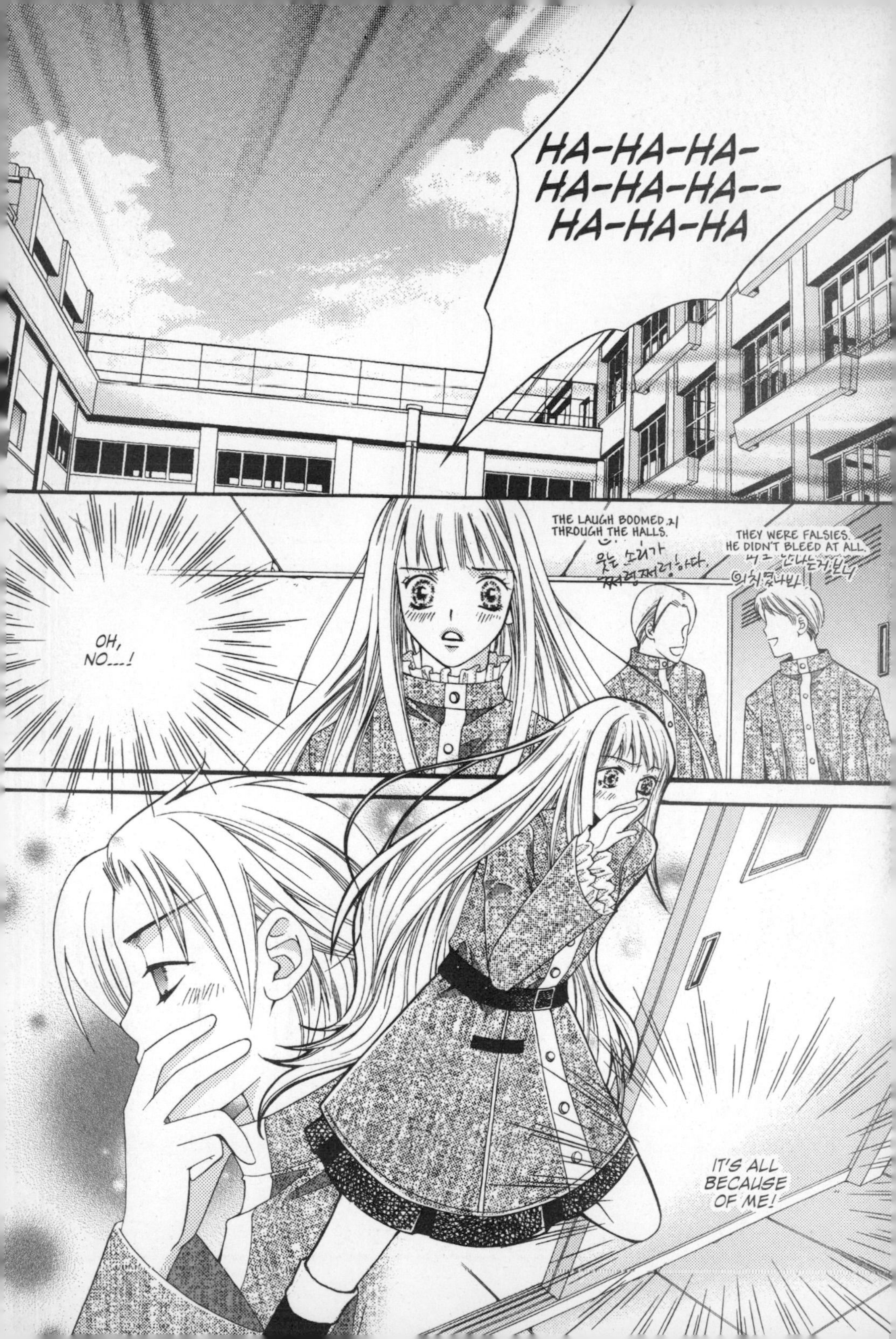
HA-HA-HA-
HA-HA-HA--
HA-HA-HA
OH, NO...!
THE LAUGH BOOMED THROUGH THE HALLS.
THEY WERE FALSIES. HE DIDN'T BLEED AT ALL.
IT'S ALL BECAUSE OF ME!

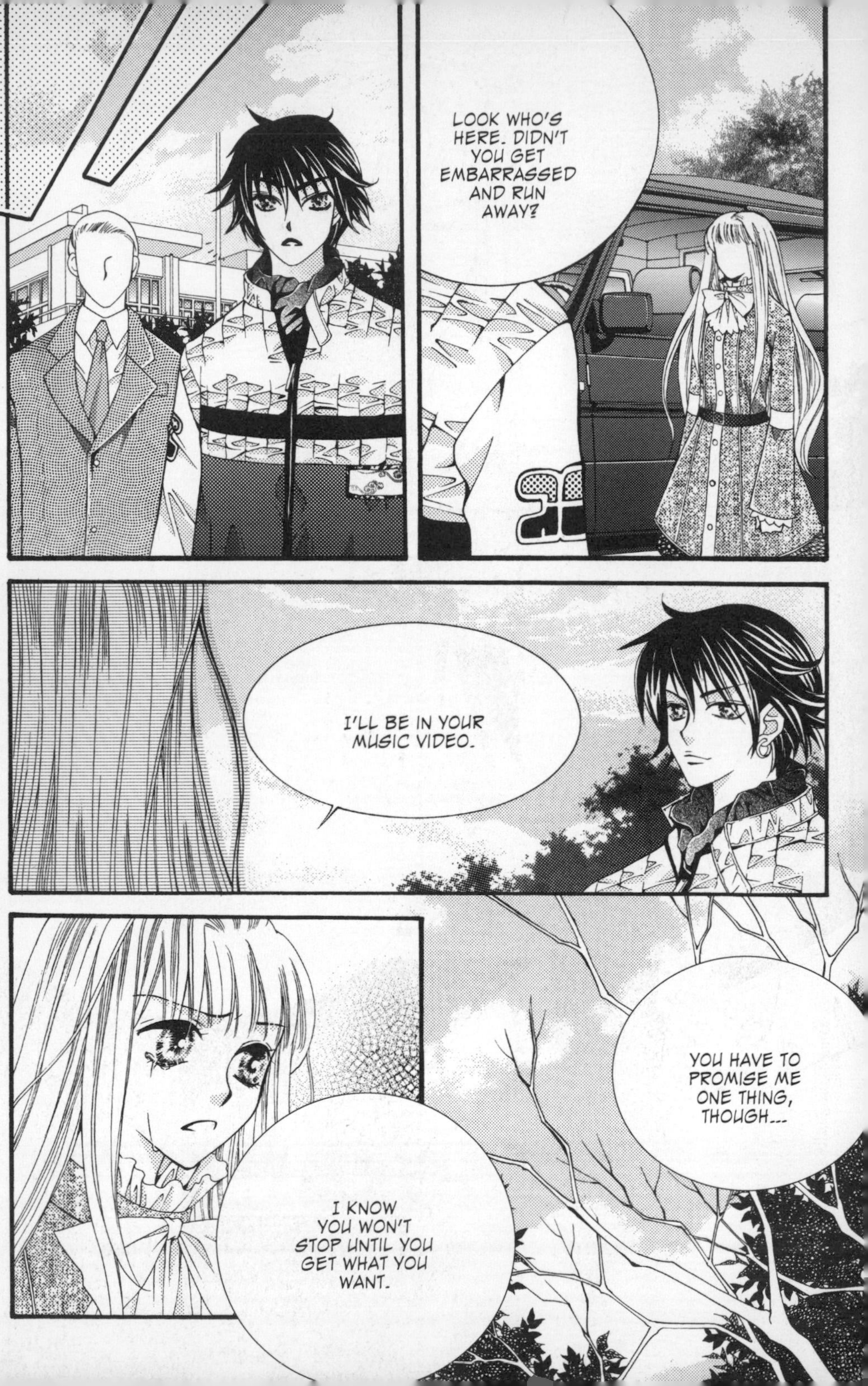
LOOK WHO'S HERE. DIDN'T YOU GET EMBARRASSED AND RUN AWAY?
I'LL BE IN YOUR MUSIC VIDEO.
I KNOW YOU WON'T STOP UNTIL YOU GET WHAT YOU WANT.
YOU HAVE TO PROMISE ME ONE THING, THOUGH...

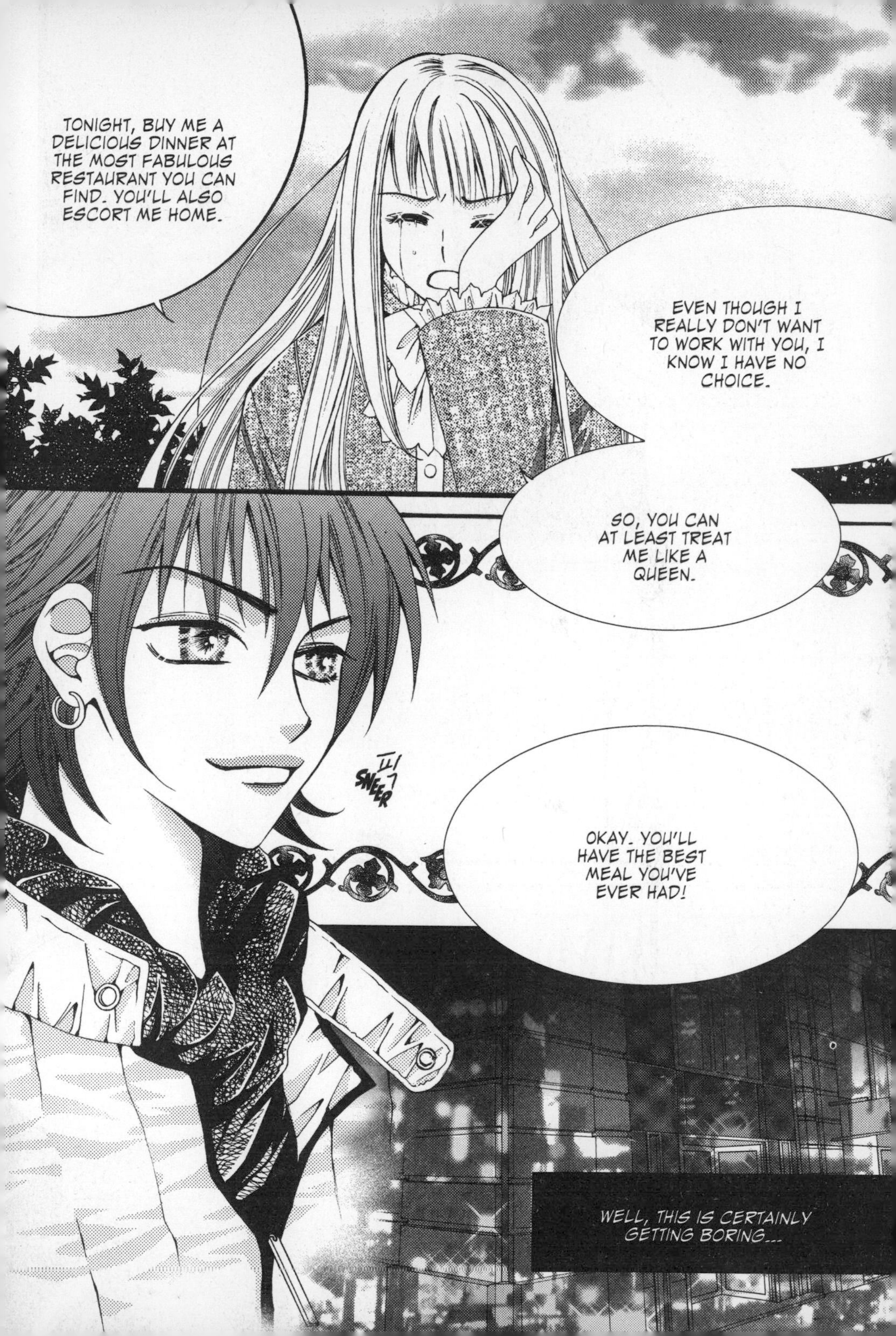
TONIGHT, BUY ME A DELICIOUS DINNER AT THE MOST FABULOUS RESTAURANT YOU CAN FIND. YOU'LL ALSO ESCORT ME HOME.
EVEN THOUGH I REALLY DON'T WANT TO WORK WITH YOU, I KNOW I HAVE NO CHOICE.
SO, YOU CAN AT LEAST TREAT ME LIKE A QUEEN.
SNEER
OKAY. YOU'LL HAVE THE BEST MEAL YOU'VE EVER HAD!
WELL, THIS IS CERTAINLY GETTING BORING...

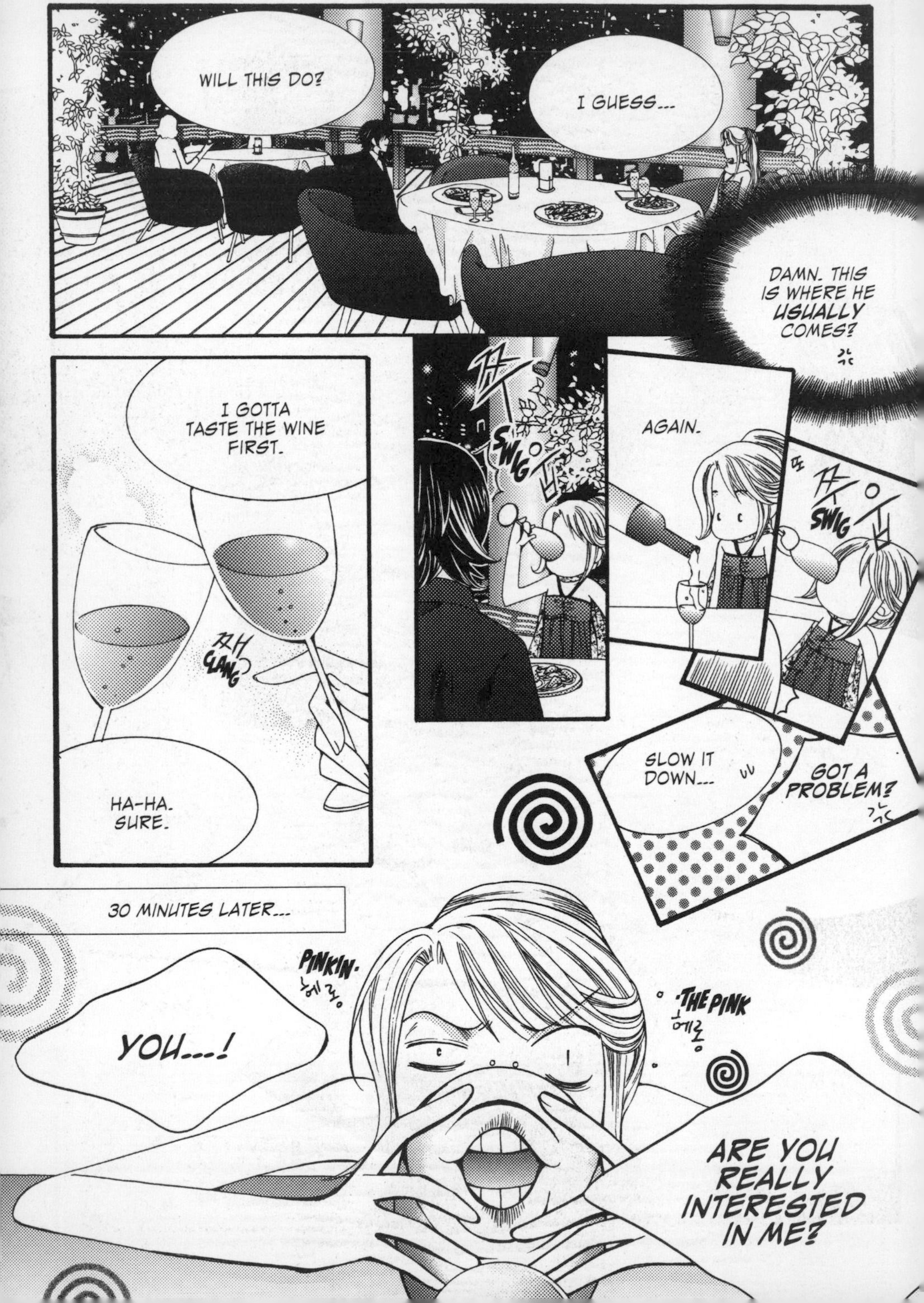
WILL THIS DO?
I GUESS...
DAMN. THIS IS WHERE HE USUALLY COMES?
I GOTTA TASTE THE WINE FIRST.
CLANG
HA-HA. SURE.
SWIG
AGAIN.
SWIG
SLOW IT DOWN...
GOT A PROBLEM?
30 MINUTES LATER...
PINKIN-
YOU...!
THE PINK
ARE YOU REALLY INTERESTED IN ME?

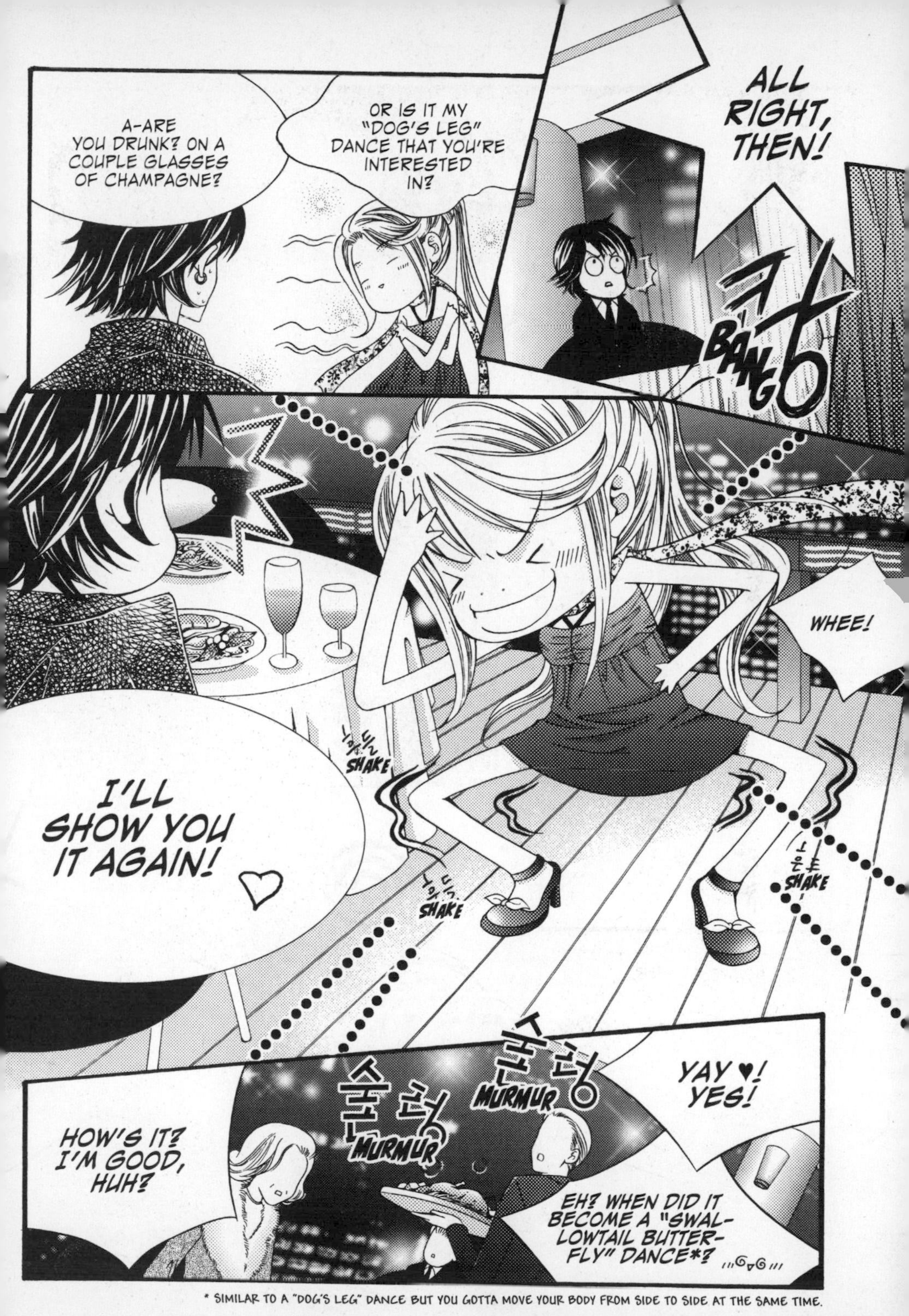
A-ARE YOU DRUNK? ON A COUPLE GLASSES OF CHAMPAGNE?
OR IS IT MY "DOG'S LEG" DANCE THAT YOU'RE INTERESTED IN?
ALL RIGHT, THEN!
BANG
I'LL SHOW YOU IT AGAIN!
WHEE!
SHAKE
SHAKE
SHAKE
HOW'S IT? I'M GOOD, HUH?
MURMUR
MURMUR
YAY♥! YES!
EH? WHEN DID IT BECOME A "SWALLOWTAIL BUTTERFLY" DANCE*?

* SIMILAR TO A "DOG'S LEG" DANCE BUT YOU GOTTA MOVE YOUR BODY FROM SIDE TO SIDE AT THE SAME TIME.

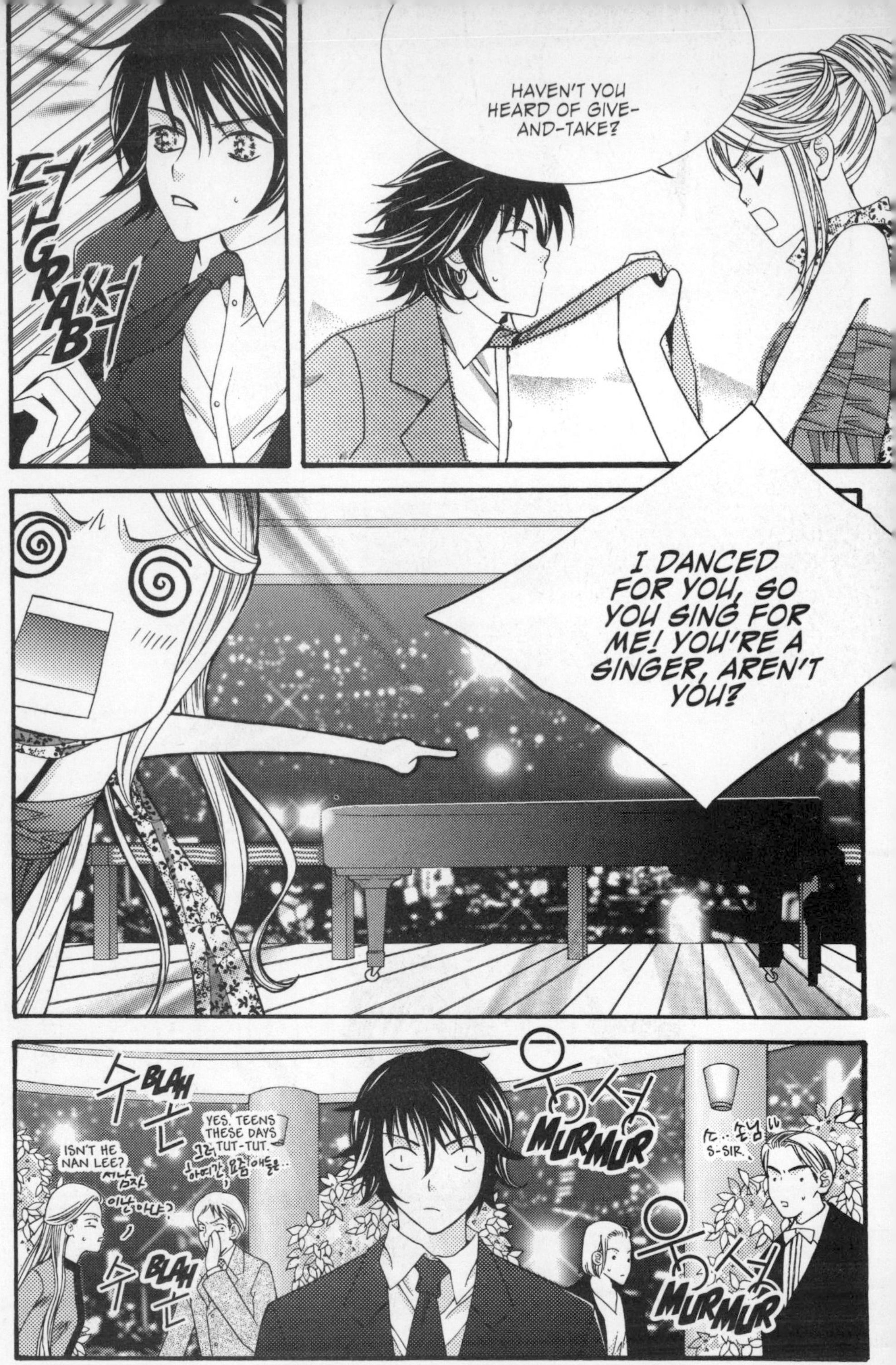
GRAB
HAVEN'T YOU HEARD OF GIVE-AND-TAKE?
I DANCED FOR YOU, SO YOU SING FOR ME! YOU'RE A SINGER, AREN'T YOU?
BLAH
ISN'T HE NAN LEE?
YES. TEENS THESE DAYS TUT-TUT.
BLAH
MURMUR
S-SIR.
MURMUR

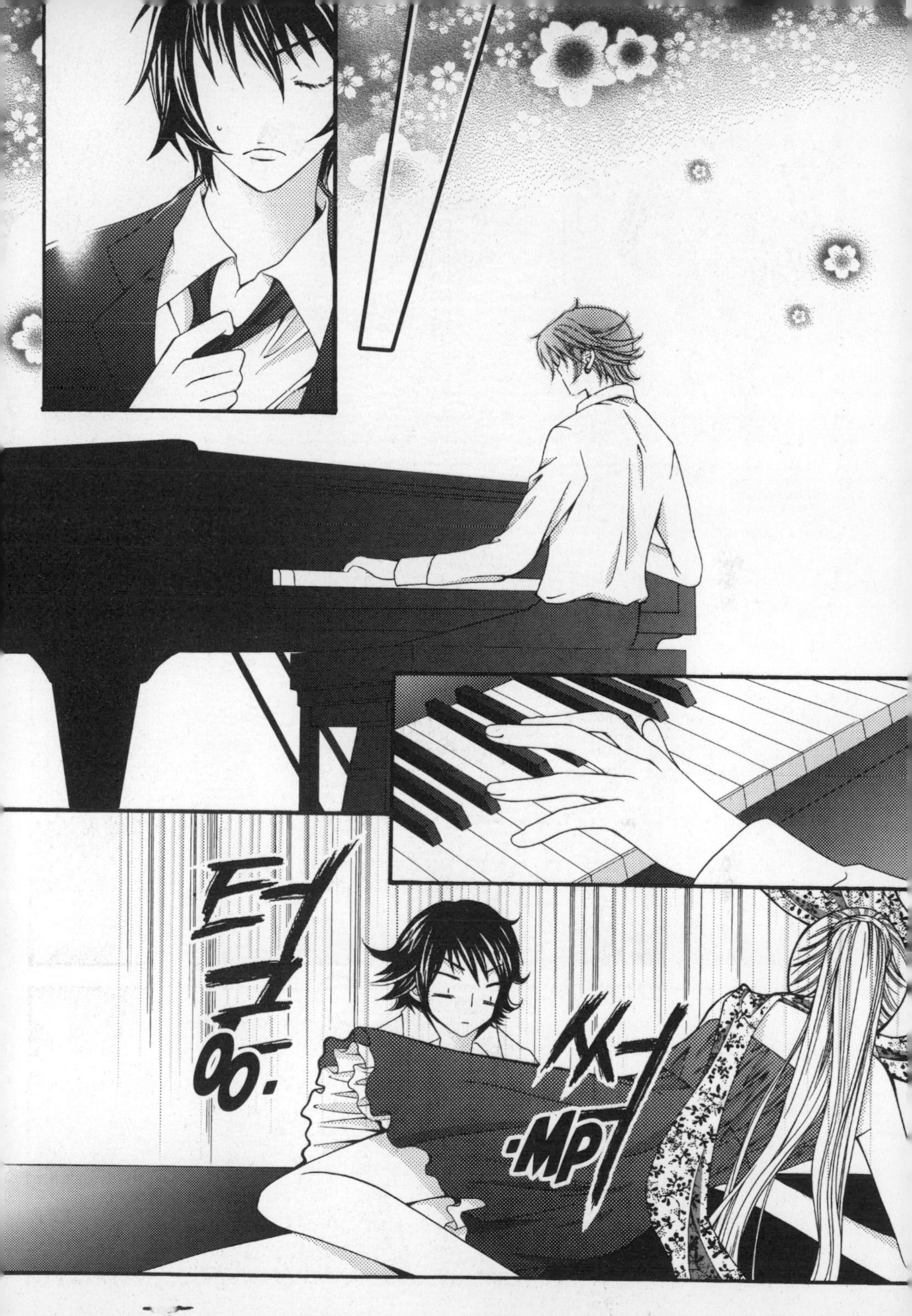
-MP

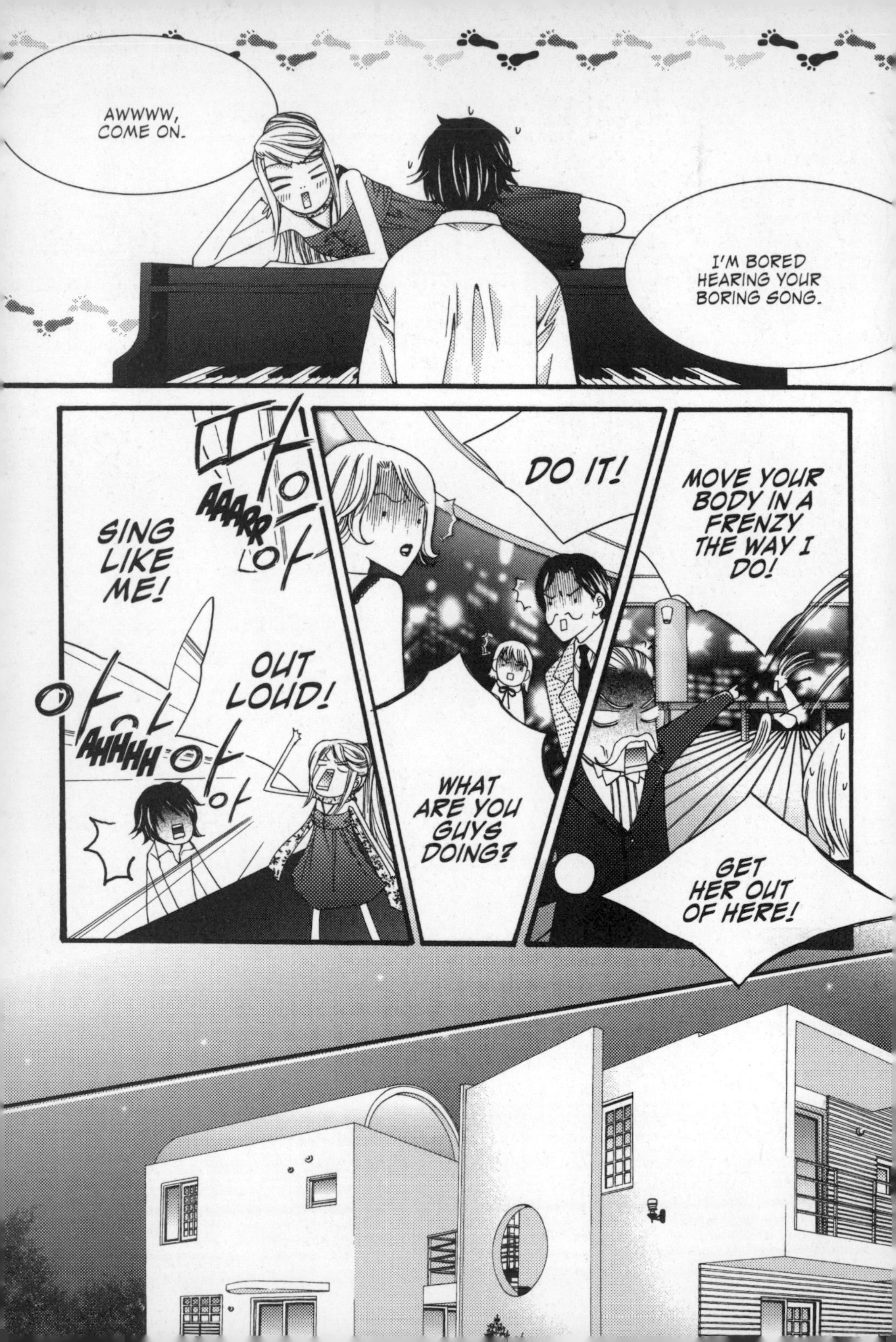

AWWWW, COME ON.
I'M BORED HEARING YOUR BORING SONG.
AAAARR
SING LIKE ME!
OUT LOUD!
AHHHH
DO IT!
WHAT ARE YOU GUYS DOING?
MOVE YOUR BODY IN A FRENZY THE WAY I DO!
GET HER OUT OF HERE!

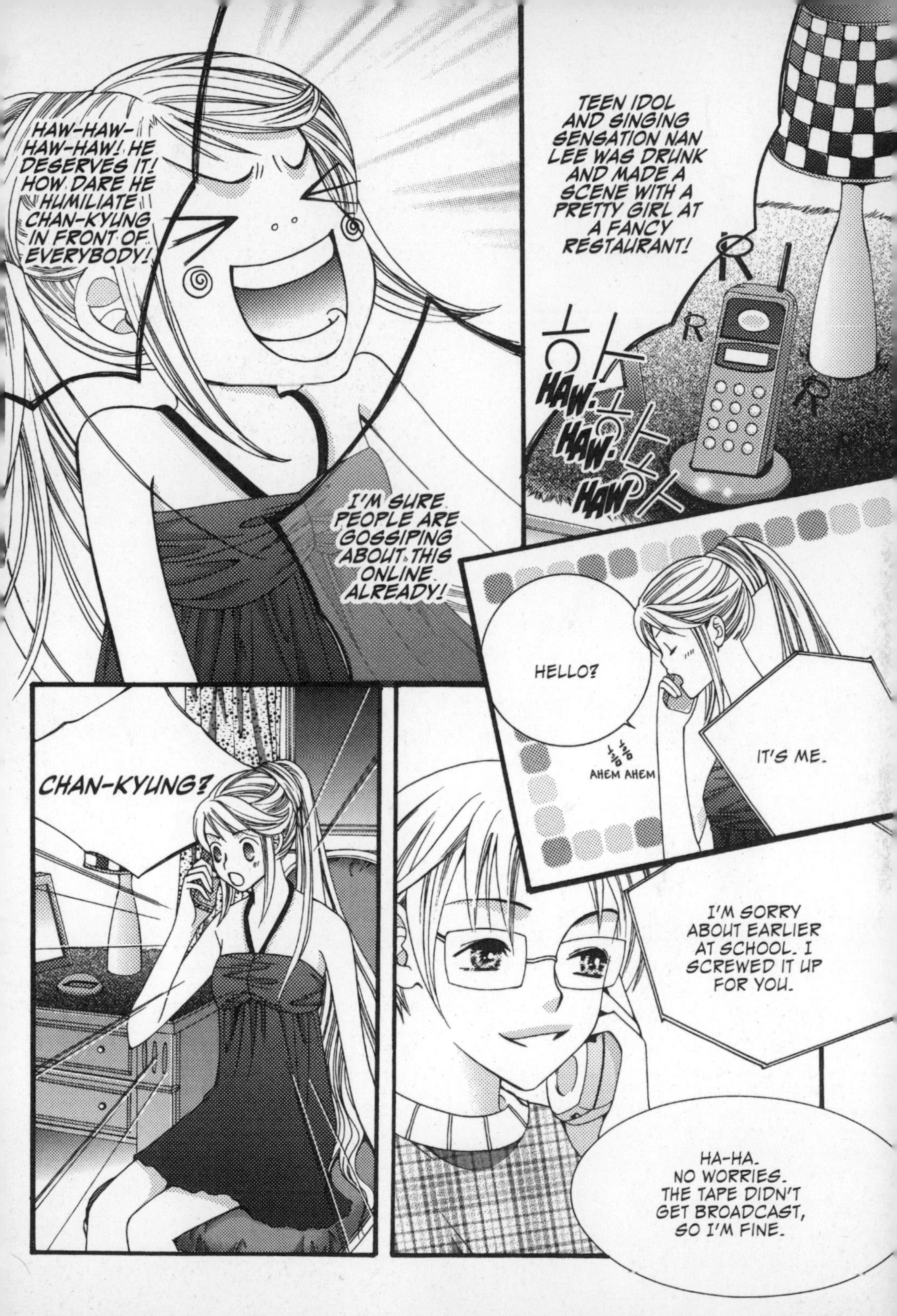

HAW-HAW-HAW-HAW! HE DESERVES IT! HOW DARE HE HUMILIATE CHAN-KYUNG IN FRONT OF EVERYBODY!
I'M SURE PEOPLE ARE GOSSIPING ABOUT THIS ONLINE ALREADY!
TEEN IDOL AND SINGING SENSATION NAN LEE WAS DRUNK AND MADE A SCENE WITH A PRETTY GIRL AT A FANCY RESTAURANT!
HAW. HAW. HAW.
HELLO?
AHEM AHEM
IT'S ME.
CHAN-KYUNG?
I'M SORRY ABOUT EARLIER AT SCHOOL. I SCREWED IT UP FOR YOU.
HA-HA. NO WORRIES. THE TAPE DIDN'T GET BROADCAST, SO I'M FINE.

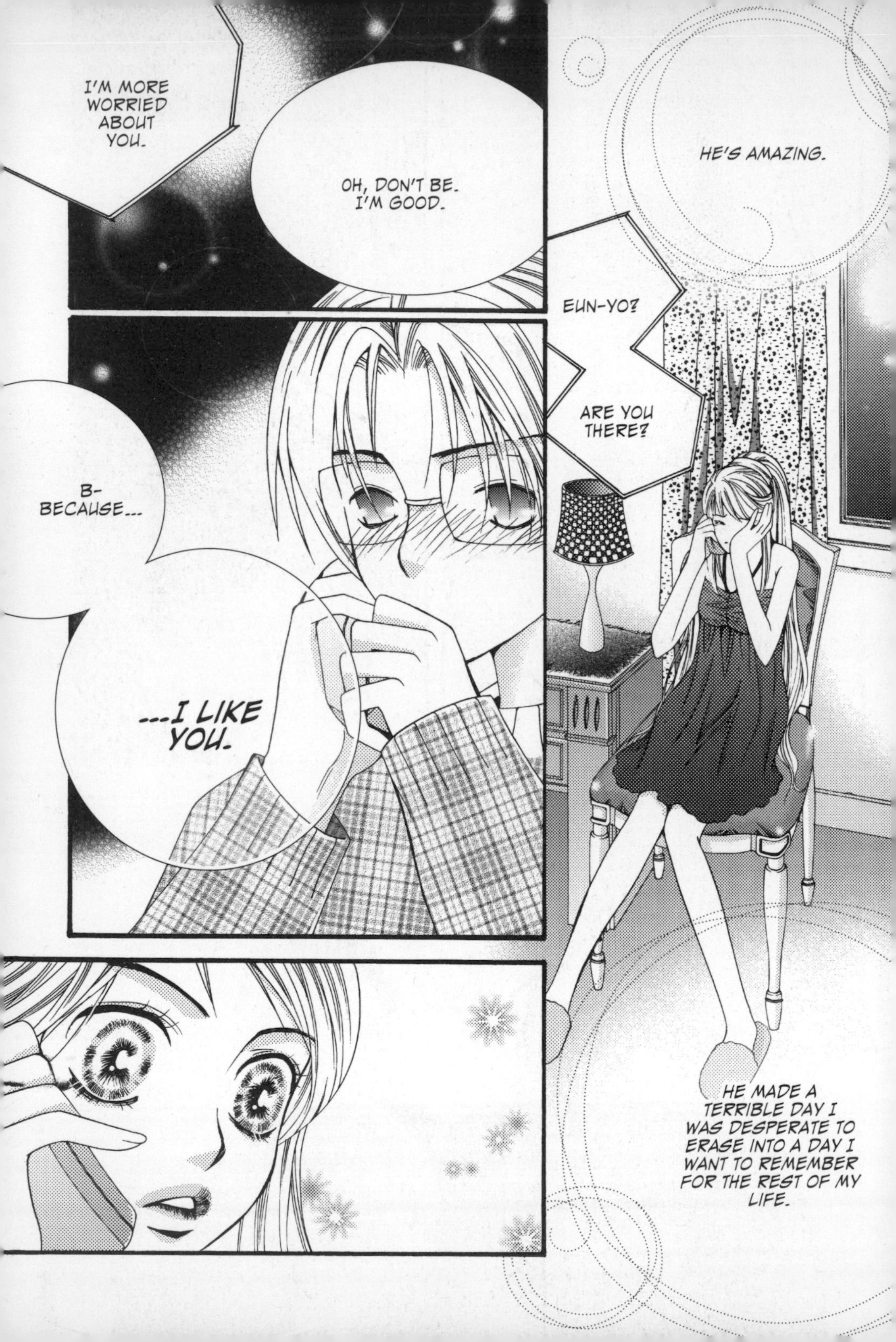

I'M MORE WORRIED ABOUT YOU.
OH, DON'T BE. I'M GOOD.
B-BECAUSE...
...I LIKE YOU.
HE'S AMAZING.
EUN-YO?
ARE YOU THERE?
HE MADE A TERRIBLE DAY I WAS DESPERATE TO ERASE INTO A DAY I WANT TO REMEMBER FOR THE REST OF MY LIFE.

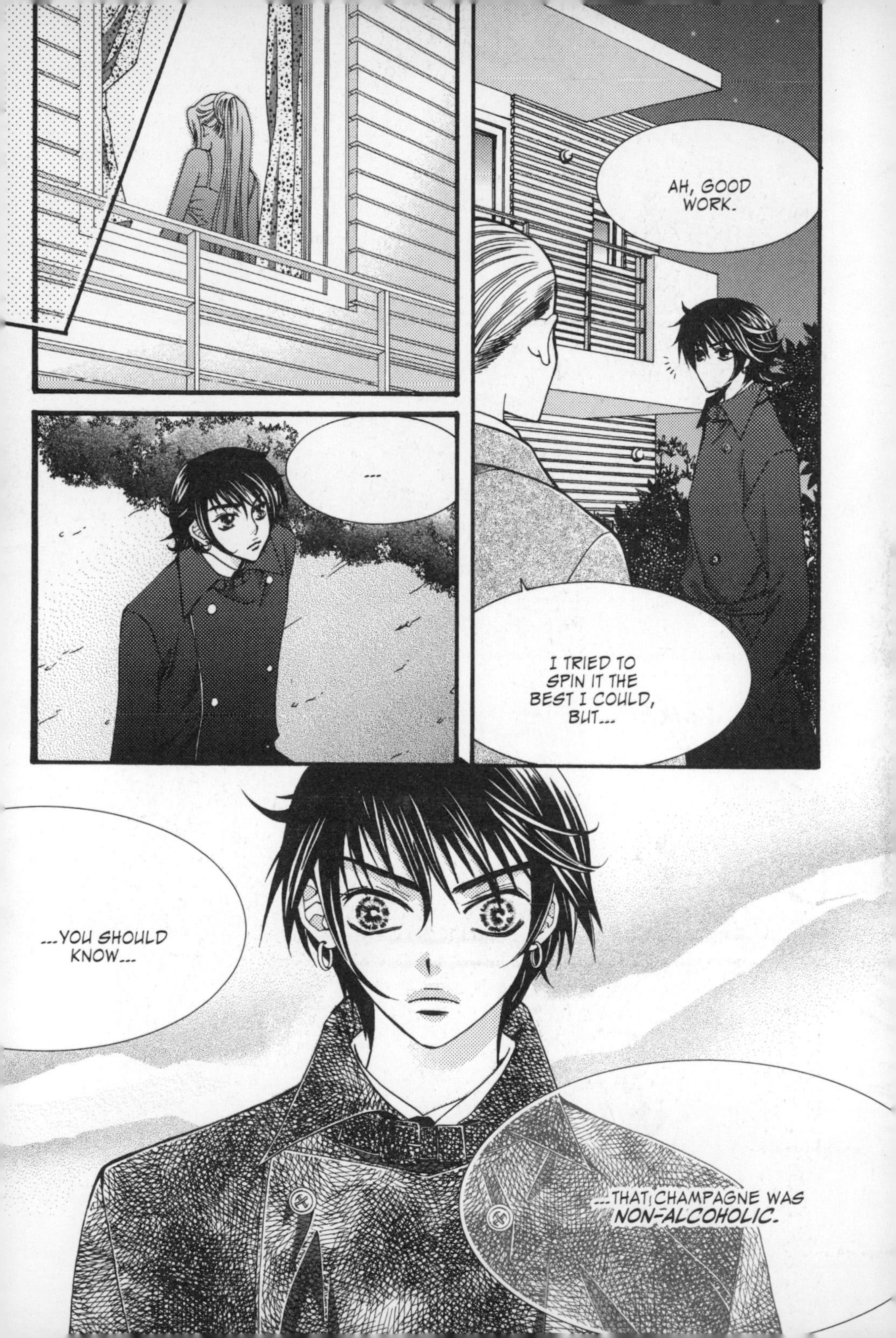
AH, GOOD WORK.
...
I TRIED TO SPIN IT THE BEST I COULD, BUT...
...YOU SHOULD KNOW...
...THAT CHAMPAGNE WAS NON-ALCOHOLIC.

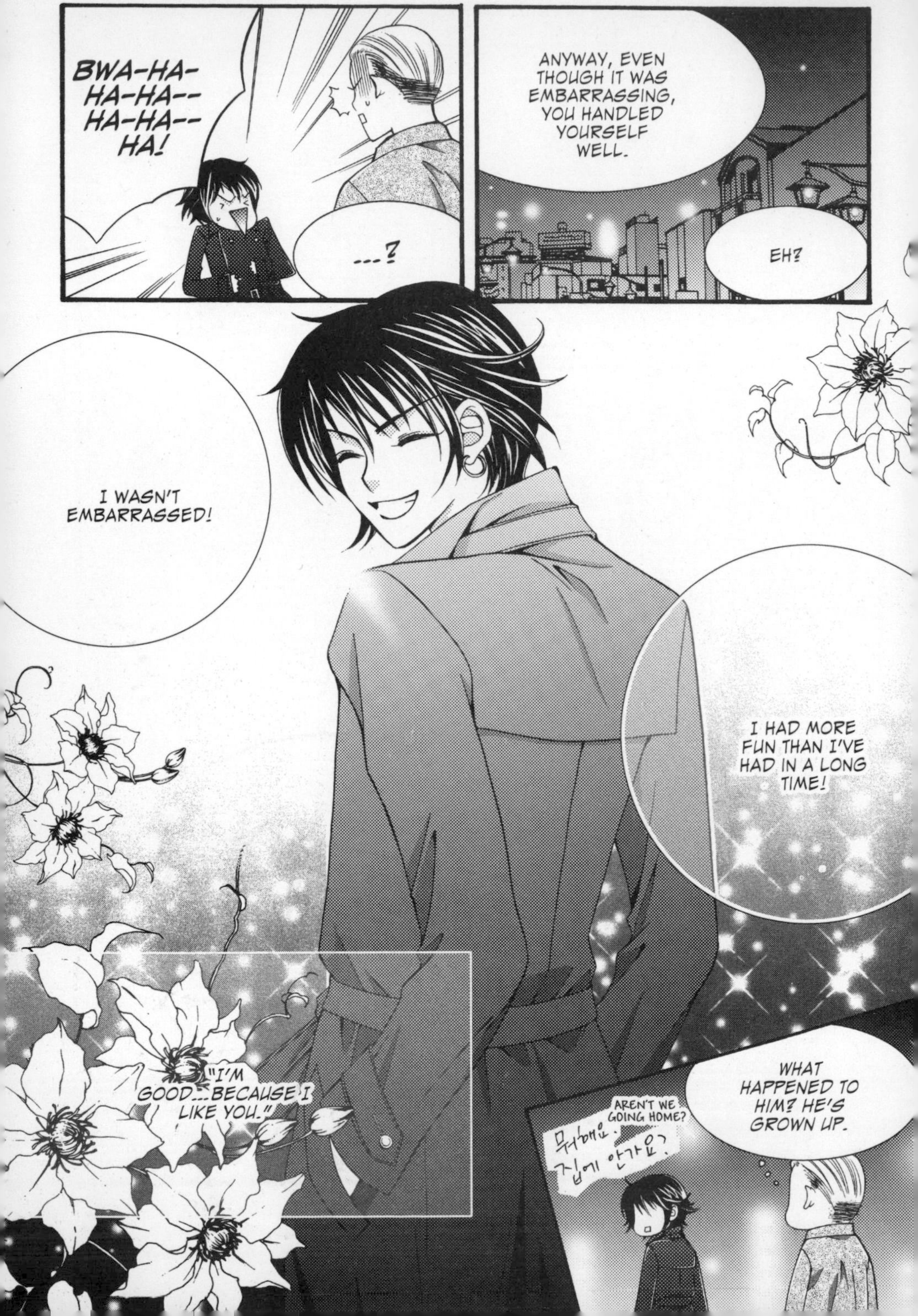
BWA-HA-HA-HA--HA-HA--HA!
...?
ANYWAY, EVEN THOUGH IT WAS EMBARRASSING, YOU HANDLED YOURSELF WELL.
EH?
I WASN'T EMBARRASSED!
I HAD MORE FUN THAN I'VE HAD IN A LONG TIME!
"I'M GOOD... BECAUSE I LIKE YOU."
AREN'T WE GOING HOME?
뭐해요. 집에 안가요?
WHAT HAPPENED TO HIM? HE'S GROWN UP.

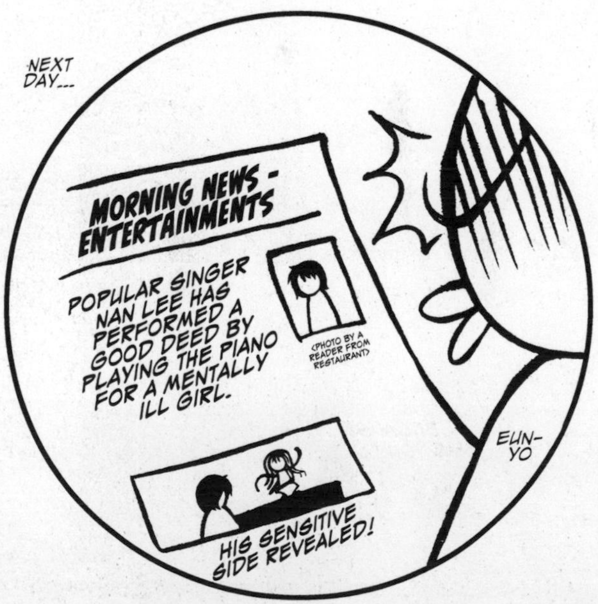
NEXT DAY...
MORNING NEWS - ENTERTAINMENTS
POPULAR SINGER NAN LEE HAS PERFORMED A GOOD DEED BY PLAYING THE PIANO FOR A MENTALLY ILL GIRL.
<PHOTO BY A READER FROM RESTAURANT>
HIS SENSITIVE SIDE REVEALED!
EUN-YO

STAR PROJECT

CHIRO 치로

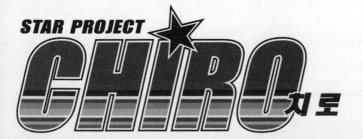

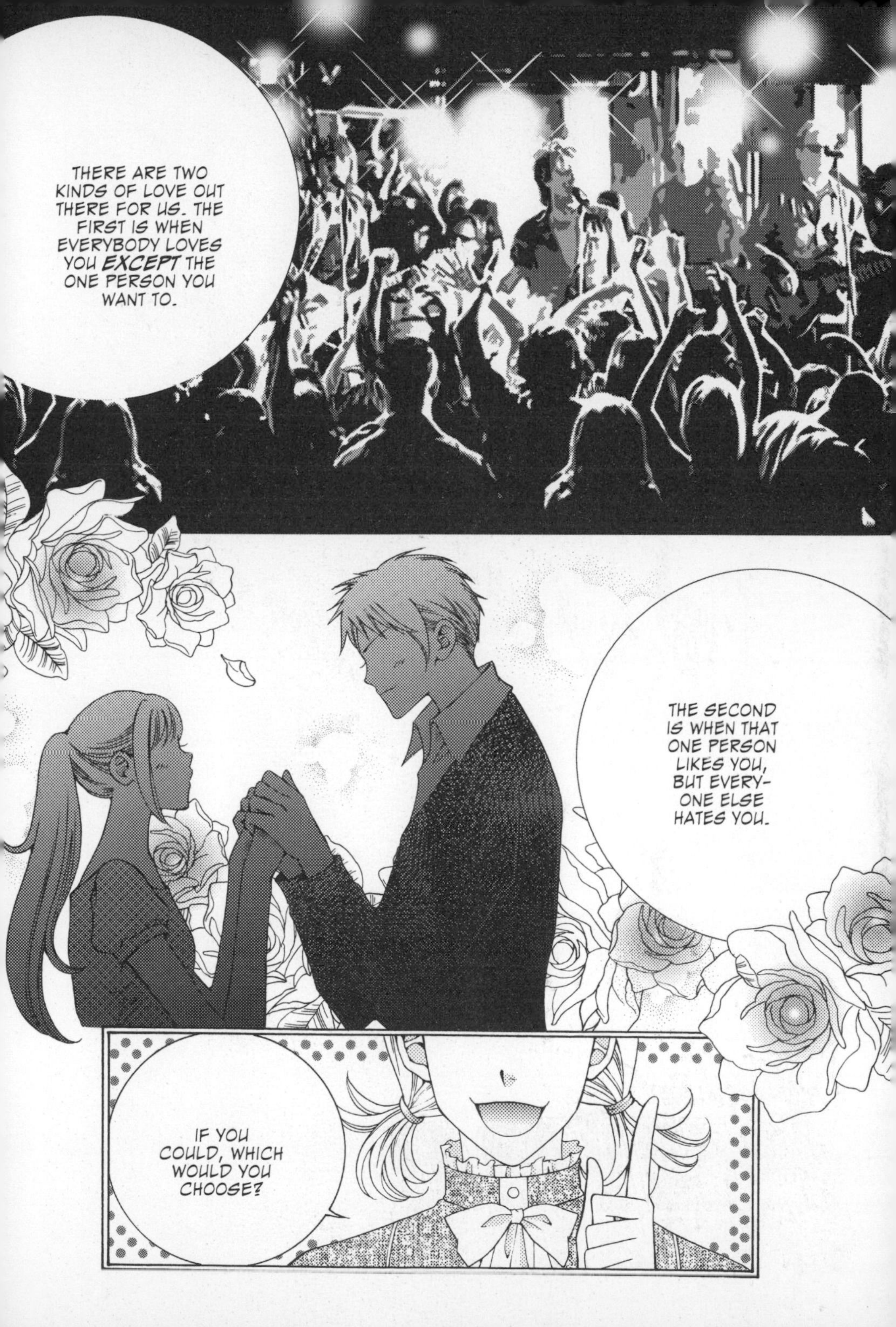
THERE ARE TWO KINDS OF LOVE OUT THERE FOR US. THE FIRST IS WHEN EVERYBODY LOVES YOU *EXCEPT* THE ONE PERSON YOU WANT TO.
THE SECOND IS WHEN THAT ONE PERSON LIKES YOU, BUT EVERY-ONE ELSE HATES YOU.
IF YOU COULD, WHICH WOULD YOU CHOOSE?

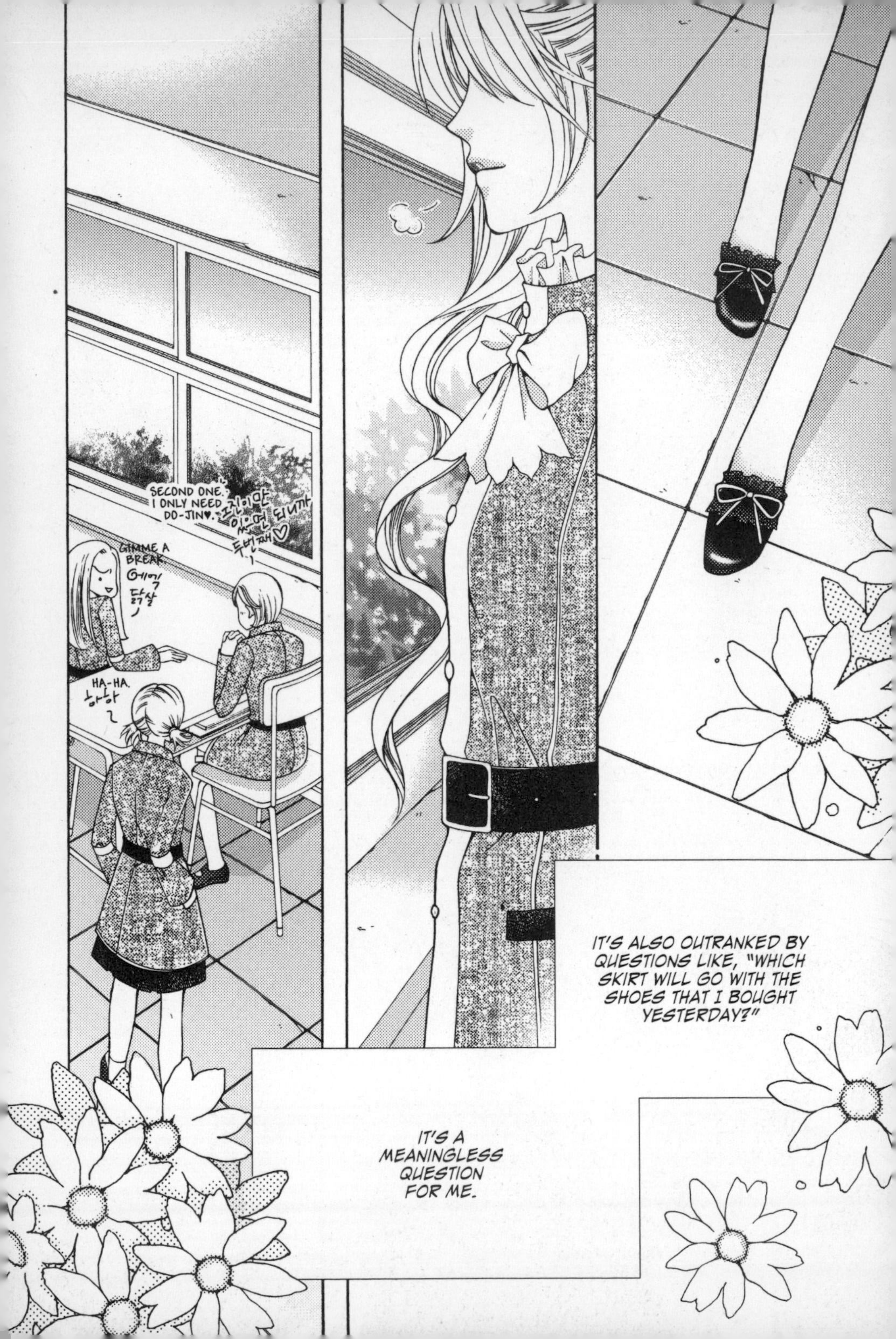
SECOND ONE. I ONLY NEED DO-JIN♥.
도진이만 있으면 되니까 두번째♥
GIMME A BREAK.
에이 닭살
HA-HA.
하하
IT'S ALSO OUTRANKED BY QUESTIONS LIKE, "WHICH SKIRT WILL GO WITH THE SHOES THAT I BOUGHT YESTERDAY?"
IT'S A MEANINGLESS QUESTION FOR ME.

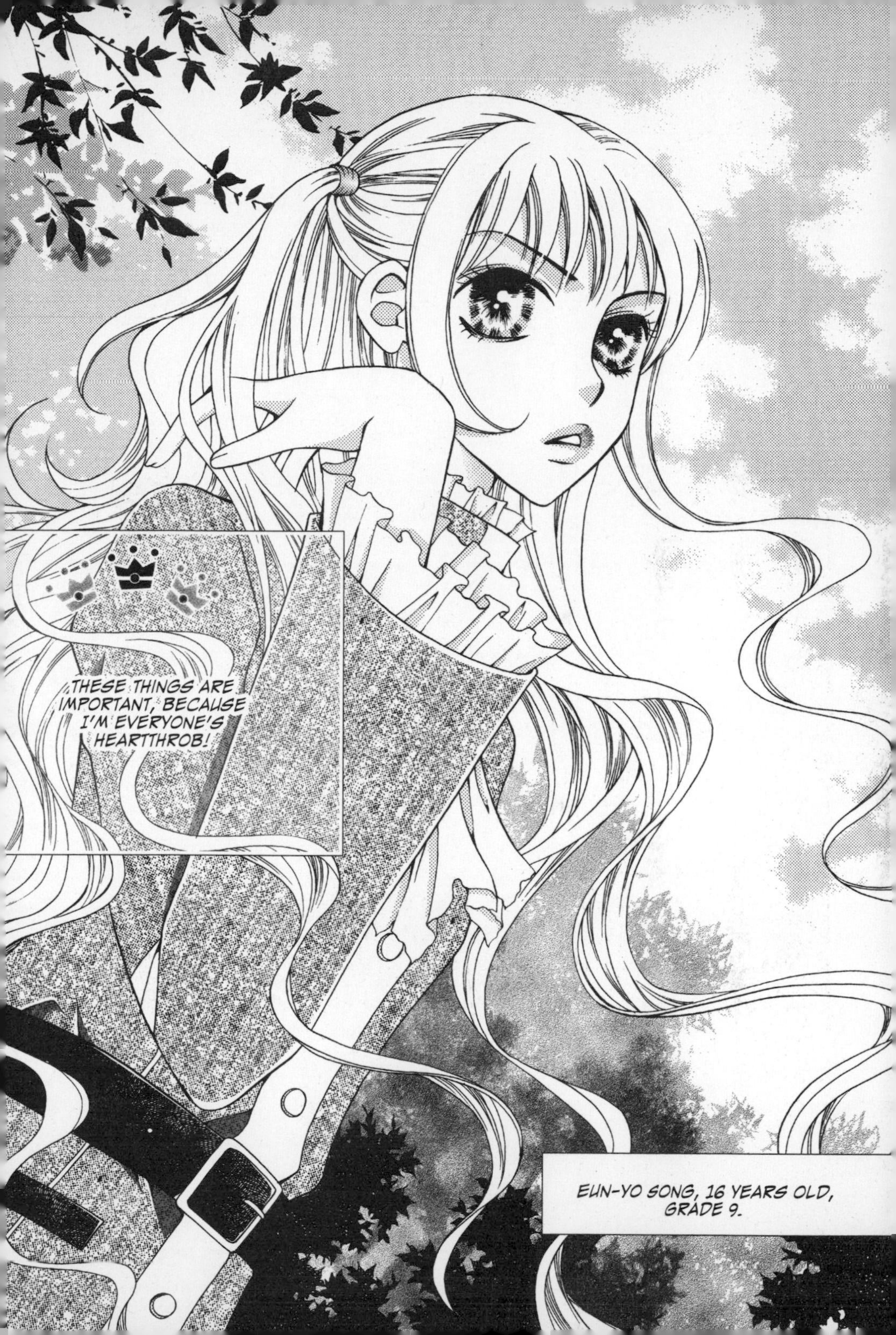
THESE THINGS ARE IMPORTANT, BECAUSE I'M EVERYONE'S HEARTTHROB!
EUN-YO SONG, 16 YEARS OLD, GRADE 9.

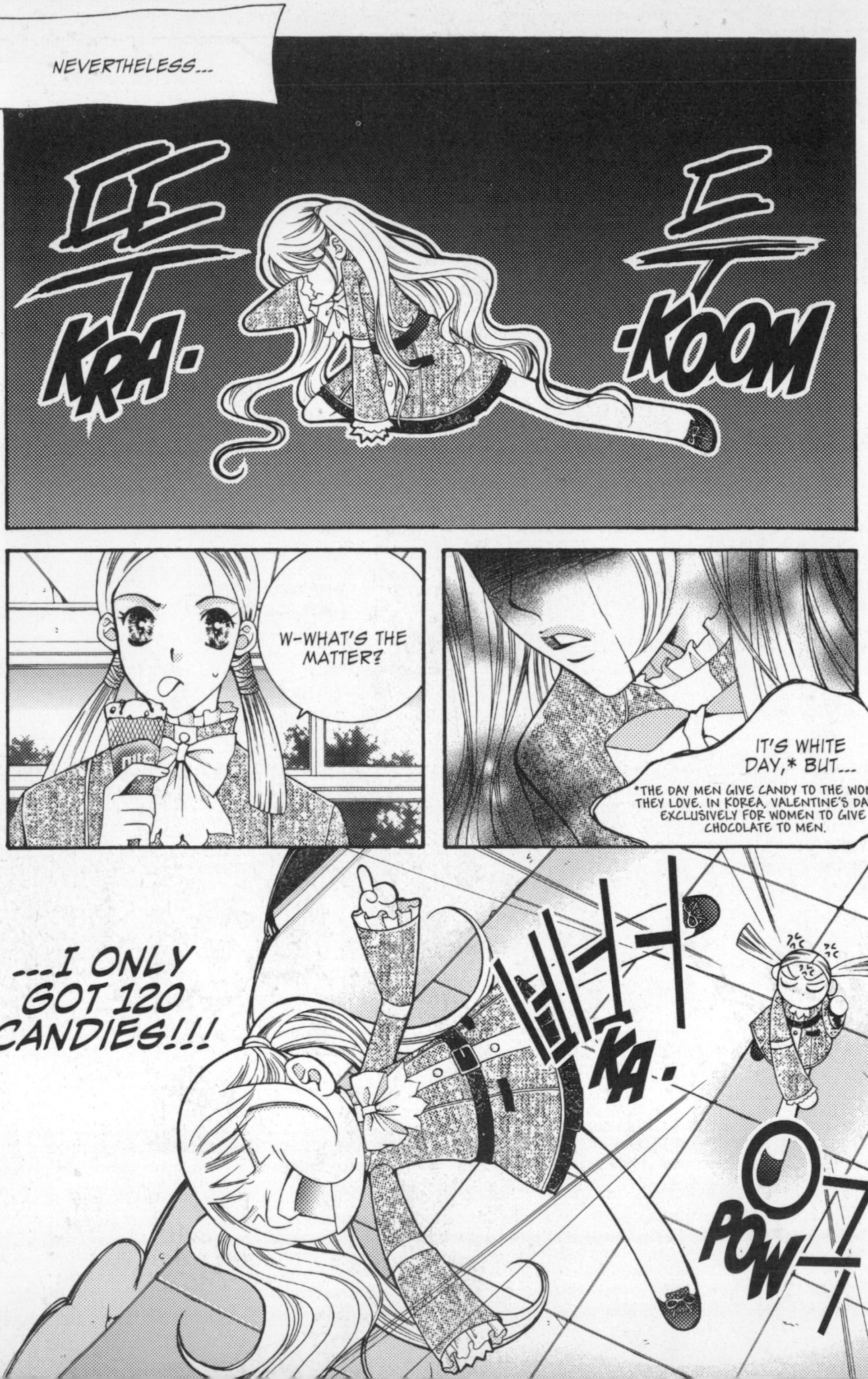
NEVERTHELESS...
KRA-
-KOOM
W-WHAT'S THE MATTER?
IT'S WHITE DAY,* BUT...
*THE DAY MEN GIVE CANDY TO THE WOMEN THEY LOVE. IN KOREA, VALENTINE'S DAY IS EXCLUSIVELY FOR WOMEN TO GIVE CHOCOLATE TO MEN.
...I ONLY GOT 120 CANDIES!!!
KA-
POW

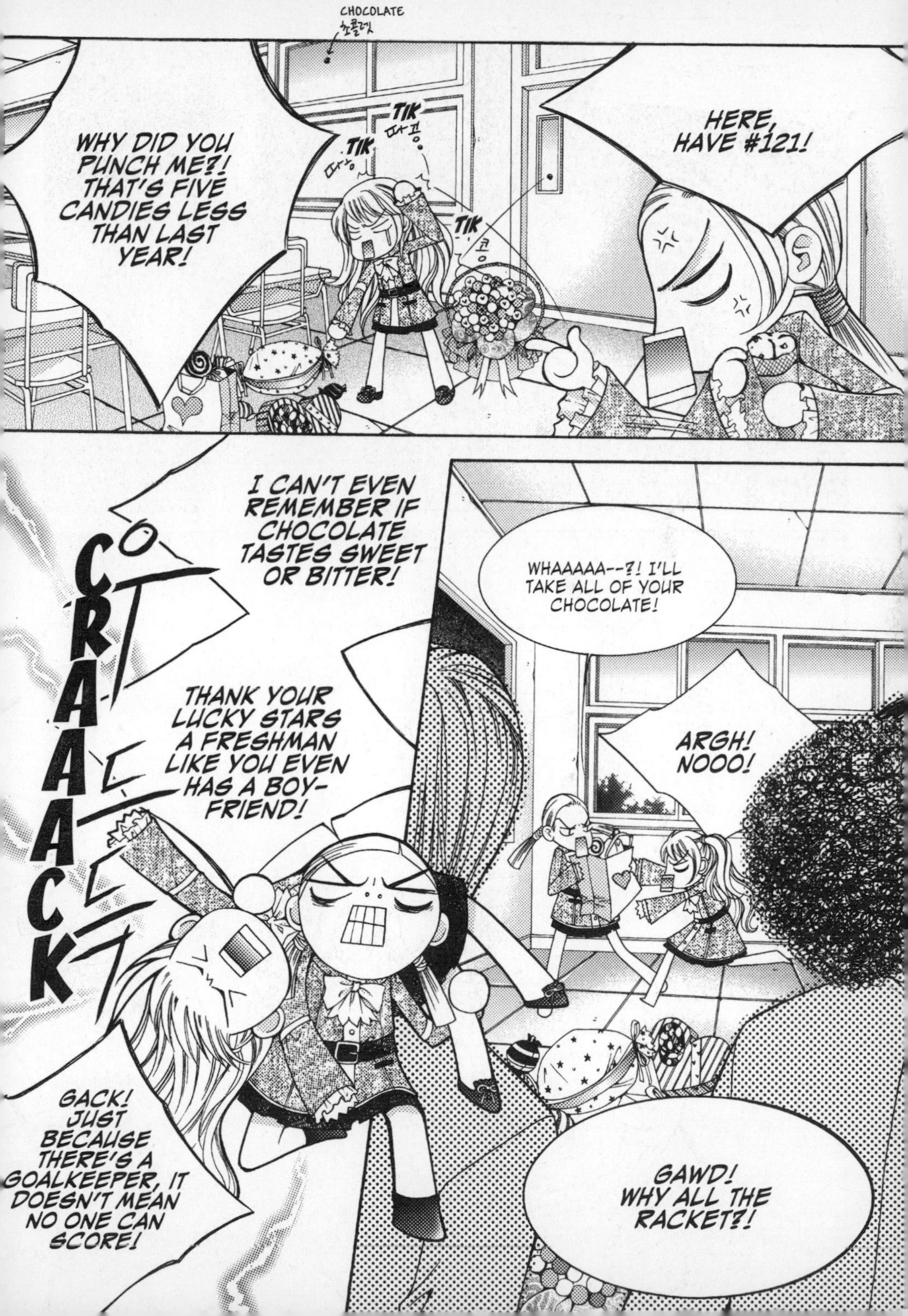
CHOCOLATE
초콜렛
WHY DID YOU PUNCH ME?! THAT'S FIVE CANDIES LESS THAN LAST YEAR!
TIK
TIK
TIK
HERE, HAVE #121!
CRAAACK
I CAN'T EVEN REMEMBER IF CHOCOLATE TASTES SWEET OR BITTER!
THANK YOUR LUCKY STARS A FRESHMAN LIKE YOU EVEN HAS A BOY-FRIEND!
GACK! JUST BECAUSE THERE'S A GOALKEEPER, IT DOESN'T MEAN NO ONE CAN SCORE!
WHAAAAA--?! I'LL TAKE ALL OF YOUR CHOCOLATE!
ARGH! NOOO!
GAWD! WHY ALL THE RACKET?!

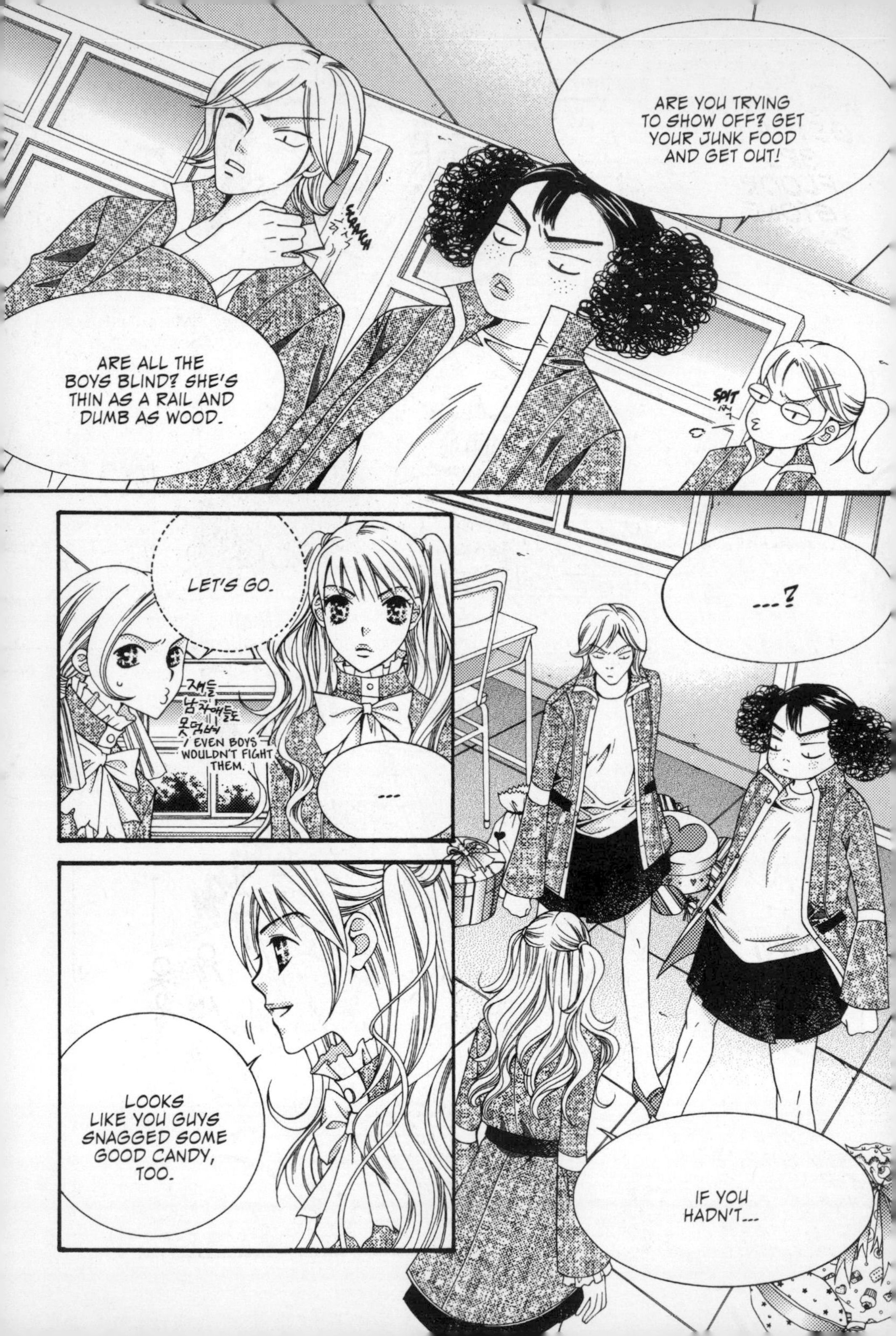
ARE YOU TRYING TO SHOW OFF? GET YOUR JUNK FOOD AND GET OUT!
ARE ALL THE BOYS BLIND? SHE'S THIN AS A RAIL AND DUMB AS WOOD.
SPIT
LET'S GO.
재들 남자애들도 못 덤벼
EVEN BOYS WOULDN'T FIGHT THEM.
...
LOOKS LIKE YOU GUYS SNAGGED SOME GOOD CANDY, TOO.
...?
IF YOU HADN'T...

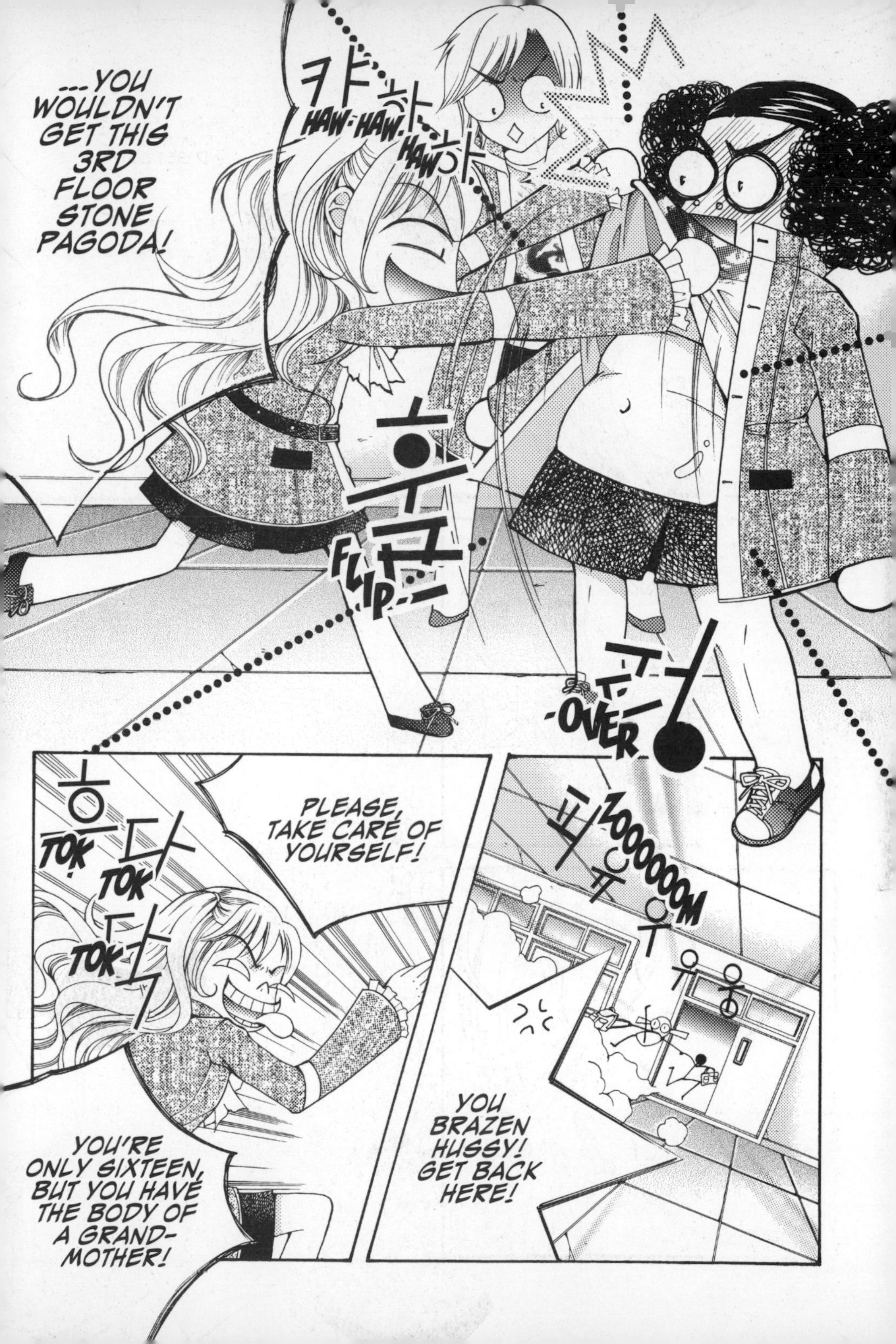
...YOU WOULDN'T GET THIS 3RD FLOOR STONE PAGODA!
HAW-HAW-HAW
FLIP-OVER
TOK TOK TOK
PLEASE, TAKE CARE OF YOURSELF!
YOU'RE ONLY SIXTEEN, BUT YOU HAVE THE BODY OF A GRAND-MOTHER!
ZOOOOOOOM
YOU BRAZEN HUSSY! GET BACK HERE!

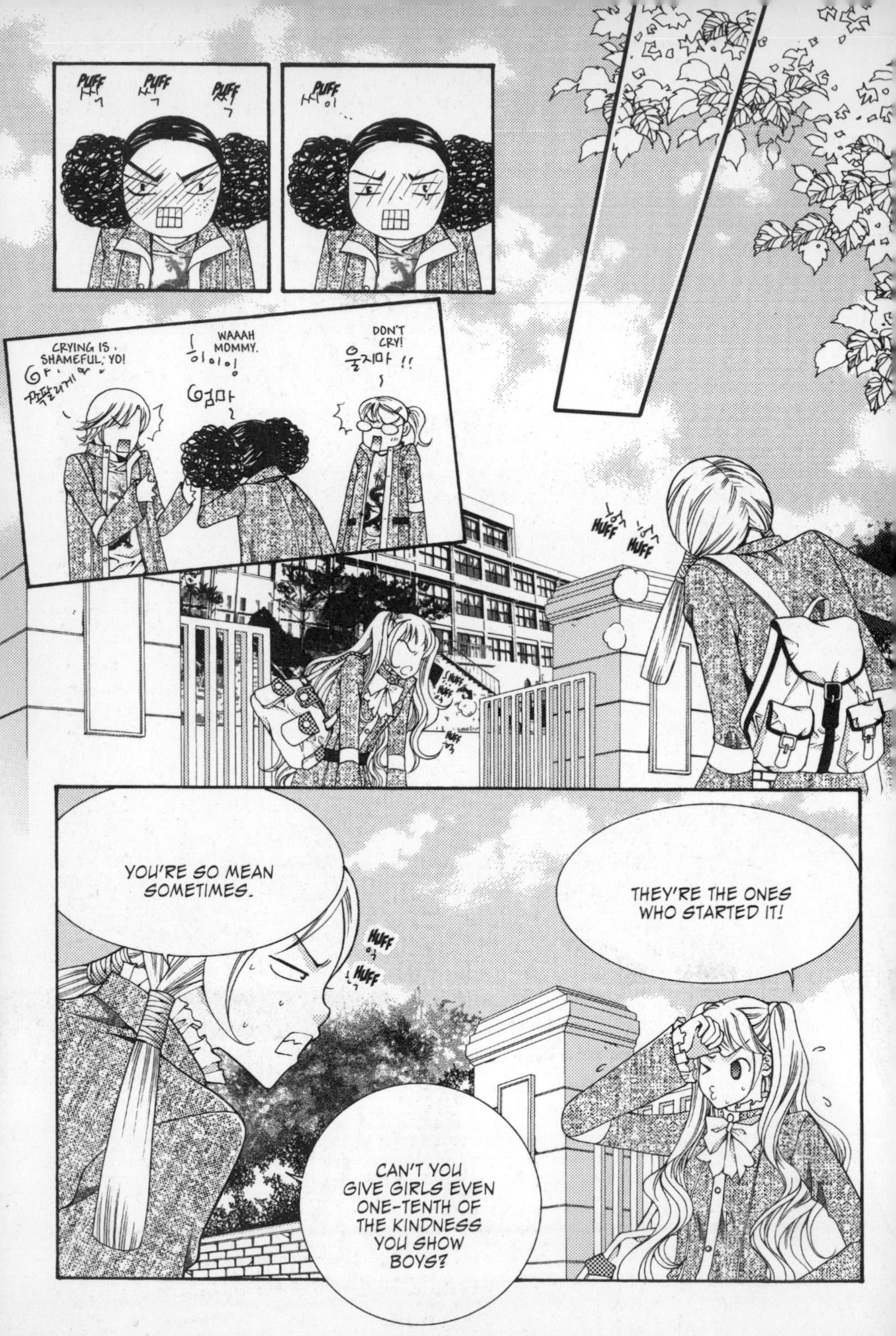

PUFF
PUFF
PUFF
PUFF
CRYING IS SHAMEFUL, YO!
WAAAH MOMMY.
이이잉
엄마
DON'T CRY!
울지마!!
HUFF
HUFF
YOU'RE SO MEAN SOMETIMES.
THEY'RE THE ONES WHO STARTED IT!
HUFF
HUFF
CAN'T YOU GIVE GIRLS EVEN ONE-TENTH OF THE KINDNESS YOU SHOW BOYS?

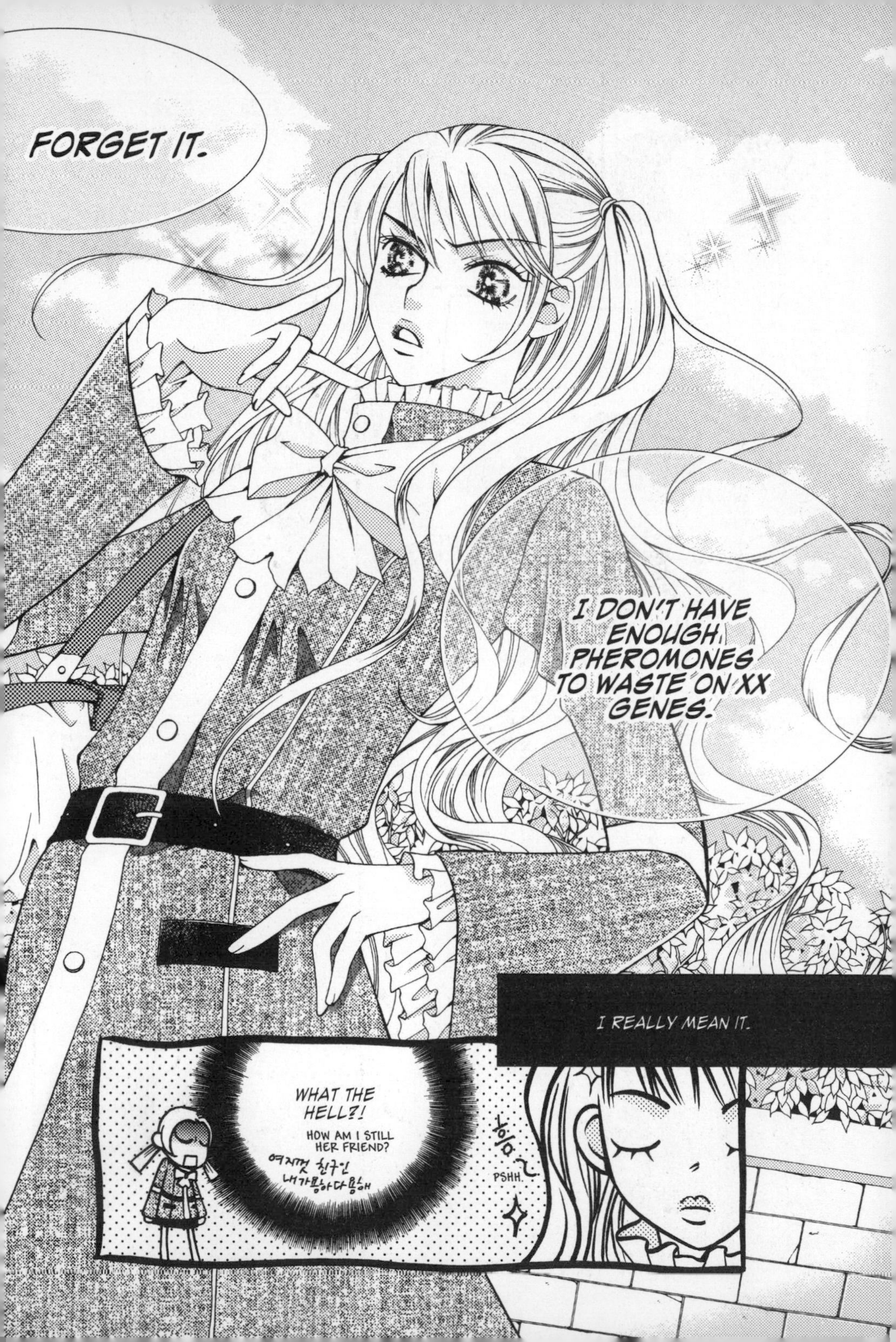
FORGET IT.
I DON'T HAVE ENOUGH PHEROMONES TO WASTE ON XX GENES.
I REALLY MEAN IT.
WHAT THE HELL?!
HOW AM I STILL HER FRIEND?
여지껏 친구인 내가용하다용해
흥~
PSHH.

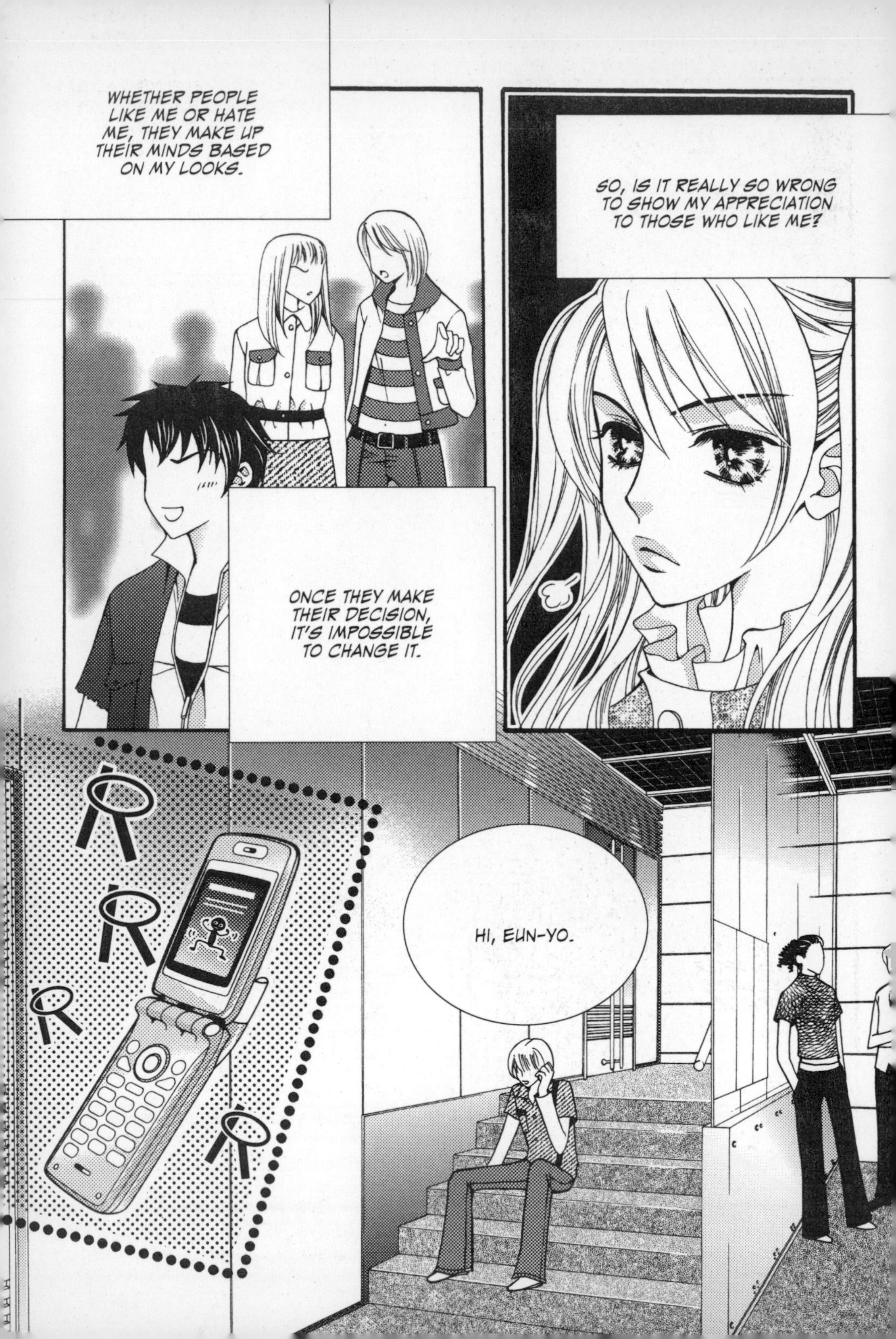
WHETHER PEOPLE LIKE ME OR HATE ME, THEY MAKE UP THEIR MINDS BASED ON MY LOOKS.
ONCE THEY MAKE THEIR DECISION, IT'S IMPOSSIBLE TO CHANGE IT.
SO, IS IT REALLY SO WRONG TO SHOW MY APPRECIATION TO THOSE WHO LIKE ME?
R R R R
HI, EUN-YO.

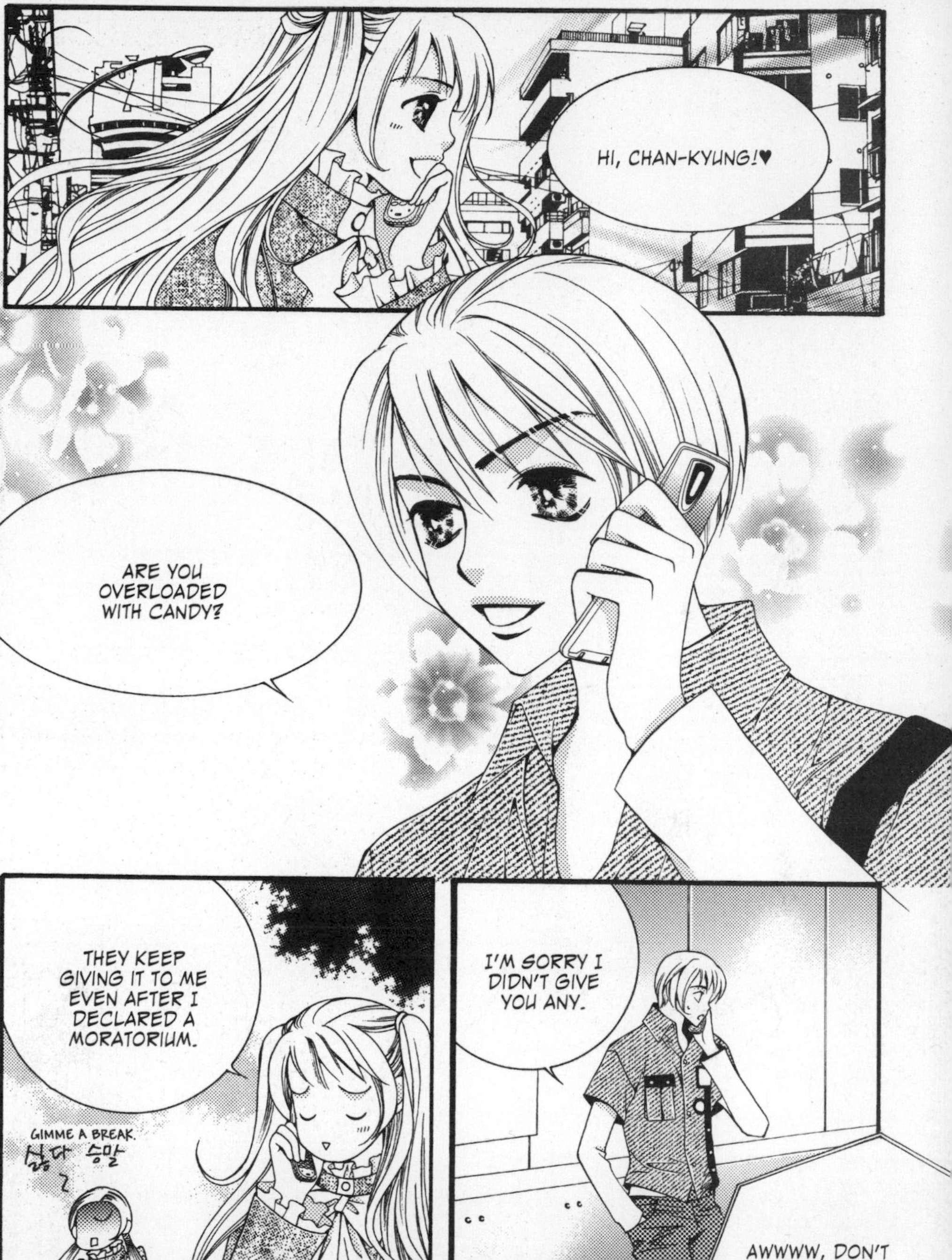
HI, CHAN-KYUNG!♥
ARE YOU OVERLOADED WITH CANDY?
THEY KEEP GIVING IT TO ME EVEN AFTER I DECLARED A MORATORIUM.
GIMME A BREAK.
I'M SORRY I DIDN'T GIVE YOU ANY.
AWWWW, DON'T WORRY. I HATE SWEET STUFF ANYWAY.

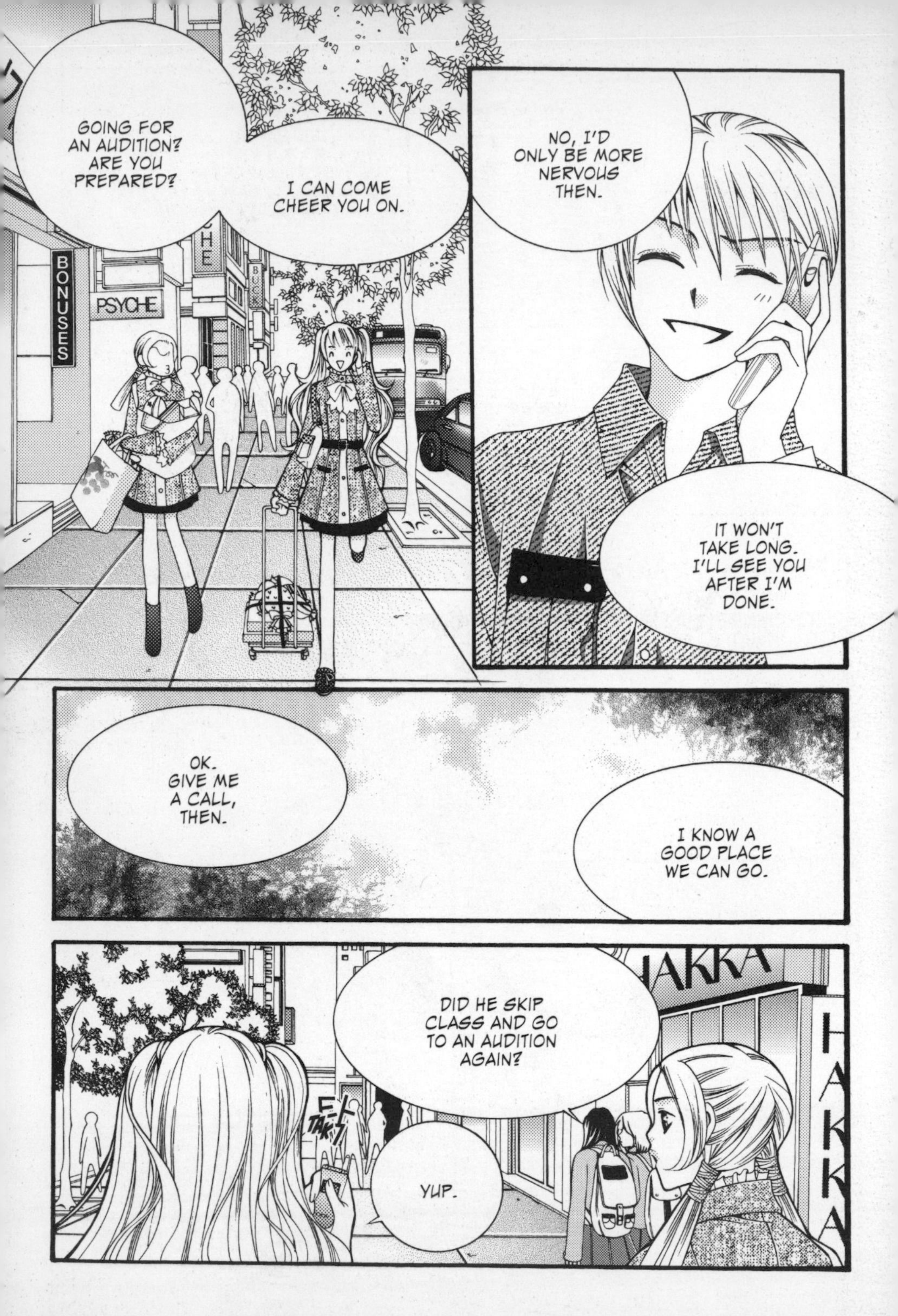
GOING FOR AN AUDITION? ARE YOU PREPARED?
I CAN COME CHEER YOU ON.
BONUSES
PSYCHE
NO, I'D ONLY BE MORE NERVOUS THEN.
IT WON'T TAKE LONG. I'LL SEE YOU AFTER I'M DONE.
OK. GIVE ME A CALL, THEN.
I KNOW A GOOD PLACE WE CAN GO.
HAKKA
DID HE SKIP CLASS AND GO TO AN AUDITION AGAIN?
TAK
YUP.
HAKKA

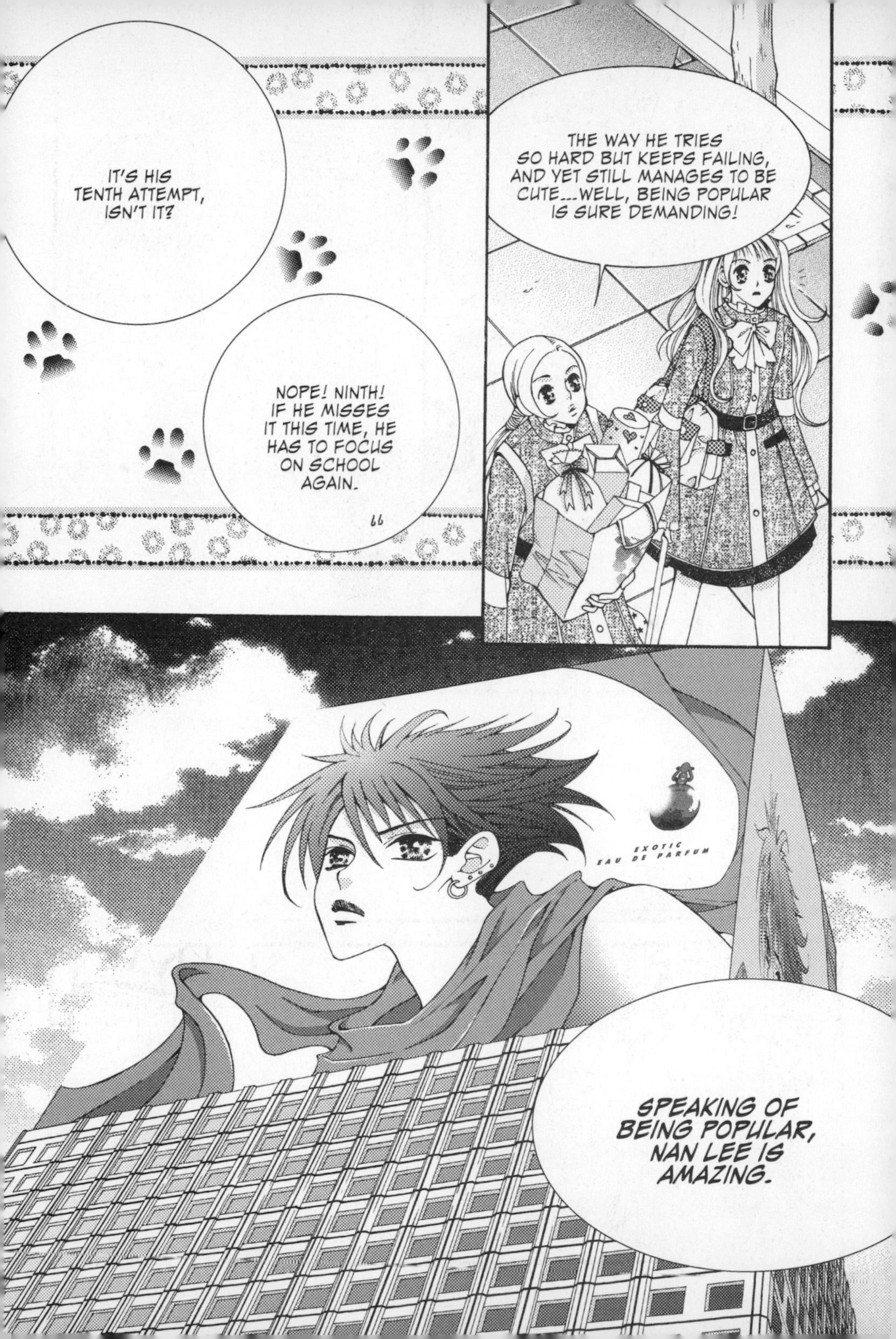
IT'S HIS TENTH ATTEMPT, ISN'T IT?
NOPE! NINTH! IF HE MISSES IT THIS TIME, HE HAS TO FOCUS ON SCHOOL AGAIN.
THE WAY HE TRIES SO HARD BUT KEEPS FAILING, AND YET STILL MANAGES TO BE CUTE...WELL, BEING POPULAR IS SURE DEMANDING!
EXOTIC EAU DE PARFUM
SPEAKING OF BEING POPULAR, NAN LEE IS AMAZING.

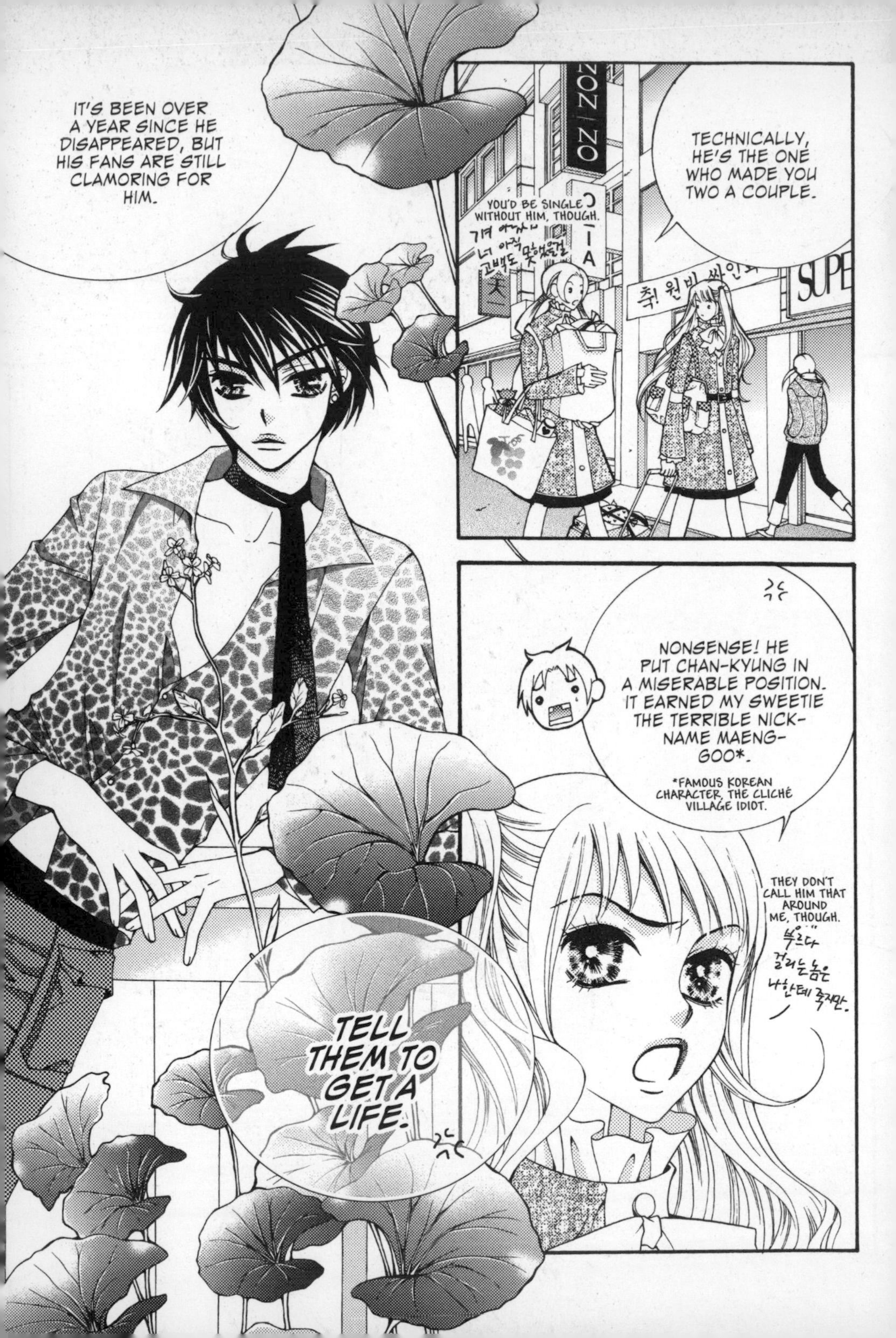
IT'S BEEN OVER A YEAR SINCE HE DISAPPEARED, BUT HIS FANS ARE STILL CLAMORING FOR HIM.
TELL THEM TO GET A LIFE.
NON NO
TECHNICALLY, HE'S THE ONE WHO MADE YOU TWO A COUPLE.
YOU'D BE SINGLE WITHOUT HIM, THOUGH.
너 아직 고백도 못했을걸
SUPE
축! 원빈 싸인회
NONSENSE! HE PUT CHAN-KYUNG IN A MISERABLE POSITION. IT EARNED MY SWEETIE THE TERRIBLE NICK-NAME MAENG-GOO*.
*FAMOUS KOREAN CHARACTER, THE CLICHÉ VILLAGE IDIOT.
THEY DON'T CALL HIM THAT AROUND ME, THOUGH.

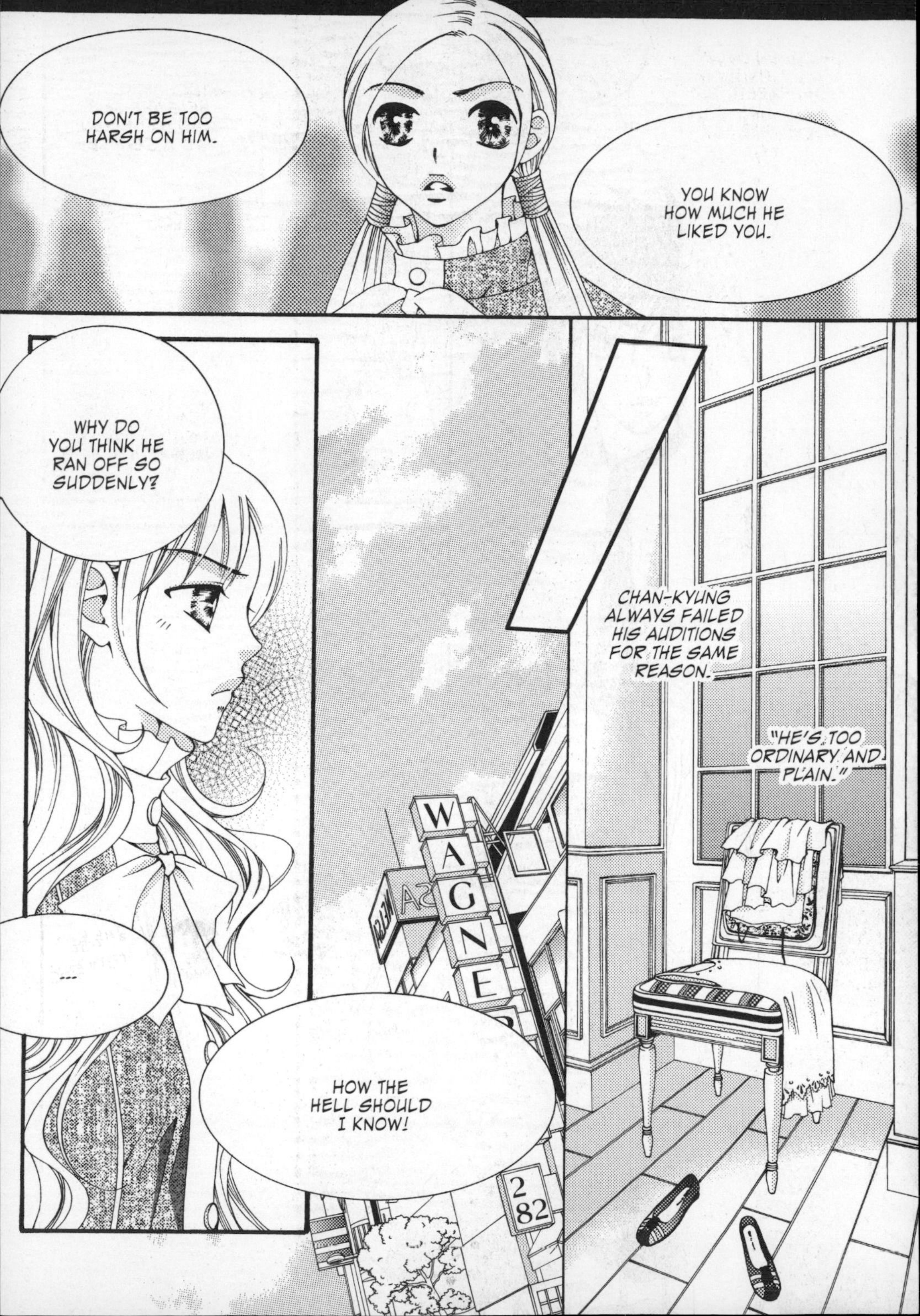
DON'T BE TOO HARSH ON HIM.
YOU KNOW HOW MUCH HE LIKED YOU.
WHY DO YOU THINK HE RAN OFF SO SUDDENLY?
...
HOW THE HELL SHOULD I KNOW!
WAGNER
2 82
CHAN-KYUNG ALWAYS FAILED HIS AUDITIONS FOR THE SAME REASON.
"HE'S TOO ORDINARY AND PLAIN."

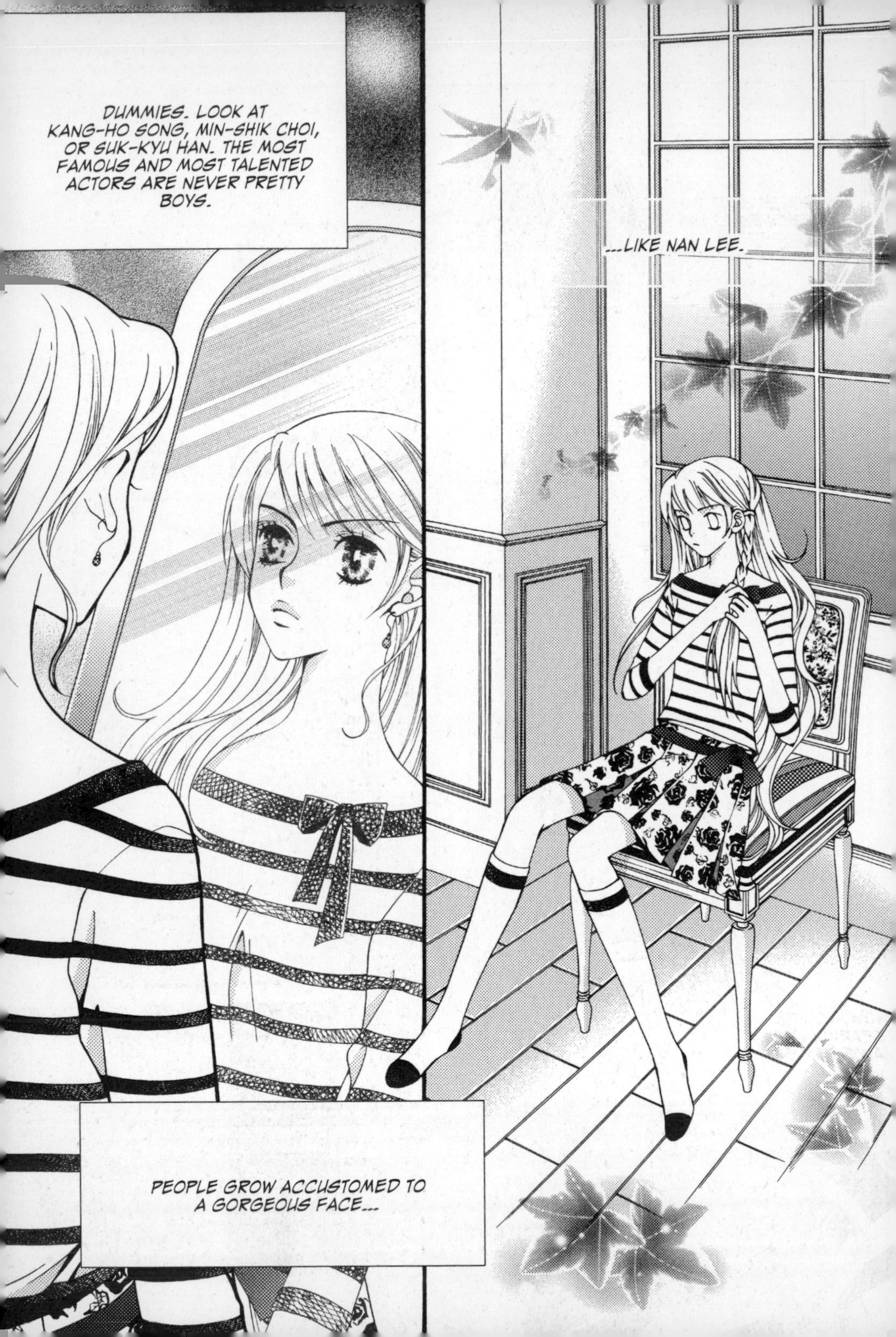
DUMMIES. LOOK AT KANG-HO SONG, MIN-SHIK CHOI, OR SUK-KYU HAN. THE MOST FAMOUS AND MOST TALENTED ACTORS ARE NEVER PRETTY BOYS.
PEOPLE GROW ACCUSTOMED TO A GORGEOUS FACE...
...LIKE NAN LEE.

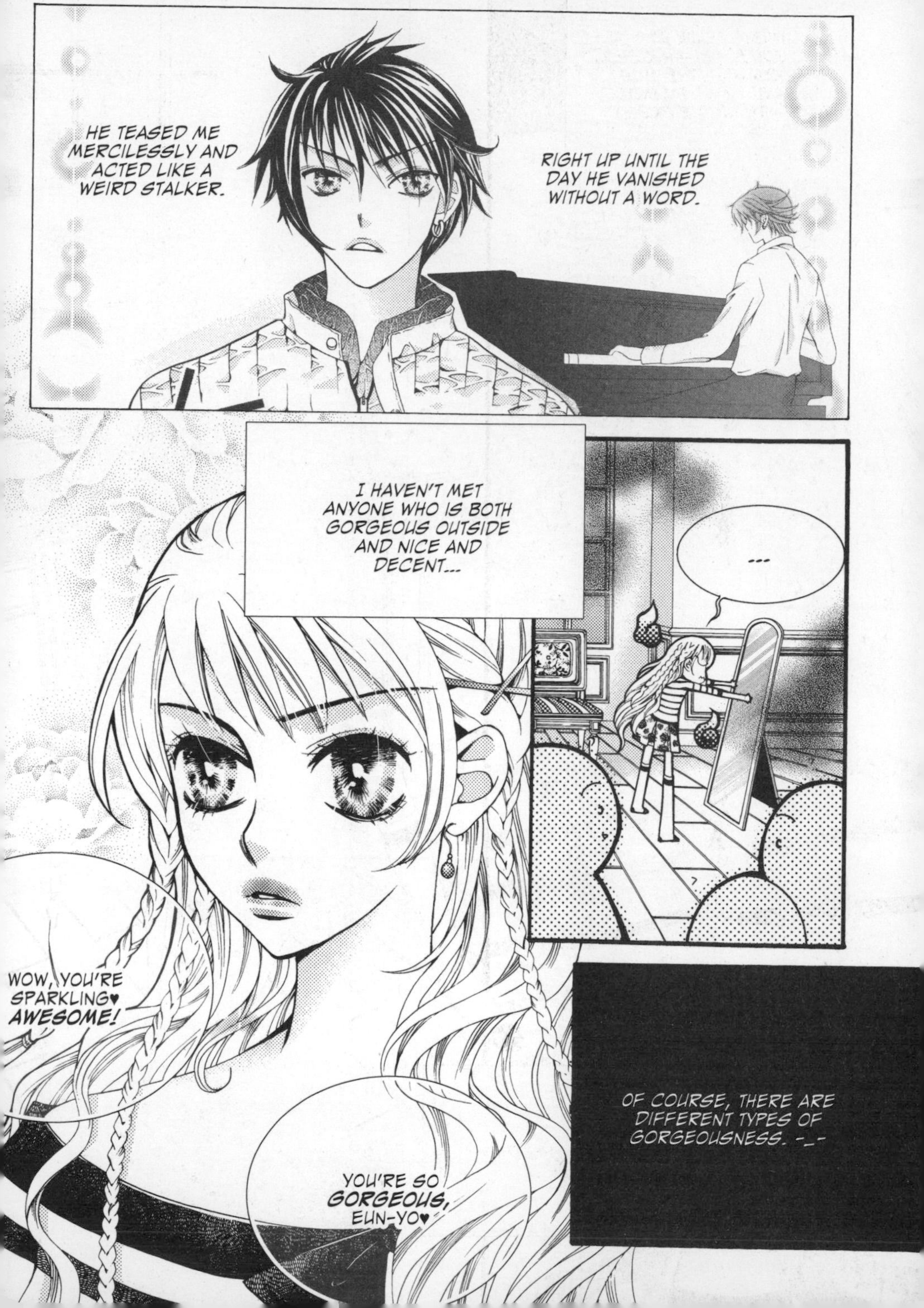
HE TEASED ME MERCILESSLY AND ACTED LIKE A WEIRD STALKER.
RIGHT UP UNTIL THE DAY HE VANISHED WITHOUT A WORD.
I HAVEN'T MET ANYONE WHO IS BOTH GORGEOUS OUTSIDE AND NICE AND DECENT...
...
WOW, YOU'RE SPARKLING♥ AWESOME!
YOU'RE SO GORGEOUS, EUN-YO♥
OF COURSE, THERE ARE DIFFERENT TYPES OF GORGEOUSNESS. -_-

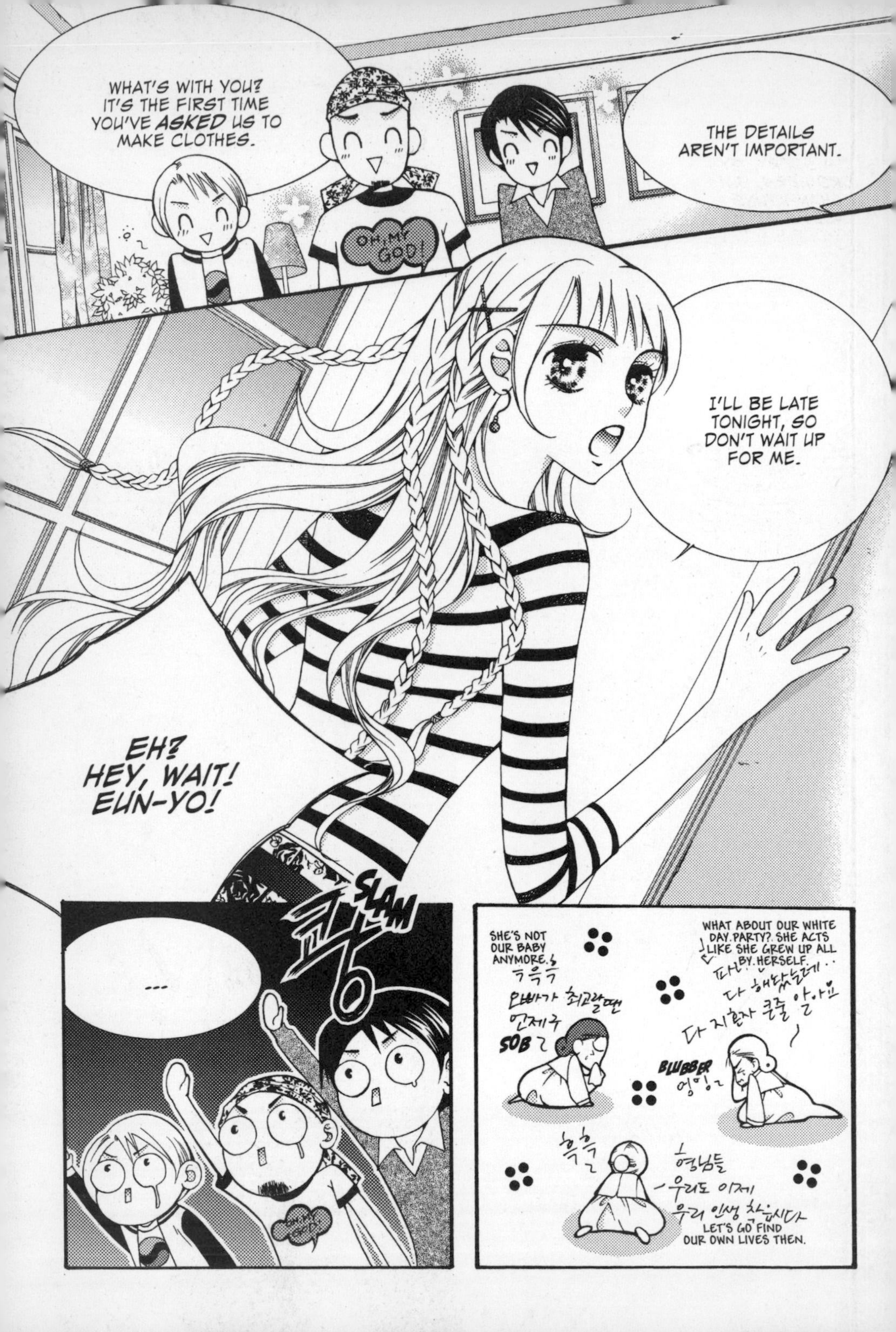

WHAT'S WITH YOU? IT'S THE FIRST TIME YOU'VE ***ASKED*** US TO MAKE CLOTHES.
OH MY GOD!
THE DETAILS AREN'T IMPORTANT.
I'LL BE LATE TONIGHT, SO DON'T WAIT UP FOR ME.
EH? HEY, WAIT! EUN-YO!
SLAM
...
SHE'S NOT OUR BABY ANYMORE.
크윽크
오빠가 최고랄땐 언제구
SOB
WHAT ABOUT OUR WHITE DAY PARTY? SHE ACTS LIKE SHE GREW UP ALL BY HERSELF.
파티 다 해놨는데..
다 지혼자 큰줄 알아요
BLUBBER
엉엉
흑흑
형님들 우리도 이제 우리 인생 찾읍시다
LET'S GO FIND OUR OWN LIVES THEN.

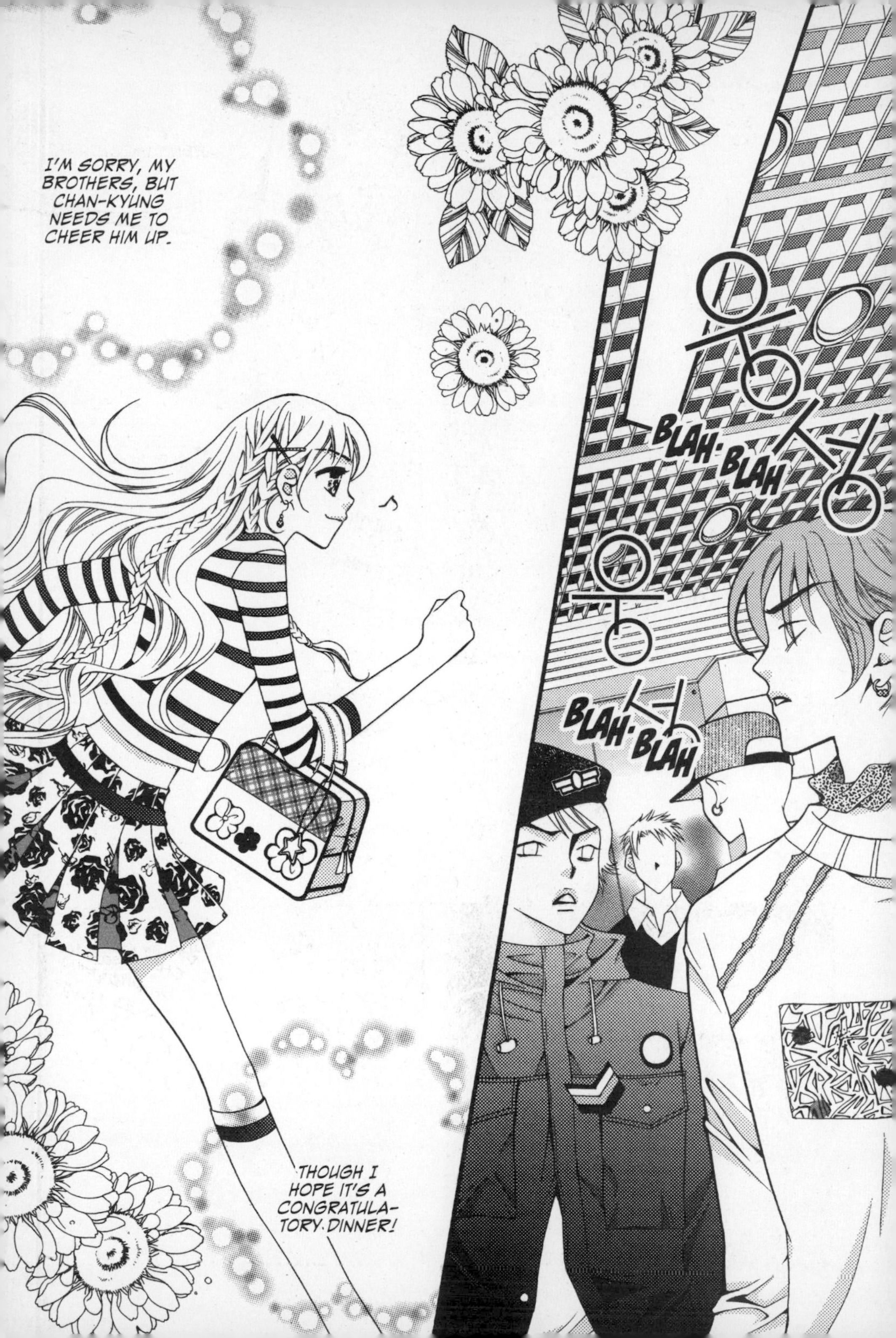
I'M SORRY, MY BROTHERS, BUT CHAN-KYUNG NEEDS ME TO CHEER HIM UP.
BLAH-BLAH
BLAH-BLAH
THOUGH I HOPE IT'S A CONGRATULA-TORY DINNER!

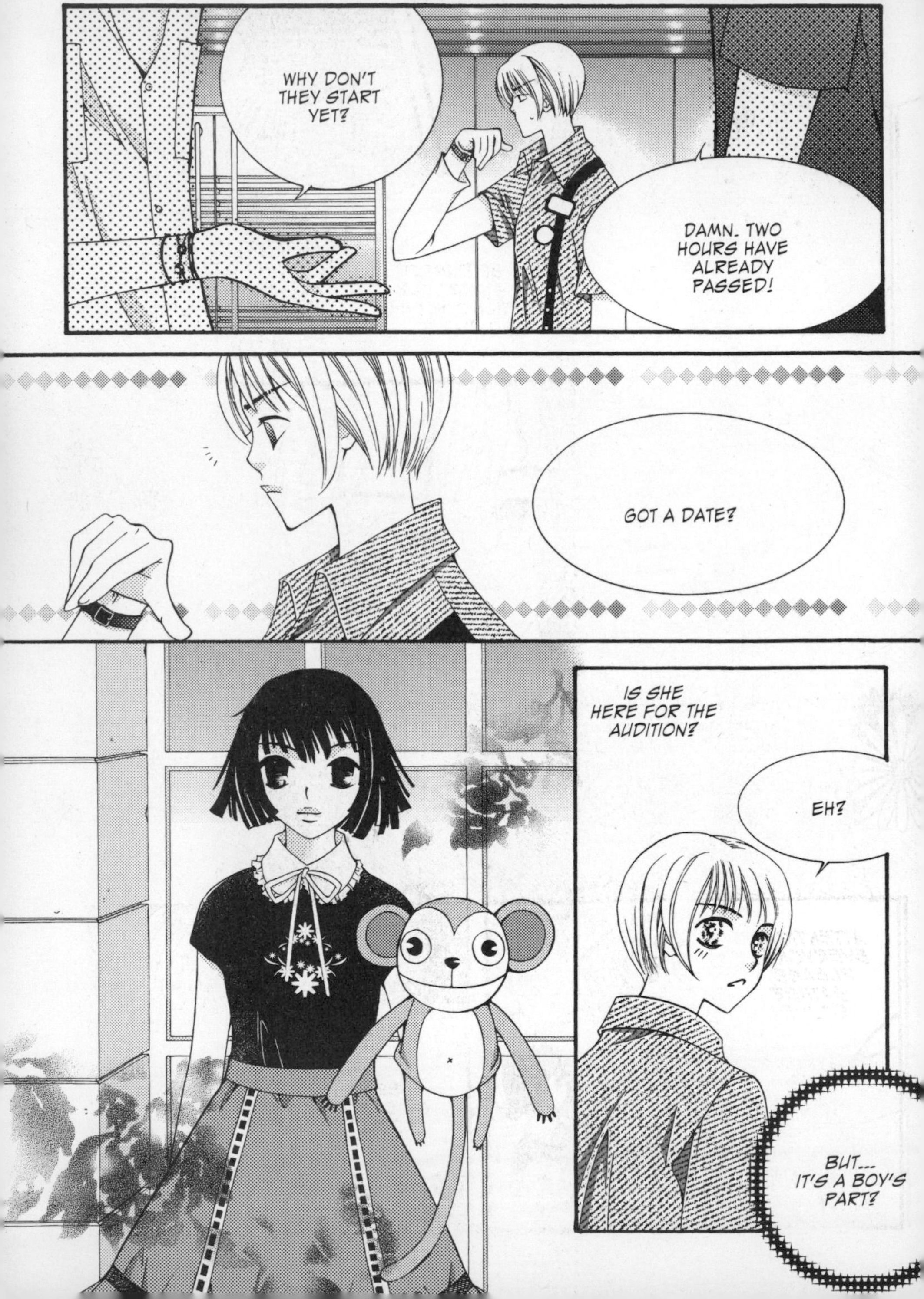
WHY DON'T THEY START YET?
DAMN. TWO HOURS HAVE ALREADY PASSED!
GOT A DATE?
IS SHE HERE FOR THE AUDITION?
EH?
BUT... IT'S A BOY'S PART?

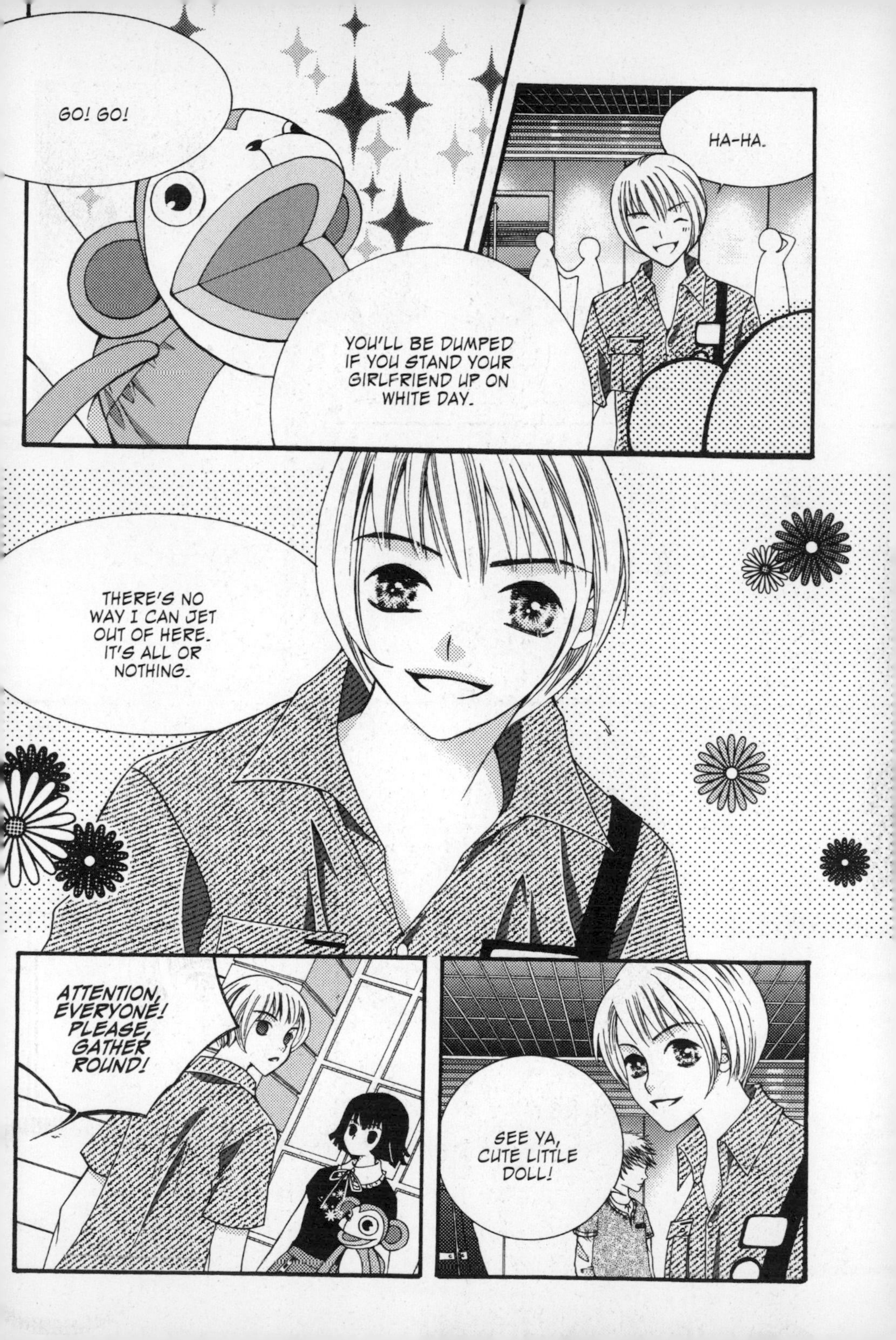
GO! GO!
HA-HA.
YOU'LL BE DUMPED IF YOU STAND YOUR GIRLFRIEND UP ON WHITE DAY.
THERE'S NO WAY I CAN JET OUT OF HERE. IT'S ALL OR NOTHING.
ATTENTION, EVERYONE! PLEASE, GATHER ROUND!
SEE YA, CUTE LITTLE DOLL!

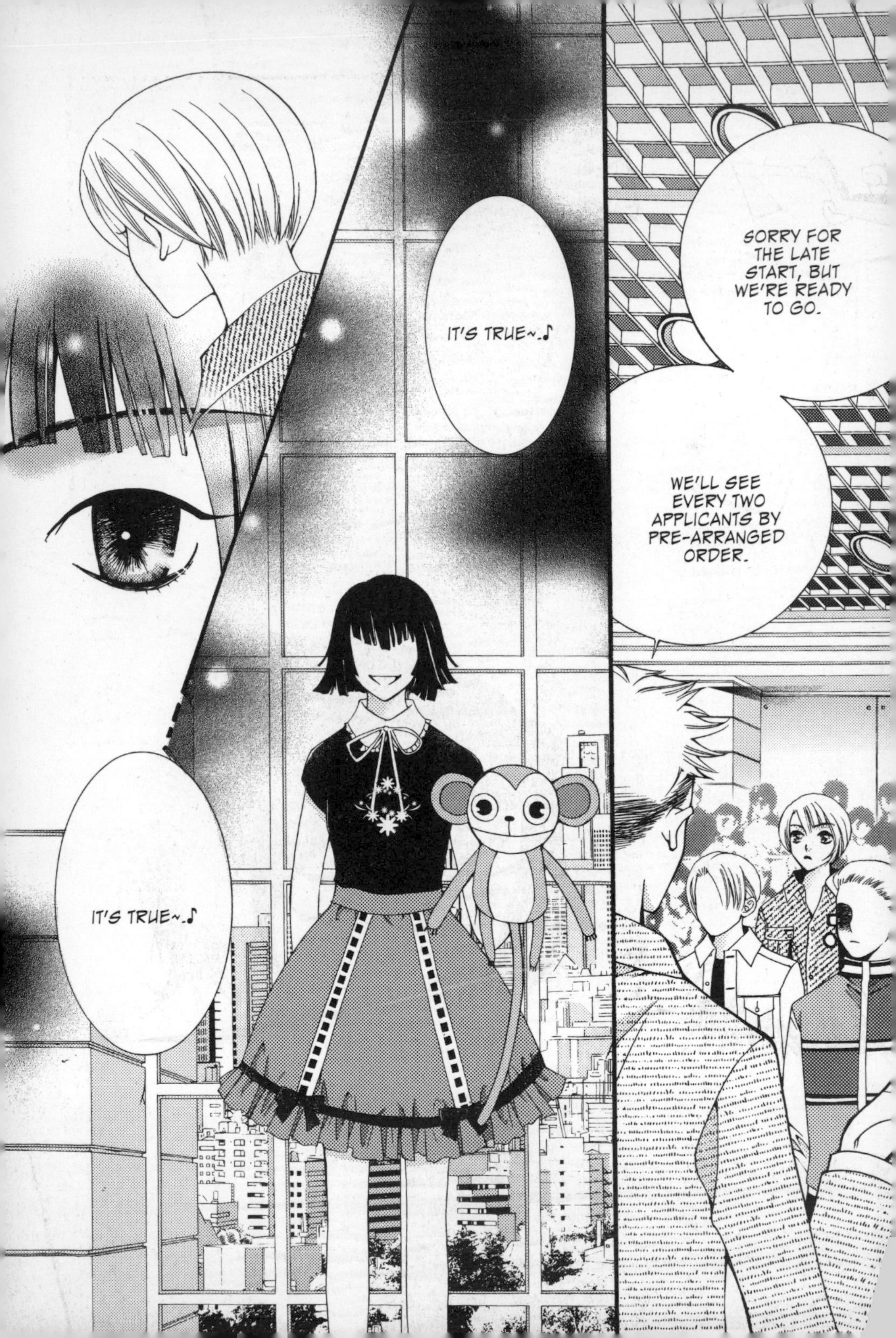
IT'S TRUE~.♪
IT'S TRUE~.♪
SORRY FOR THE LATE START, BUT WE'RE READY TO GO.
WE'LL SEE EVERY TWO APPLICANTS BY PRE-ARRANGED ORDER.

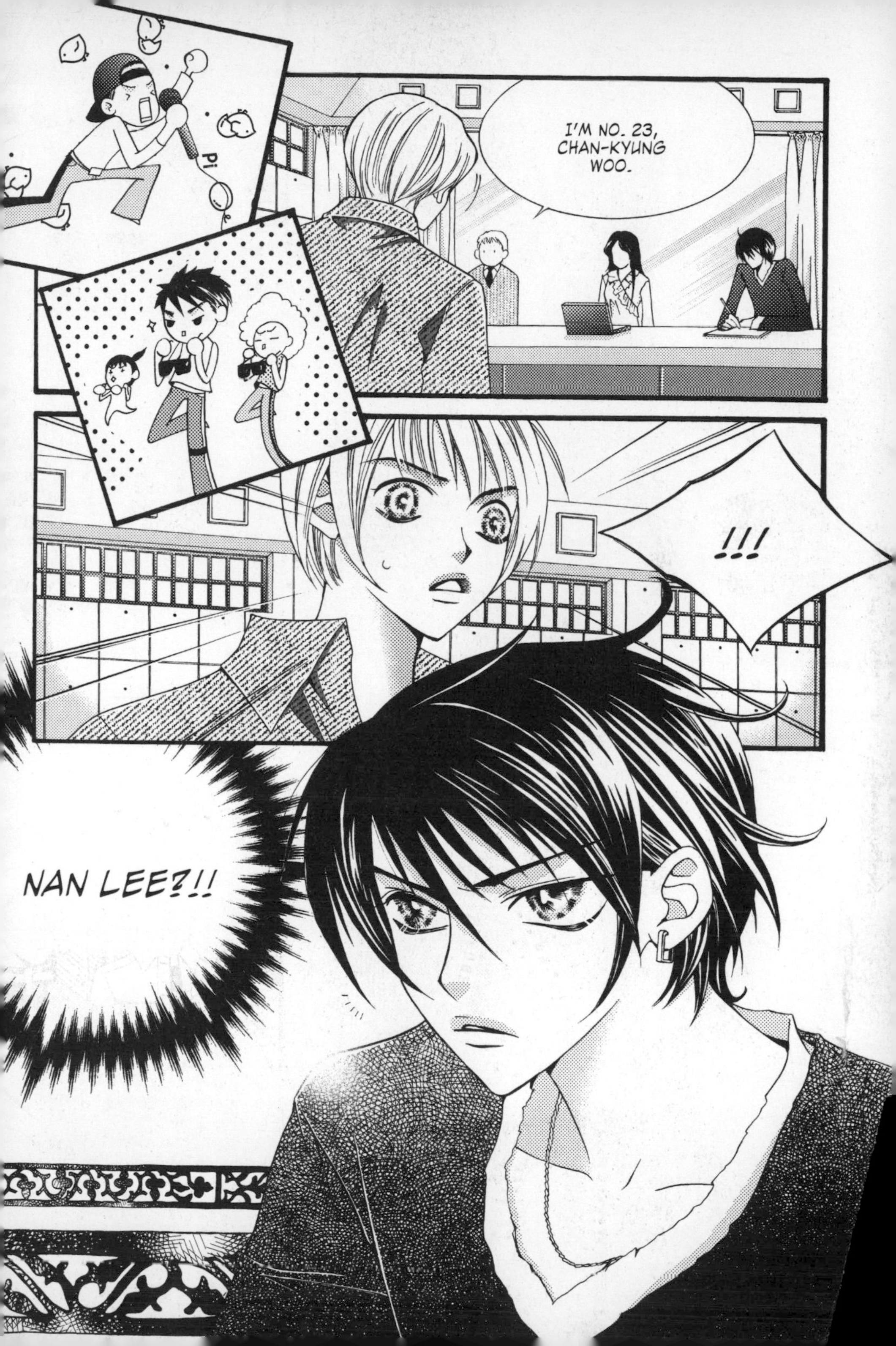
PI
I'M NO. 23, CHAN-KYUNG WOO.
!!!
NAN LEE?!!

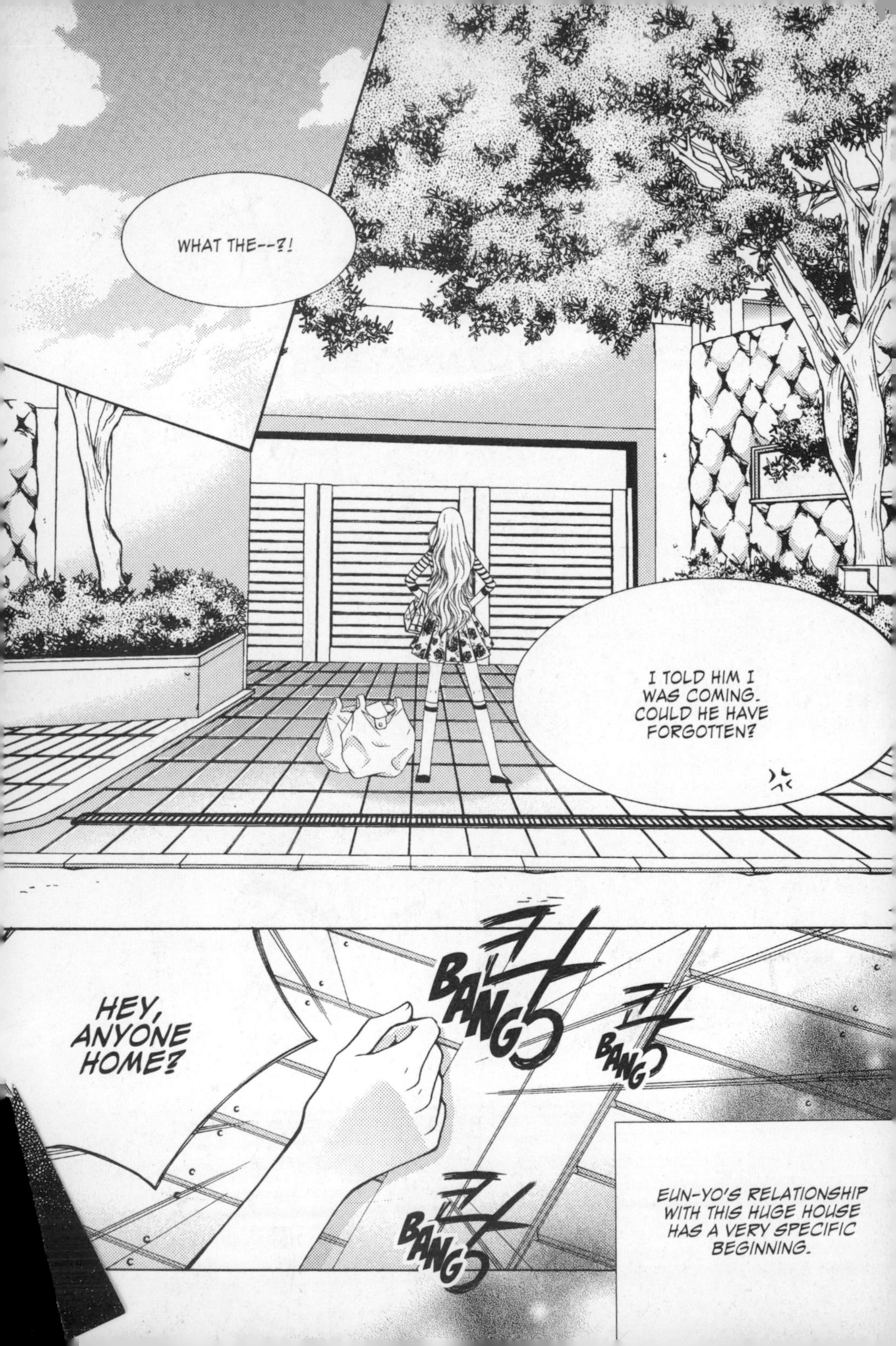
WHAT THE--?!
I TOLD HIM I WAS COMING. COULD HE HAVE FORGOTTEN?
HEY, ANYONE HOME?
BANG
BANG
BANG
EUN-YO'S RELATIONSHIP WITH THIS HUGE HOUSE HAS A VERY SPECIFIC BEGINNING.

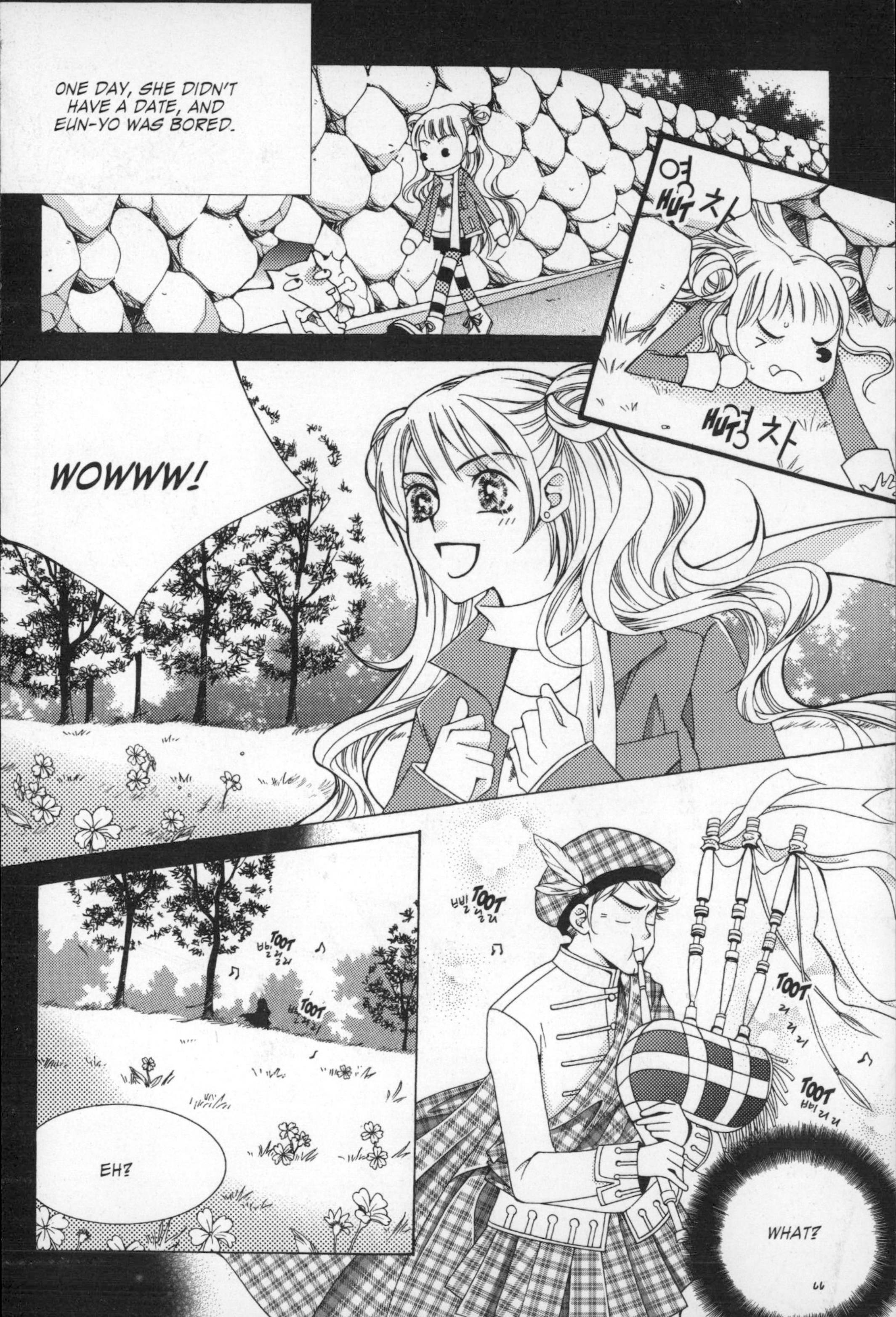
ONE DAY, SHE DIDN'T HAVE A DATE, AND EUN-YO WAS BORED.
영 HUT 차
HUT영 차
WOWWW!
EH?
TOOT
TOOT
TOOT
TOOT
TOOT
WHAT?

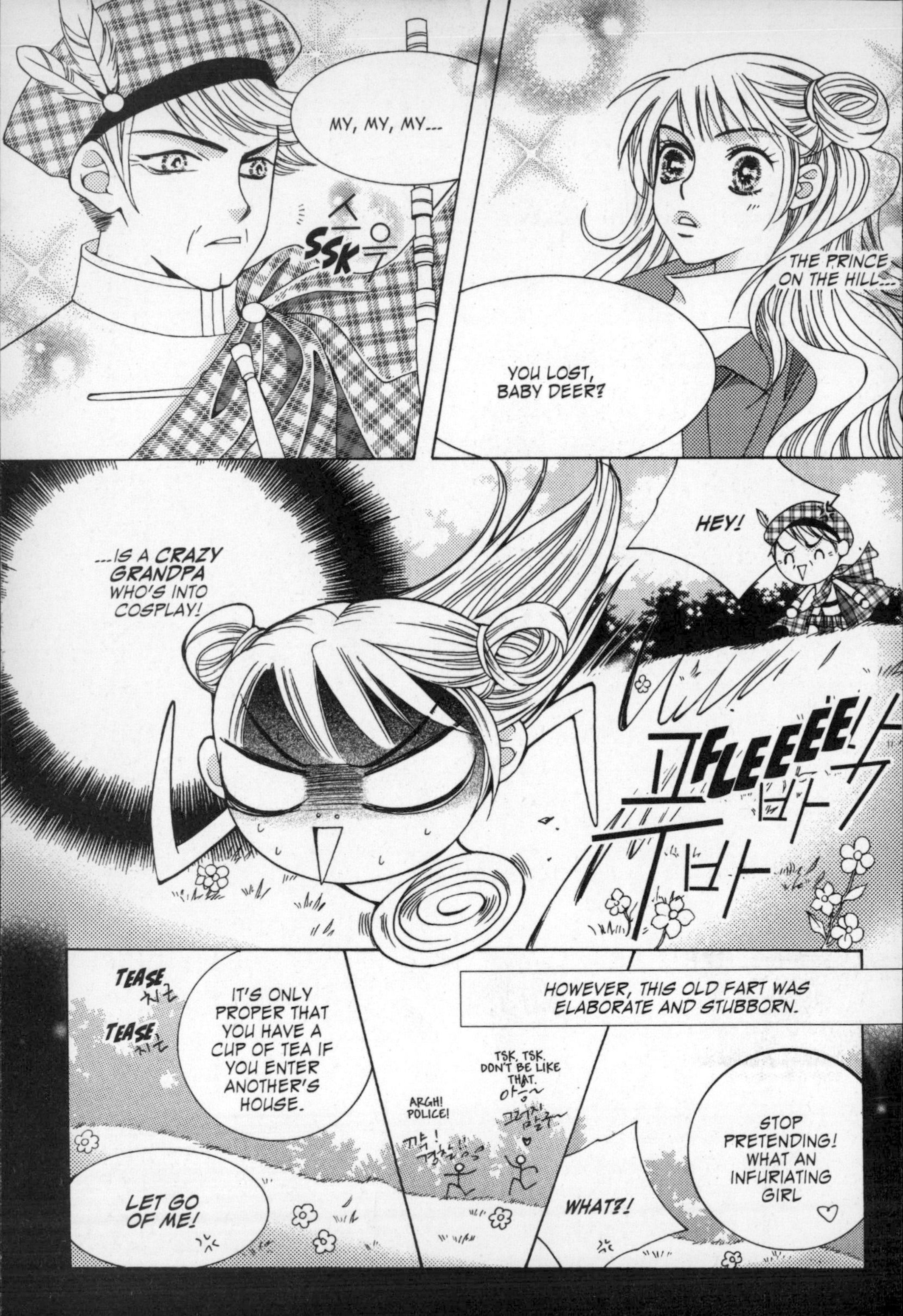
MY, MY, MY...
SSK
YOU LOST, BABY DEER?
THE PRINCE ON THE HILL...
...IS A CRAZY GRANDPA WHO'S INTO COSPLAY!
HEY!
FLEEEEE!
TEASE
TEASE
IT'S ONLY PROPER THAT YOU HAVE A CUP OF TEA IF YOU ENTER ANOTHER'S HOUSE.
LET GO OF ME!
ARGH! POLICE!
TSK, TSK. DON'T BE LIKE THAT.
HOWEVER, THIS OLD FART WAS ELABORATE AND STUBBORN.
WHAT?!
STOP PRETENDING! WHAT AN INFURIATING GIRL

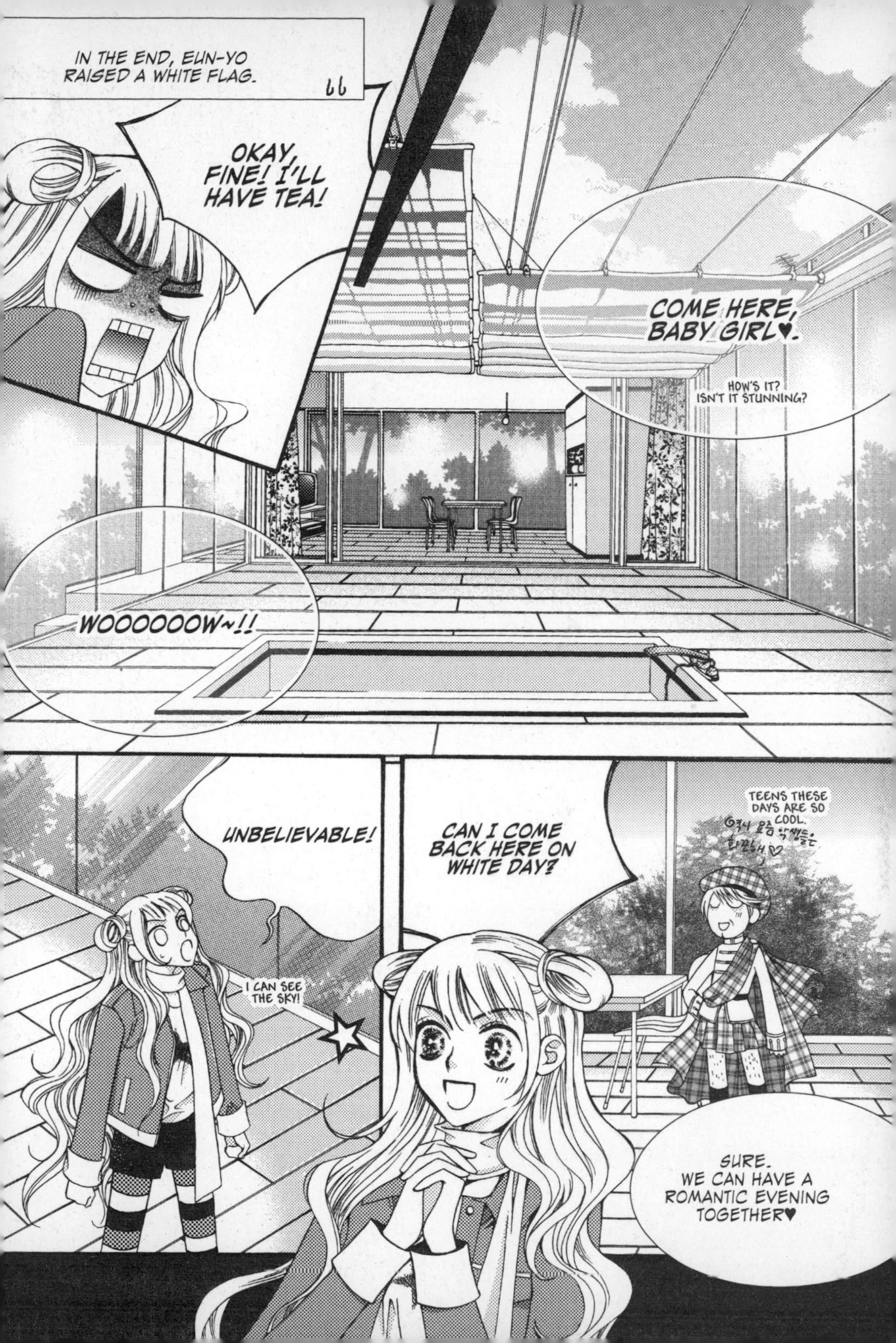
IN THE END, EUN-YO RAISED A WHITE FLAG.
OKAY, FINE! I'LL HAVE TEA!
COME HERE, BABY GIRL♥.
HOW'S IT? ISN'T IT STUNNING?
WOOOOOOW~!!
UNBELIEVABLE!
I CAN SEE THE SKY!
CAN I COME BACK HERE ON WHITE DAY?
TEENS THESE DAYS ARE SO COOL.
SURE. WE CAN HAVE A ROMANTIC EVENING TOGETHER♥

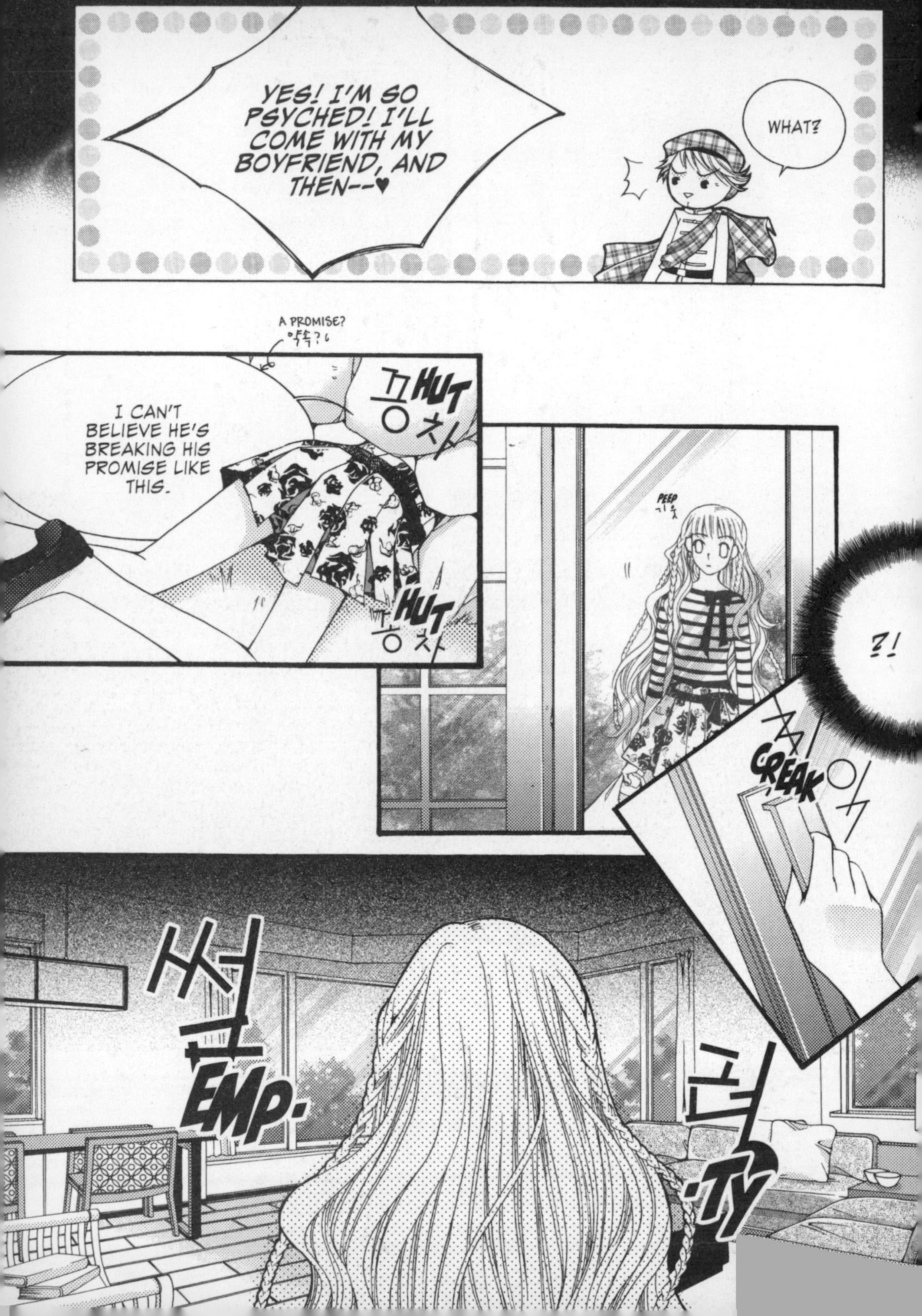

YES! I'M SO PSYCHED! I'LL COME WITH MY BOYFRIEND, AND THEN--♥
WHAT?
A PROMISE?
약속?!
I CAN'T BELIEVE HE'S BREAKING HIS PROMISE LIKE THIS.
HUT
HUT
PEEP
?!
CREAK
EMP-
-TY

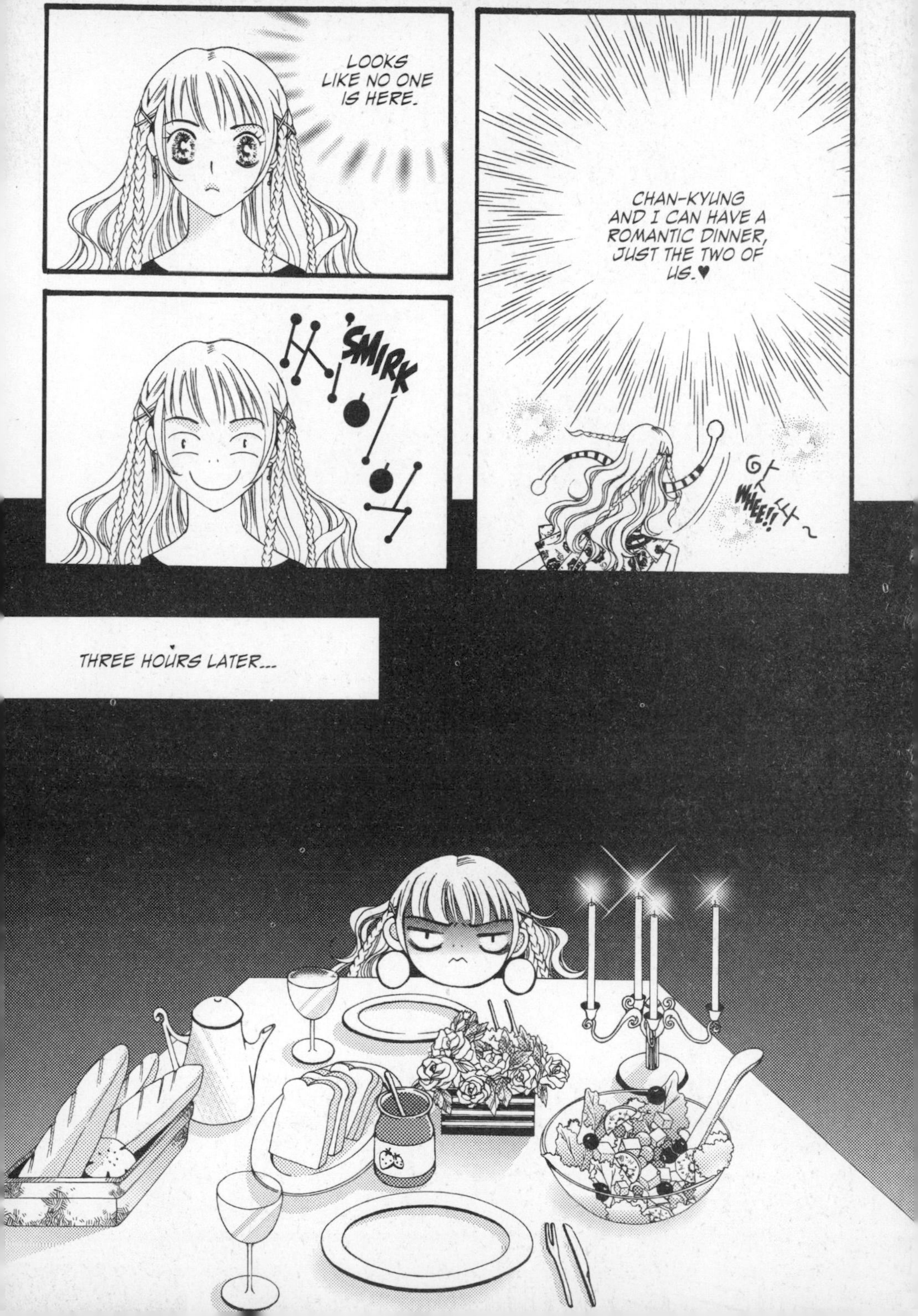
LOOKS LIKE NO ONE IS HERE.
SMIRK
CHAN-KYUNG AND I CAN HAVE A ROMANTIC DINNER, JUST THE TWO OF US.♥
앗싸~
WHEE!!
THREE HOURS LATER...

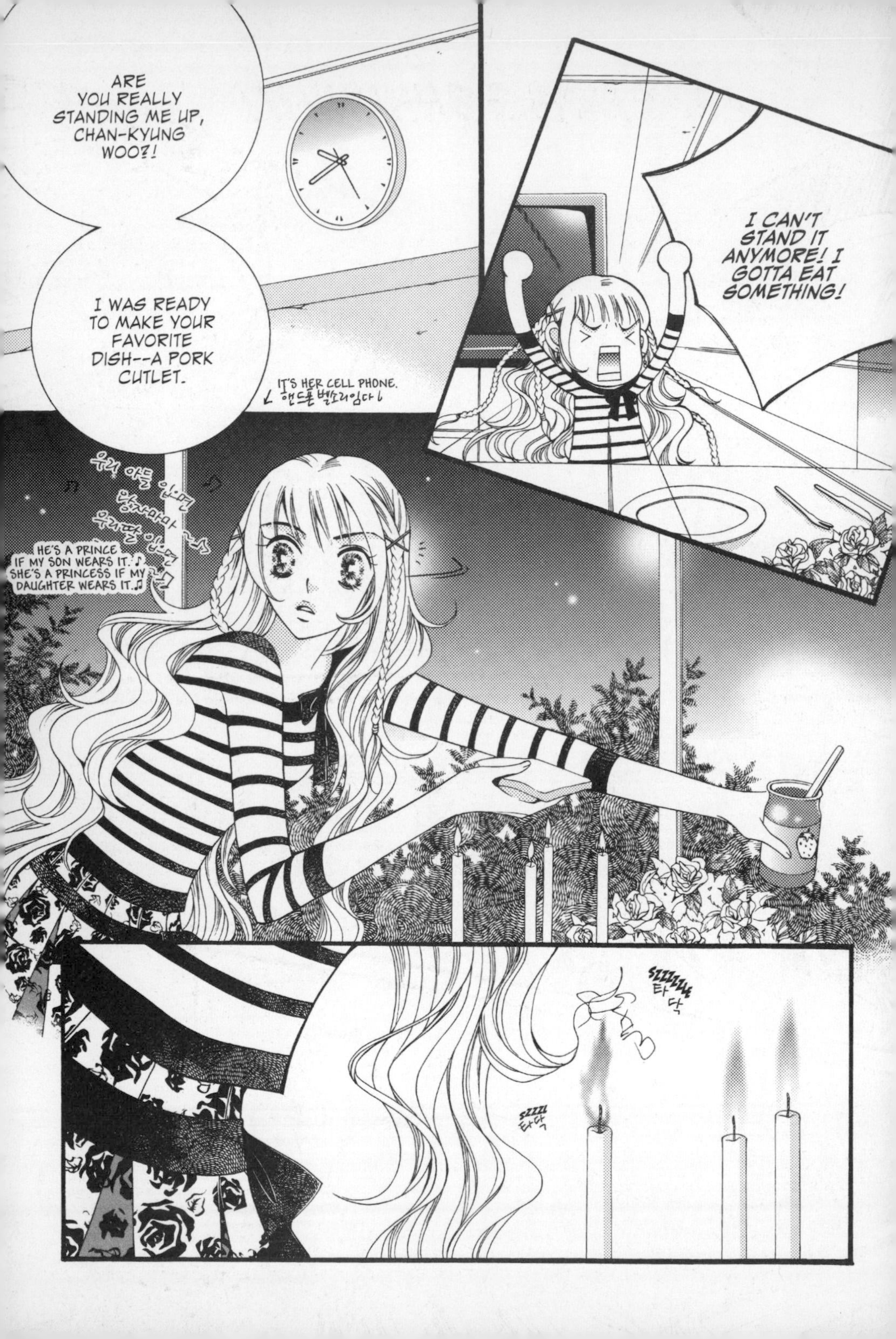
ARE YOU REALLY STANDING ME UP, CHAN-KYUNG WOO?!
I WAS READY TO MAKE YOUR FAVORITE DISH--A PORK CUTLET.
I CAN'T STAND IT ANYMORE! I GOTTA EAT SOMETHING!
IT'S HER CELL PHONE.
핸드폰 벨소리임다
우리 아들 입으면 왕자마마~ 우리딸 입으면~
HE'S A PRINCE IF MY SON WEARS IT. ♪ SHE'S A PRINCESS IF MY DAUGHTER WEARS IT. ♫
SZZZZZZ
타닥
SZZZZ
타닥

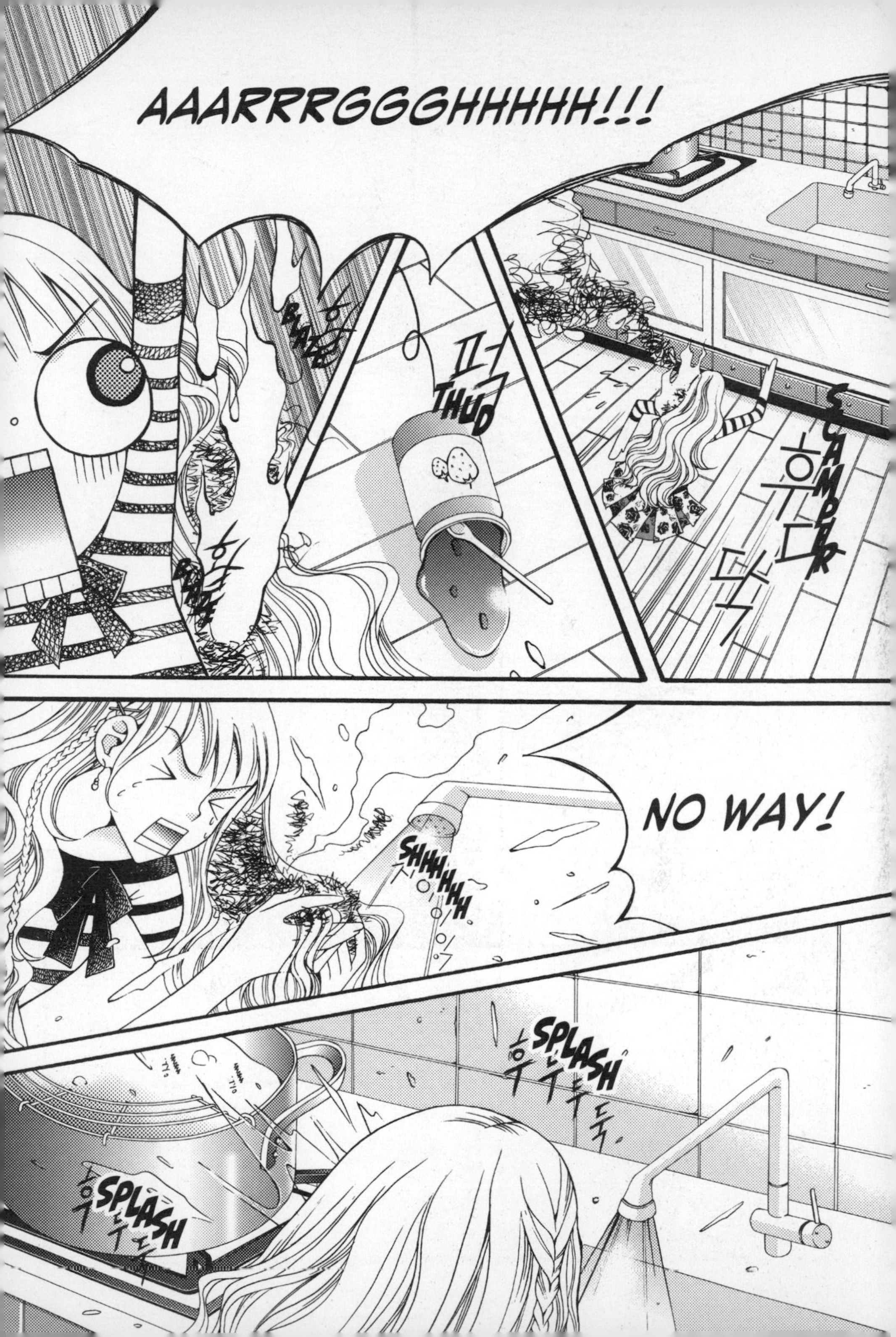
AAARRRGGGHHHHH!!!
THUD
SCAMPER
NO WAY!
SHHHHHH
SPLASH
SPLASH

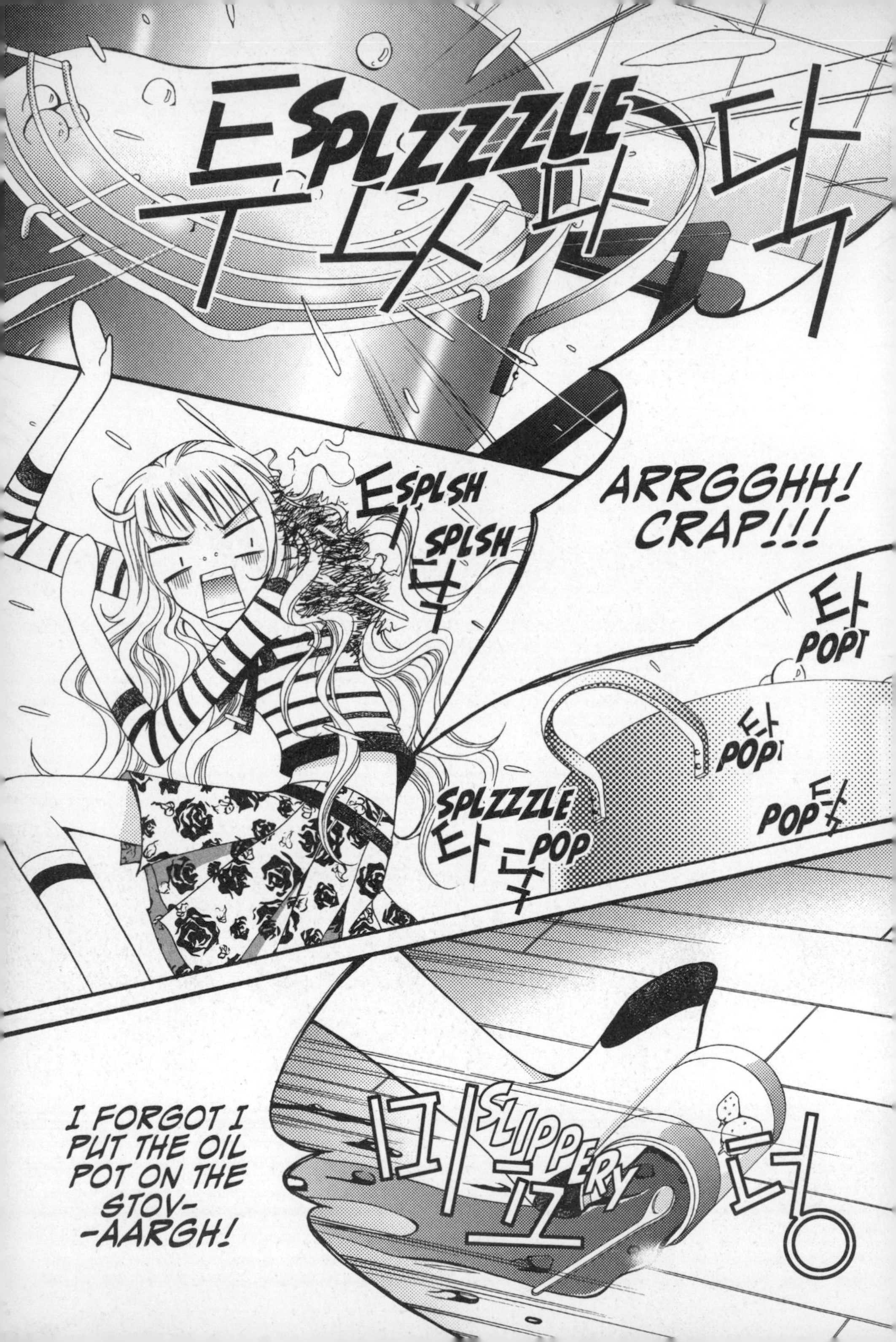

SPLZZZZLE
SPLSH
SPLSH
ARRGGHH! CRAP!!!
타
POP
POP
POP
SPLZZZLE
POP
SLIPPERY
I FORGOT I PUT THE OIL POT ON THE STOV- -AARGH!

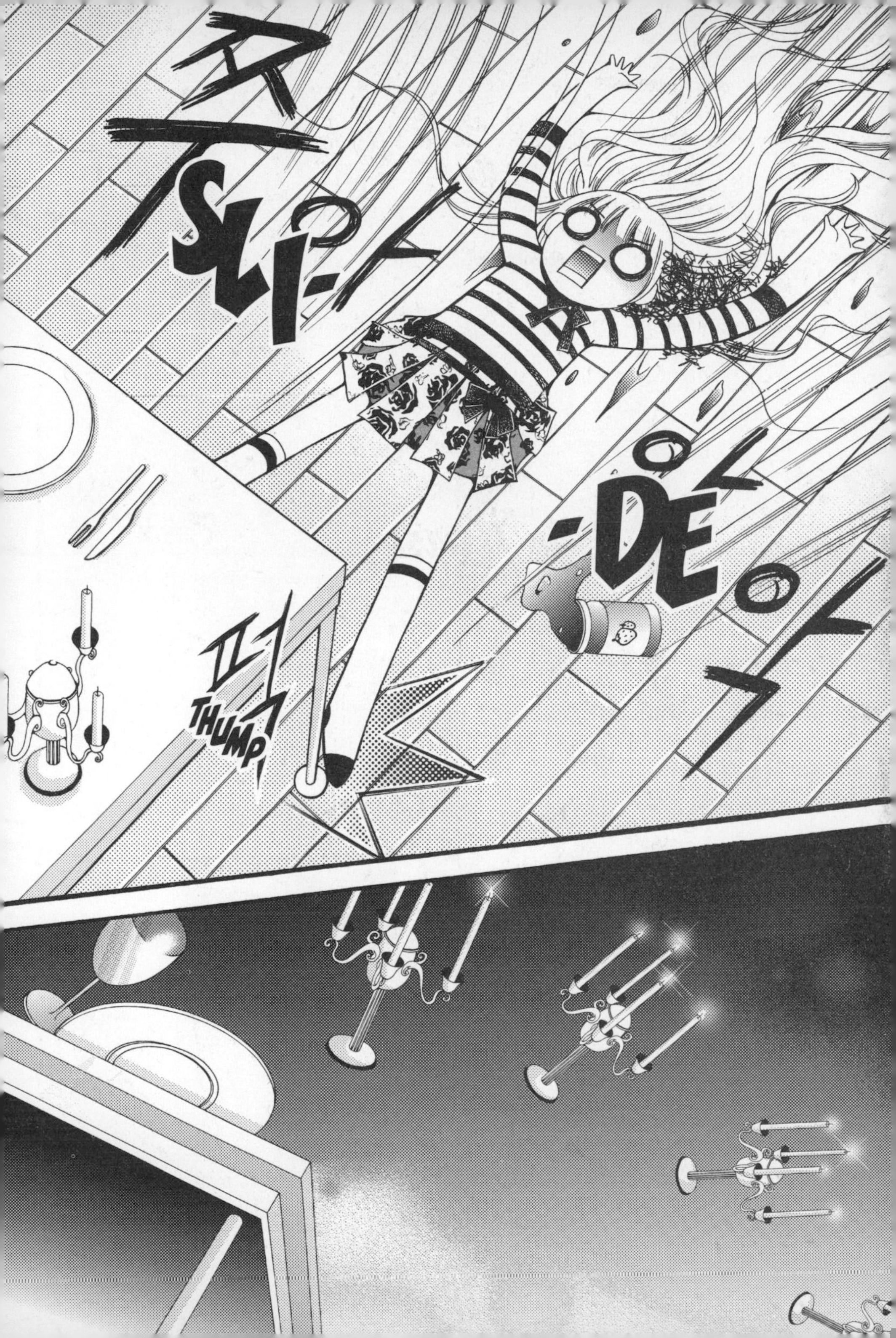
SLI-
-DE
THUMP

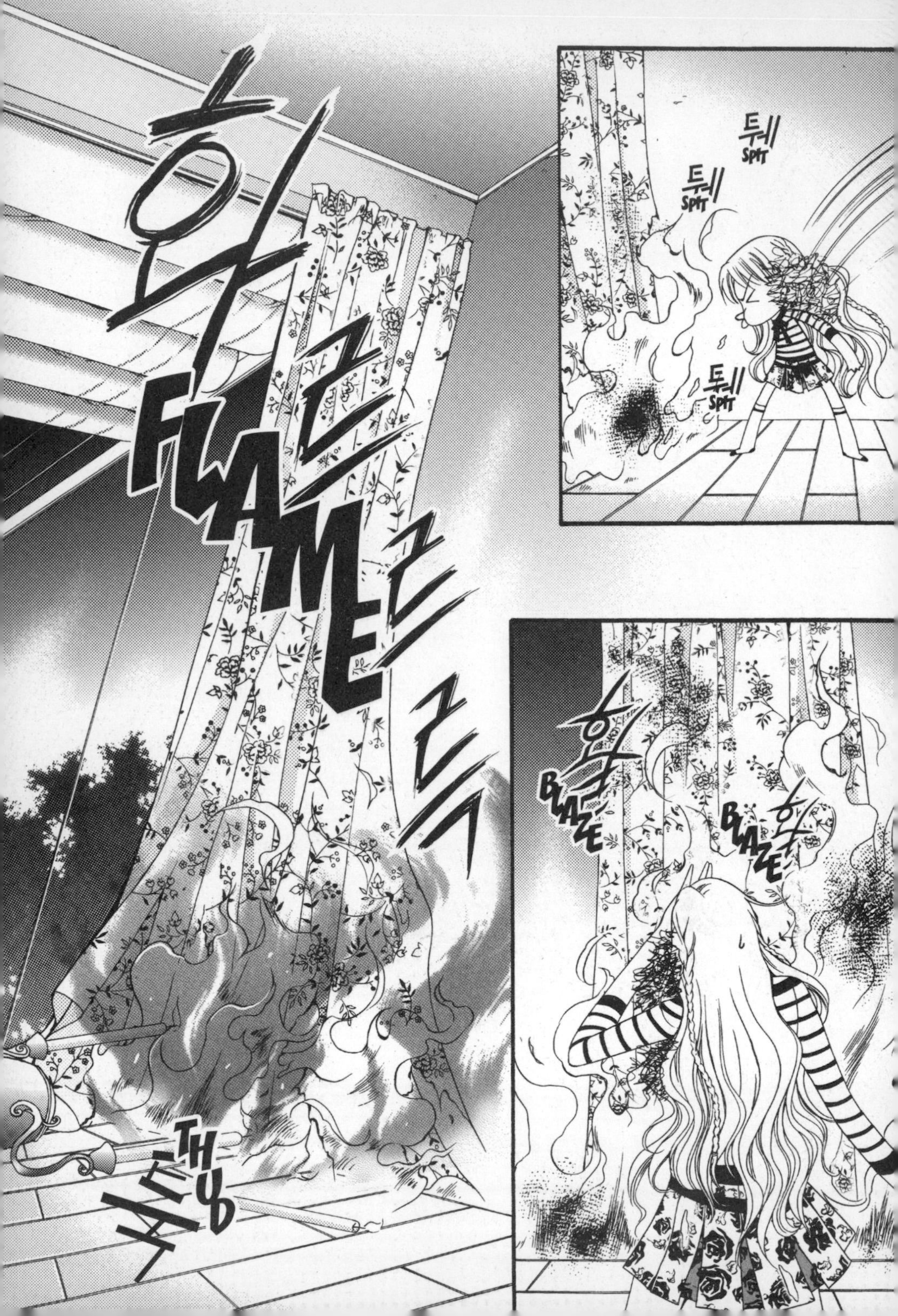
화르르륵
FLAME
탁
THUD
퉤
SPIT
퉤
SPIT
퉤
SPIT
확
BLAZE
확
BLAZE

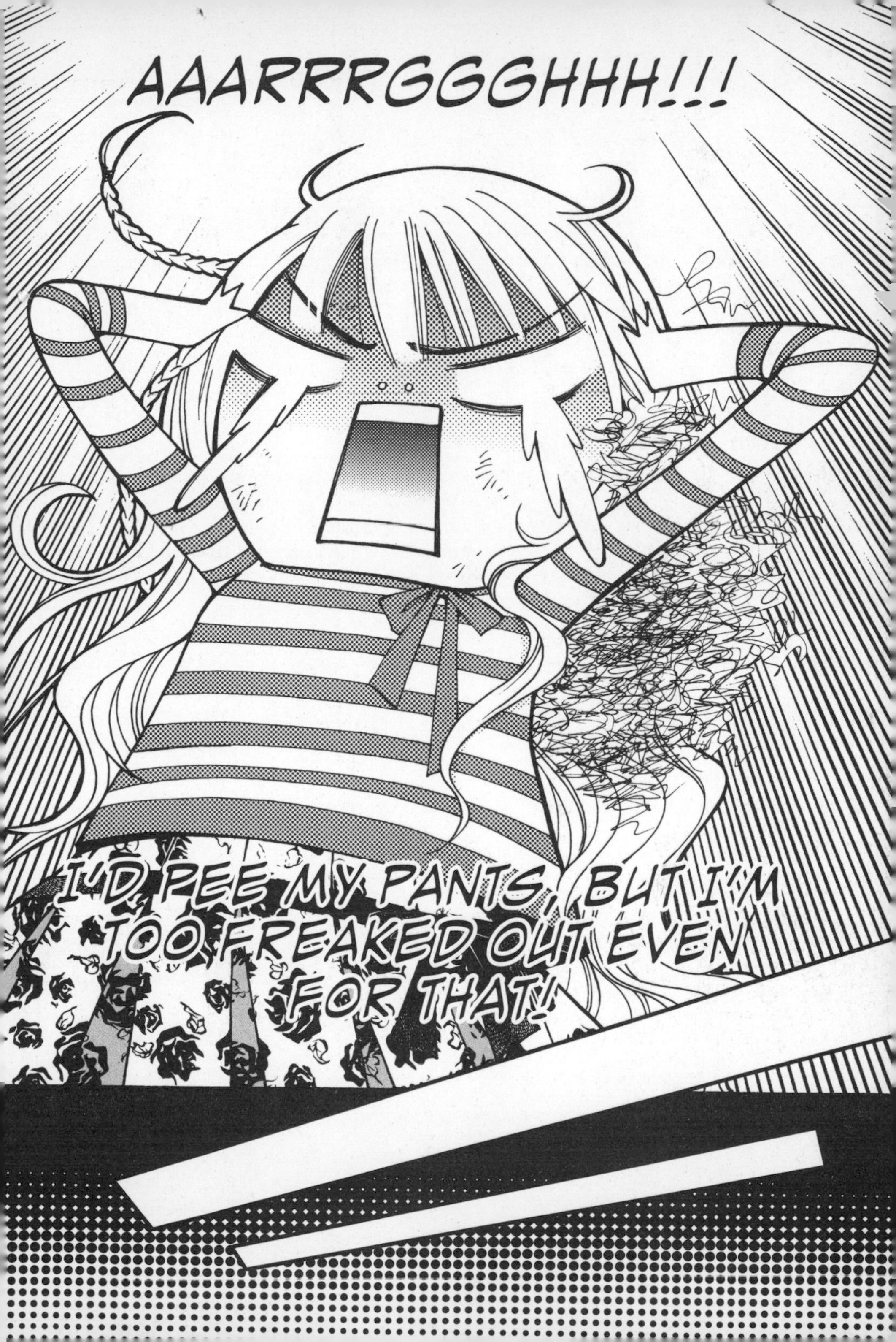
AAARRRGGGHHH!!!
I'D PEE MY PANTS, BUT I'M TOO FREAKED OUT EVEN FOR THAT!

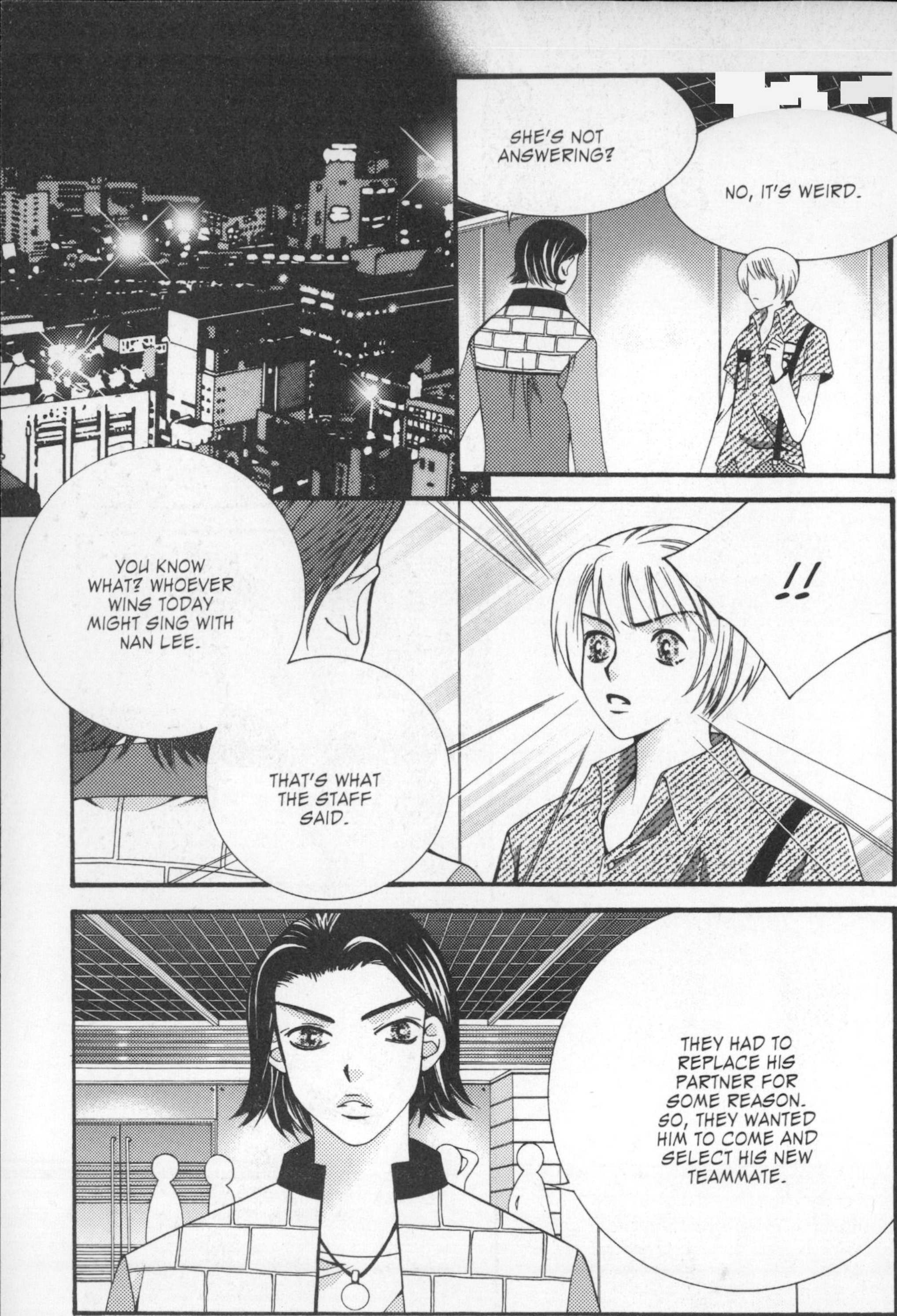
SHE'S NOT ANSWERING?
NO, IT'S WEIRD.
YOU KNOW WHAT? WHOEVER WINS TODAY MIGHT SING WITH NAN LEE.
THAT'S WHAT THE STAFF SAID.
!!
THEY HAD TO REPLACE HIS PARTNER FOR SOME REASON. SO, THEY WANTED HIM TO COME AND SELECT HIS NEW TEAMMATE.

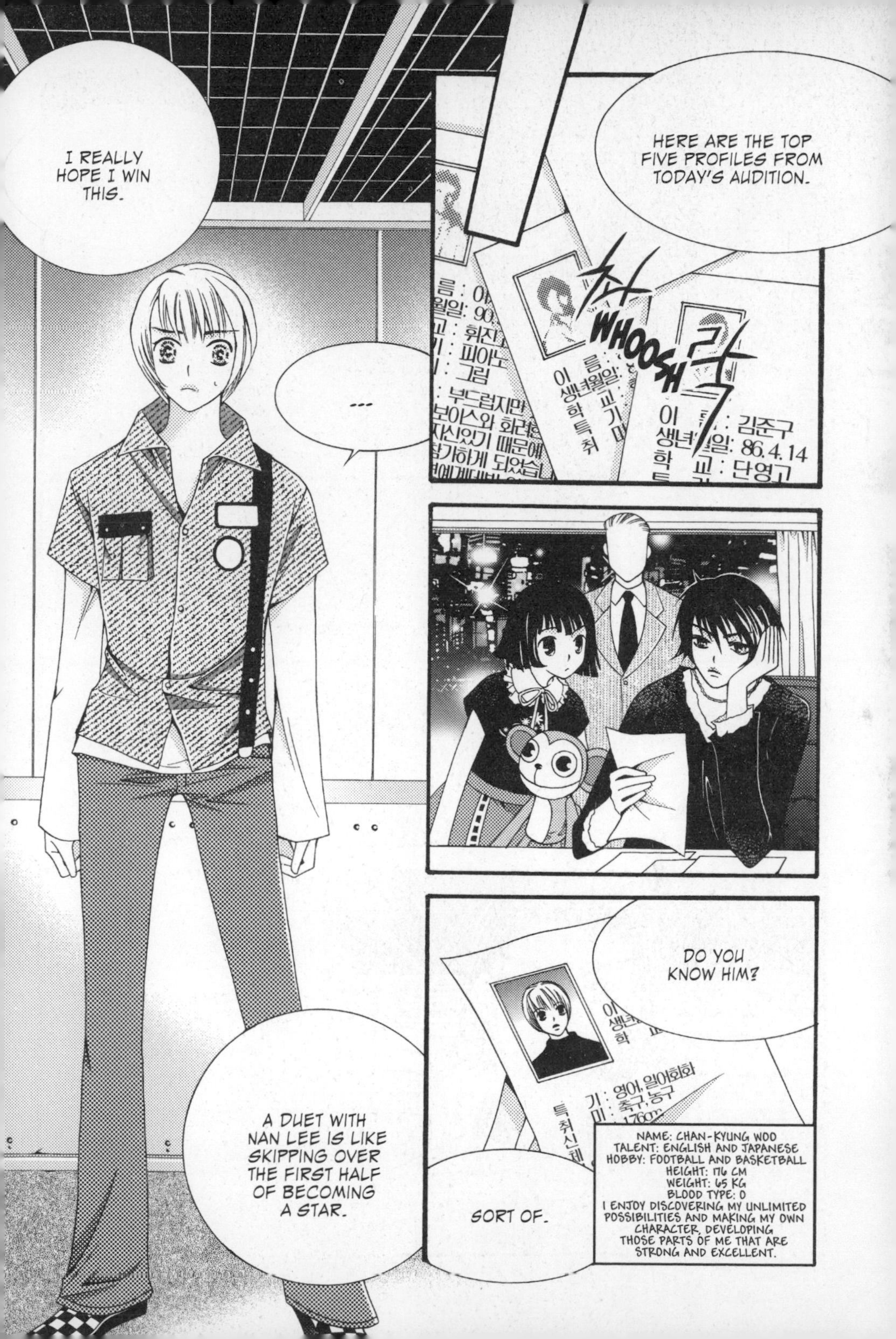
I REALLY HOPE I WIN THIS.
...
A DUET WITH NAN LEE IS LIKE SKIPPING OVER THE FIRST HALF OF BECOMING A STAR.
HERE ARE THE TOP FIVE PROFILES FROM TODAY'S AUDITION.
WHOOSH
이 름 : 김준구
생년월일: 86.4.14
학 교 : 단영고
DO YOU KNOW HIM?
SORT OF.
NAME: CHAN-KYUNG WOO
TALENT: ENGLISH AND JAPANESE
HOBBY: FOOTBALL AND BASKETBALL
HEIGHT: 176 CM
WEIGHT: 65 KG
BLOOD TYPE: O
I ENJOY DISCOVERING MY UNLIMITED POSSIBILITIES AND MAKING MY OWN CHARACTER, DEVELOPING THOSE PARTS OF ME THAT ARE STRONG AND EXCELLENT.

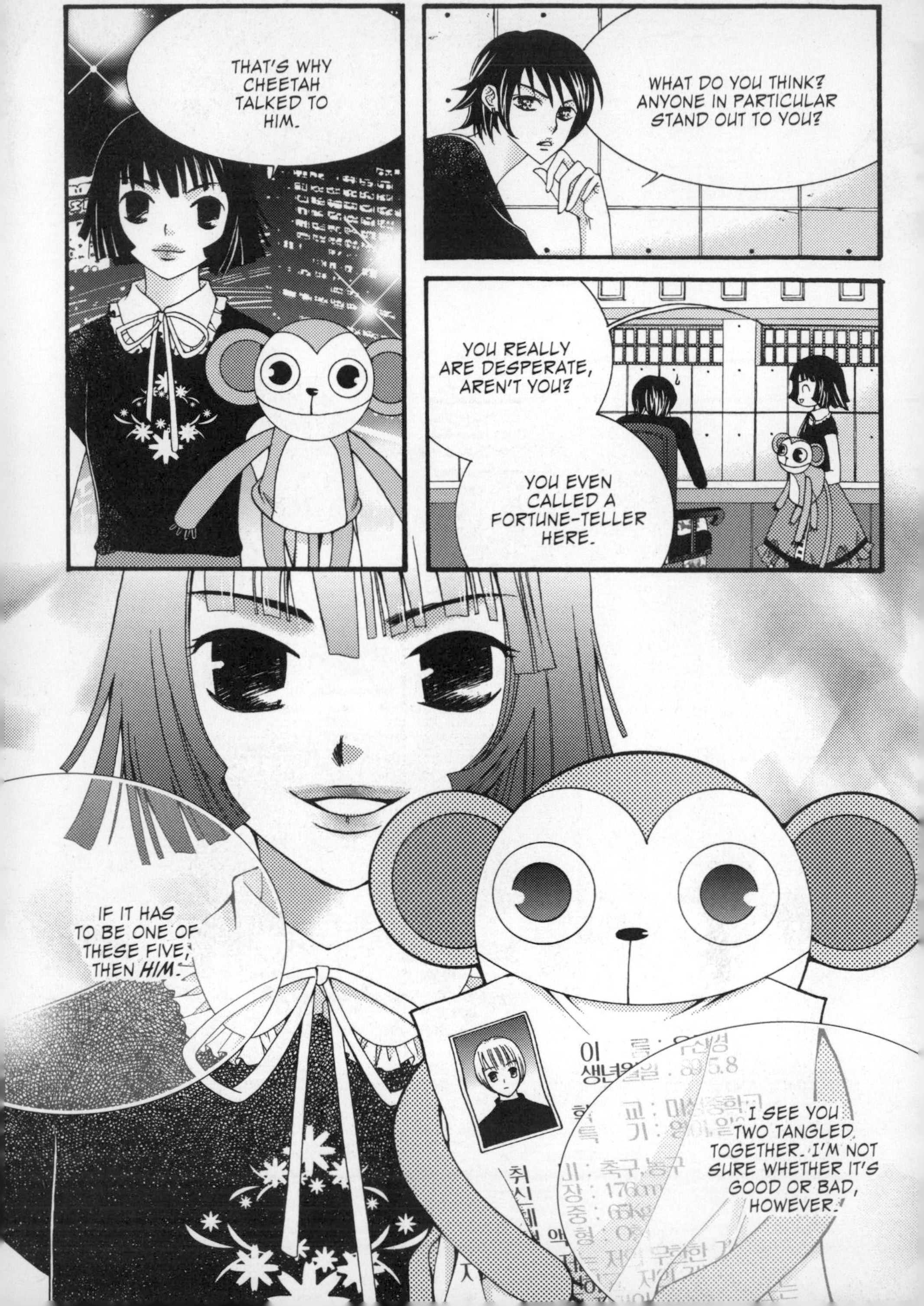
THAT'S WHY CHEETAH TALKED TO HIM.
WHAT DO YOU THINK? ANYONE IN PARTICULAR STAND OUT TO YOU?
YOU REALLY ARE DESPERATE, AREN'T YOU?
YOU EVEN CALLED A FORTUNE-TELLER HERE.
IF IT HAS TO BE ONE OF THESE FIVE, THEN *HIM*.
I SEE YOU TWO TANGLED TOGETHER. I'M NOT SURE WHETHER IT'S GOOD OR BAD, HOWEVER.

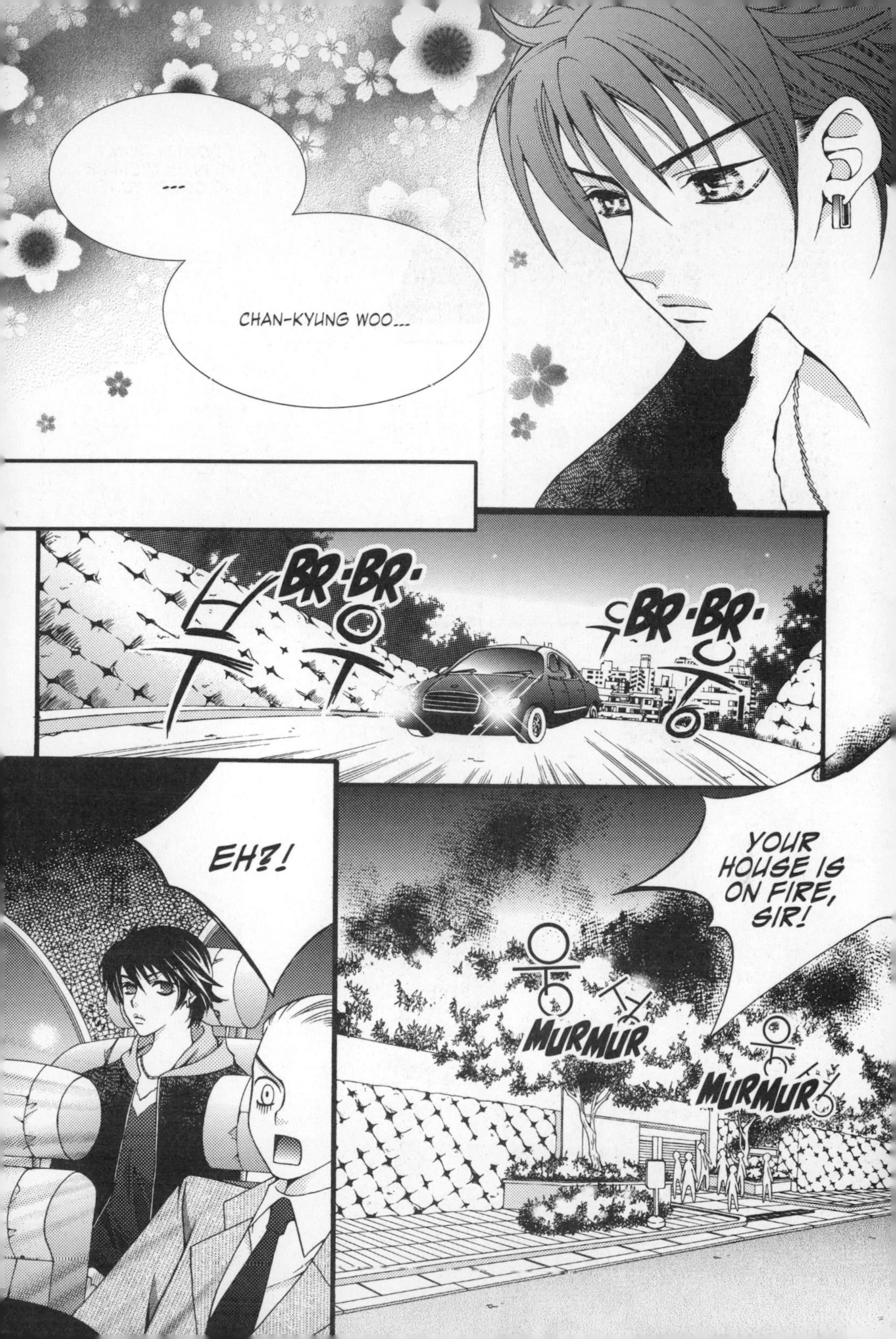
...
CHAN-KYUNG WOO...
BR-BR-
BR-BR-
EH?!
YOUR HOUSE IS ON FIRE, SIR!
MURMUR
MURMUR

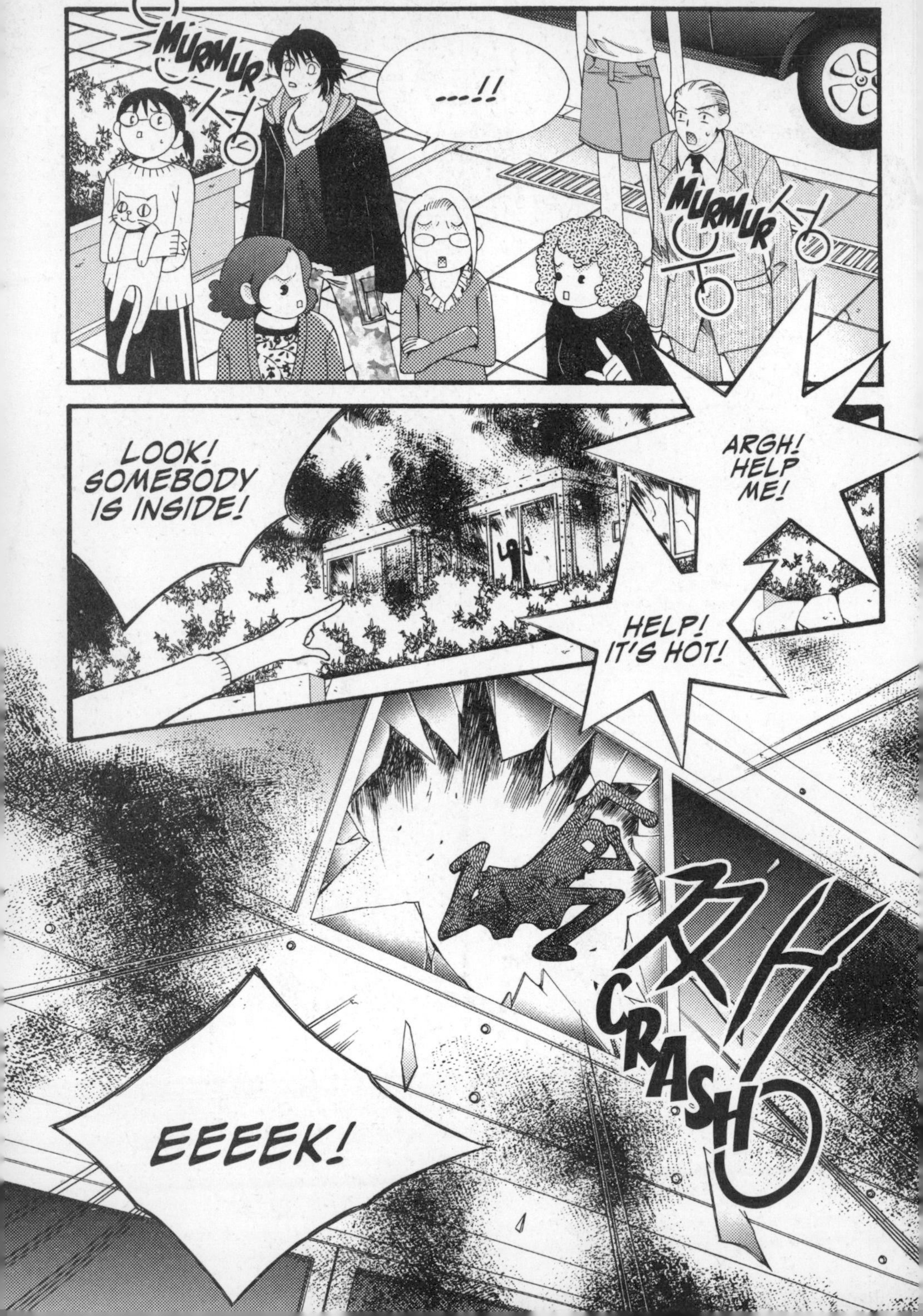
MURMUR
...!!
MURMUR
LOOK! SOMEBODY IS INSIDE!
ARGH! HELP ME!
HELP! IT'S HOT!
EEEEK!
CRASH

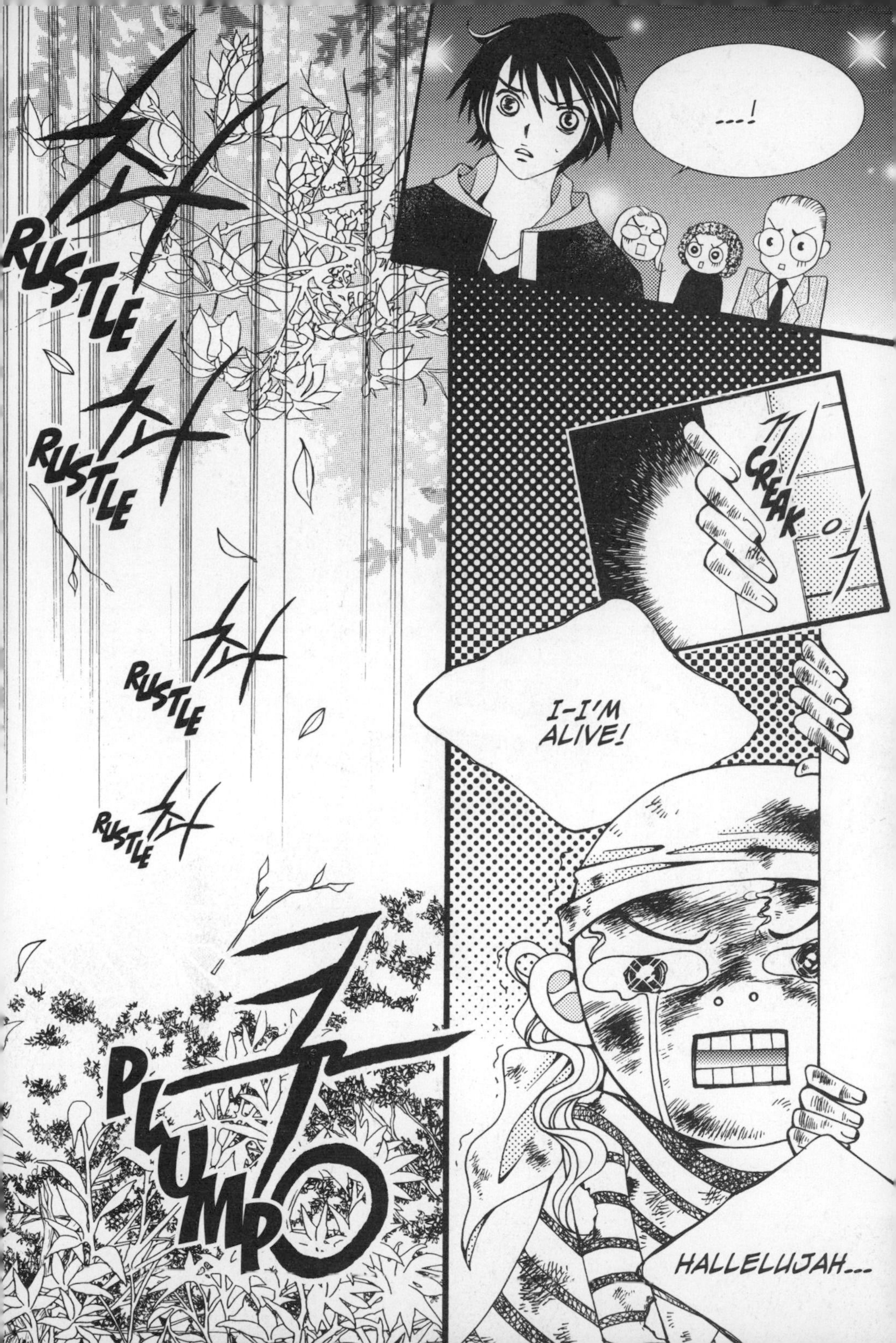
RUSTLE
RUSTLE
RUSTLE
RUSTLE
PLUMP
...!
CREAK
I-I'M ALIVE!
HALLELUJAH...

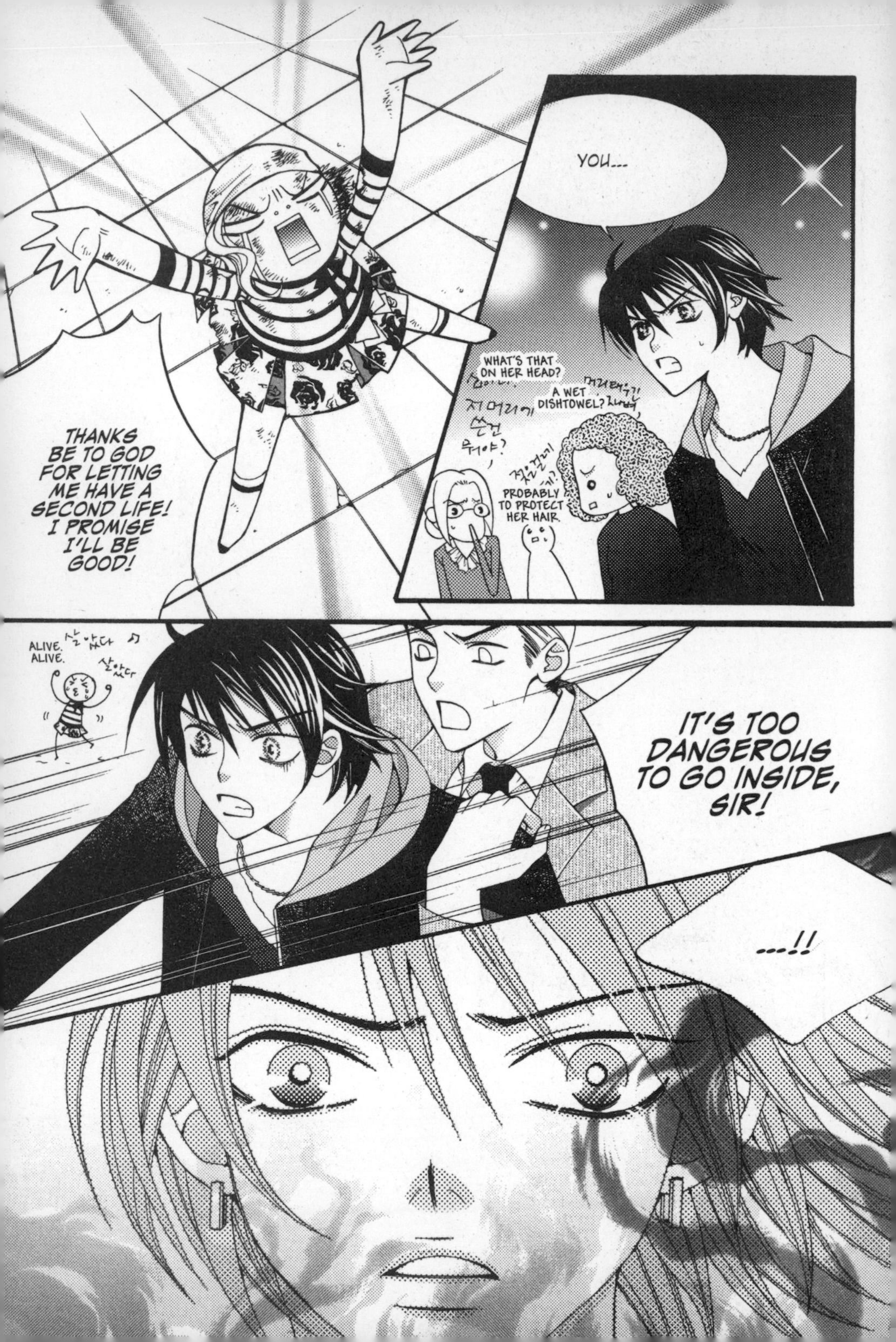
THANKS BE TO GOD FOR LETTING ME HAVE A SECOND LIFE! I PROMISE I'LL BE GOOD!
YOU...
WHAT'S THAT ON HER HEAD?
A WET DISHTOWEL?
PROBABLY TO PROTECT HER HAIR.
ALIVE. ALIVE.
IT'S TOO DANGEROUS TO GO INSIDE, SIR!
...!!

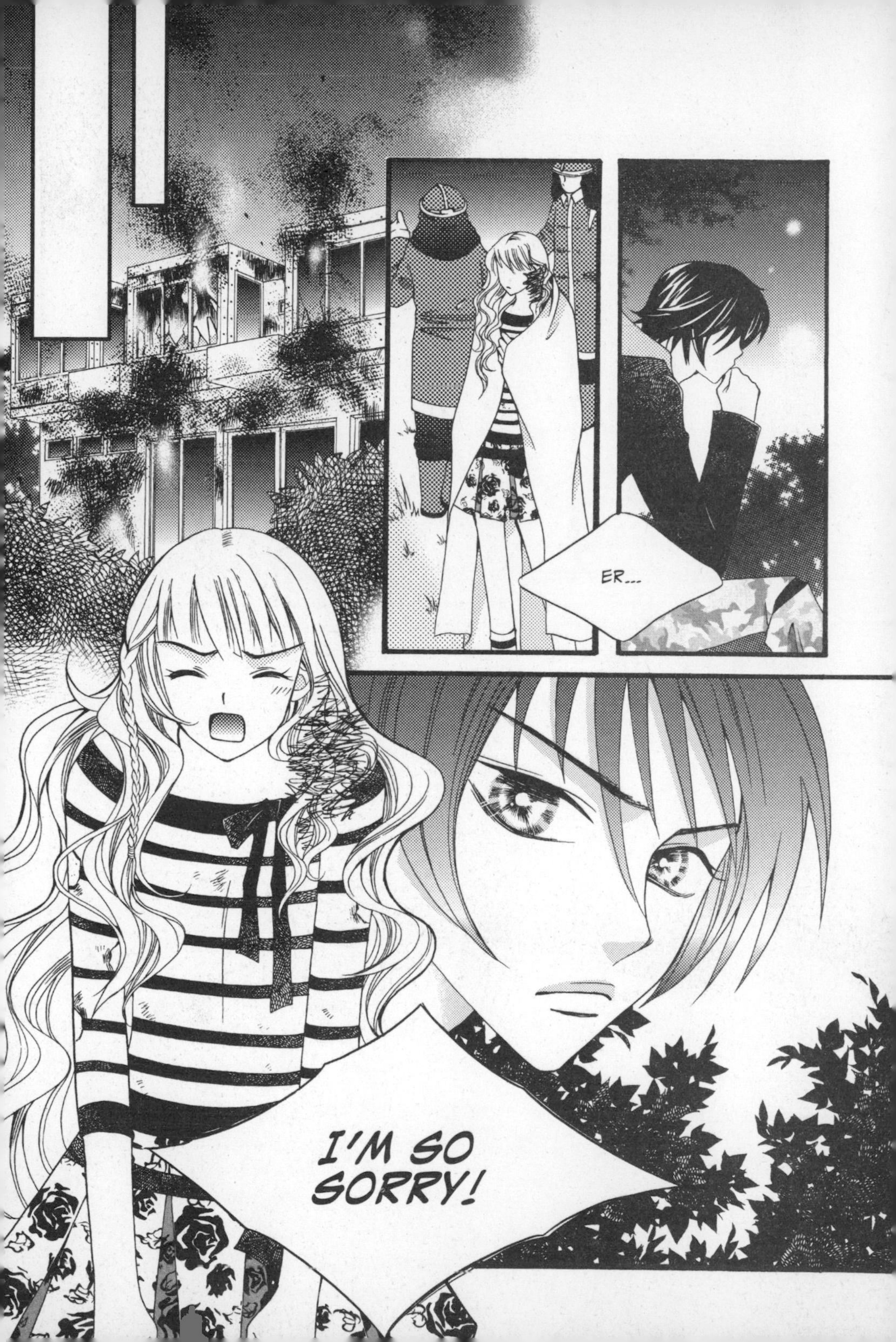
ER...
I'M SO SORRY!

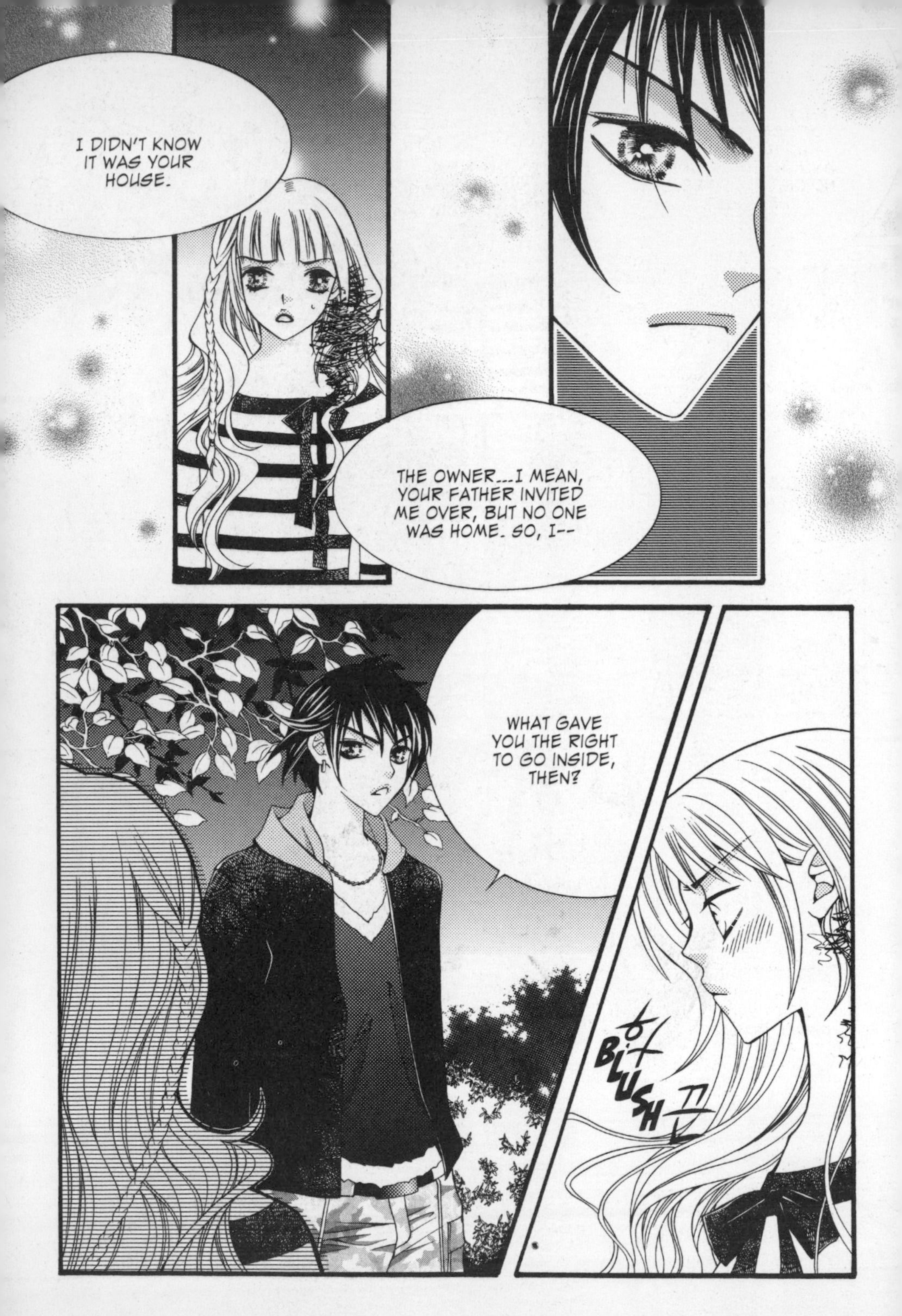
I DIDN'T KNOW IT WAS YOUR HOUSE.
THE OWNER...I MEAN, YOUR FATHER INVITED ME OVER, BUT NO ONE WAS HOME. SO, I--
WHAT GAVE YOU THE RIGHT TO GO INSIDE, THEN?
BLUSH

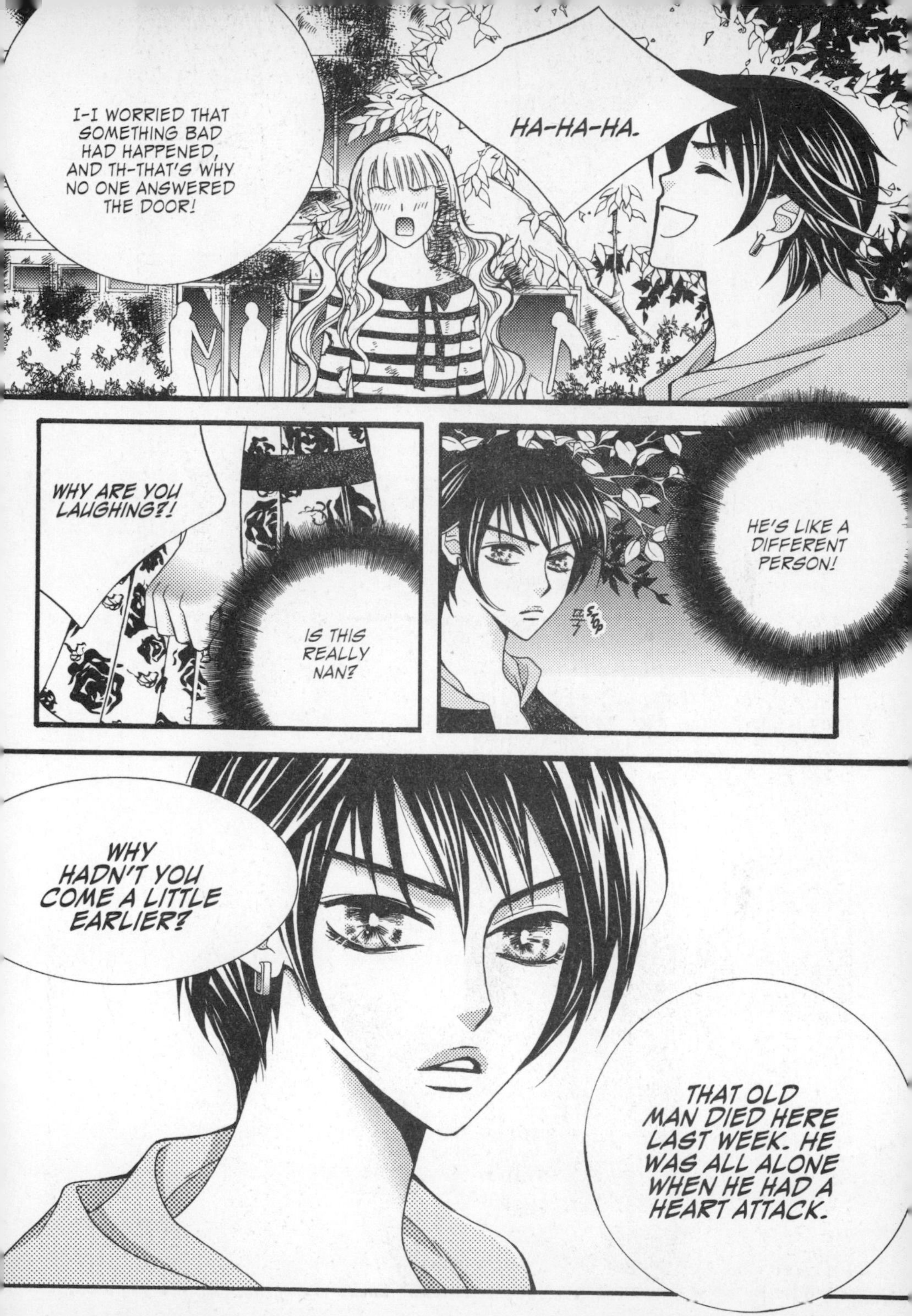
I-I WORRIED THAT SOMETHING BAD HAD HAPPENED, AND TH-THAT'S WHY NO ONE ANSWERED THE DOOR!
HA-HA-HA.
WHY ARE YOU LAUGHING?!
IS THIS REALLY NAN?
HE'S LIKE A DIFFERENT PERSON!
WHY HADN'T YOU COME A LITTLE EARLIER?
THAT OLD MAN DIED HERE LAST WEEK. HE WAS ALL ALONE WHEN HE HAD A HEART ATTACK.

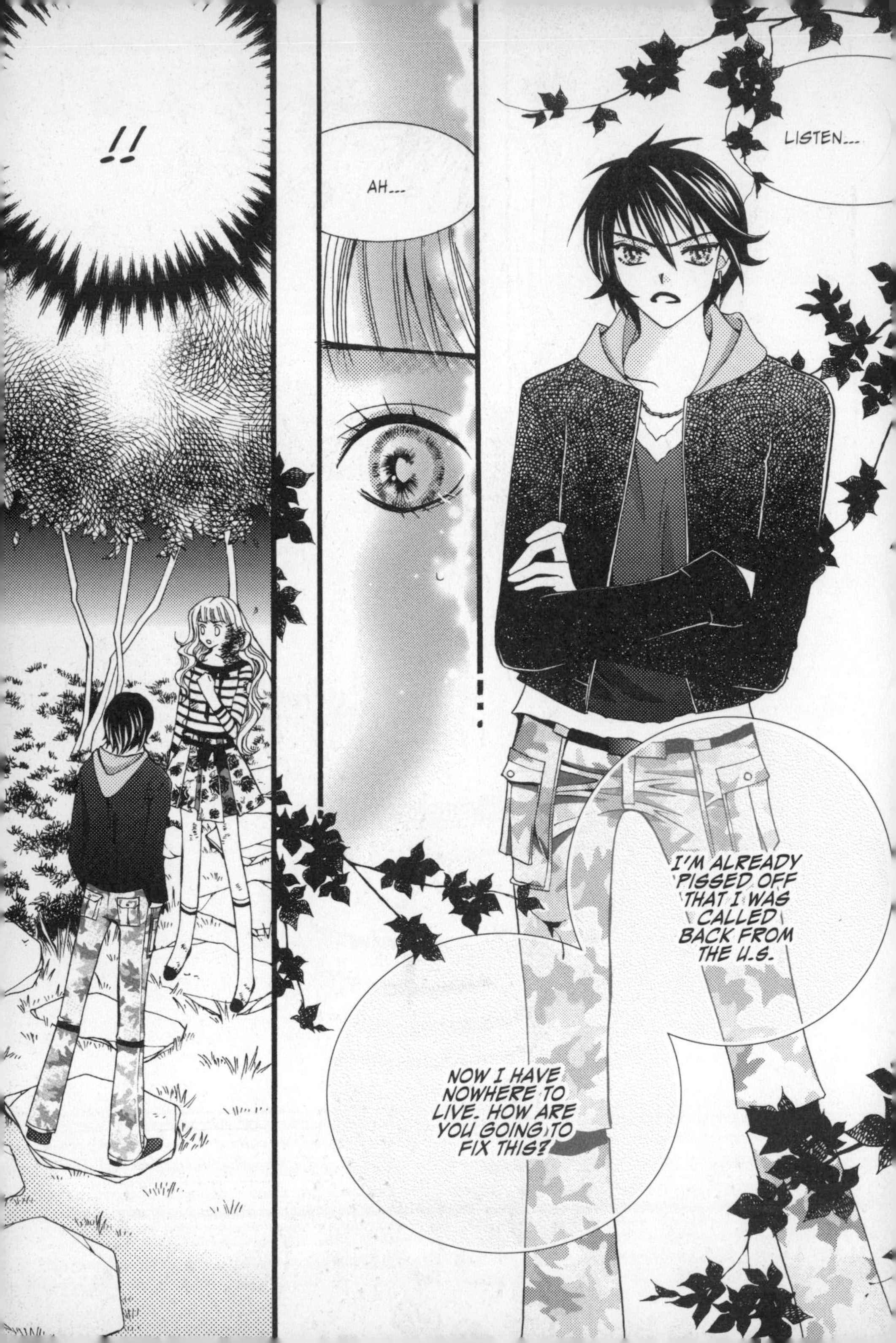
!!
AH...
!
LISTEN...
I'M ALREADY PISSED OFF THAT I WAS CALLED BACK FROM THE U.S.
NOW I HAVE NOWHERE TO LIVE. HOW ARE YOU GOING TO FIX THIS?

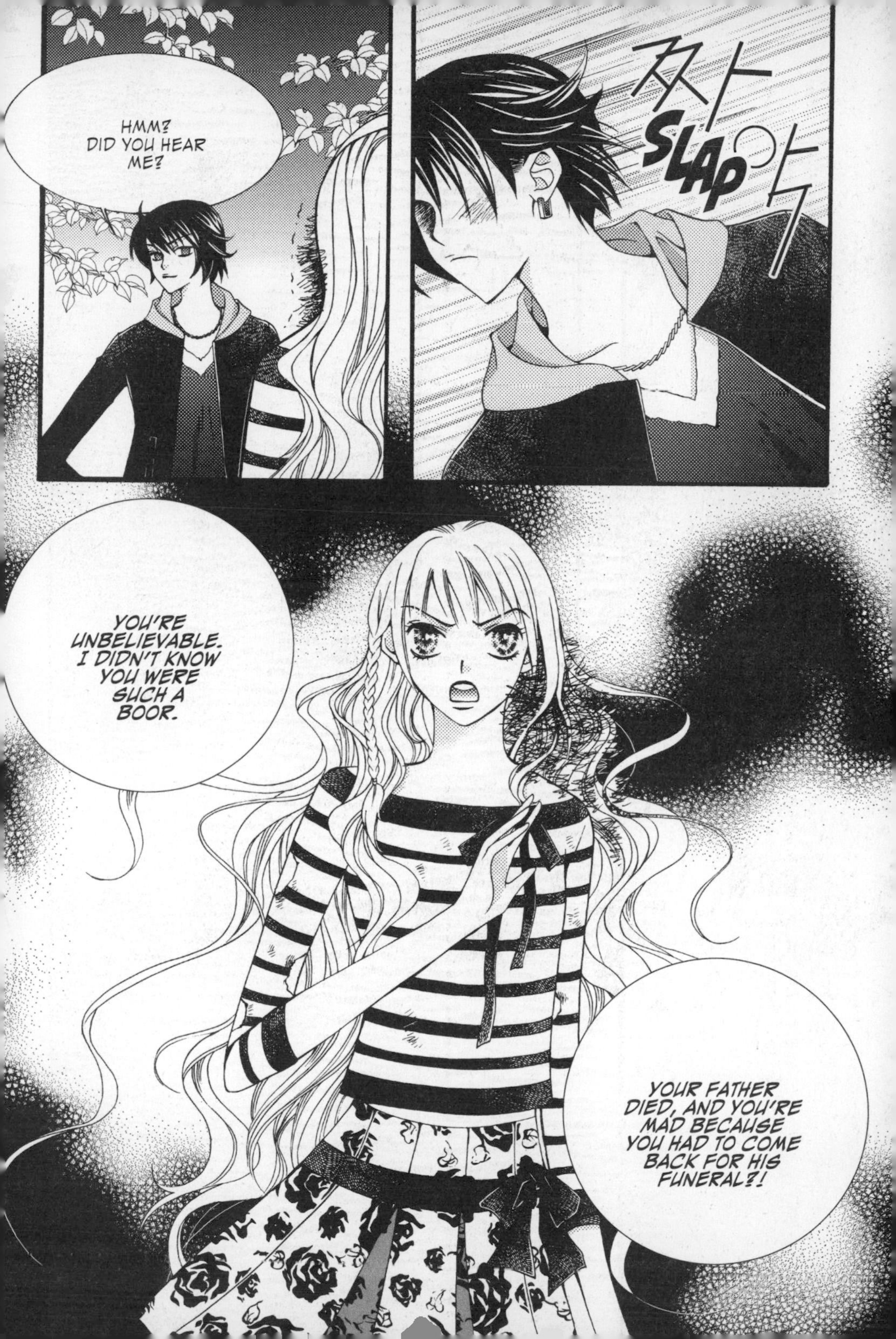
HMM? DID YOU HEAR ME?
SLAP
YOU'RE UNBELIEVABLE. I DIDN'T KNOW YOU WERE SUCH A BOOR.
YOUR FATHER DIED, AND YOU'RE MAD BECAUSE YOU HAD TO COME BACK FOR HIS FUNERAL?!

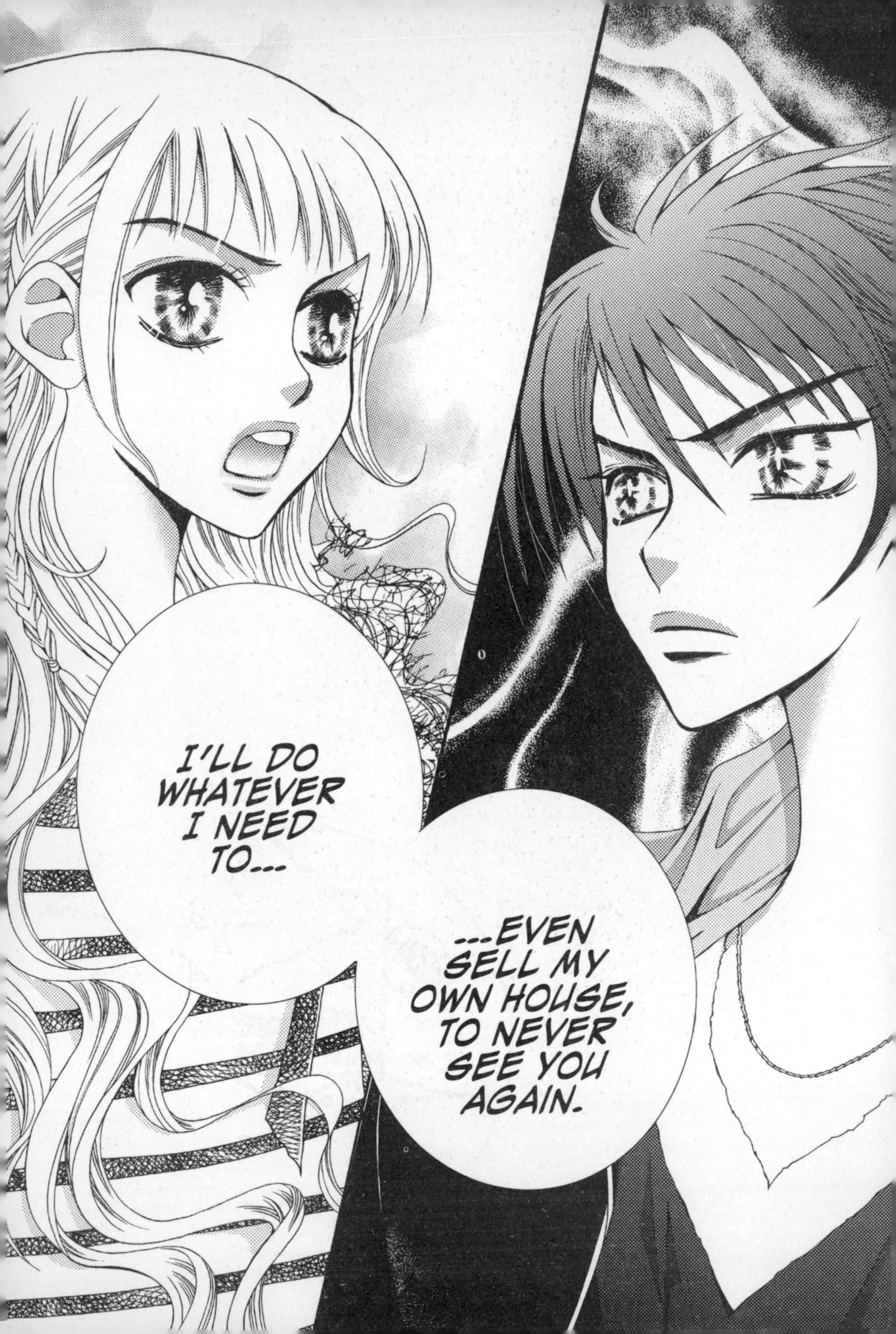
I'LL DO WHATEVER I NEED TO...
...EVEN SELL MY OWN HOUSE, TO NEVER SEE YOU AGAIN.

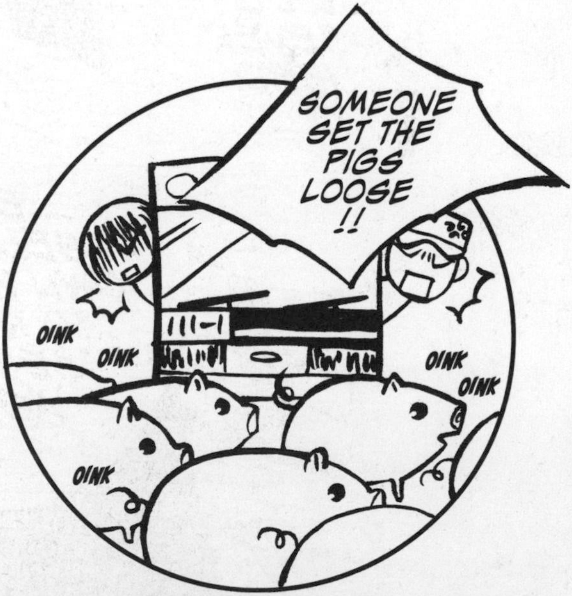
SOMEONE SET THE PIGS LOOSE !!
OINK
OINK
OINK
OINK
OINK
CHAN-KYUNG WAS FAR AWAY.

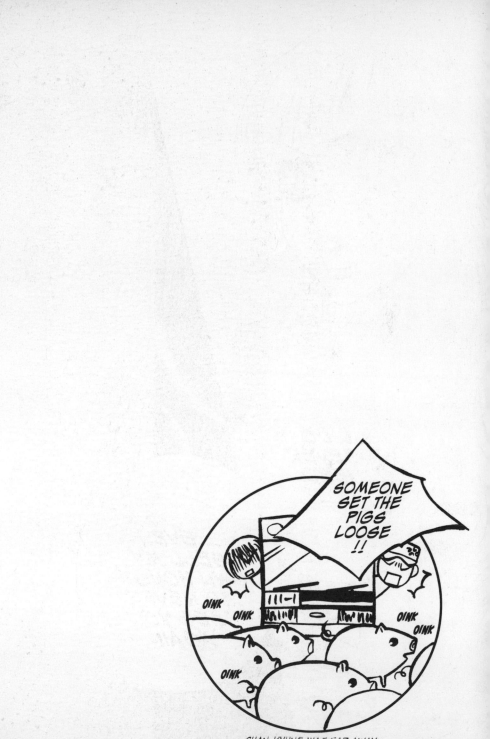

STAR PROJECT
CHIRO 치로

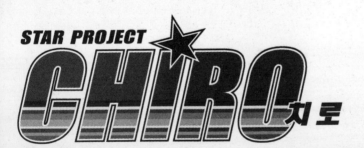

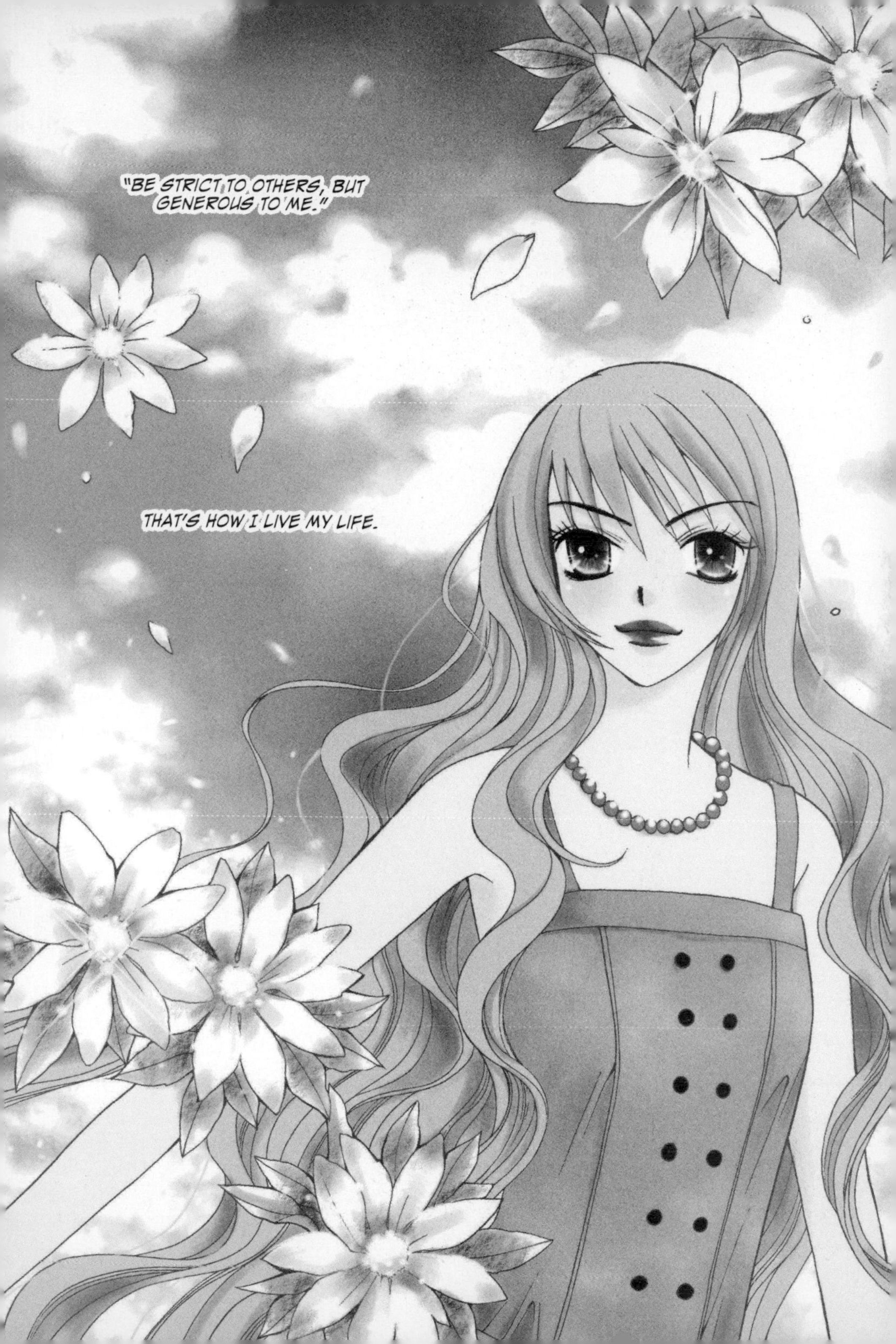
"BE STRICT TO OTHERS, BUT GENEROUS TO ME."
THAT'S HOW I LIVE MY LIFE.

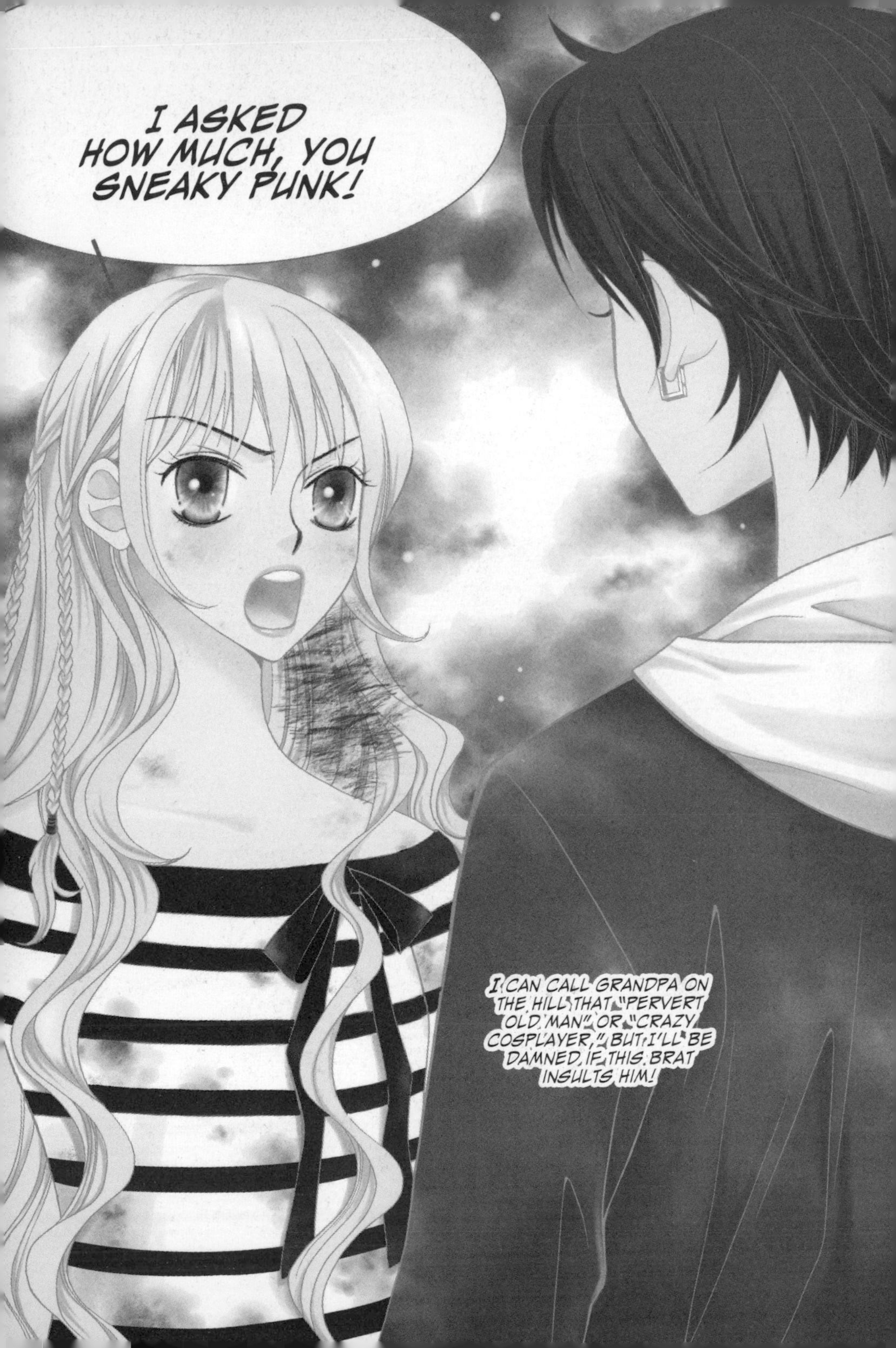
I ASKED HOW MUCH, YOU SNEAKY PUNK!
I CAN CALL GRANDPA ON THE HILL THAT "PERVERT OLD MAN" OR "CRAZY COSPLAYER," BUT I'LL BE DAMNED IF THIS BRAT INSULTS HIM!

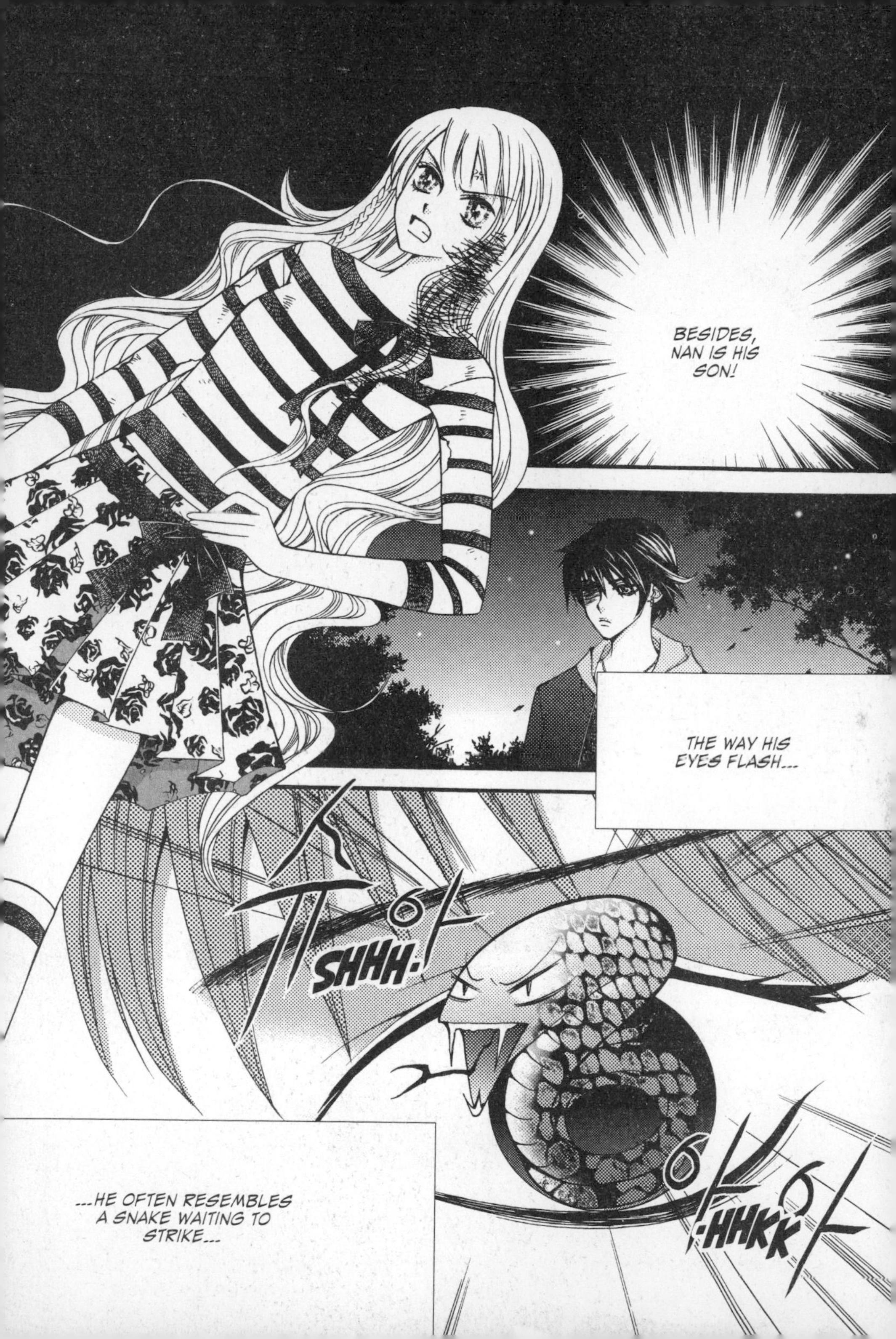
BESIDES, NAN IS HIS SON!
THE WAY HIS EYES FLASH...
SHHH-!
...HE OFTEN RESEMBLES A SNAKE WAITING TO STRIKE...
-HHKK

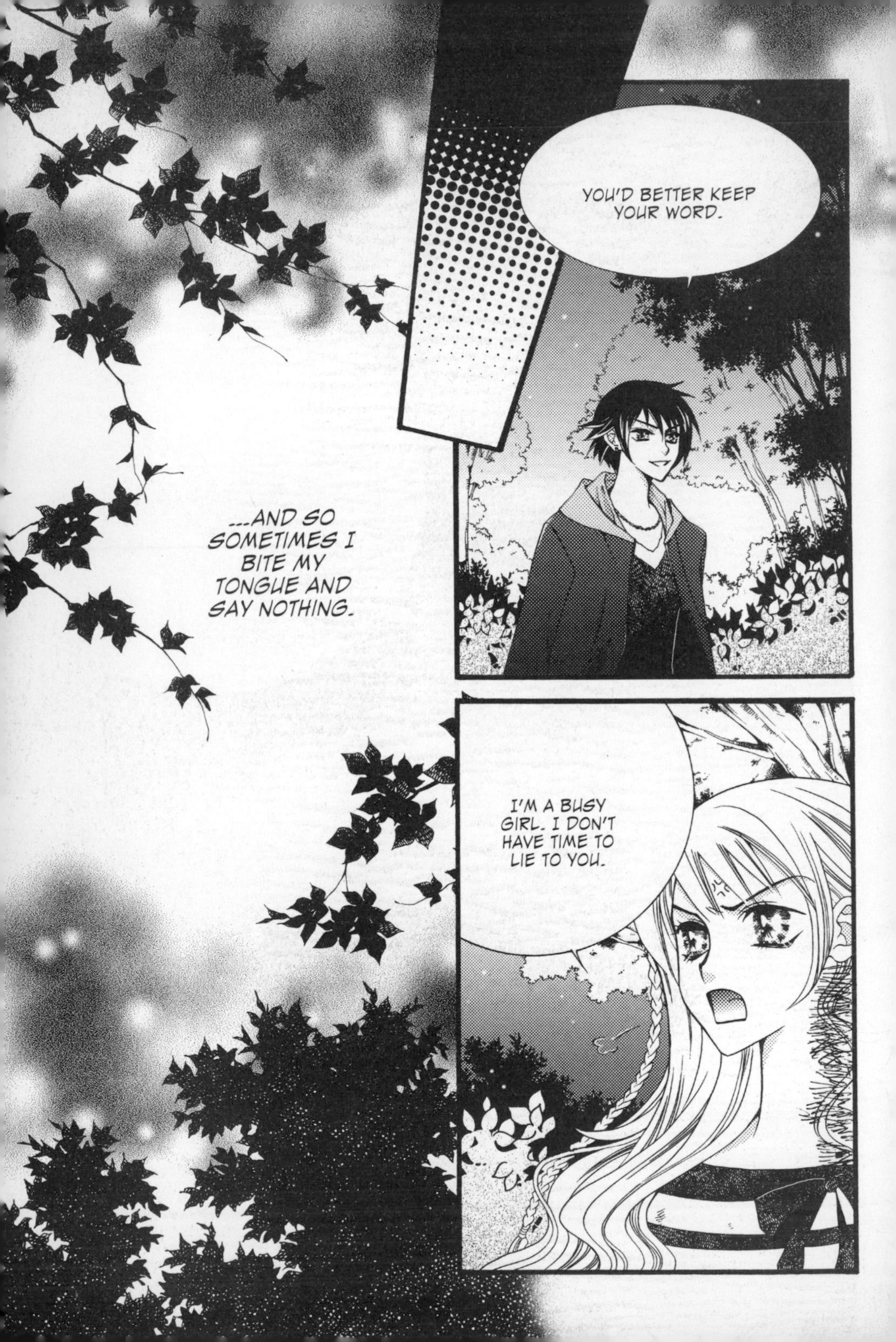
...AND SO SOMETIMES I BITE MY TONGUE AND SAY NOTHING.
YOU'D BETTER KEEP YOUR WORD.
I'M A BUSY GIRL. I DON'T HAVE TIME TO LIE TO YOU.

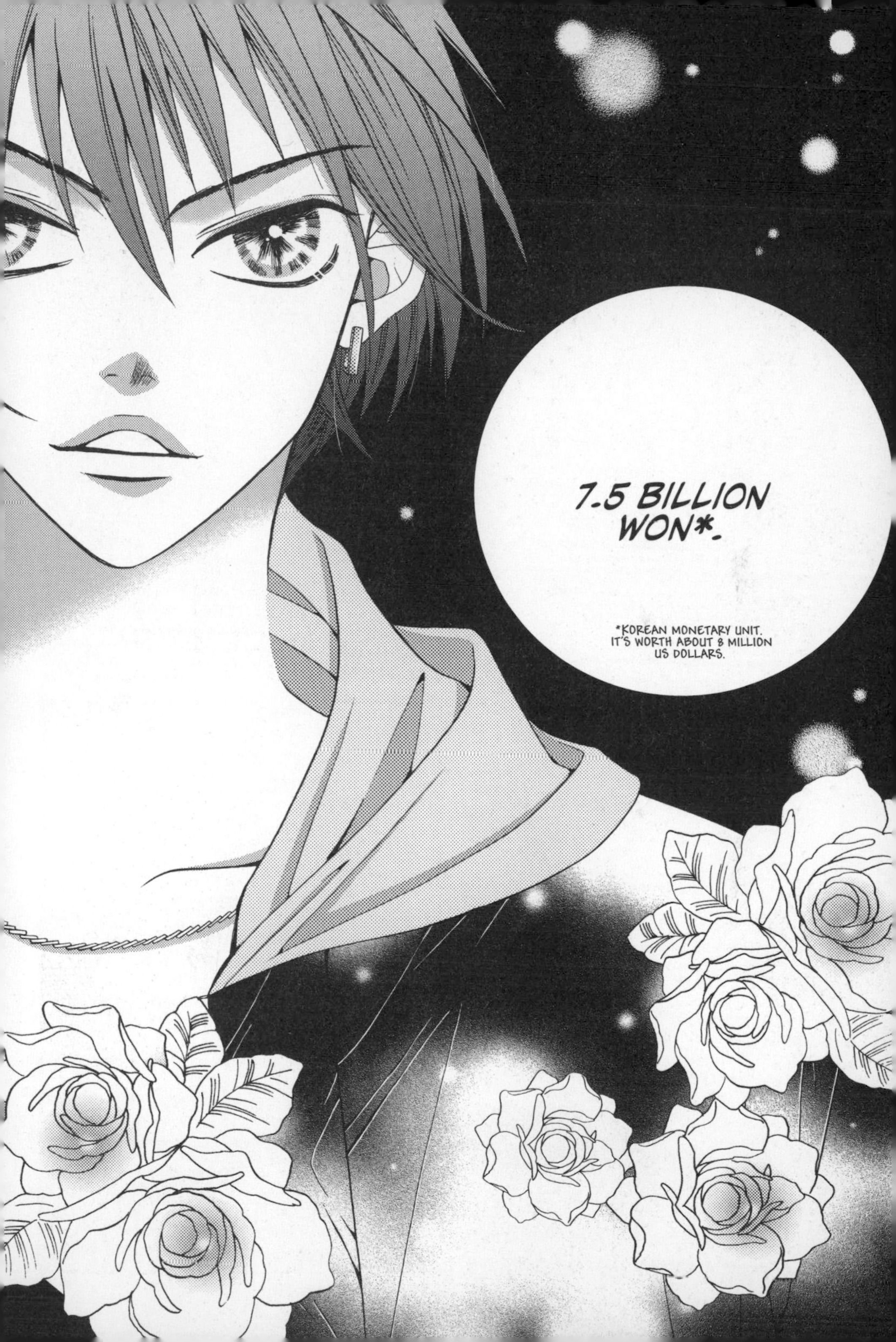
7.5 BILLION WON*.
*KOREAN MONETARY UNIT. IT'S WORTH ABOUT 8 MILLION US DOLLARS.

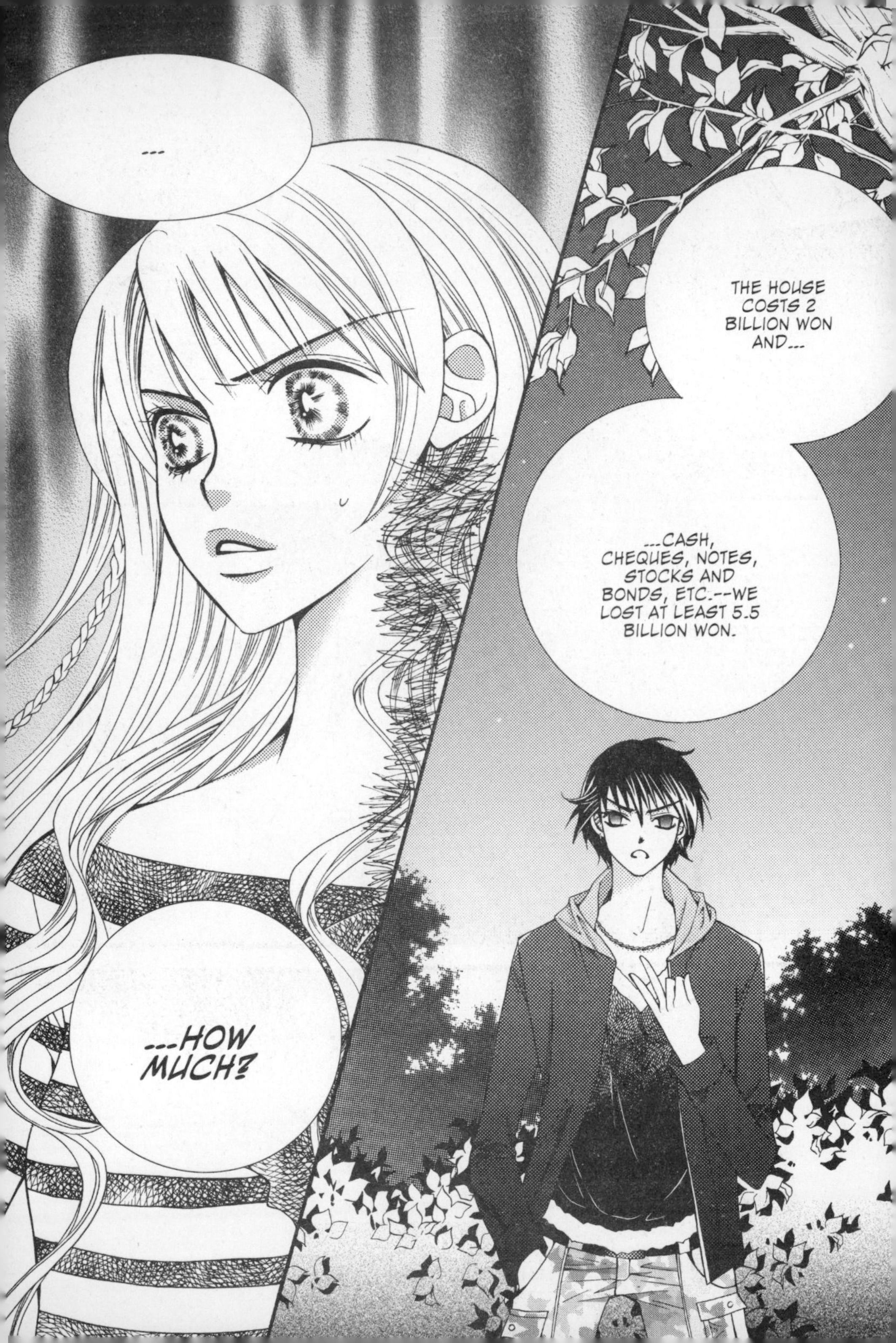
...
...HOW MUCH?
THE HOUSE COSTS 2 BILLION WON AND...
...CASH, CHEQUES, NOTES, STOCKS AND BONDS, ETC.--WE LOST AT LEAST 5.5 BILLION WON.

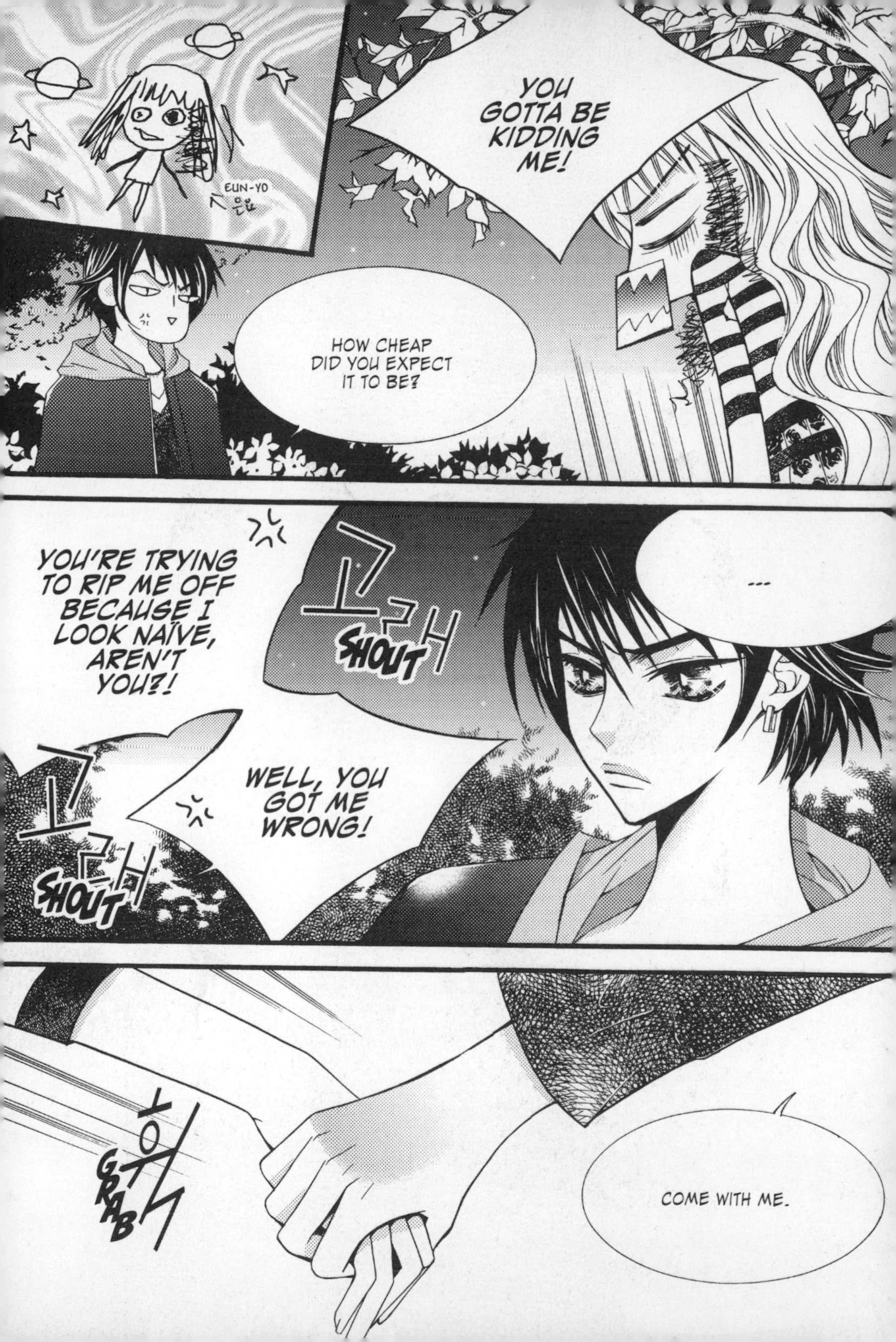
EUN-YO
YOU GOTTA BE KIDDING ME!
HOW CHEAP DID YOU EXPECT IT TO BE?
YOU'RE TRYING TO RIP ME OFF BECAUSE I LOOK NAÏVE, AREN'T YOU?!
SHOUT
...
WELL, YOU GOT ME WRONG!
SHOUT
GRAB
COME WITH ME.

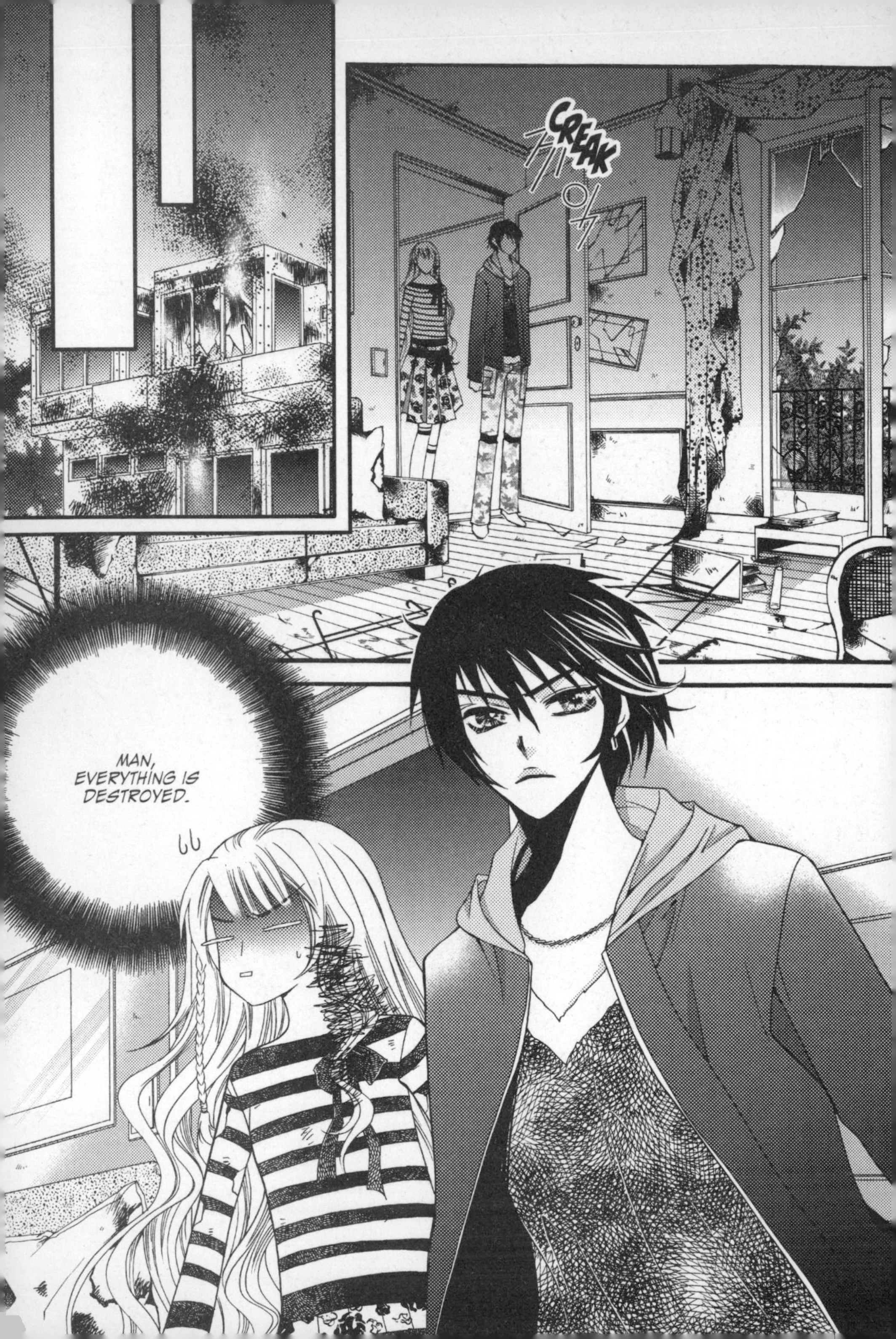
CREAK
MAN, EVERYTHING IS DESTROYED.

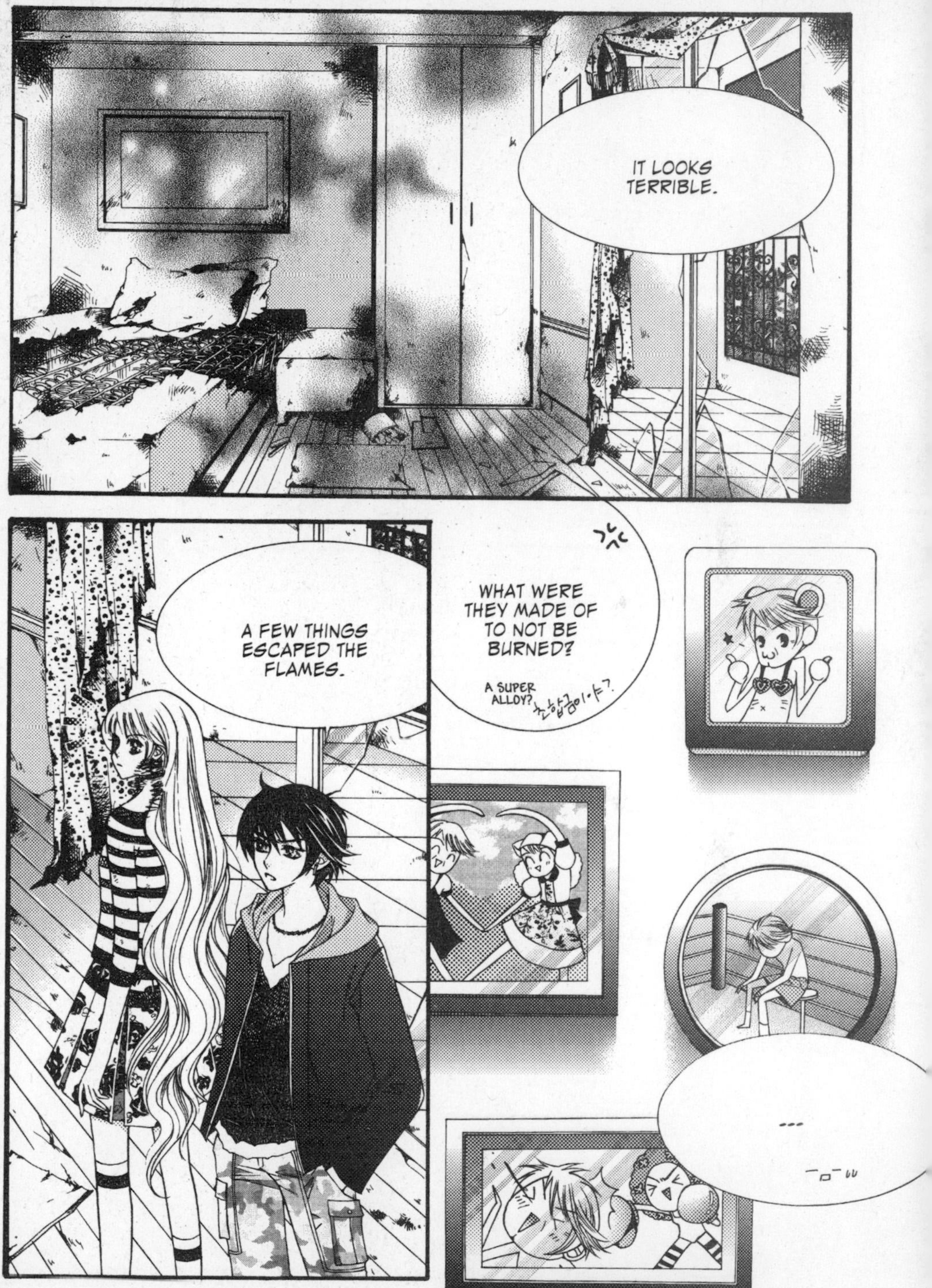
IT LOOKS TERRIBLE.
A FEW THINGS ESCAPED THE FLAMES.
WHAT WERE THEY MADE OF TO NOT BE BURNED?
A SUPER ALLOY? 초합금이냐?
...

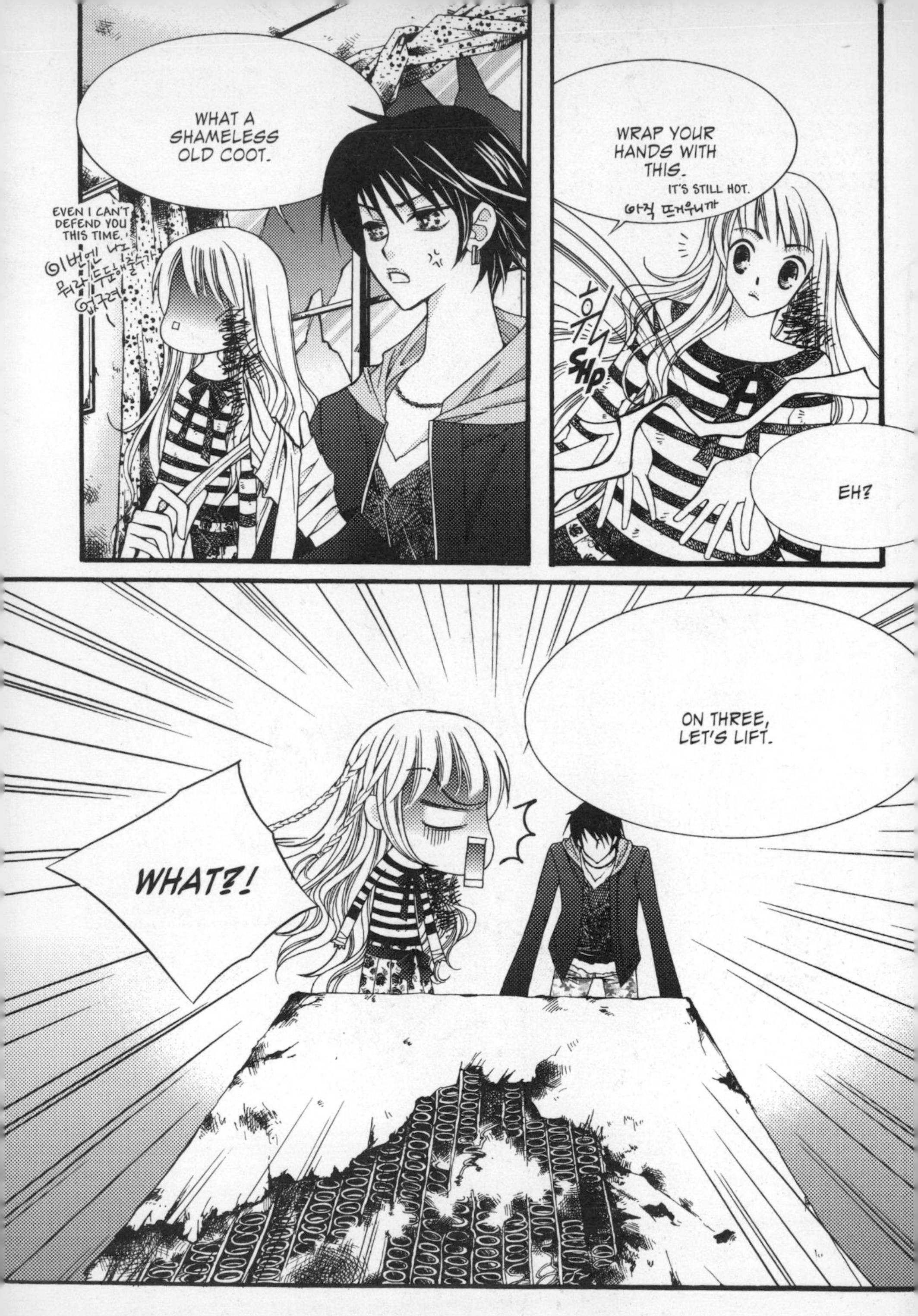
WHAT A SHAMELESS OLD COOT.
EVEN I CAN'T DEFEND YOU THIS TIME.
이번엔 나도 뭐라 두둔해줄수가 없구려
WRAP YOUR HANDS WITH THIS.
IT'S STILL HOT.
아직 뜨거우니까
SHP
EH?
WHAT?!
ON THREE, LET'S LIFT.

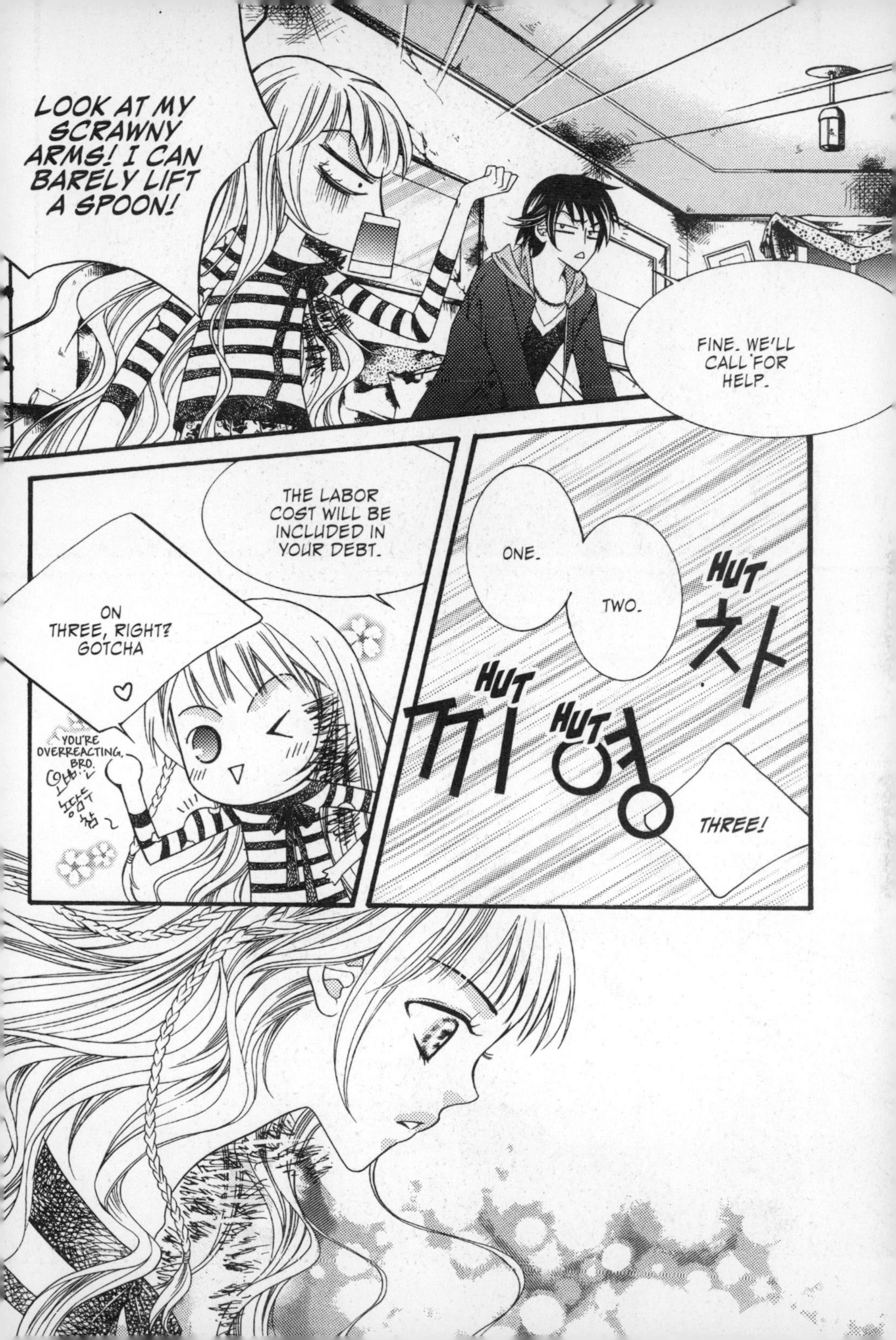
LOOK AT MY SCRAWNY ARMS! I CAN BARELY LIFT A SPOON!
FINE. WE'LL CALL FOR HELP.
THE LABOR COST WILL BE INCLUDED IN YOUR DEBT.
ON THREE, RIGHT? GOTCHA
♡
YOU'RE OVERREACTING, BRO.
ONE.
TWO.
HUT
HUT
HUT
THREE!

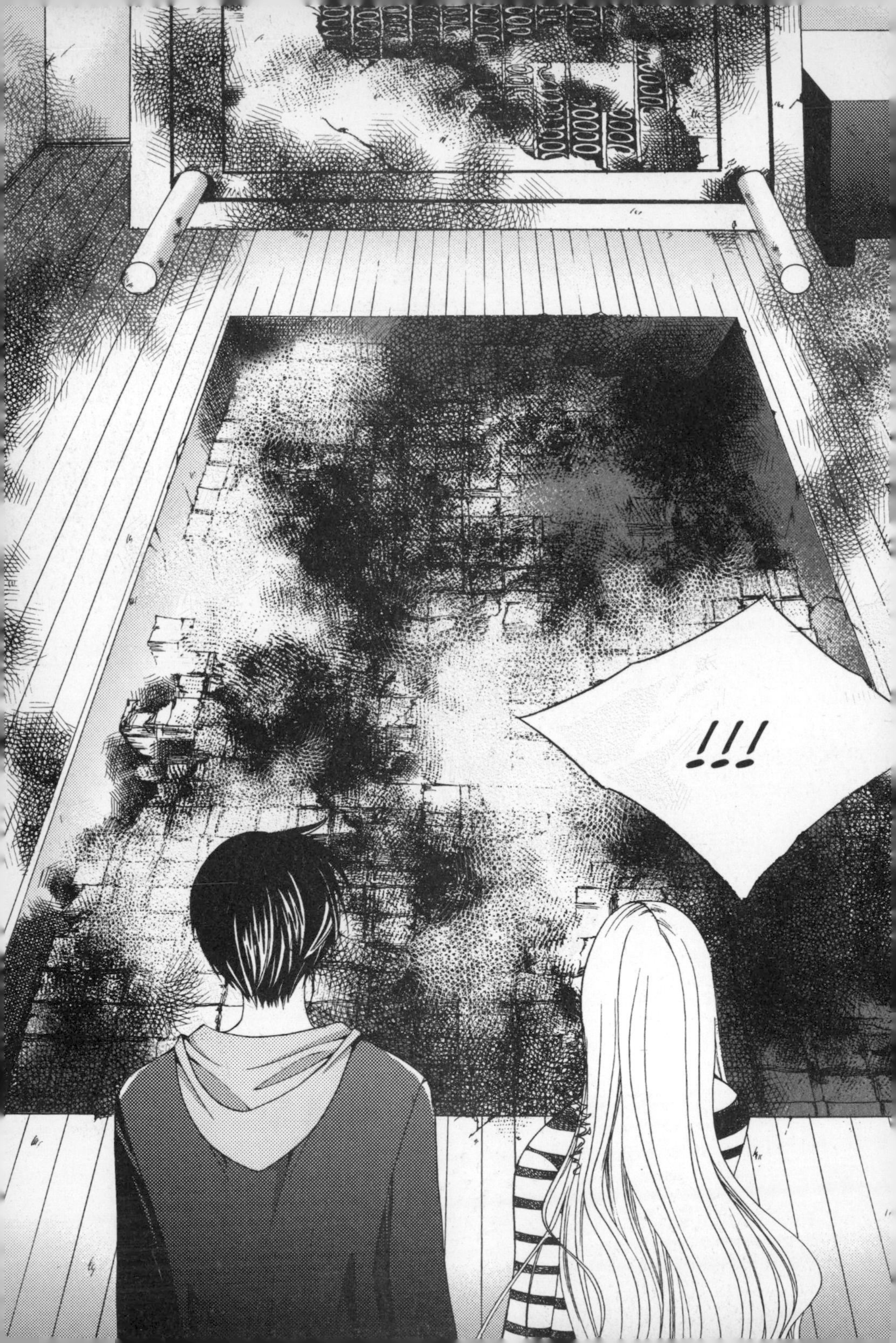
!!!

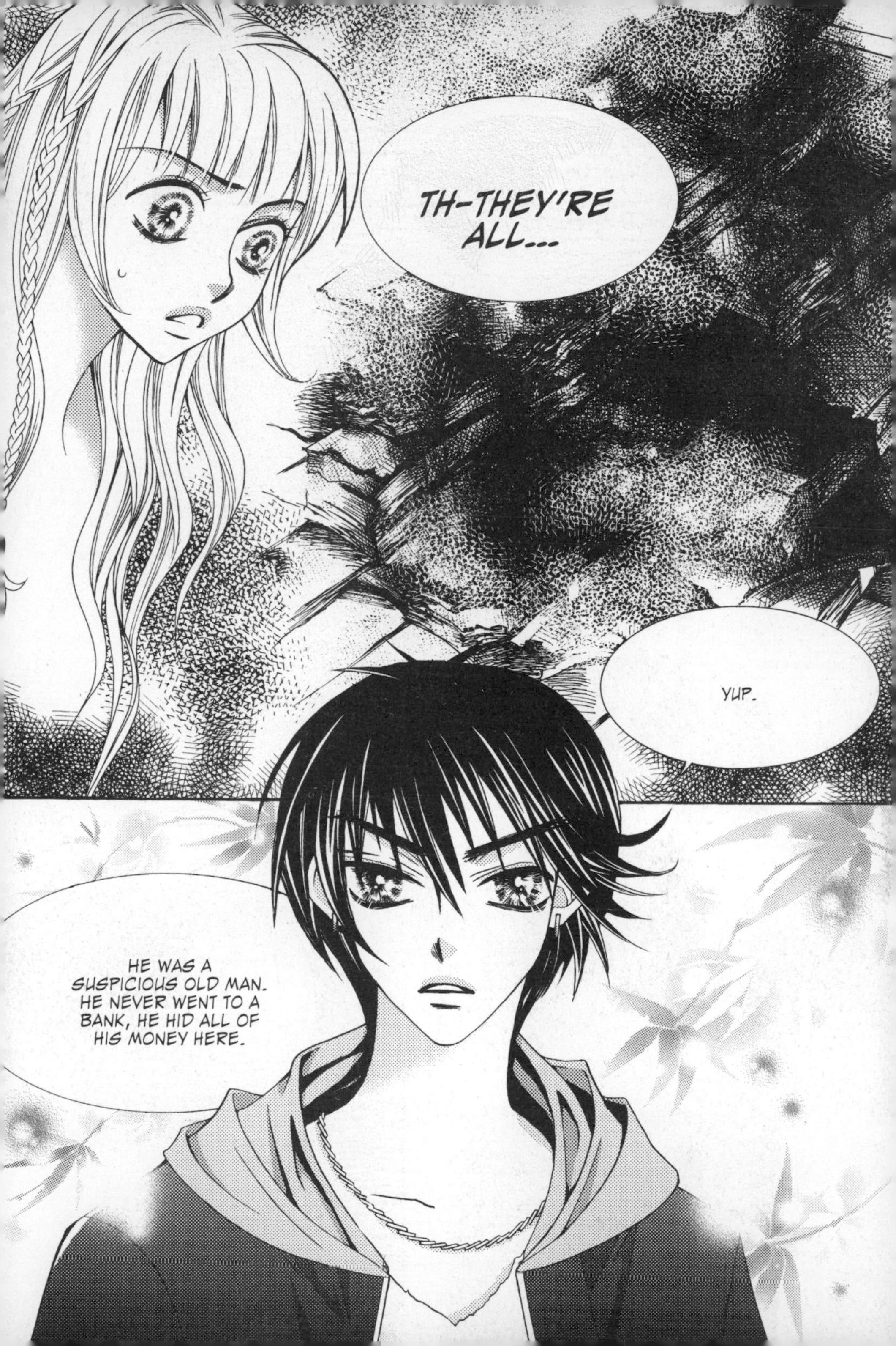
TH-THEY'RE ALL...
YUP.
HE WAS A SUSPICIOUS OLD MAN. HE NEVER WENT TO A BANK, HE HID ALL OF HIS MONEY HERE.

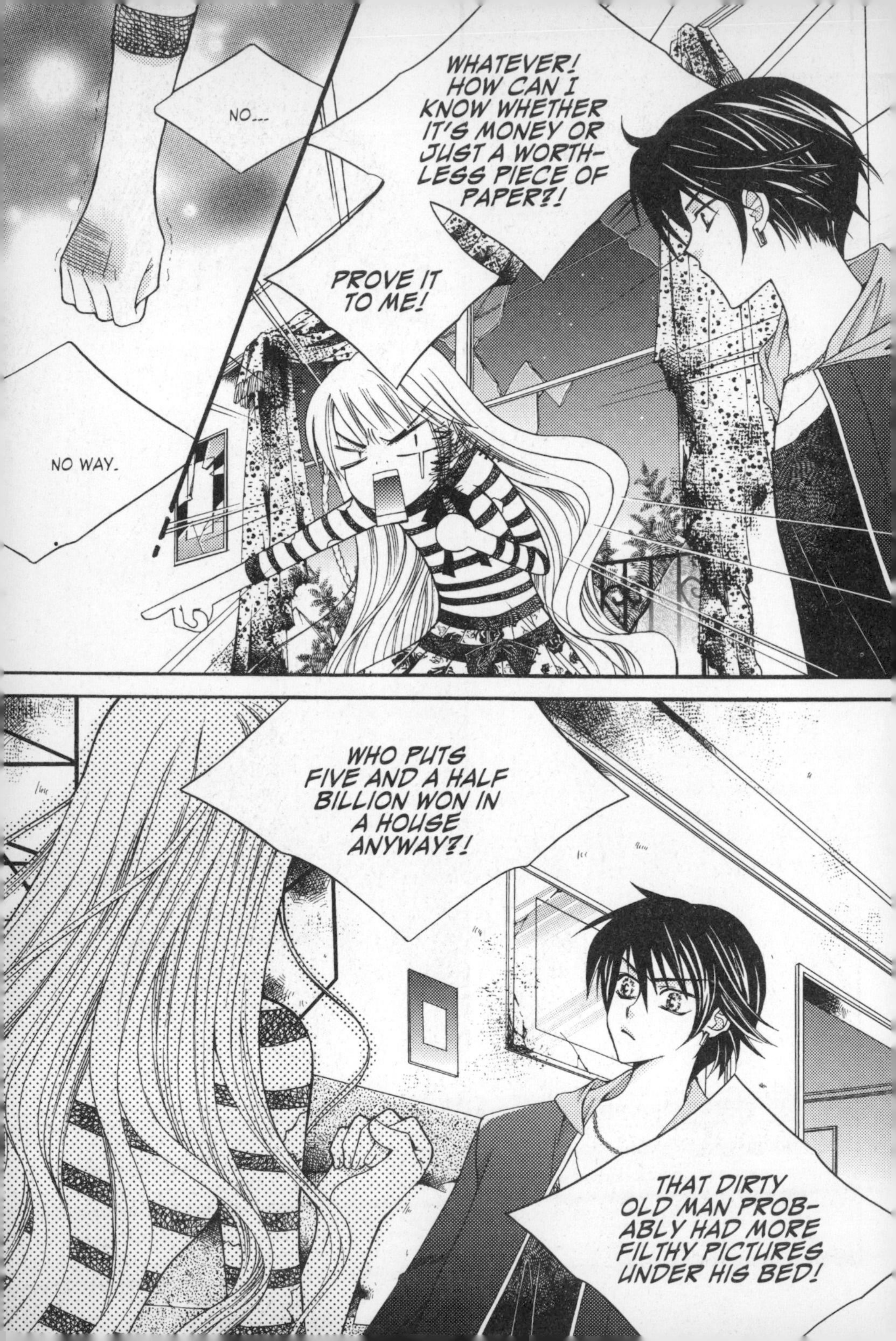
NO...
WHATEVER! HOW CAN I KNOW WHETHER IT'S MONEY OR JUST A WORTH-LESS PIECE OF PAPER?!
PROVE IT TO ME!
NO WAY.
WHO PUTS FIVE AND A HALF BILLION WON IN A HOUSE ANYWAY?!
THAT DIRTY OLD MAN PROB-ABLY HAD MORE FILTHY PICTURES UNDER HIS BED!

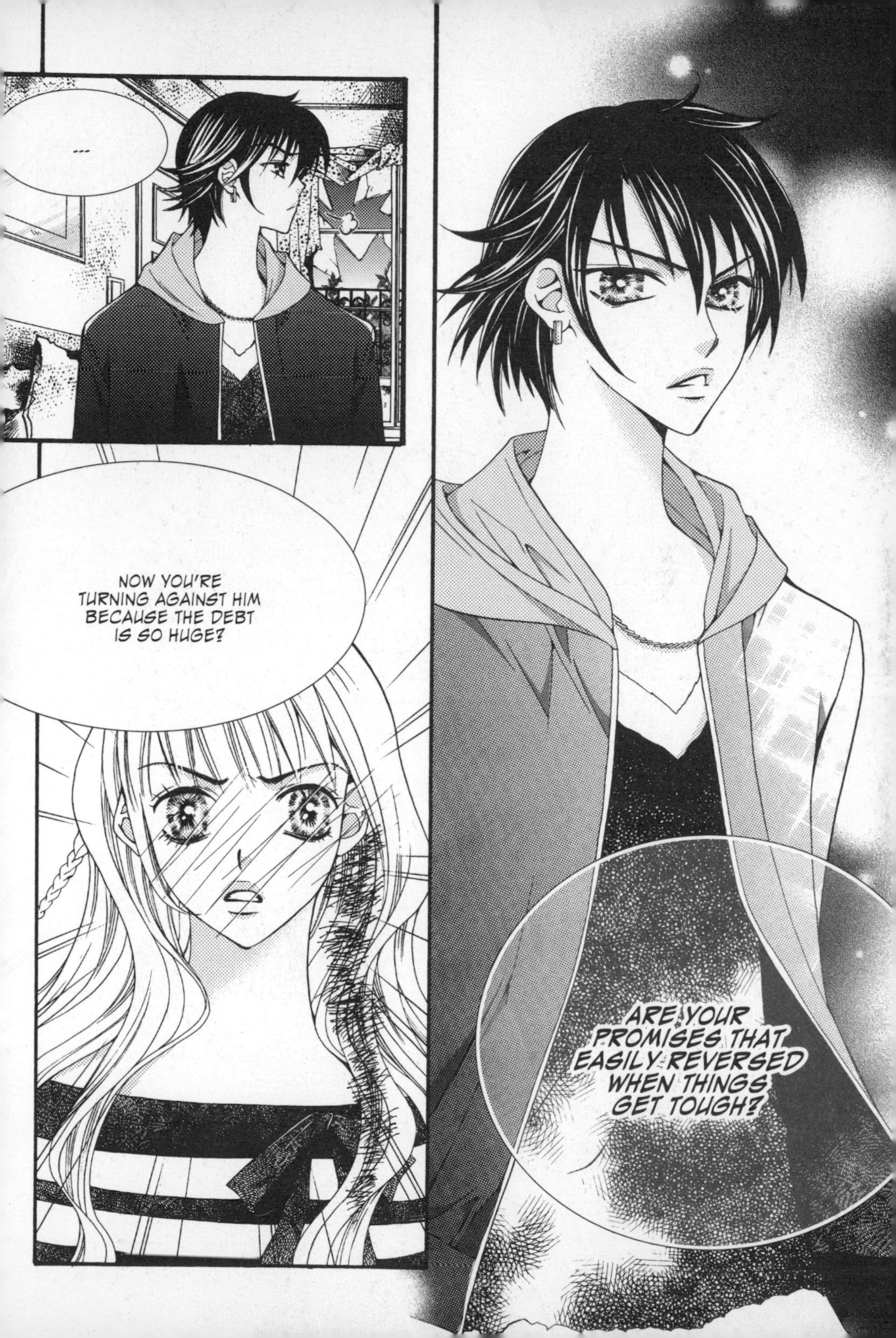
...
NOW YOU'RE TURNING AGAINST HIM BECAUSE THE DEBT IS SO HUGE?
ARE YOUR PROMISES THAT EASILY REVERSED WHEN THINGS GET TOUGH?

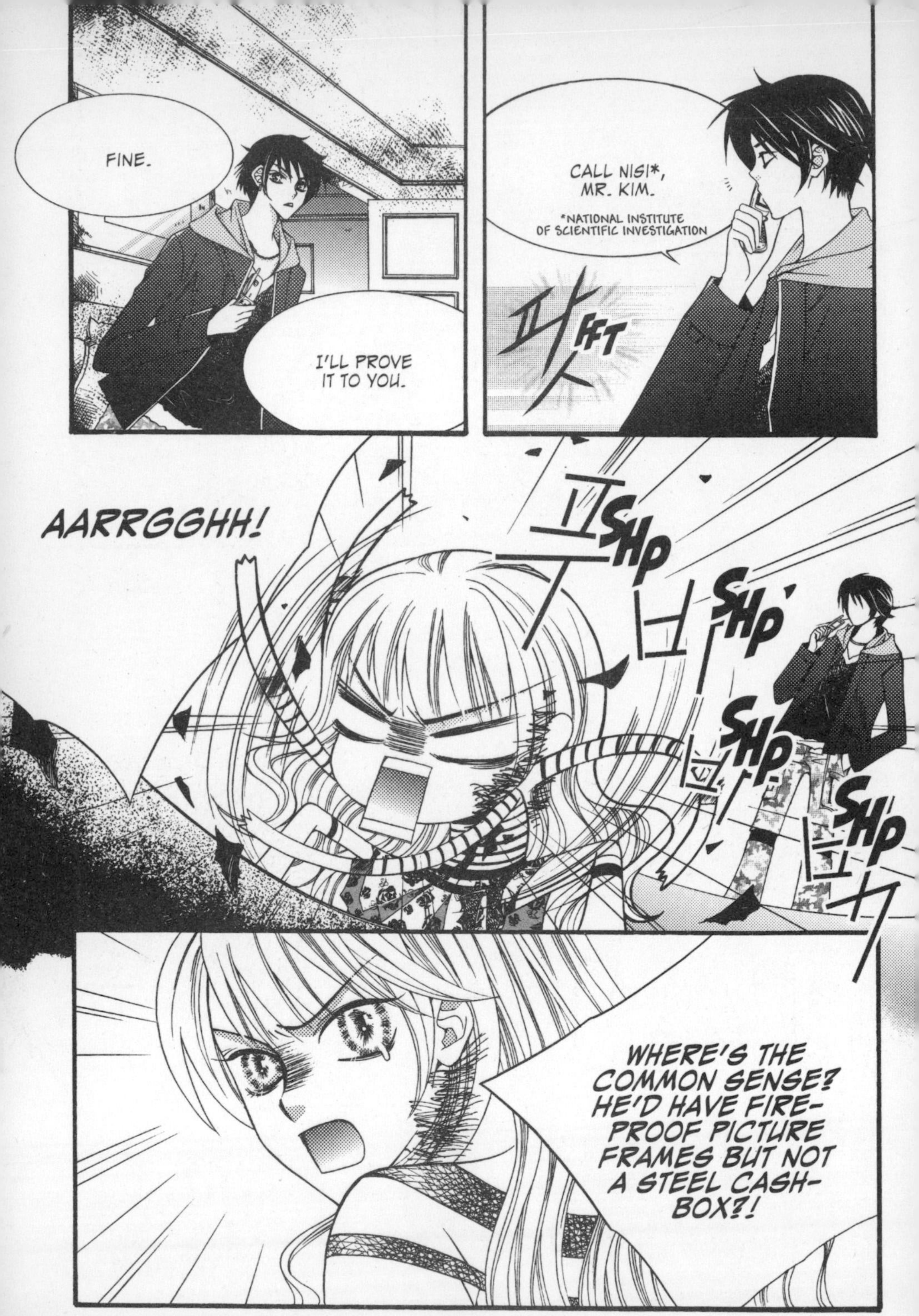
FINE.
I'LL PROVE IT TO YOU.
CALL NISI*, MR. KIM.
*NATIONAL INSTITUTE OF SCIENTIFIC INVESTIGATION
PFFT
AARRGGHH!
SHP
SHP
SHP
SHP
WHERE'S THE COMMON SENSE? HE'D HAVE FIRE-PROOF PICTURE FRAMES BUT NOT A STEEL CASH-BOX?!

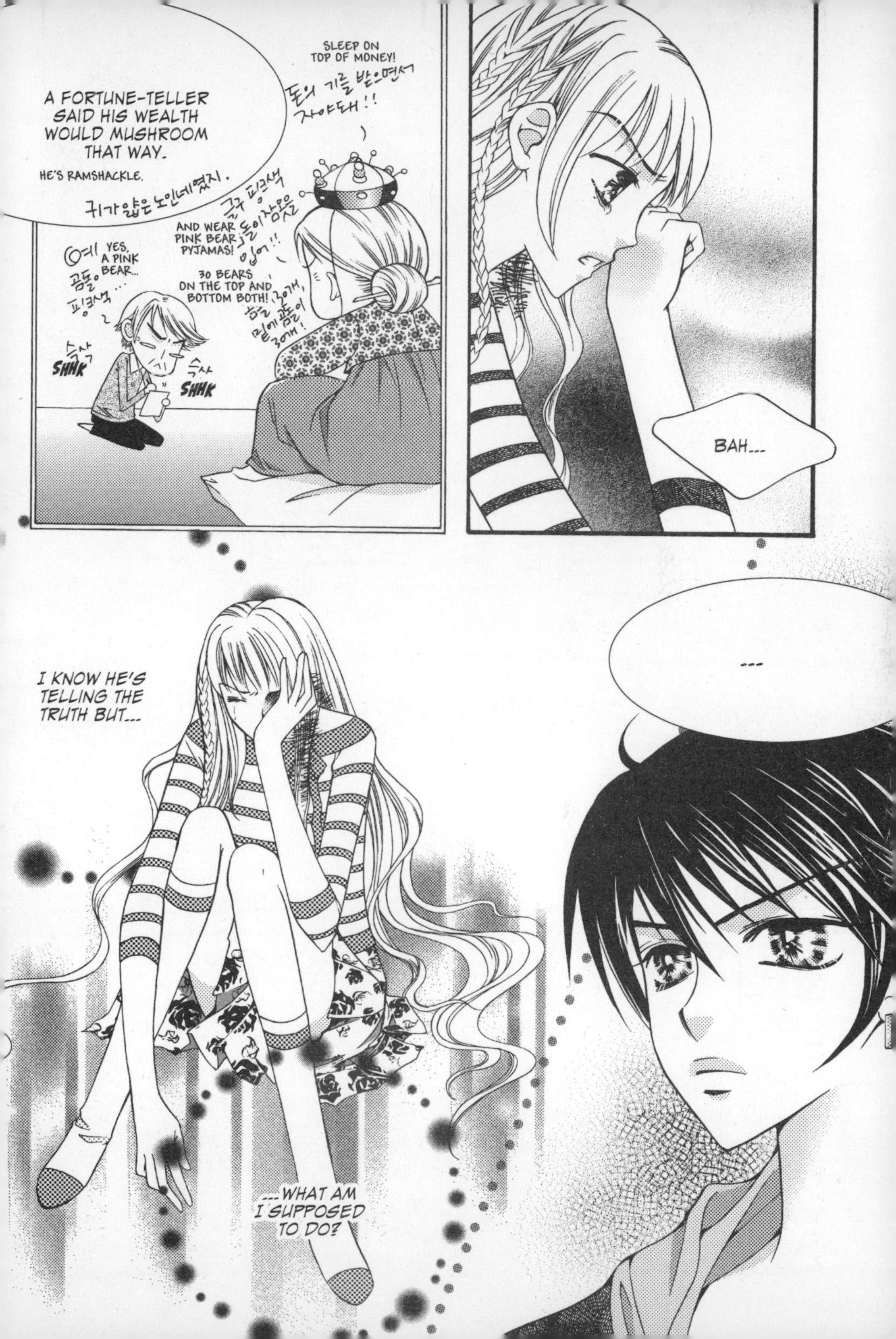

A FORTUNE-TELLER SAID HIS WEALTH WOULD MUSHROOM THAT WAY.
HE'S RAMSHACKLE.
귀가얇은 노인네였지.
SLEEP ON TOP OF MONEY!
돈의 기를 받으면서 자야돼!!
AND WEAR PINK BEAR PYJAMAS!
30 BEARS ON THE TOP AND BOTTOM BOTH!
YES, A PINK BEAR...
SHHK
SHHK
BAH...
I KNOW HE'S TELLING THE TRUTH BUT...
...
...WHAT AM I SUPPOSED TO DO?

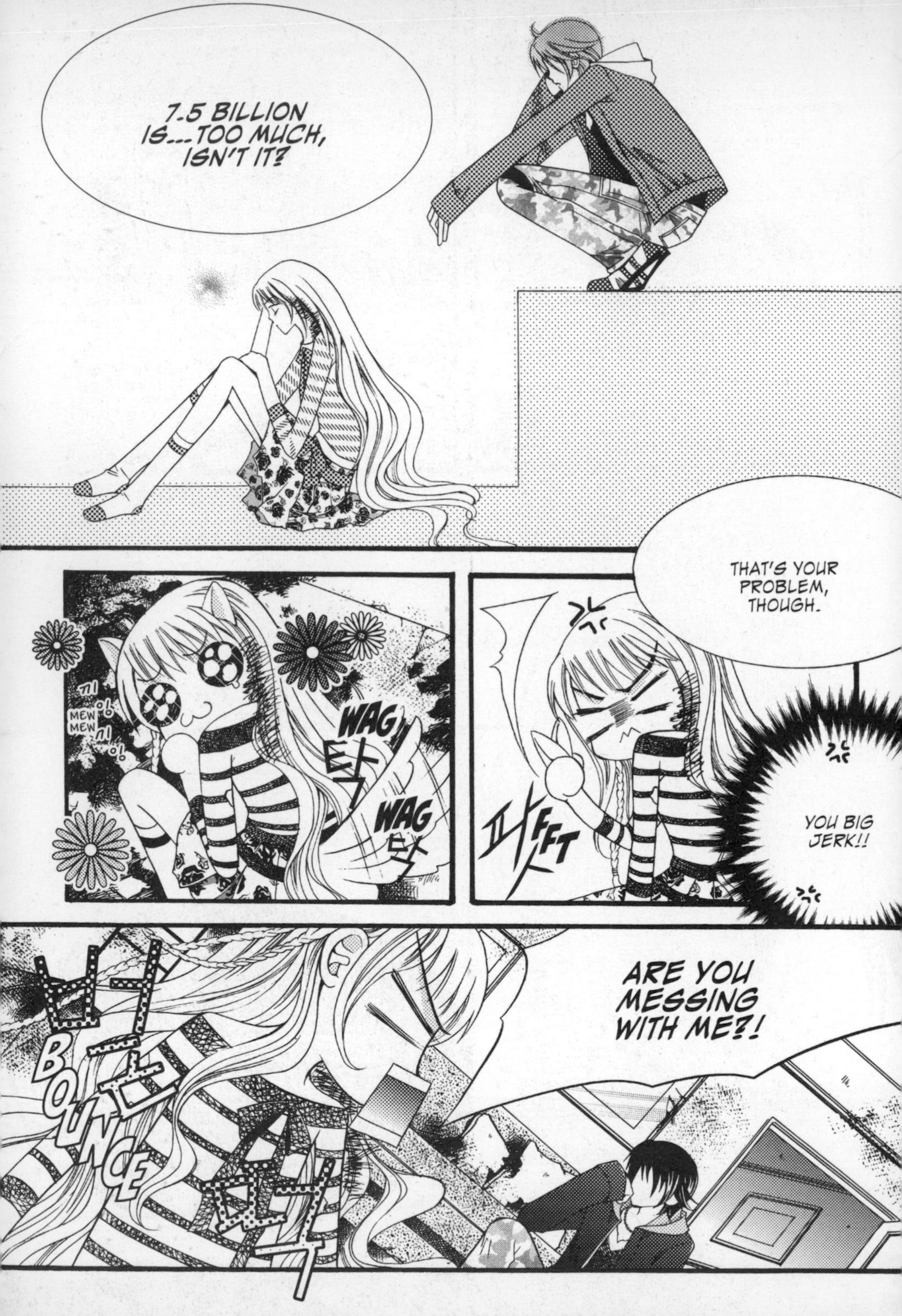
7.5 BILLION IS... TOO MUCH, ISN'T IT?
끼잉
끼잉
MEW MEW
WAG
탁
WAG
탁
THAT'S YOUR PROBLEM, THOUGH.
FFFT
YOU BIG JERK!!
BOUNCE
ARE YOU MESSING WITH ME?!

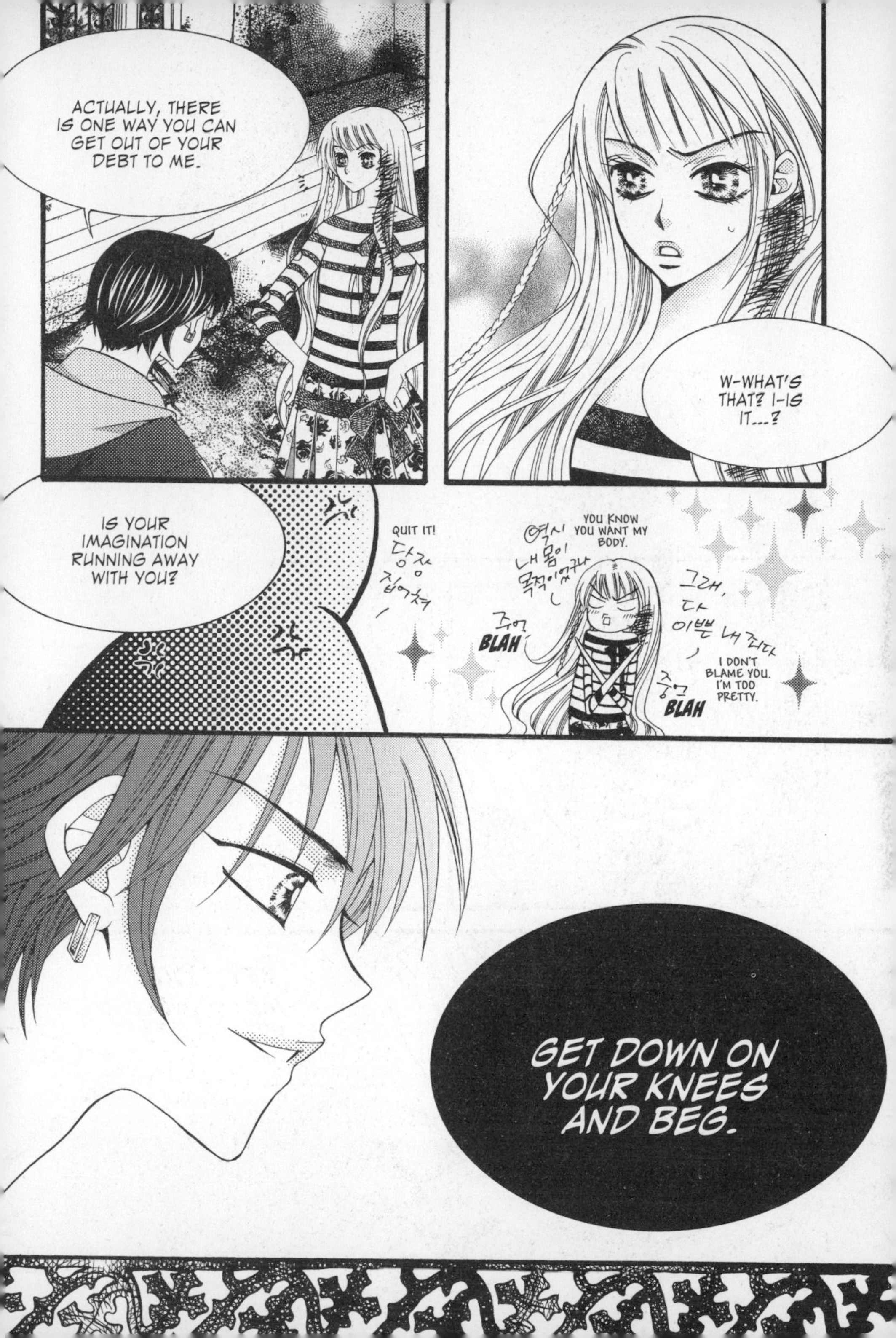
ACTUALLY, THERE IS ONE WAY YOU CAN GET OUT OF YOUR DEBT TO ME.
W-WHAT'S THAT? I-IS IT...?
IS YOUR IMAGINATION RUNNING AWAY WITH YOU?
QUIT IT!
당장 집어쳐!
역시 내 몸이 목적이었구나!
YOU KNOW YOU WANT MY BODY.
BLAH
그래, 다 이쁜 내 죄다!
I DON'T BLAME YOU. I'M TOO PRETTY.
BLAH
GET DOWN ON YOUR KNEES AND BEG.

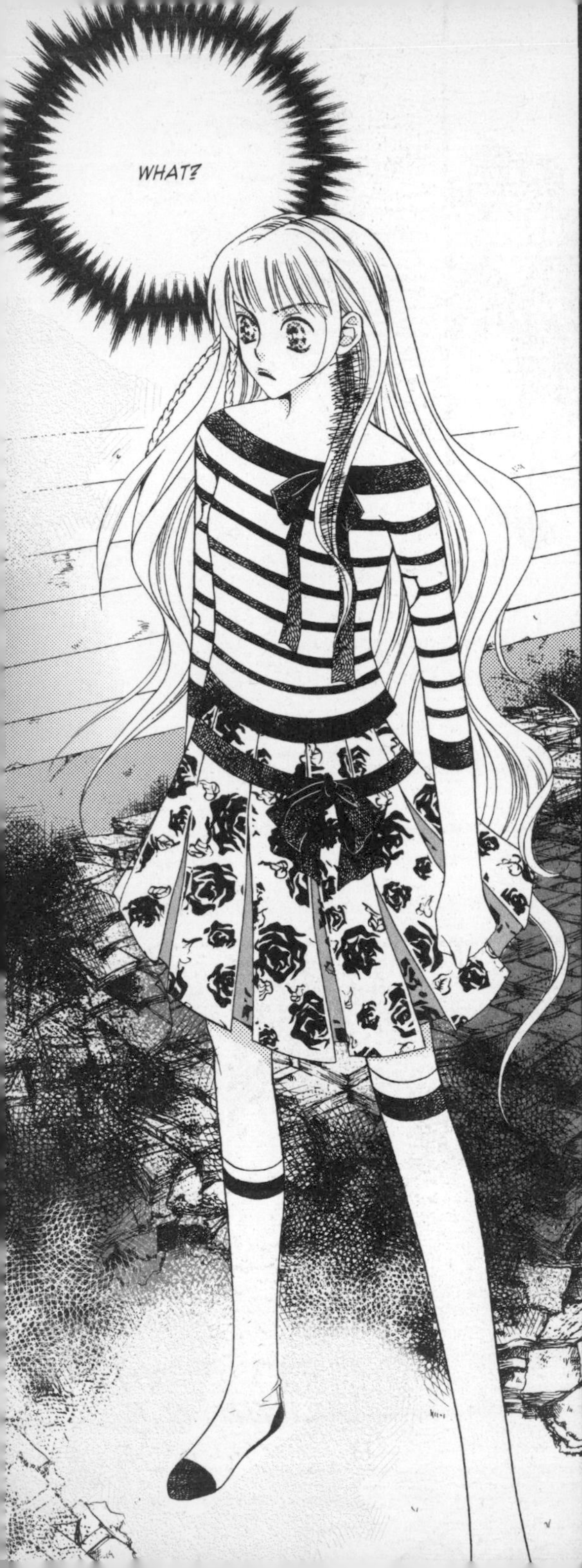
WHAT?
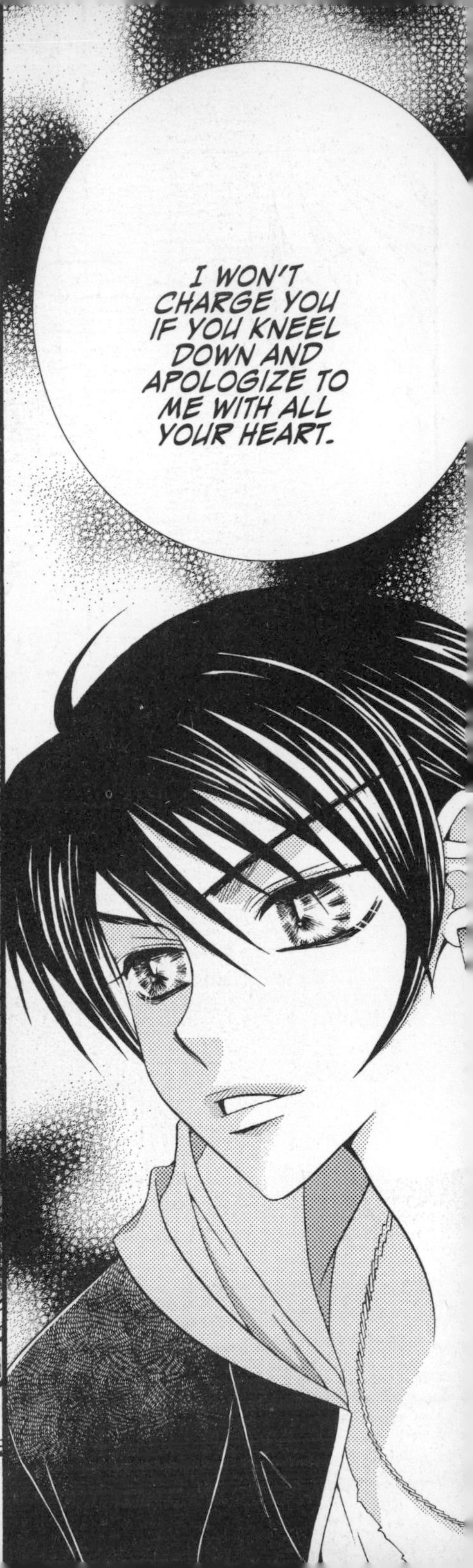
I WON'T CHARGE YOU IF YOU KNEEL DOWN AND APOLOGIZE TO ME WITH ALL YOUR HEART.

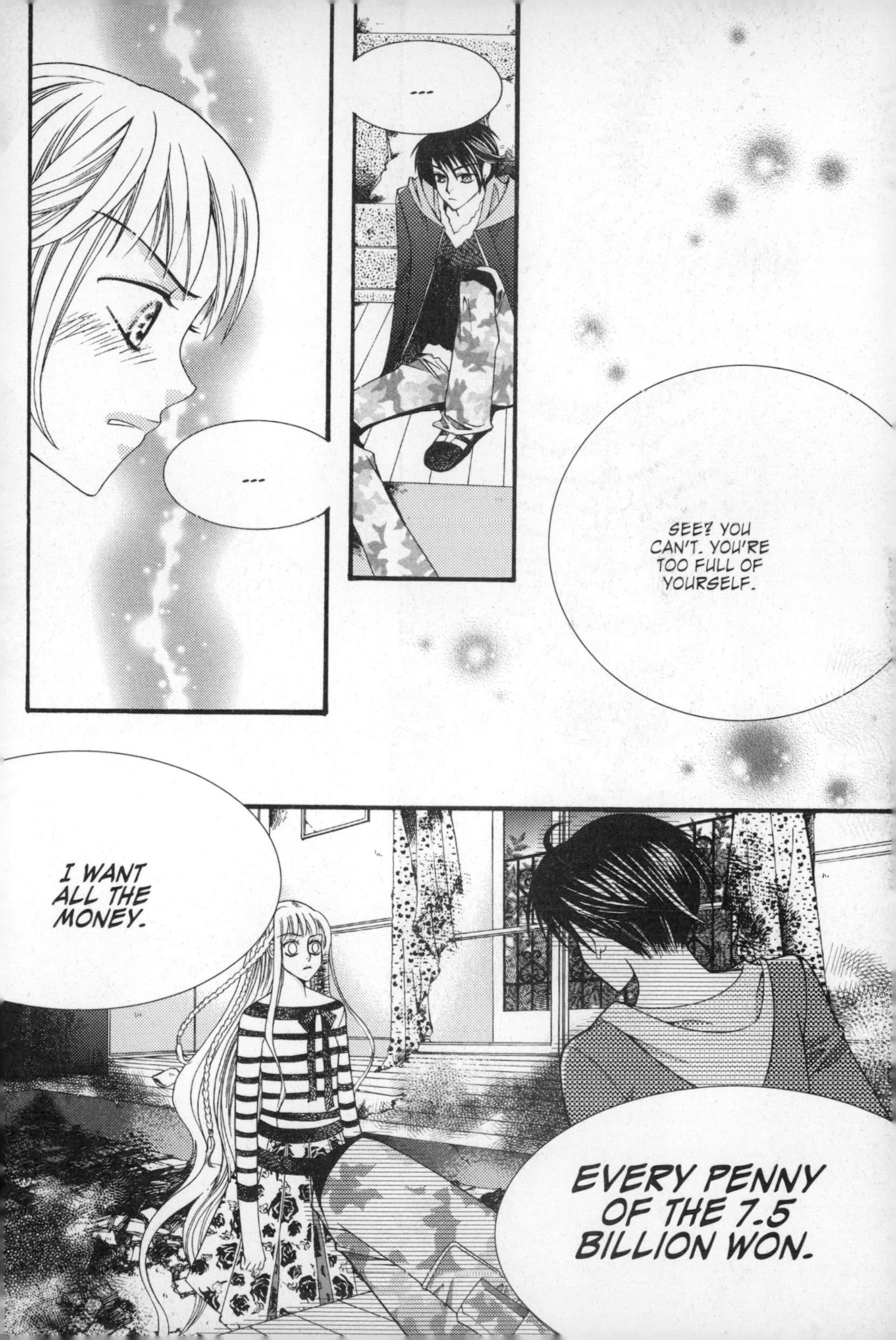
...
...
SEE? YOU CAN'T. YOU'RE TOO FULL OF YOURSELF.
I WANT ALL THE MONEY.
EVERY PENNY OF THE 7.5 BILLION WON.

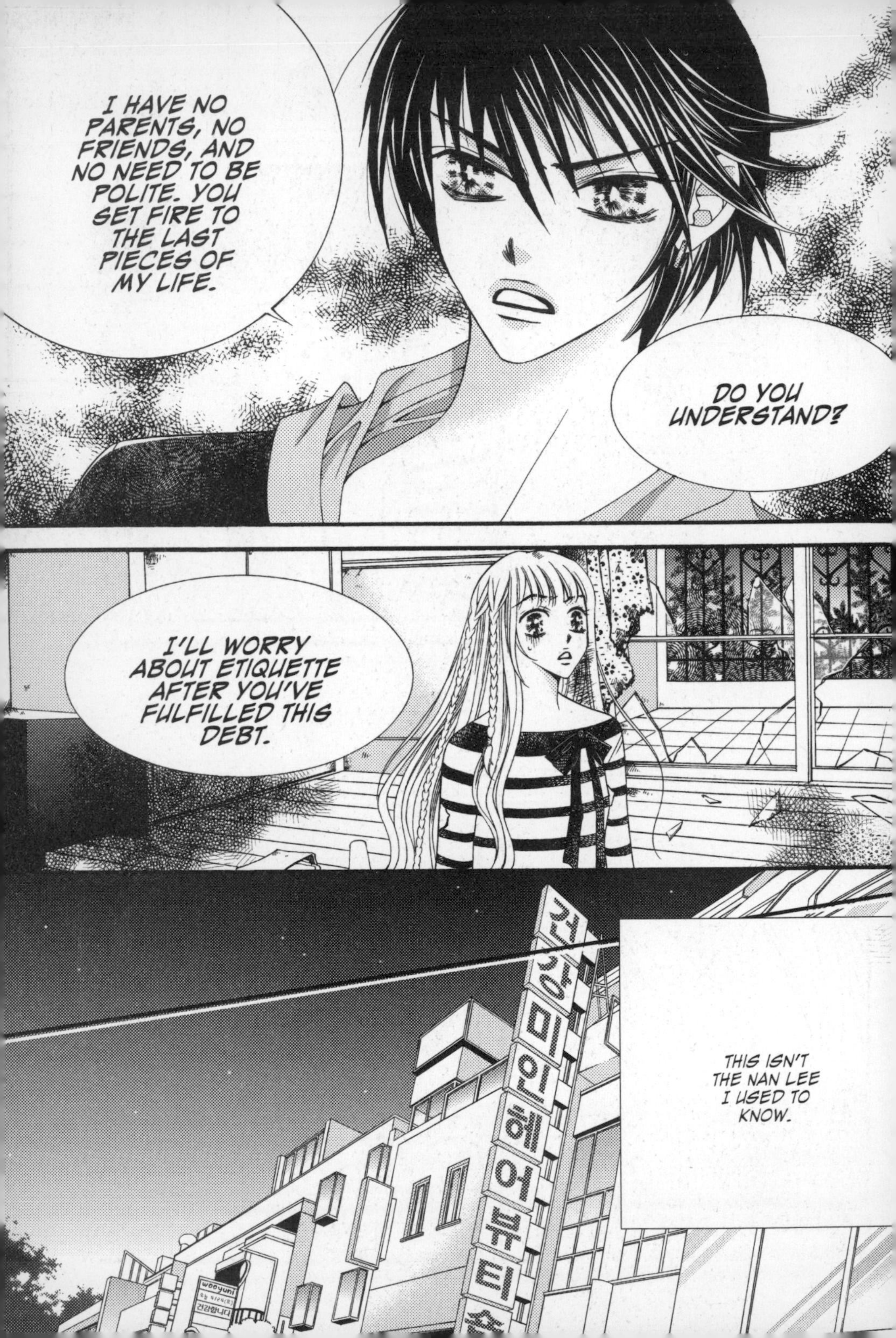
I HAVE NO PARENTS, NO FRIENDS, AND NO NEED TO BE POLITE. YOU SET FIRE TO THE LAST PIECES OF MY LIFE.
DO YOU UNDERSTAND?
I'LL WORRY ABOUT ETIQUETTE AFTER YOU'VE FULFILLED THIS DEBT.
건강미인헤어뷰티
THIS ISN'T THE NAN LEE I USED TO KNOW.

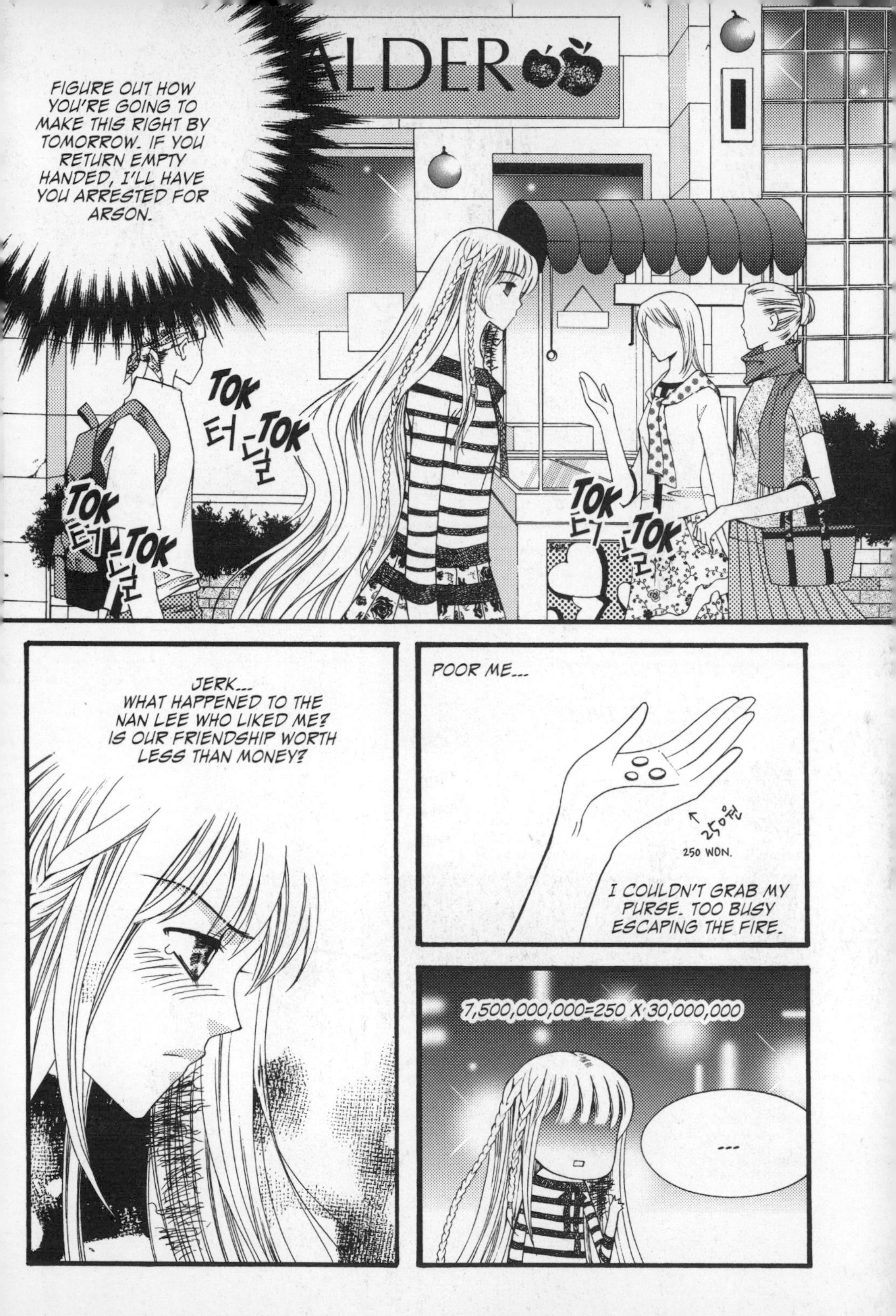
ALDER
FIGURE OUT HOW YOU'RE GOING TO MAKE THIS RIGHT BY TOMORROW. IF YOU RETURN EMPTY HANDED, I'LL HAVE YOU ARRESTED FOR ARSON.
TOK TOK
TOK TOK
TOK TOK
JERK... WHAT HAPPENED TO THE NAN LEE WHO LIKED ME? IS OUR FRIENDSHIP WORTH LESS THAN MONEY?
POOR ME...
250원
250 WON.
I COULDN'T GRAB MY PURSE. TOO BUSY ESCAPING THE FIRE.
7,500,000,000=250 X 30,000,000
...

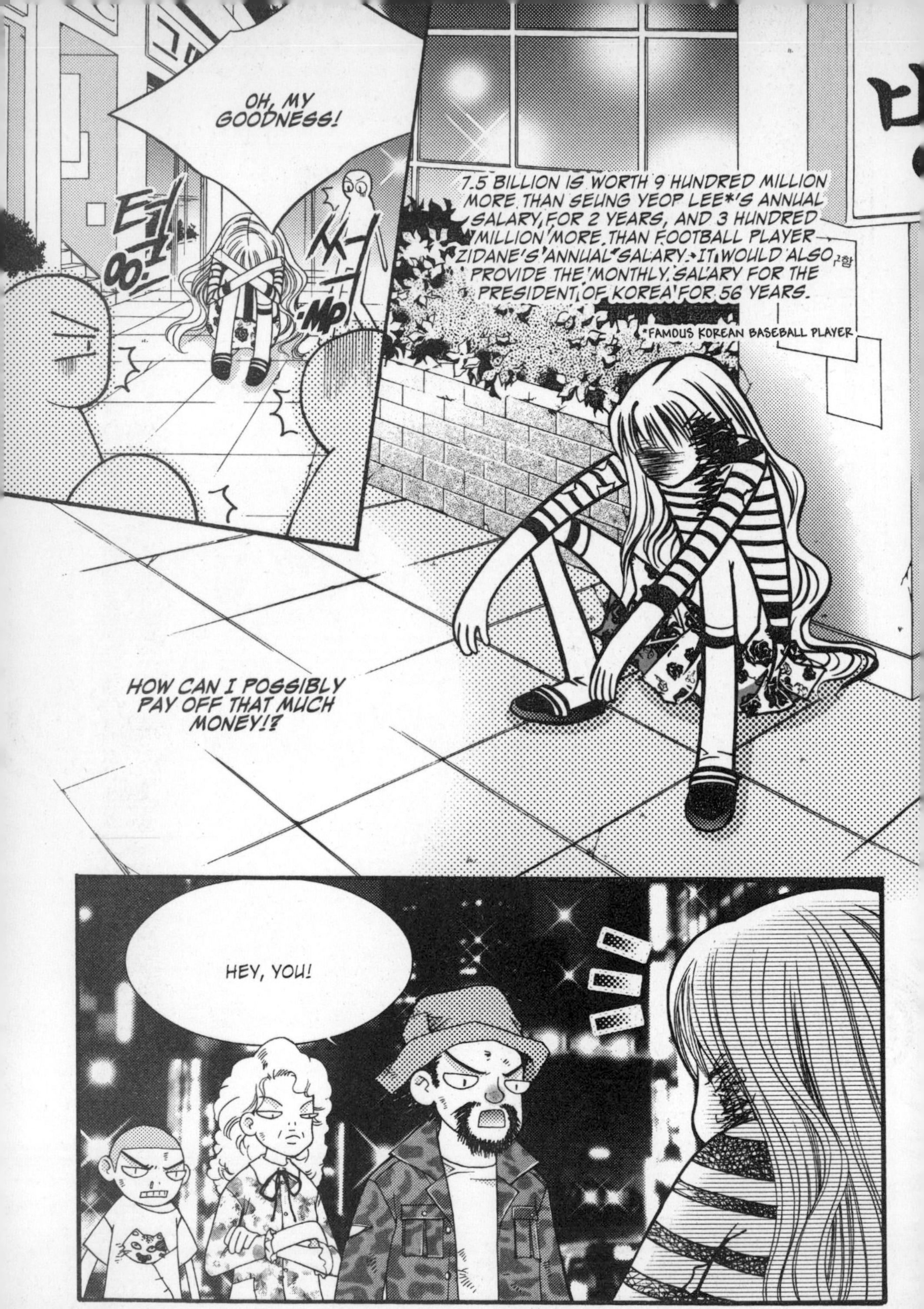
OH, MY GOODNESS!
7.5 BILLION IS WORTH 9 HUNDRED MILLION MORE THAN SEUNG YEOP LEE*'S ANNUAL SALARY, FOR 2 YEARS, AND 3 HUNDRED MILLION MORE THAN FOOTBALL PLAYER ZIDANE'S ANNUAL SALARY. IT WOULD ALSO PROVIDE THE MONTHLY SALARY FOR THE PRESIDENT OF KOREA FOR 56 YEARS.
*FAMOUS KOREAN BASEBALL PLAYER
HOW CAN I POSSIBLY PAY OFF THAT MUCH MONEY!?
HEY, YOU!

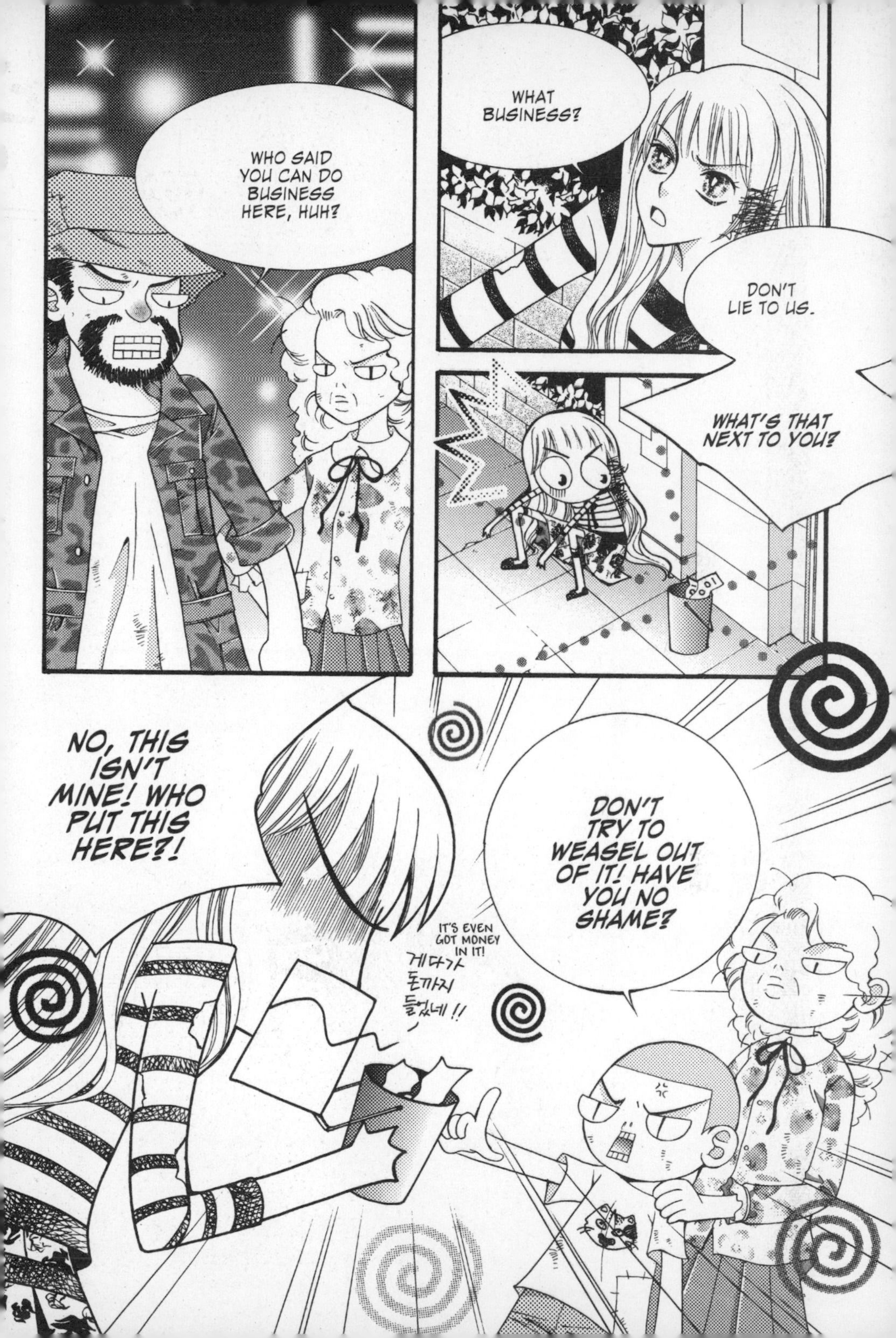
WHO SAID YOU CAN DO BUSINESS HERE, HUH?
WHAT BUSINESS?
DON'T LIE TO US.
WHAT'S THAT NEXT TO YOU?
NO, THIS ISN'T MINE! WHO PUT THIS HERE?!
DON'T TRY TO WEASEL OUT OF IT! HAVE YOU NO SHAME?
IT'S EVEN GOT MONEY IN IT!
게다가 돈까지 들었네!!

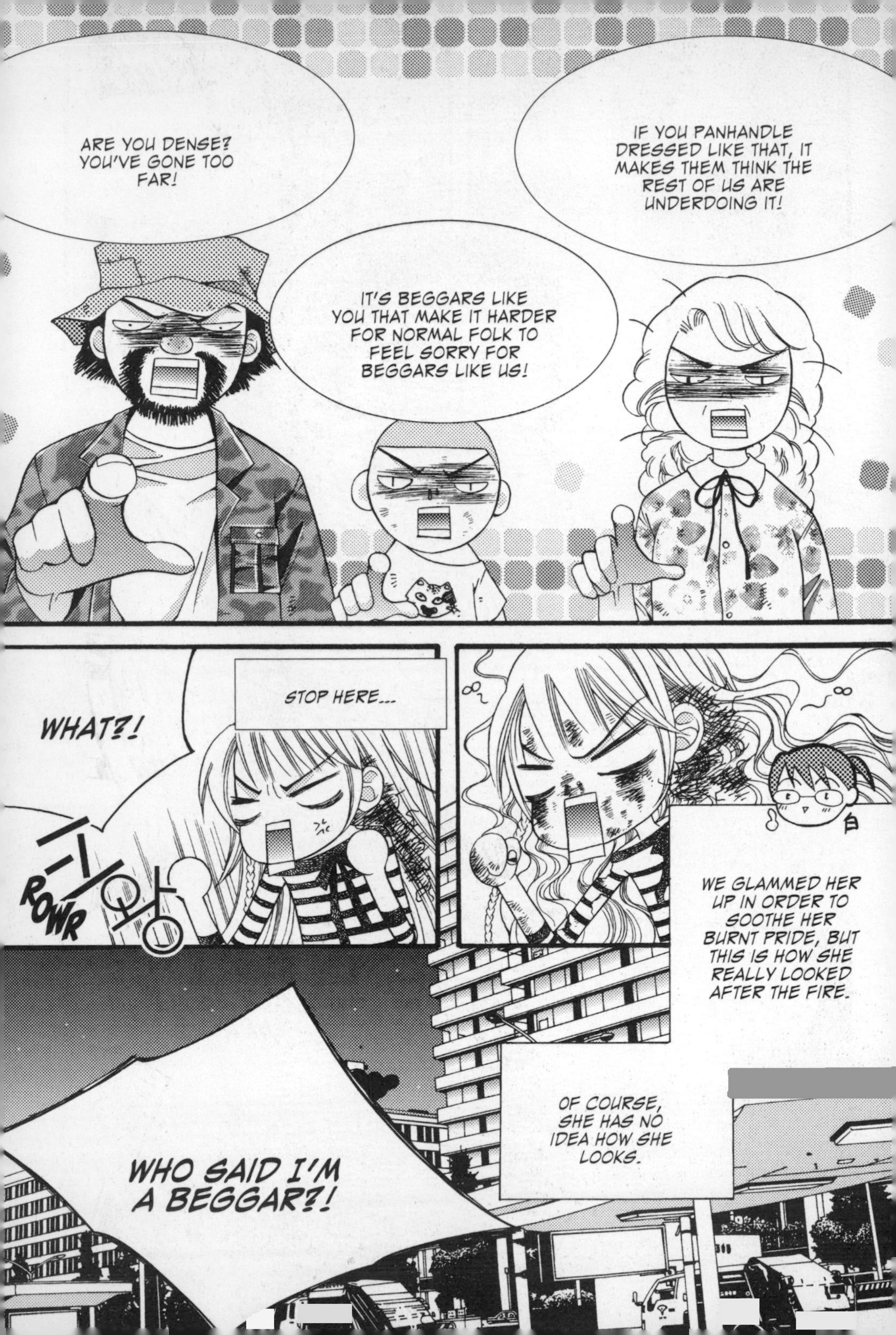
ARE YOU DENSE? YOU'VE GONE TOO FAR!
IT'S BEGGARS LIKE YOU THAT MAKE IT HARDER FOR NORMAL FOLK TO FEEL SORRY FOR BEGGARS LIKE US!
IF YOU PANHANDLE DRESSED LIKE THAT, IT MAKES THEM THINK THE REST OF US ARE UNDERDOING IT!
WHAT?!
STOP HERE...
ROWR
白
WE GLAMMED HER UP IN ORDER TO SOOTHE HER BURNT PRIDE, BUT THIS IS HOW SHE REALLY LOOKED AFTER THE FIRE.
WHO SAID I'M A BEGGAR?!
OF COURSE, SHE HAS NO IDEA HOW SHE LOOKS.

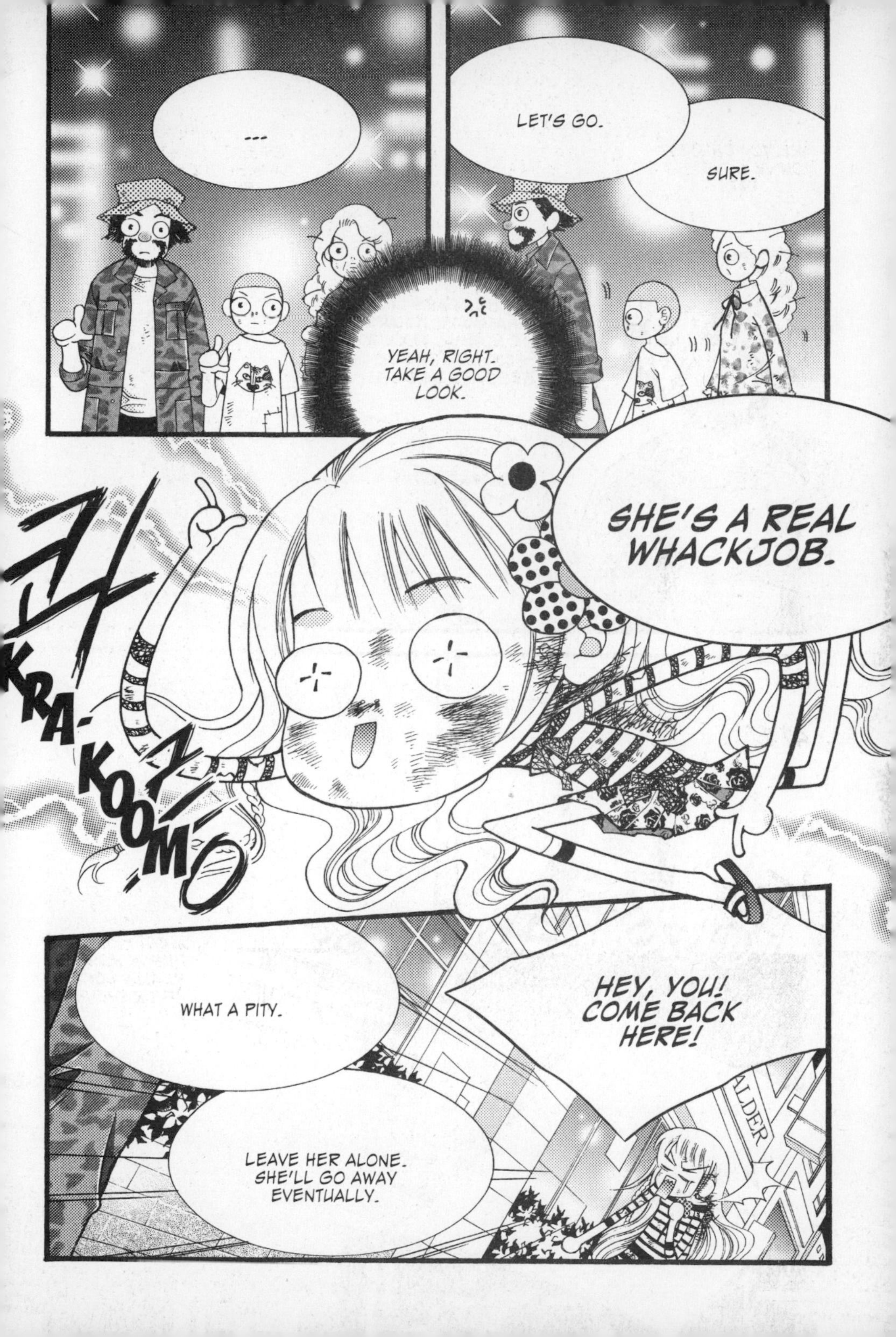
...
LET'S GO.
SURE.
YEAH, RIGHT. TAKE A GOOD LOOK.
SHE'S A REAL WHACKJOB.
ZZ KRA-KOOM
WHAT A PITY.
HEY, YOU! COME BACK HERE!
LEAVE HER ALONE. SHE'LL GO AWAY EVENTUALLY.
ALDER

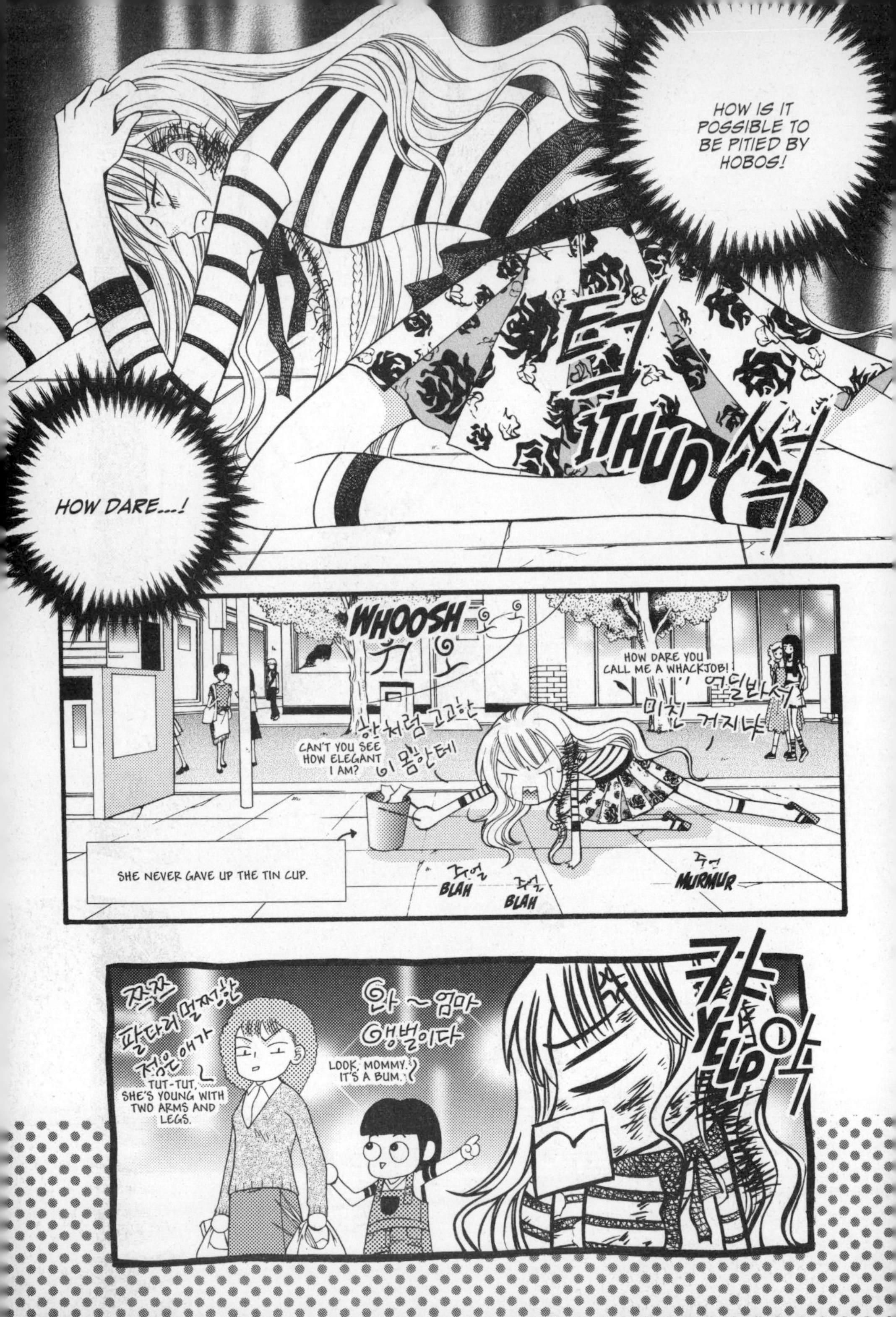
HOW IS IT POSSIBLE TO BE PITIED BY HOBOS!
털썩
THUD
HOW DARE...!
WHOOSH
학처럼 고고한 이 몸한테
CAN'T YOU SEE HOW ELEGANT I AM?
HOW DARE YOU CALL ME A WHACKJOB!
미친 거지냐
SHE NEVER GAVE UP THE TIN CUP.
BLAH
BLAH
MURMUR
쯧쯧 팔다리 멀쩡한 젊은 애가
TUT-TUT, SHE'S YOUNG WITH TWO ARMS AND LEGS.
LOOK, MOMMY. IT'S A BUM.
YELP

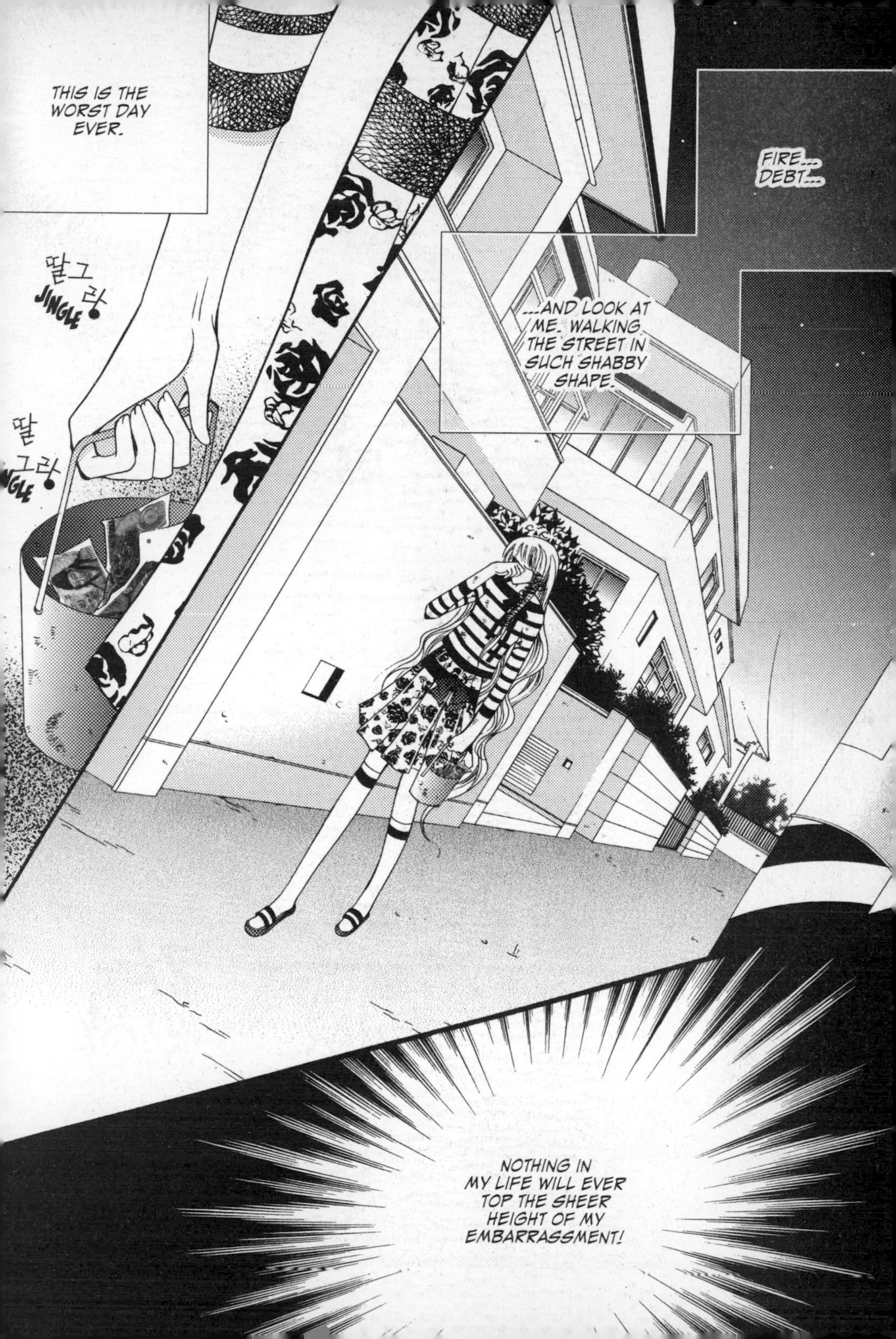

THIS IS THE WORST DAY EVER.
딸그랑 JINGLE
딸그랑 JINGLE
FIRE... DEBT...
...AND LOOK AT ME. WALKING THE STREET IN SUCH SHABBY SHAPE.
NOTHING IN MY LIFE WILL EVER TOP THE SHEER HEIGHT OF MY EMBARRASSMENT!

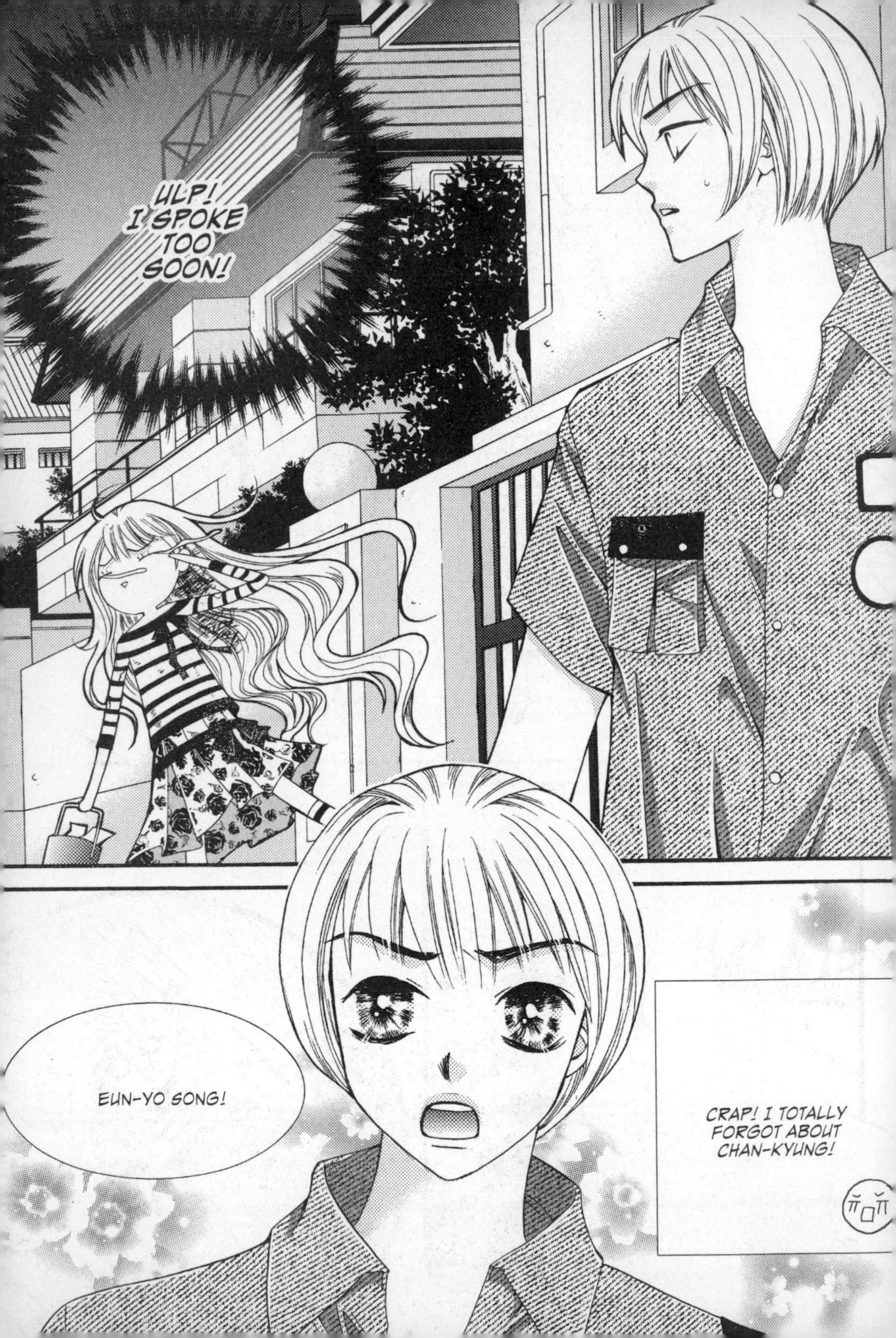
ULP! I SPOKE TOO SOON!
EUN-YO SONG!
CRAP! I TOTALLY FORGOT ABOUT CHAN-KYUNG!
π□π

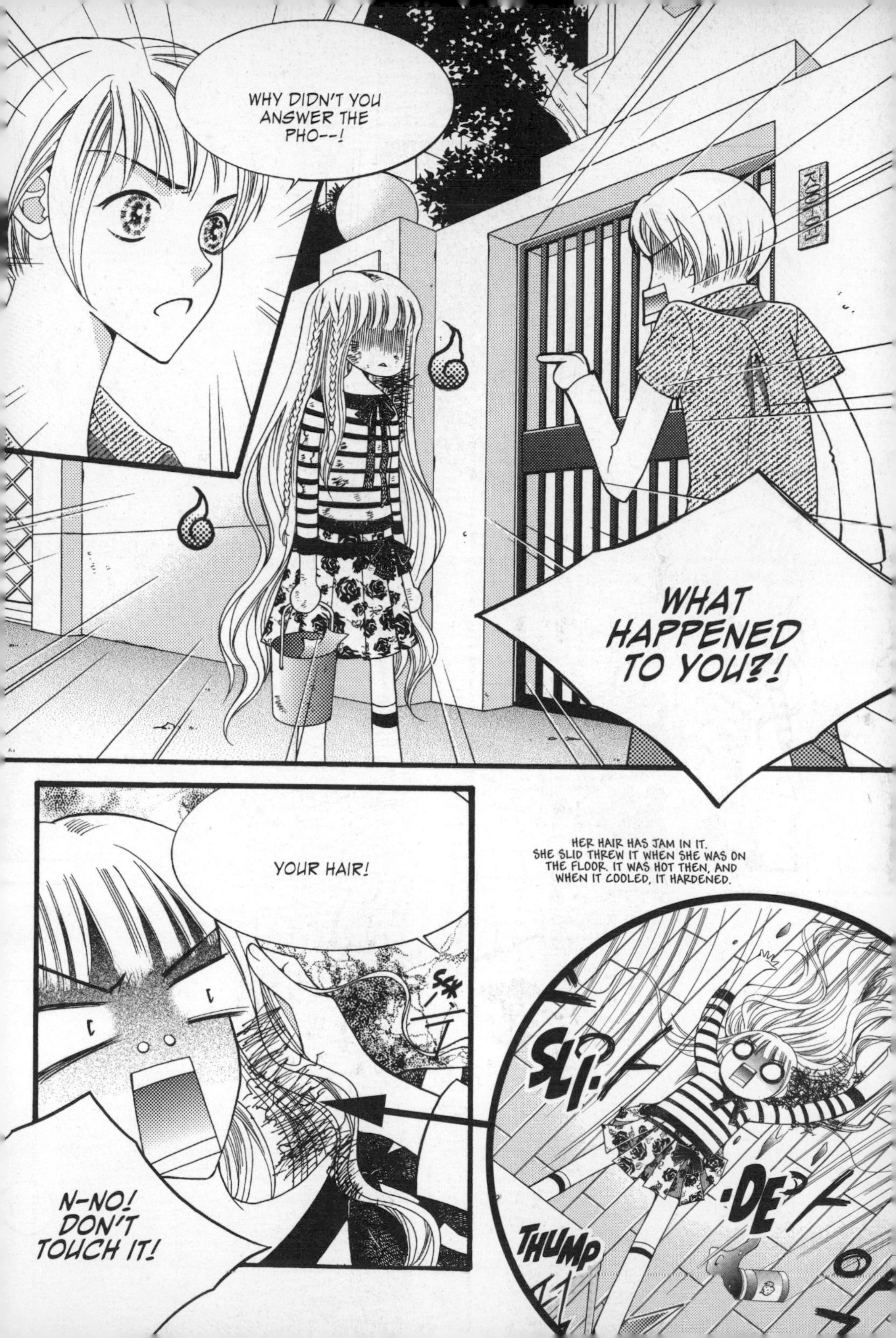
WHY DIDN'T YOU ANSWER THE PHO--!
WHAT HAPPENED TO YOU?!
YOUR HAIR!
N-NO! DON'T TOUCH IT!
HER HAIR HAS JAM IN IT. SHE SLID THREW IT WHEN SHE WAS ON THE FLOOR. IT WAS HOT THEN, AND WHEN IT COOLED, IT HARDENED.
THUMP

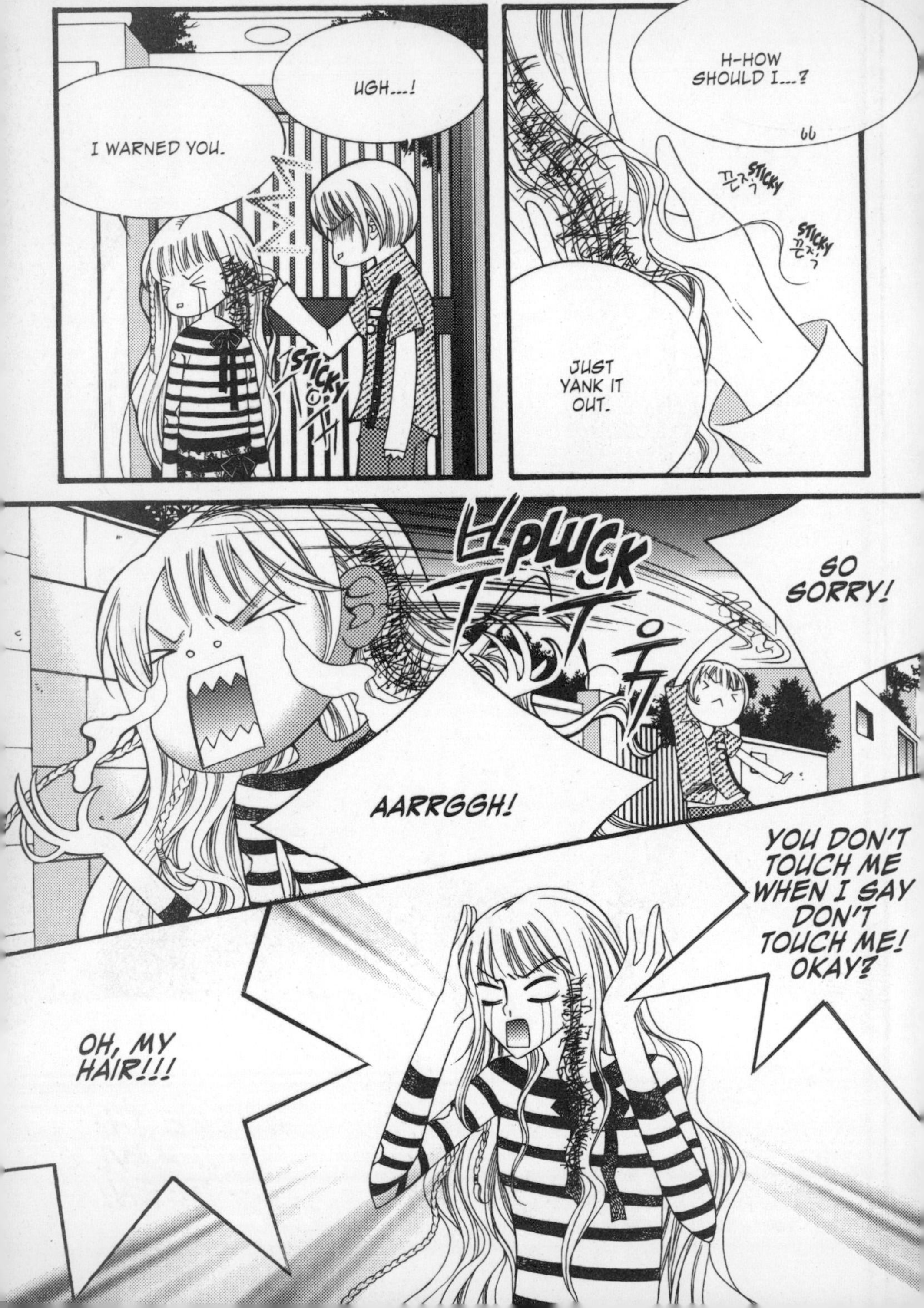
I WARNED YOU.
UGH...!
STICKY
H-HOW SHOULD I...?
STICKY
STICKY
JUST YANK IT OUT.
PLUCK
SO SORRY!
AARRGGH!
YOU DON'T TOUCH ME WHEN I SAY DON'T TOUCH ME! OKAY?
OH, MY HAIR!!!

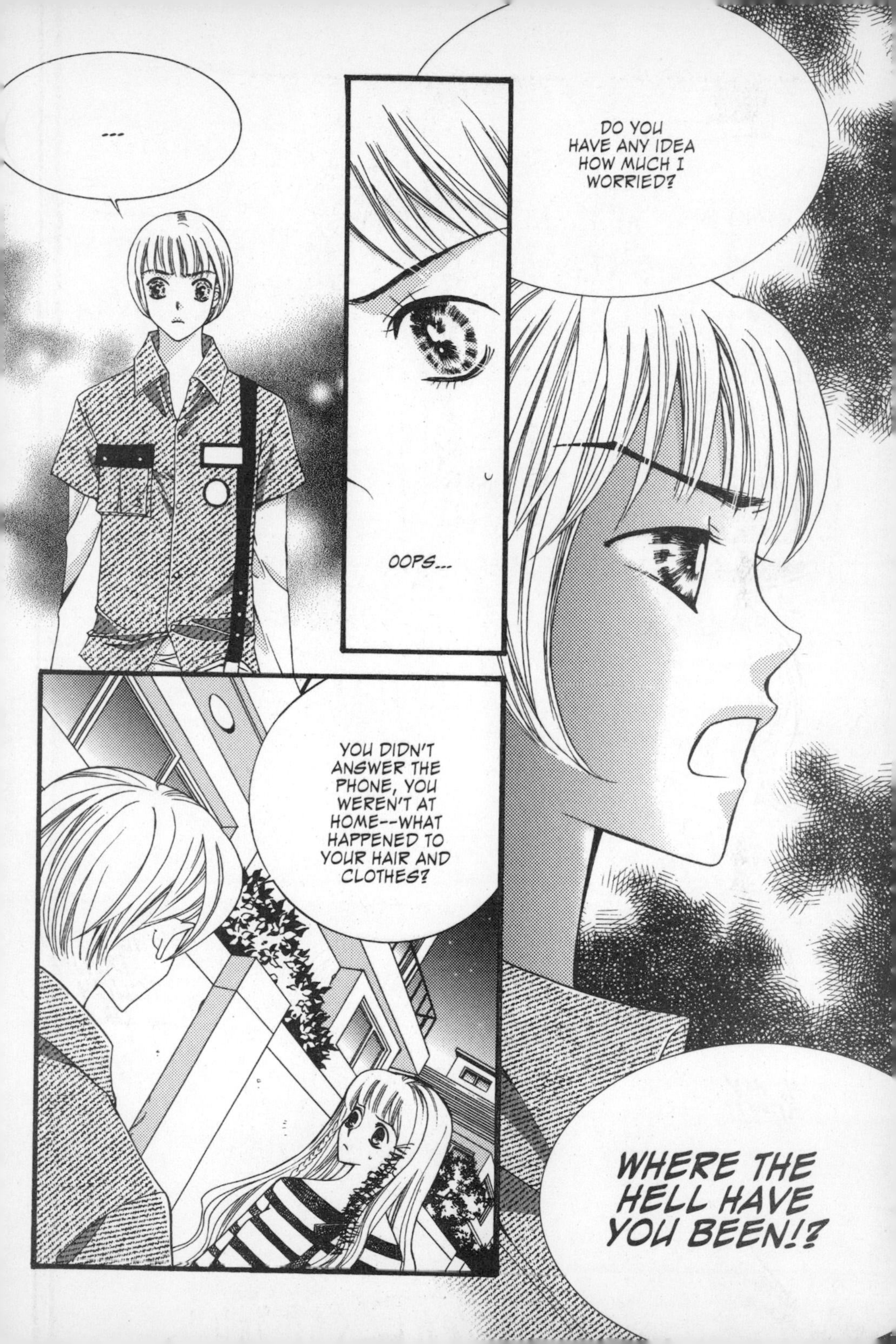
...
OOPS...
YOU DIDN'T ANSWER THE PHONE, YOU WEREN'T AT HOME--WHAT HAPPENED TO YOUR HAIR AND CLOTHES?
DO YOU HAVE ANY IDEA HOW MUCH I WORRIED?
WHERE THE HELL HAVE YOU BEEN!?

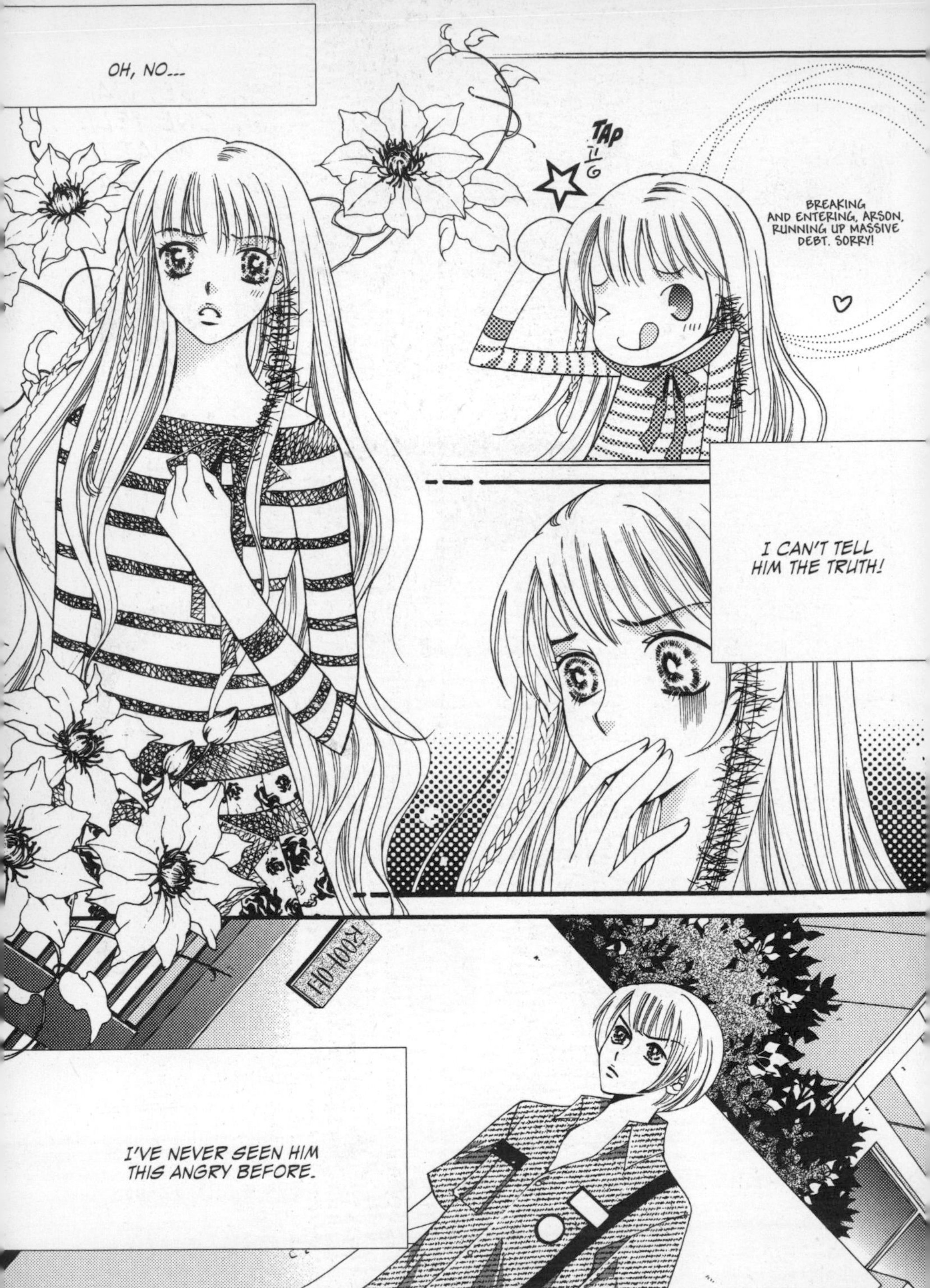
OH, NO...
TAP
BREAKING AND ENTERING, ARSON, RUNNING UP MASSIVE DEBT. SORRY!
I CAN'T TELL HIM THE TRUTH!
I'VE NEVER SEEN HIM THIS ANGRY BEFORE.

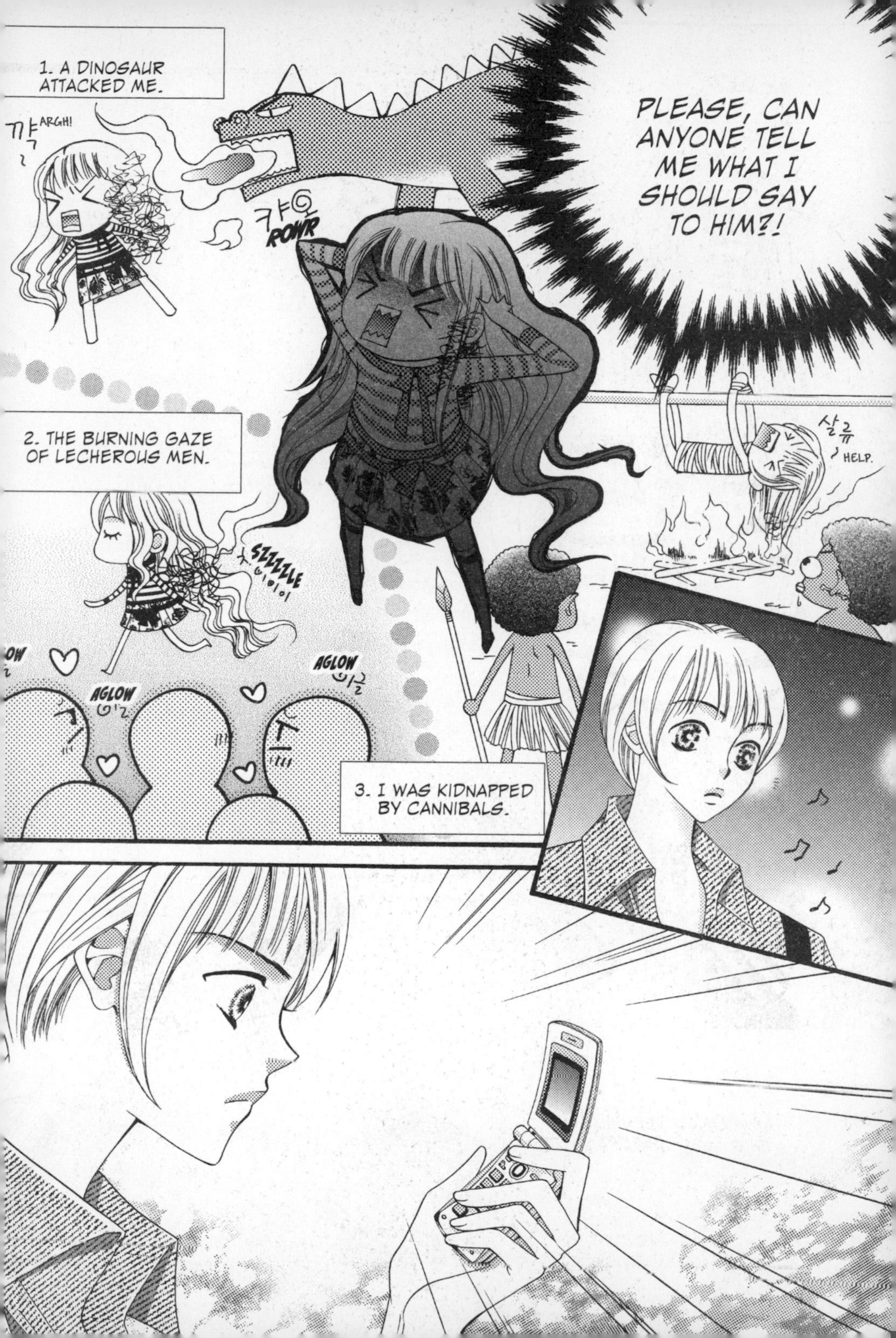

1. A DINOSAUR ATTACKED ME.
까ARGH!
크ROWR
PLEASE, CAN ANYONE TELL ME WHAT I SHOULD SAY TO HIM?!
2. THE BURNING GAZE OF LECHEROUS MEN.
SZZZZZLE
살려 HELP.
AGLOW
AGLOW
AGLOW
3. I WAS KIDNAPPED BY CANNIBALS.

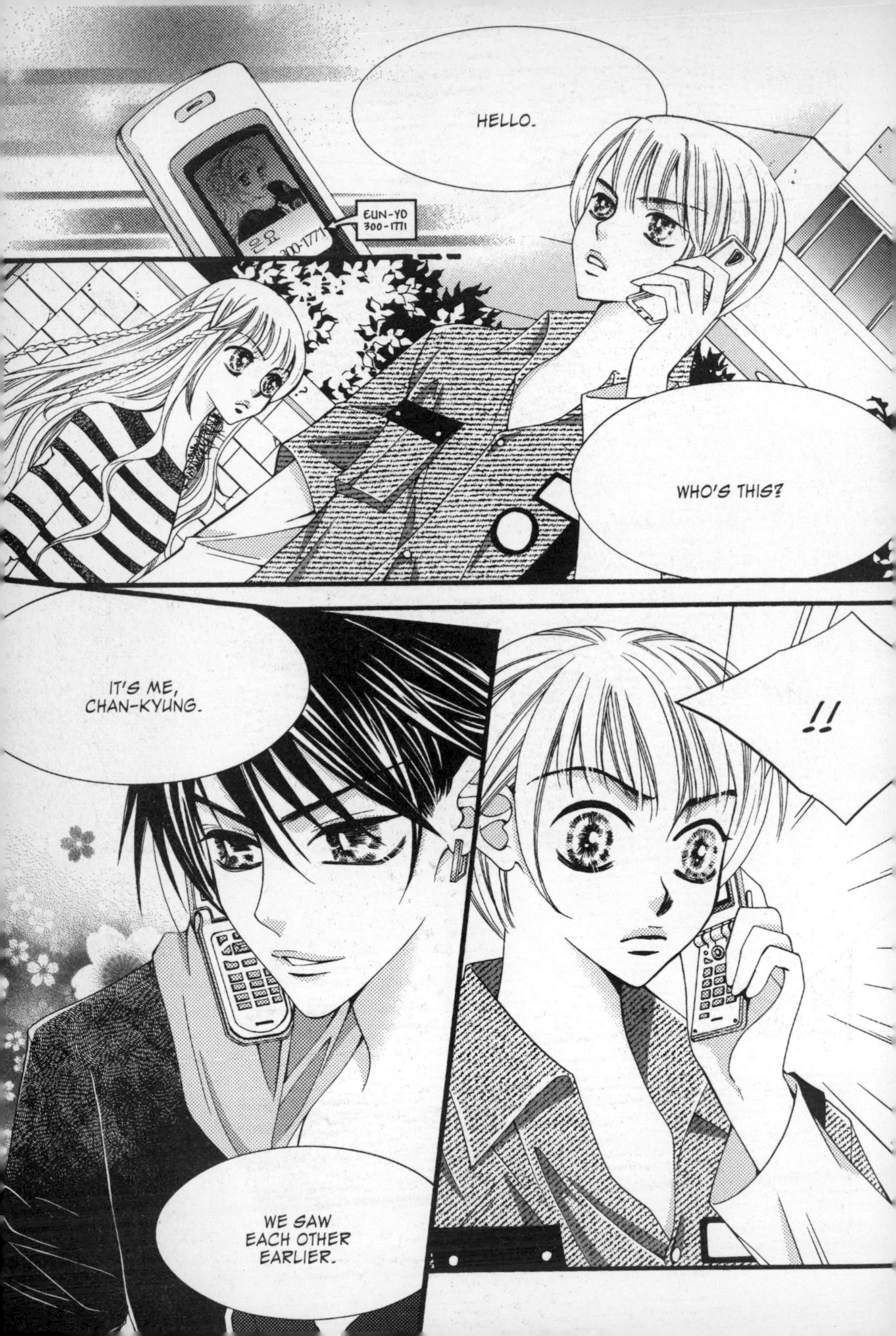
HELLO.
EUN-YO 300-1771
은요 300-1771
?
WHO'S THIS?
IT'S ME, CHAN-KYUNG.
!!
WE SAW EACH OTHER EARLIER.

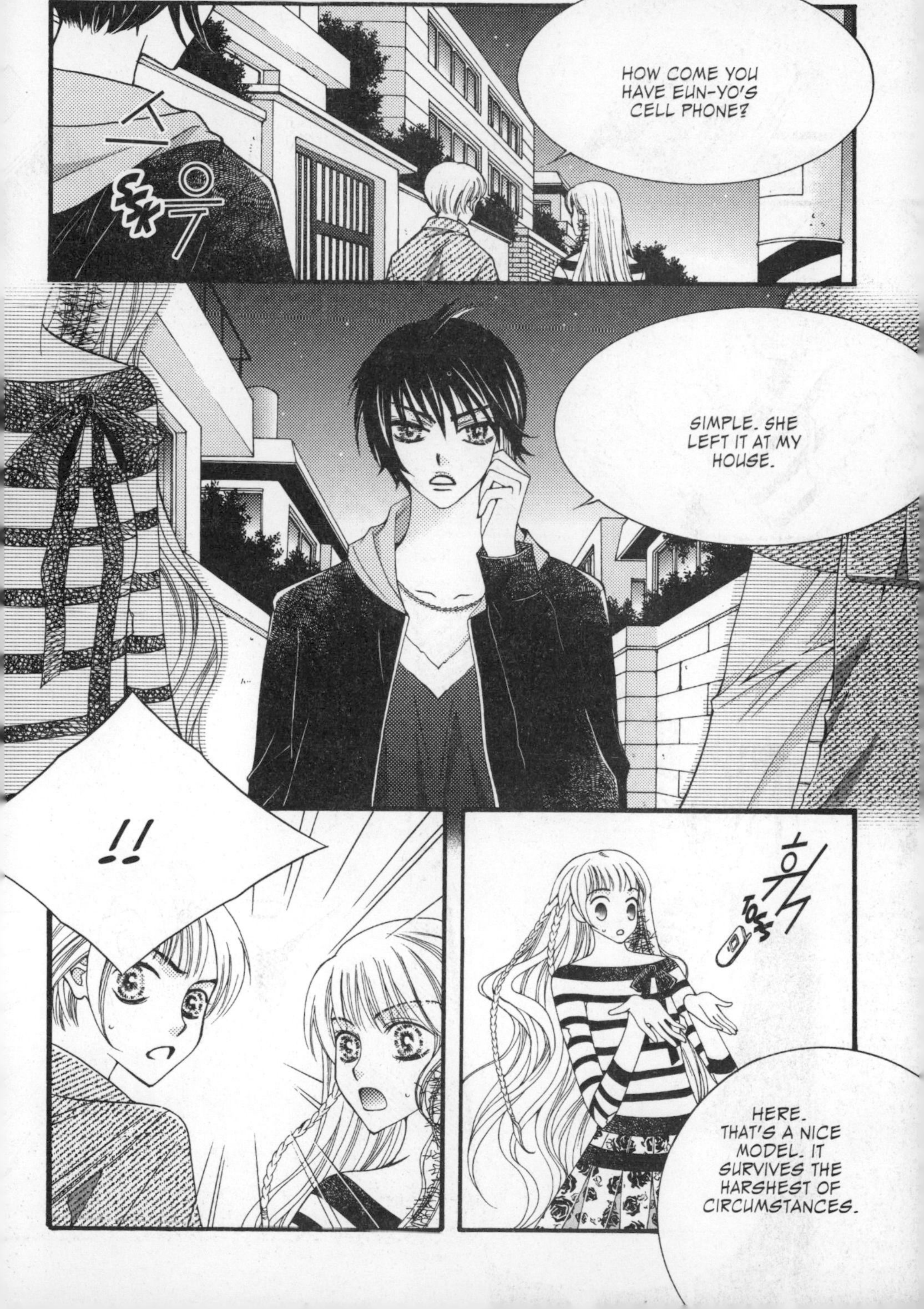
SK
HOW COME YOU HAVE EUN-YO'S CELL PHONE?
SIMPLE. SHE LEFT IT AT MY HOUSE.
!!
TOSS
HERE. THAT'S A NICE MODEL. IT SURVIVES THE HARSHEST OF CIRCUMSTANCES.

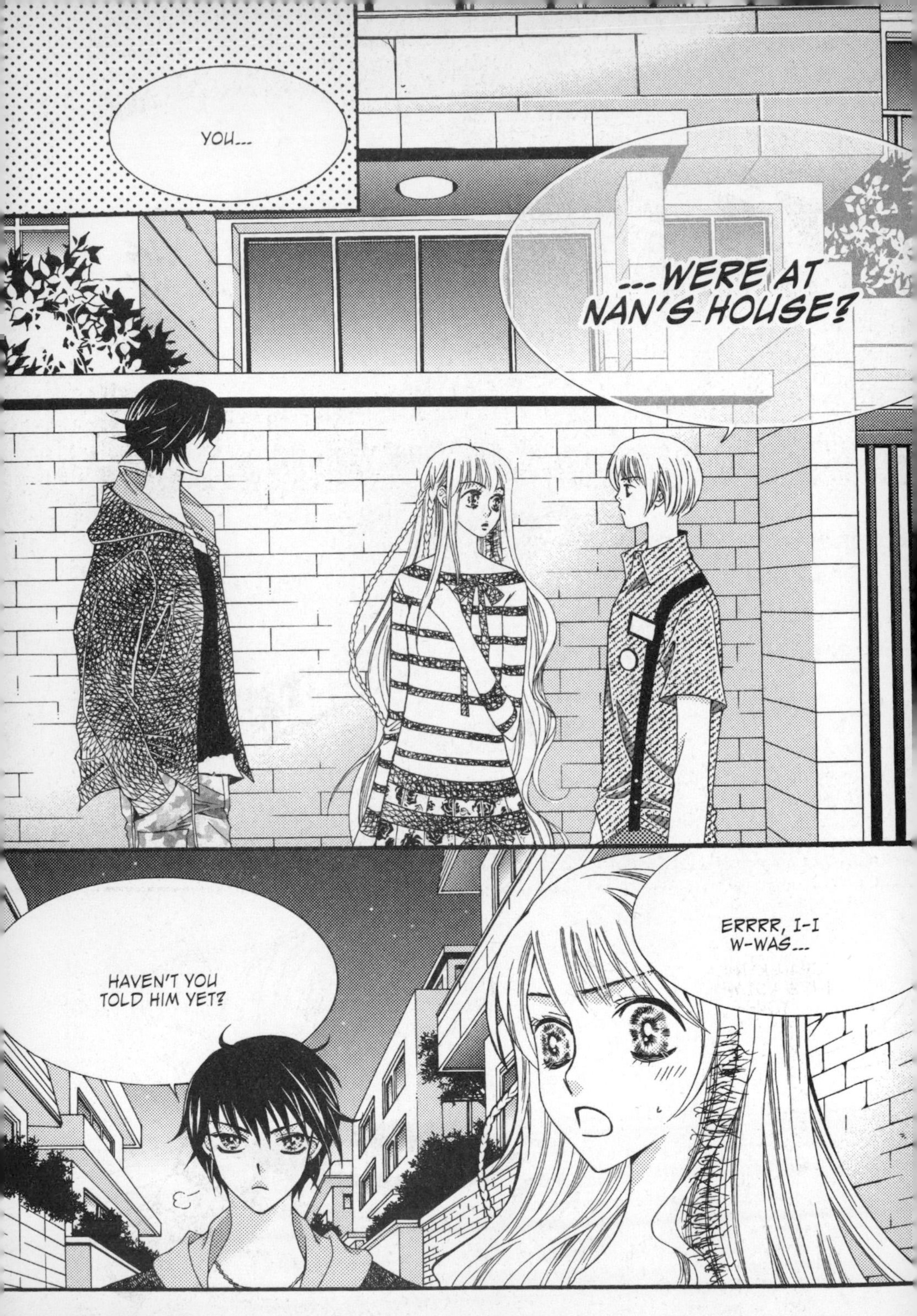
YOU...
...WERE AT NAN'S HOUSE?
HAVEN'T YOU TOLD HIM YET?
ERRRR, I-I W-WAS...

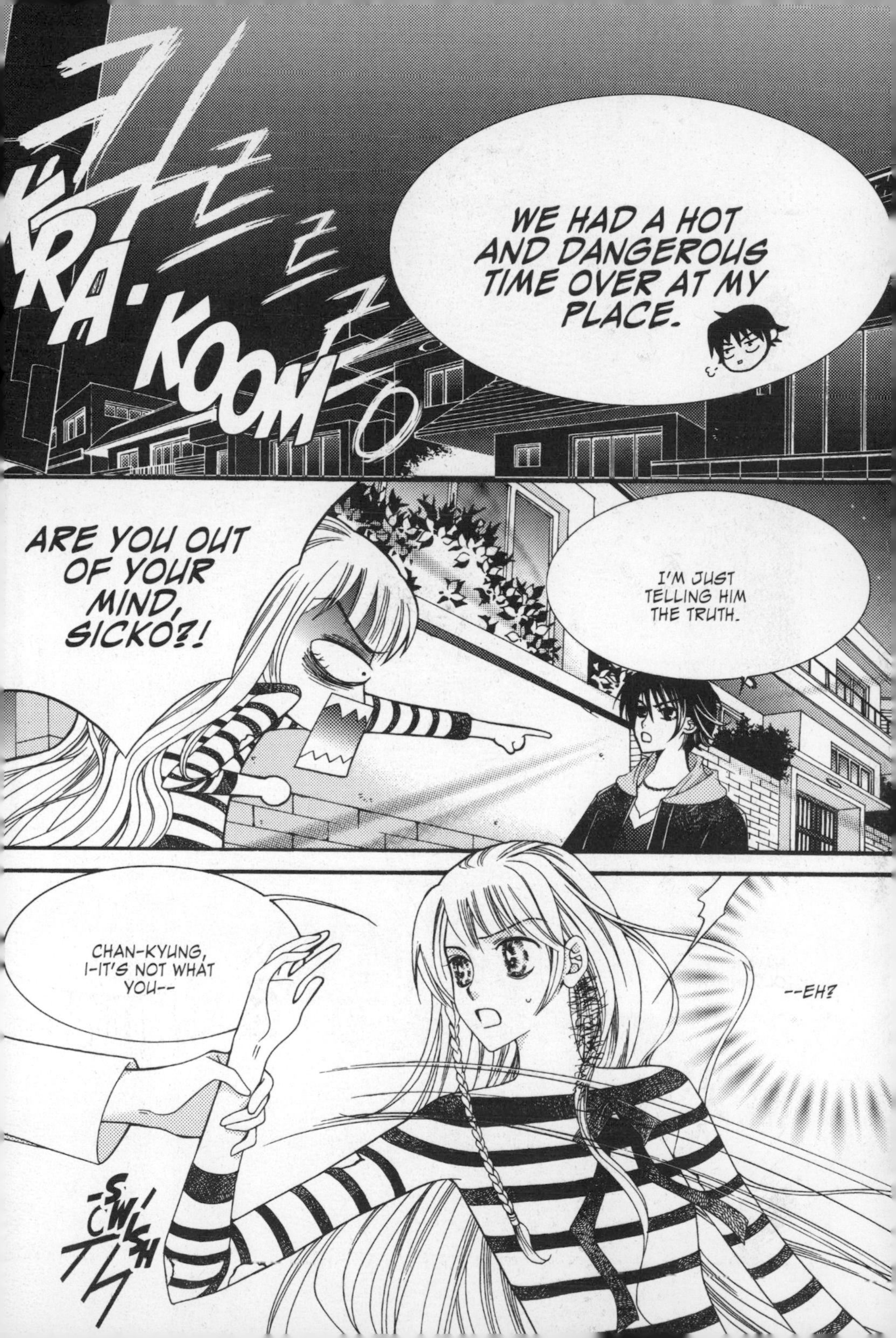
KRA-KOOM
WE HAD A HOT AND DANGEROUS TIME OVER AT MY PLACE.
ARE YOU OUT OF YOUR MIND, SICKO?!
I'M JUST TELLING HIM THE TRUTH.
CHAN-KYUNG, I-IT'S NOT WHAT YOU--
--EH?
SWISH

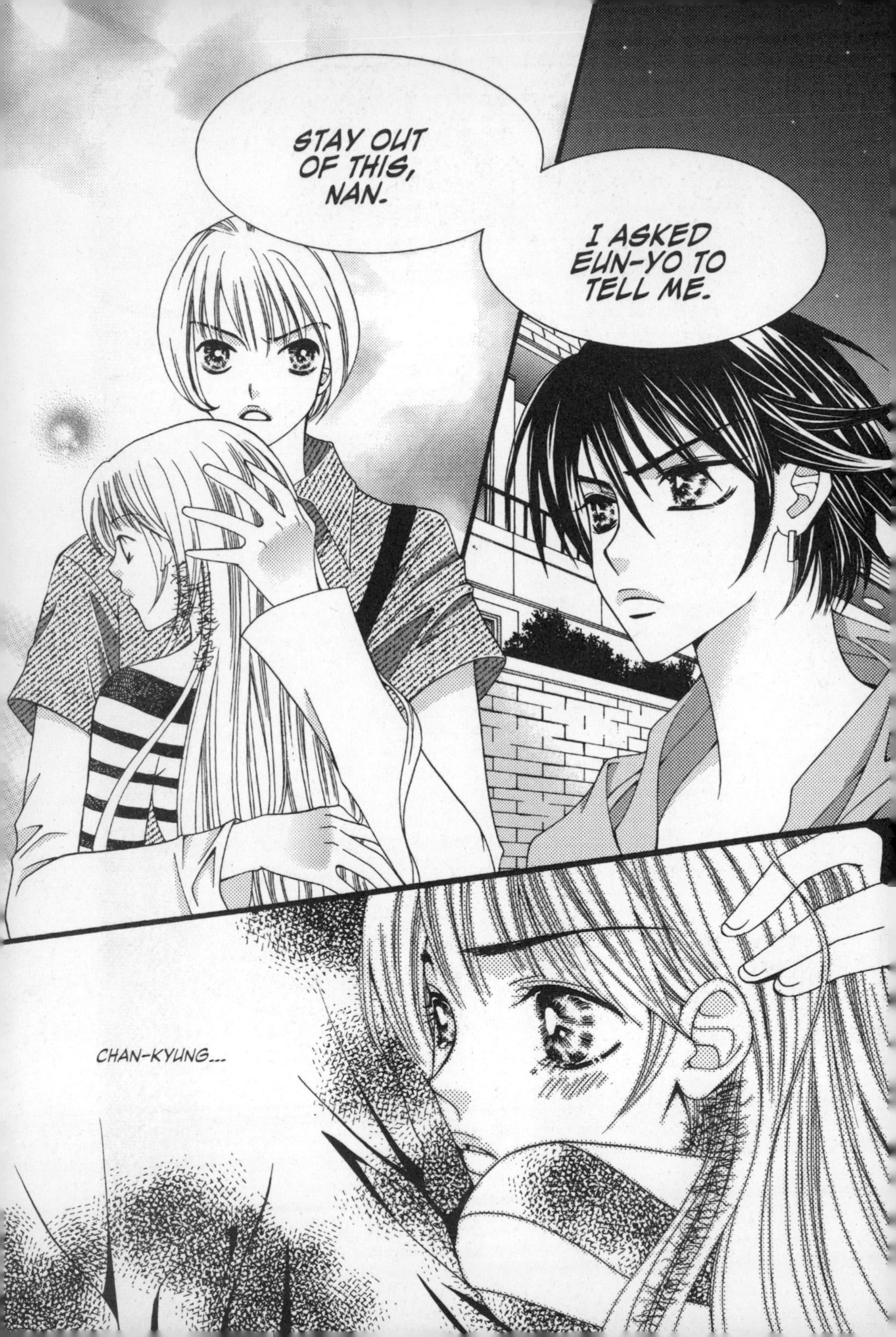
STAY OUT OF THIS, NAN.
I ASKED EUN-YO TO TELL ME.
CHAN-KYUNG...

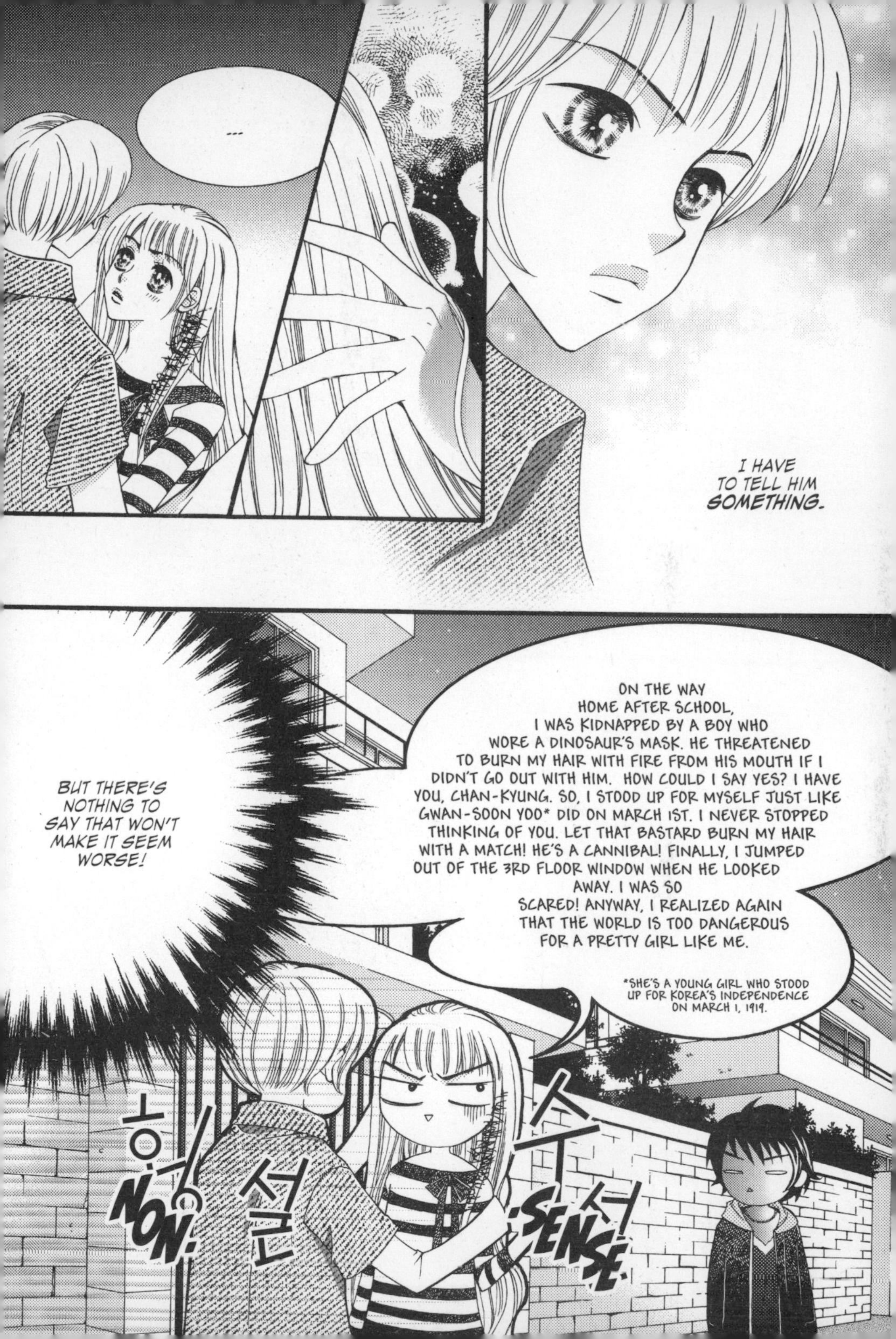
...
I HAVE TO TELL HIM SOMETHING.
BUT THERE'S NOTHING TO SAY THAT WON'T MAKE IT SEEM WORSE!
ON THE WAY HOME AFTER SCHOOL, I WAS KIDNAPPED BY A BOY WHO WORE A DINOSAUR'S MASK. HE THREATENED TO BURN MY HAIR WITH FIRE FROM HIS MOUTH IF I DIDN'T GO OUT WITH HIM. HOW COULD I SAY YES? I HAVE YOU, CHAN-KYUNG. SO, I STOOD UP FOR MYSELF JUST LIKE GWAN-SOON YOO* DID ON MARCH 1ST. I NEVER STOPPED THINKING OF YOU. LET THAT BASTARD BURN MY HAIR WITH A MATCH! HE'S A CANNIBAL! FINALLY, I JUMPED OUT OF THE 3RD FLOOR WINDOW WHEN HE LOOKED AWAY. I WAS SO SCARED! ANYWAY, I REALIZED AGAIN THAT THE WORLD IS TOO DANGEROUS FOR A PRETTY GIRL LIKE ME.
*SHE'S A YOUNG GIRL WHO STOOD UP FOR KOREA'S INDEPENDENCE ON MARCH 1, 1919.
NON-SENSE.

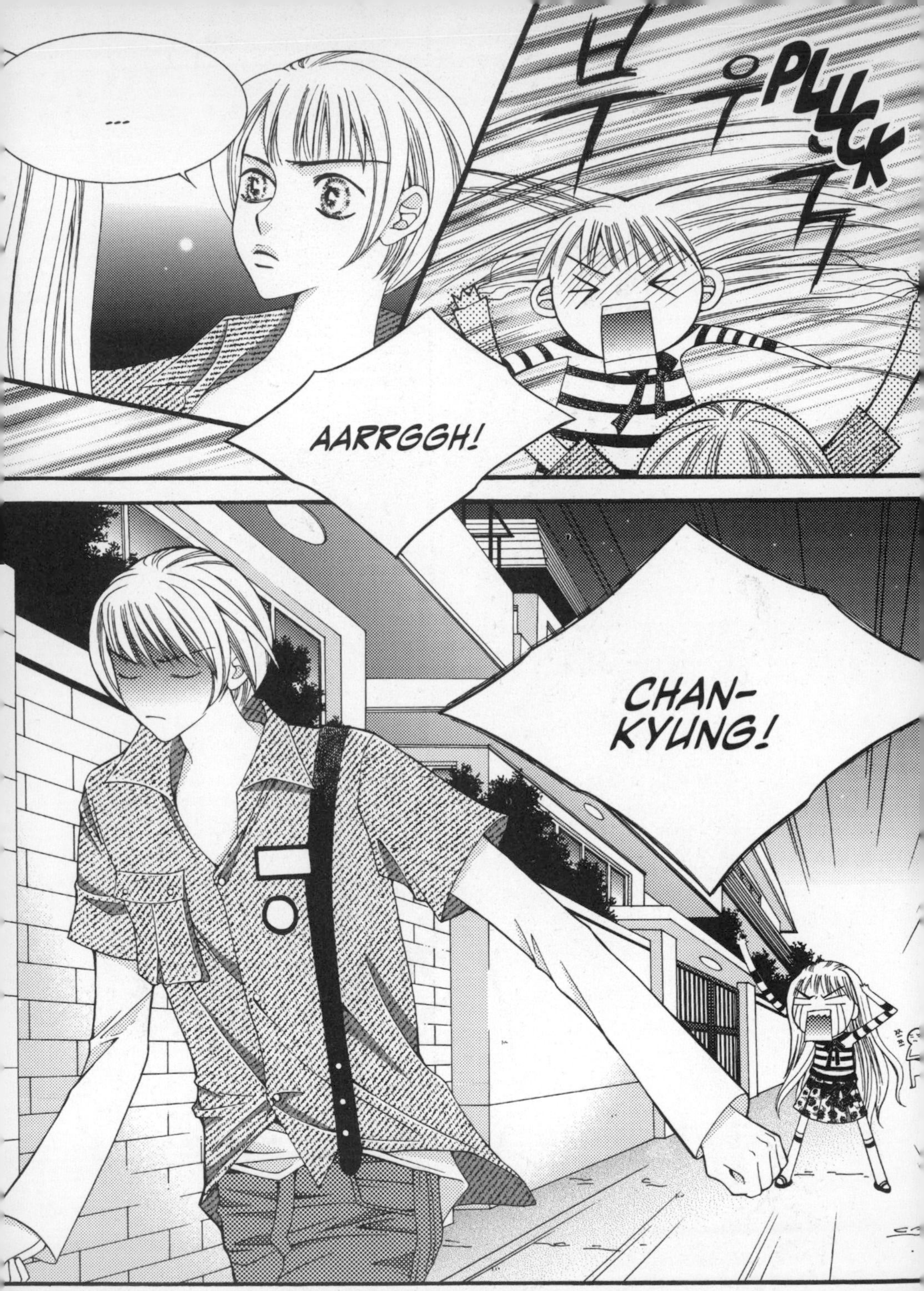
...
PLUCK
AARRGGH!
CHAN-KYUNG!

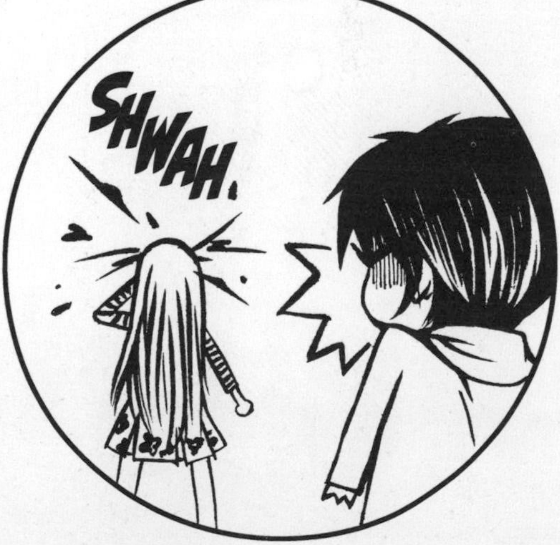
SHWAH.

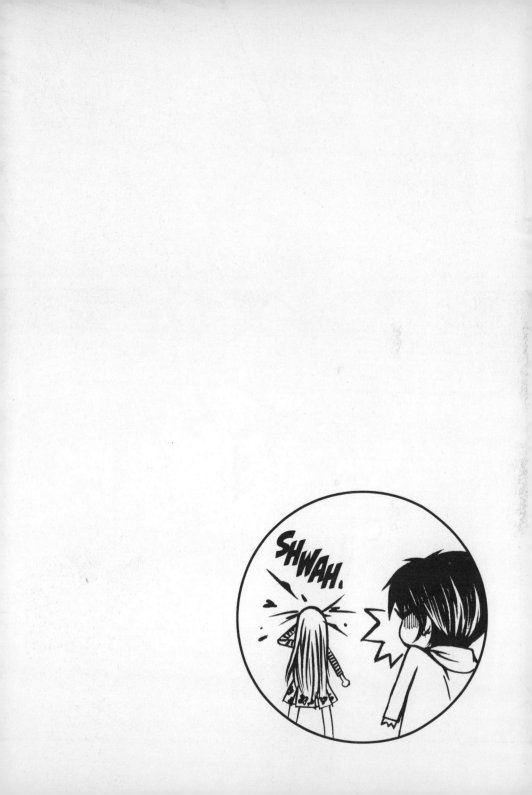

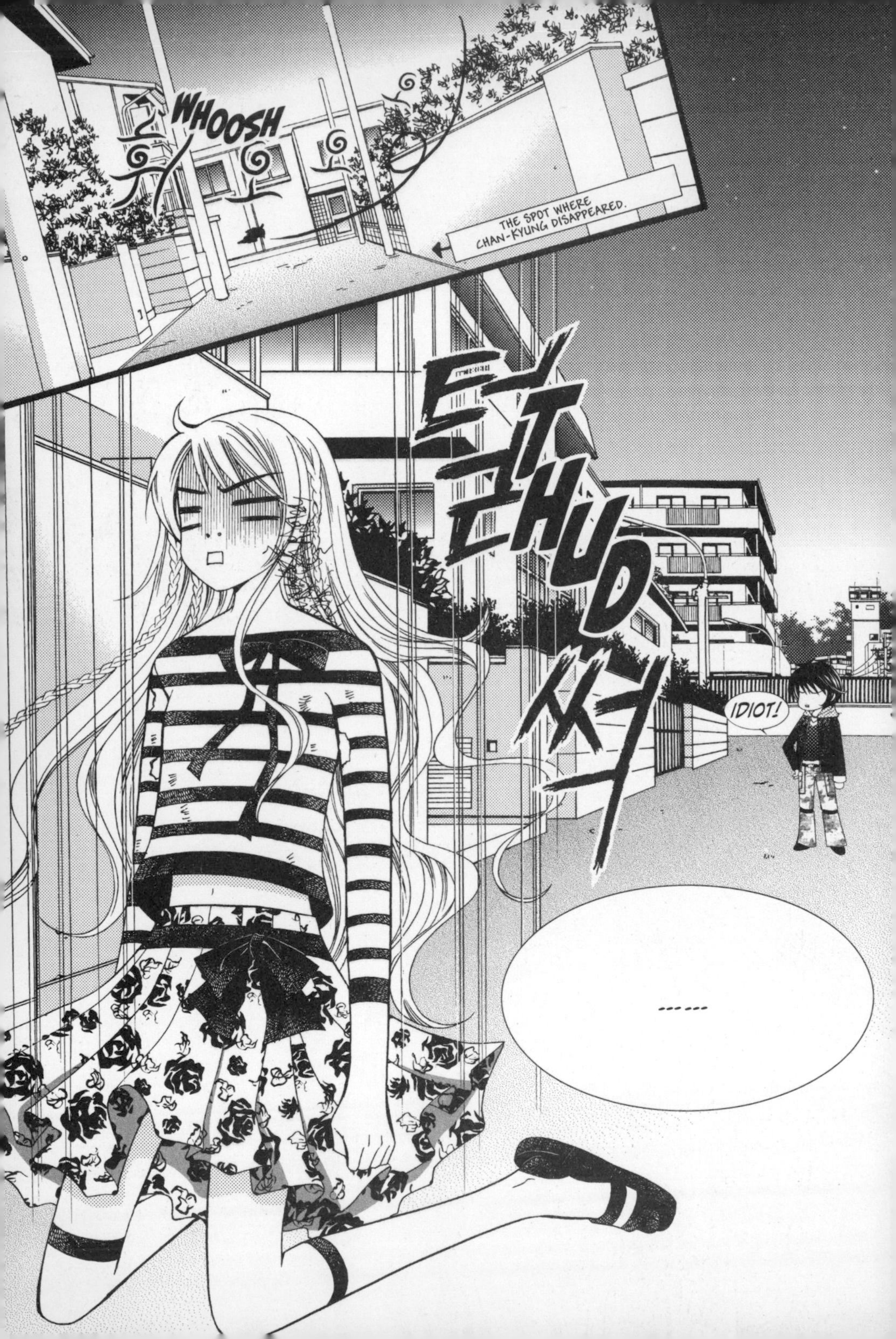
WHOOSH
THE SPOT WHERE CHAN-KYUNG DISAPPEARED.
THUD
IDIOT!
......

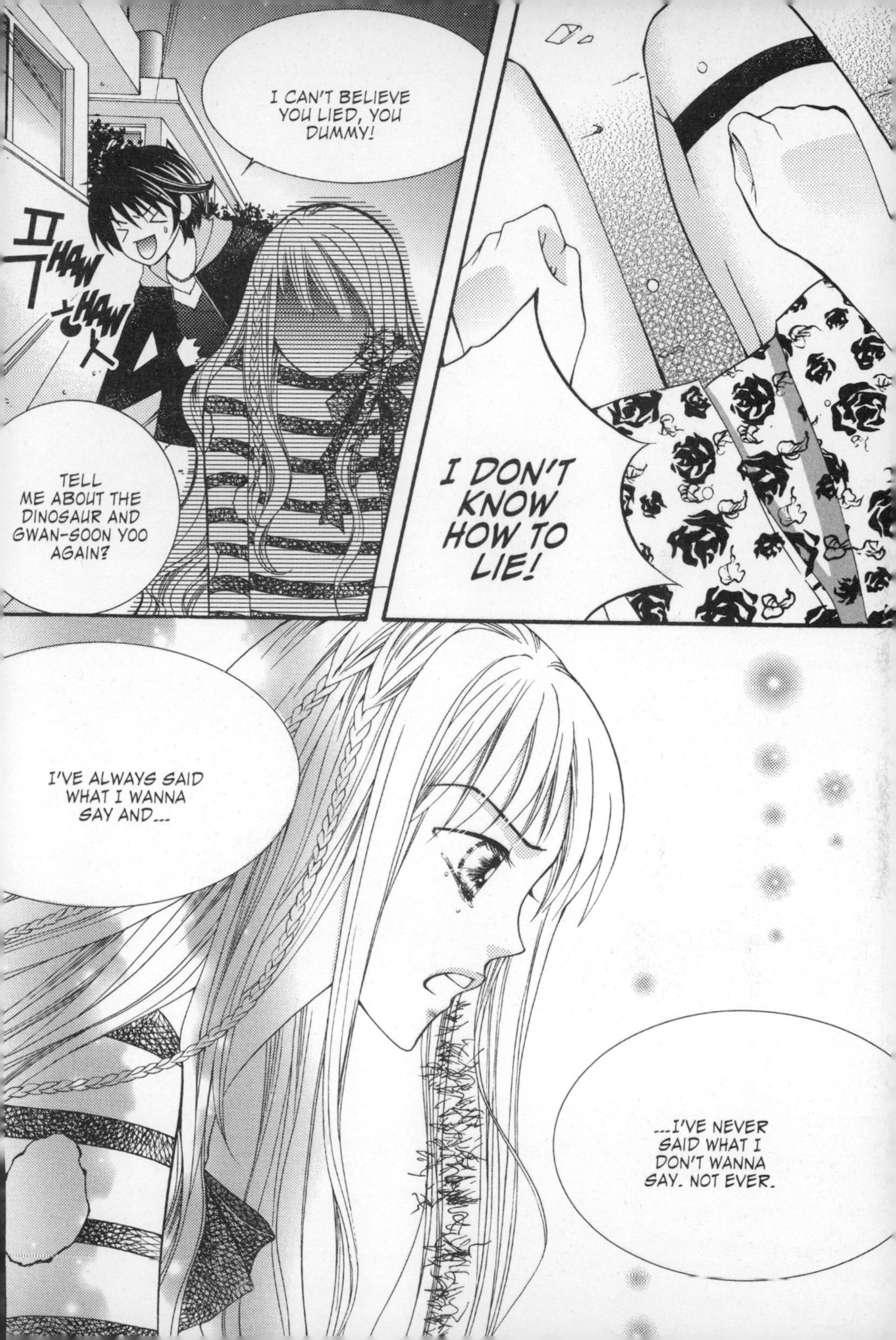
I CAN'T BELIEVE YOU LIED, YOU DUMMY!
HAW HAW
TELL ME ABOUT THE DINOSAUR AND GWAN-SOON YOO AGAIN?
I DON'T KNOW HOW TO LIE!
I'VE ALWAYS SAID WHAT I WANNA SAY AND...
...I'VE NEVER SAID WHAT I DON'T WANNA SAY. NOT EVER.

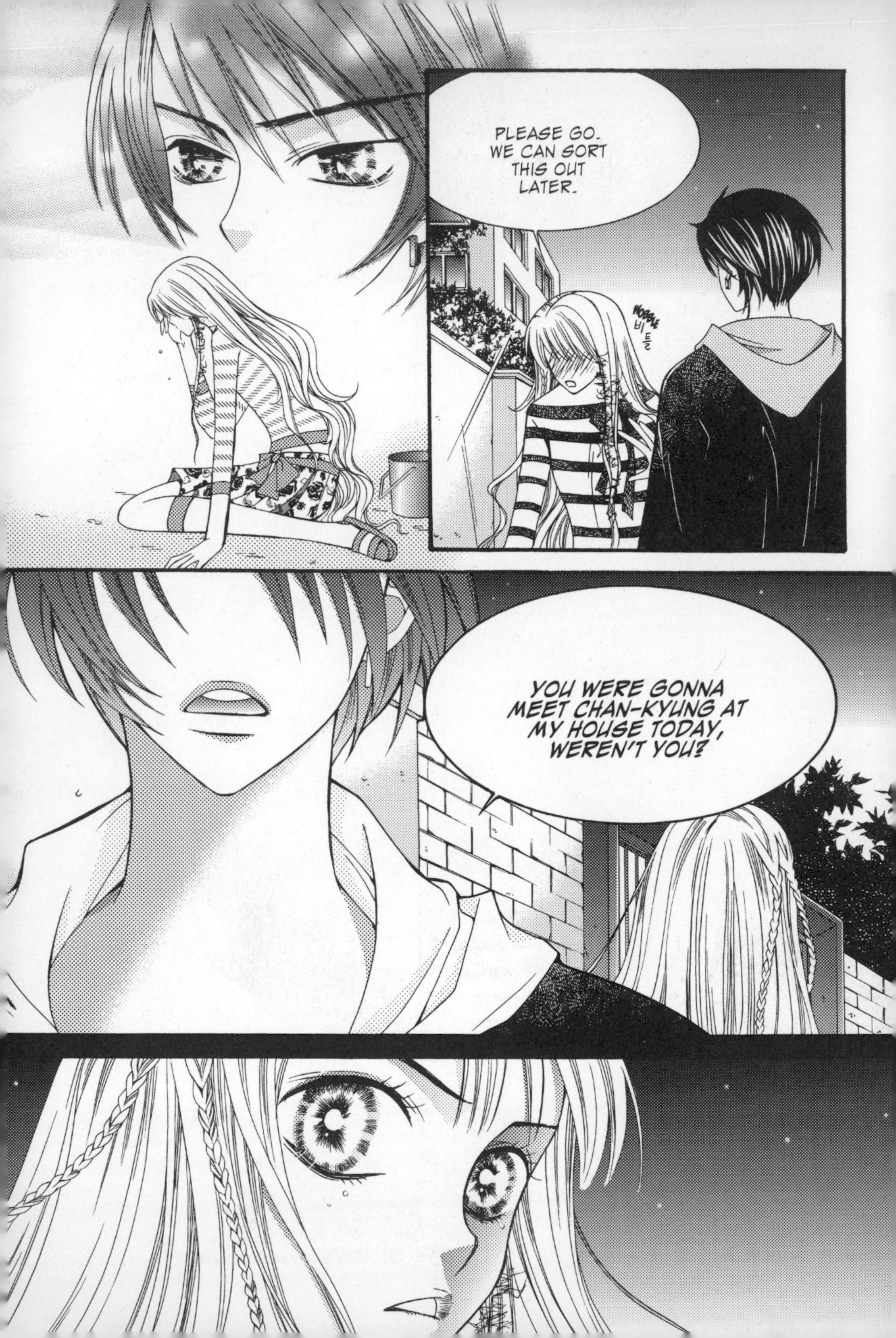
PLEASE GO. WE CAN SORT THIS OUT LATER.
WOBBLE
YOU WERE GONNA MEET CHAN-KYUNG AT MY HOUSE TODAY, WEREN'T YOU?

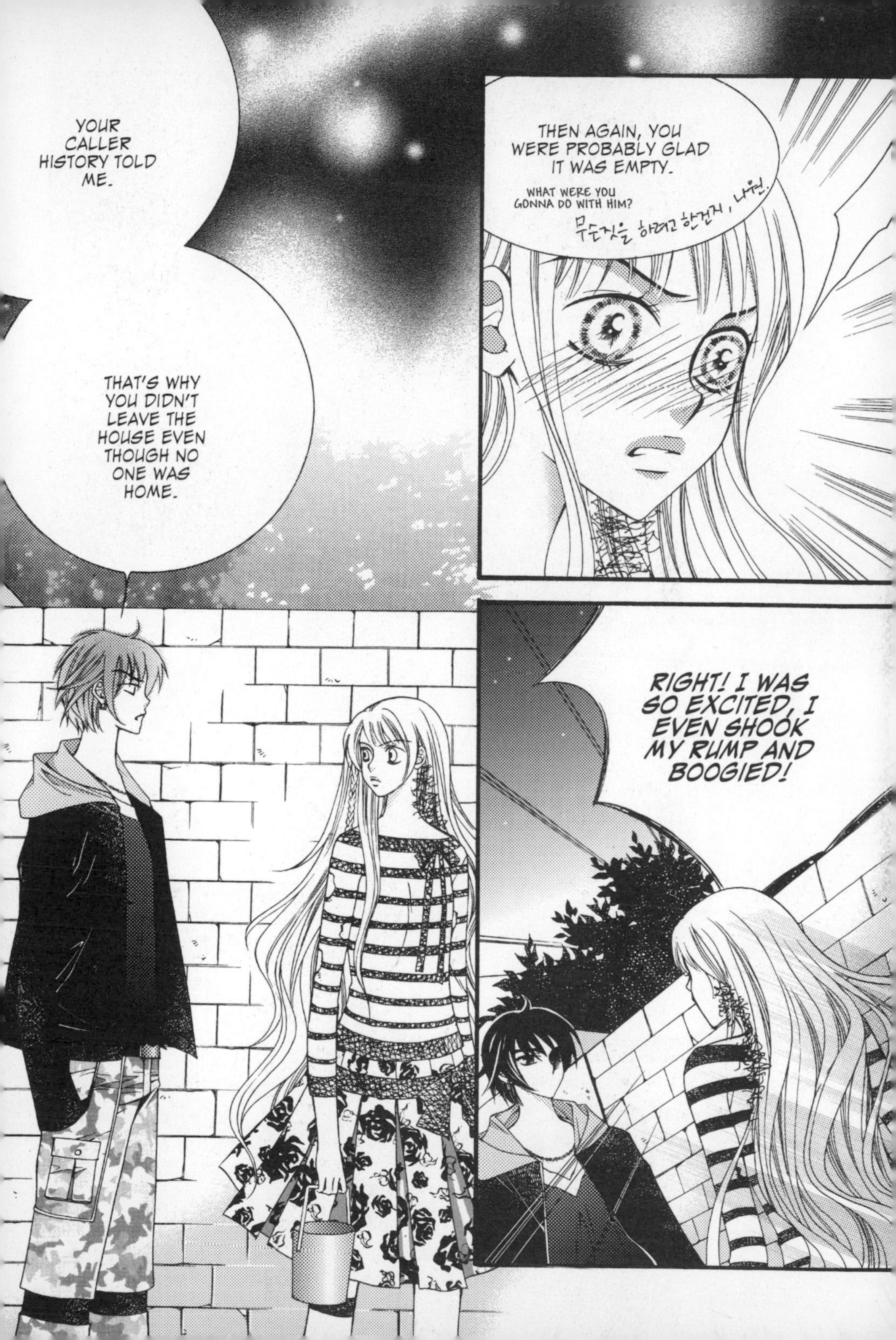
YOUR CALLER HISTORY TOLD ME.
THAT'S WHY YOU DIDN'T LEAVE THE HOUSE EVEN THOUGH NO ONE WAS HOME.
THEN AGAIN, YOU WERE PROBABLY GLAD IT WAS EMPTY.
WHAT WERE YOU GONNA DO WITH HIM?
무슨짓을 하려고 한건지, 나원.
RIGHT! I WAS SO EXCITED, I EVEN SHOOK MY RUMP AND BOOGIED!

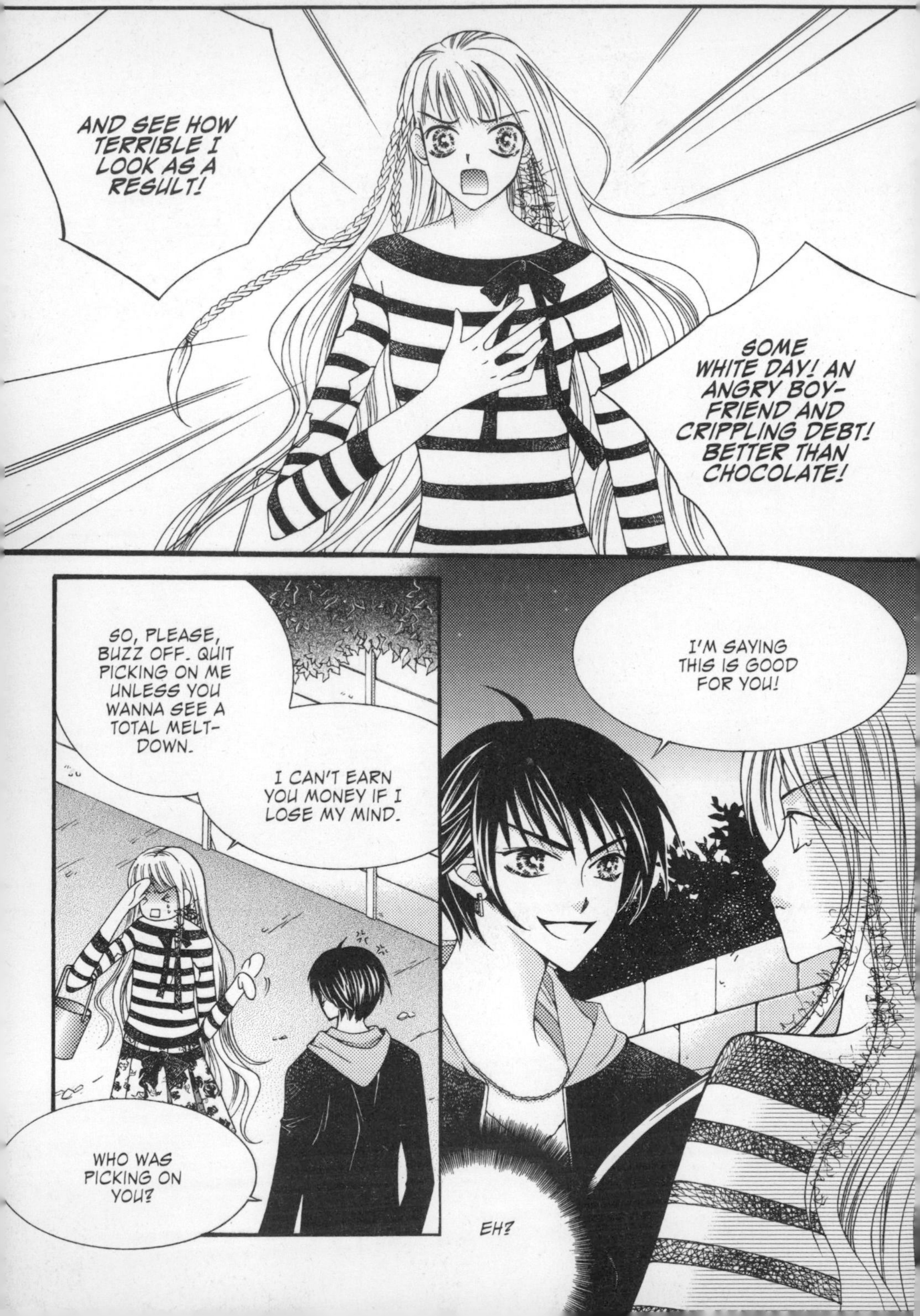
AND SEE HOW TERRIBLE I LOOK AS A RESULT!
SOME WHITE DAY! AN ANGRY BOY-FRIEND AND CRIPPLING DEBT! BETTER THAN CHOCOLATE!
SO, PLEASE, BUZZ OFF. QUIT PICKING ON ME UNLESS YOU WANNA SEE A TOTAL MELT-DOWN.
I CAN'T EARN YOU MONEY IF I LOSE MY MIND.
WHO WAS PICKING ON YOU?
I'M SAYING THIS IS GOOD FOR YOU!
EH?

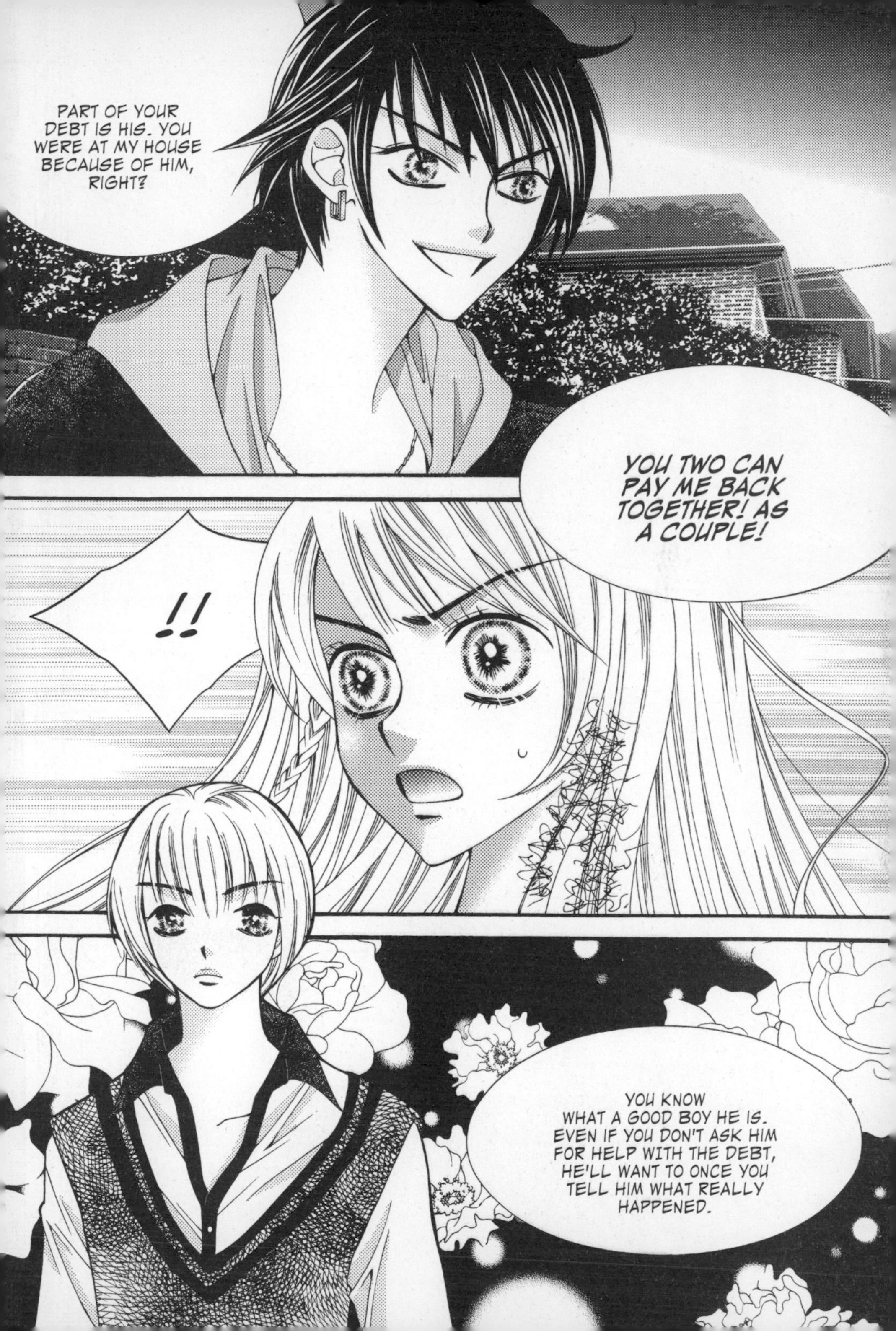
PART OF YOUR DEBT IS HIS. YOU WERE AT MY HOUSE BECAUSE OF HIM, RIGHT?
!!
YOU TWO CAN PAY ME BACK TOGETHER! AS A COUPLE!
YOU KNOW WHAT A GOOD BOY HE IS. EVEN IF YOU DON'T ASK HIM FOR HELP WITH THE DEBT, HE'LL WANT TO ONCE YOU TELL HIM WHAT REALLY HAPPENED.

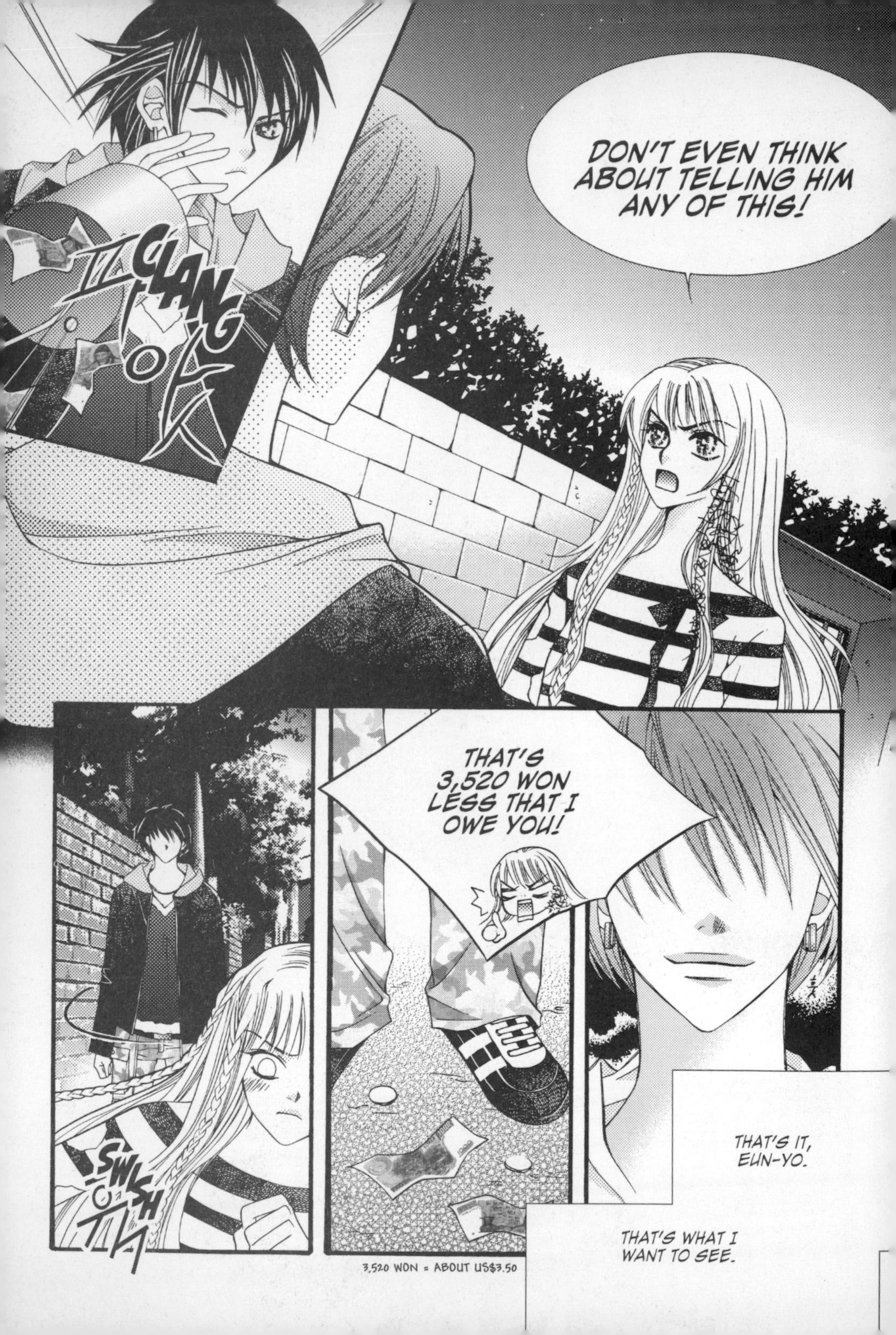
CLANG
DON'T EVEN THINK ABOUT TELLING HIM ANY OF THIS!
SWISH
THAT'S 3,520 WON LESS THAT I OWE YOU!
THAT'S IT, EUN-YO.
THAT'S WHAT I WANT TO SEE.
3,520 WON = ABOUT US$3.50

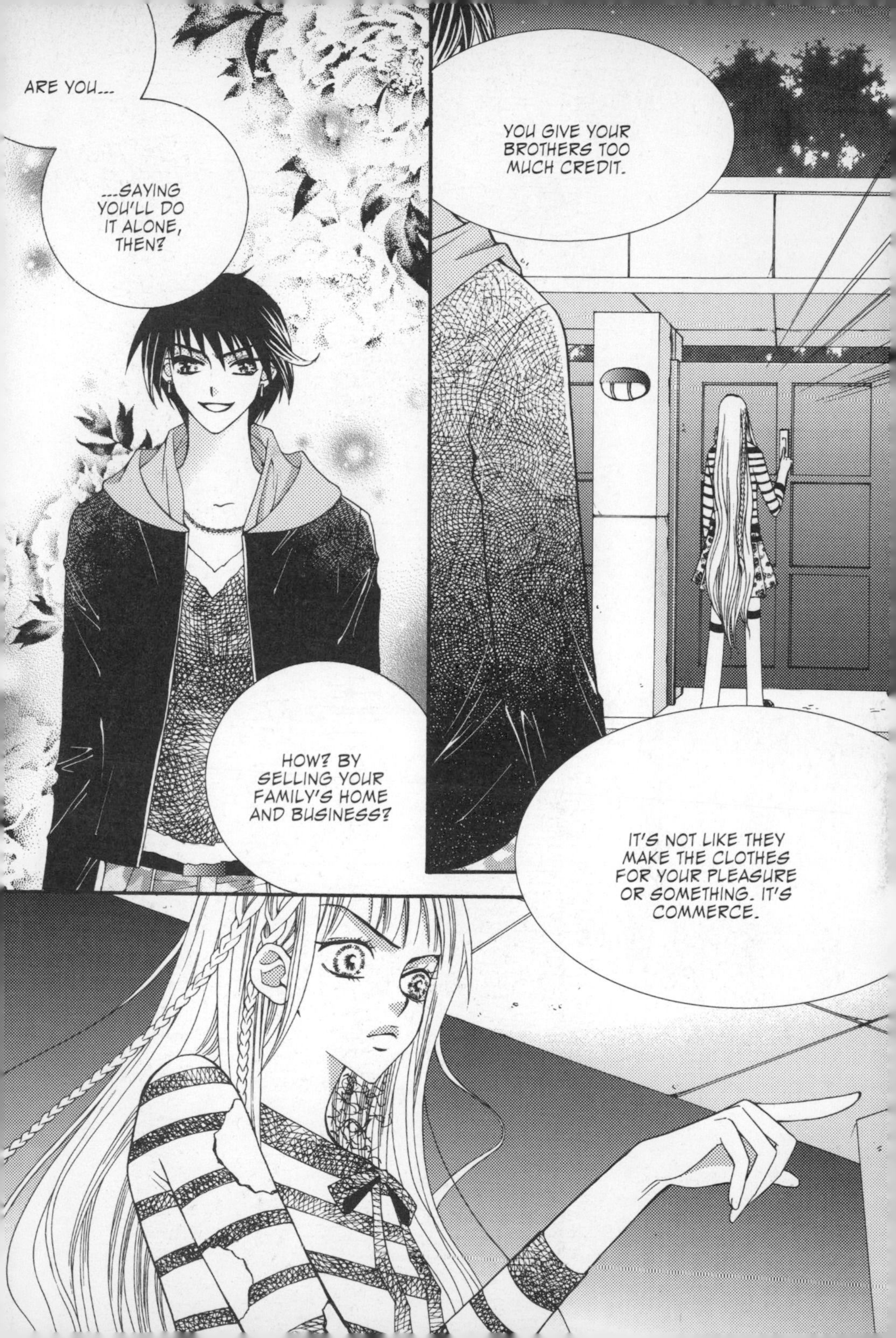
ARE YOU...
...SAYING YOU'LL DO IT ALONE, THEN?
HOW? BY SELLING YOUR FAMILY'S HOME AND BUSINESS?
YOU GIVE YOUR BROTHERS TOO MUCH CREDIT.
IT'S NOT LIKE THEY MAKE THE CLOTHES FOR YOUR PLEASURE OR SOMETHING. IT'S COMMERCE.

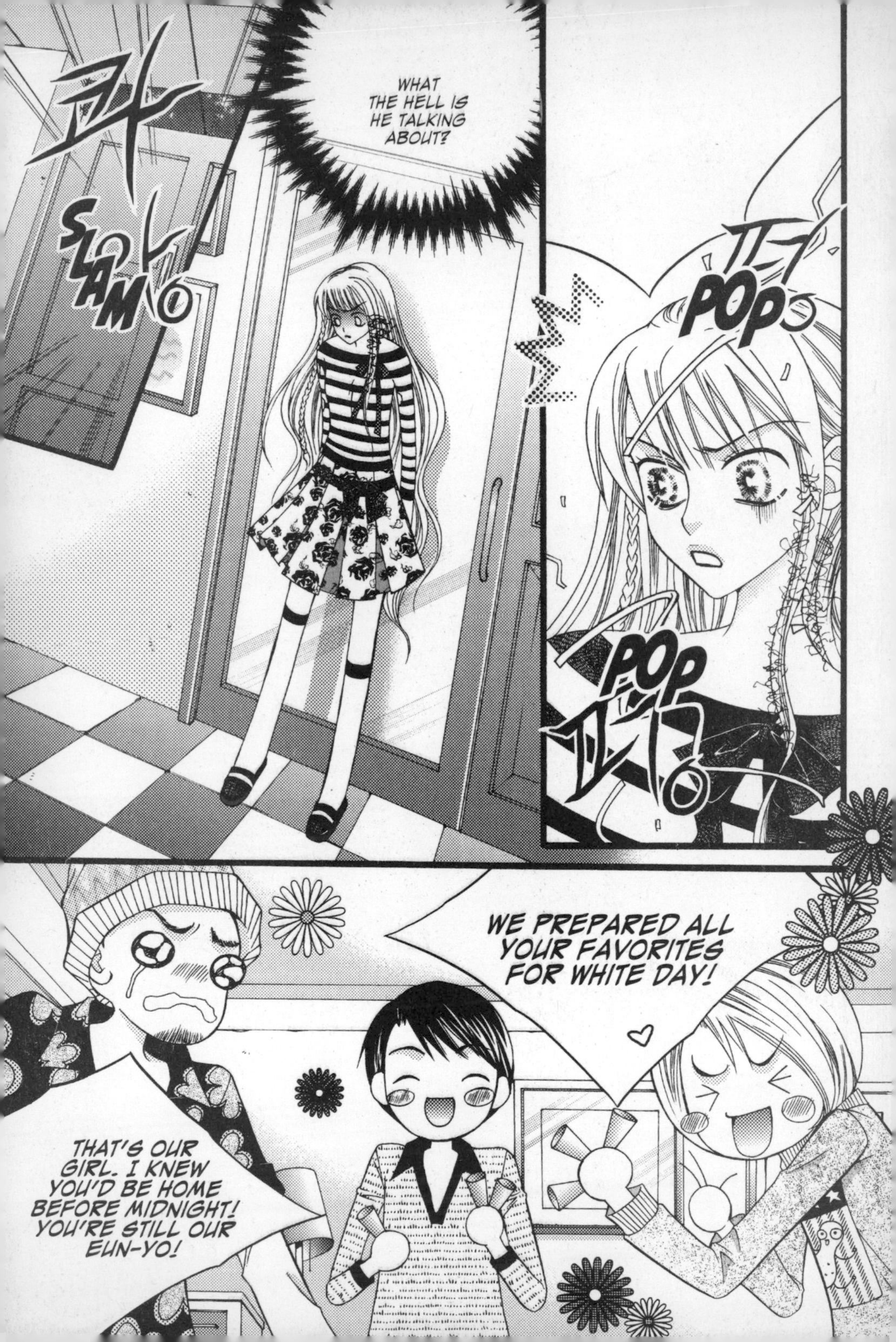
SLAM
WHAT THE HELL IS HE TALKING ABOUT?
POP
POP
WE PREPARED ALL YOUR FAVORITES FOR WHITE DAY!
THAT'S OUR GIRL. I KNEW YOU'D BE HOME BEFORE MIDNIGHT! YOU'RE STILL OUR EUN-YO!

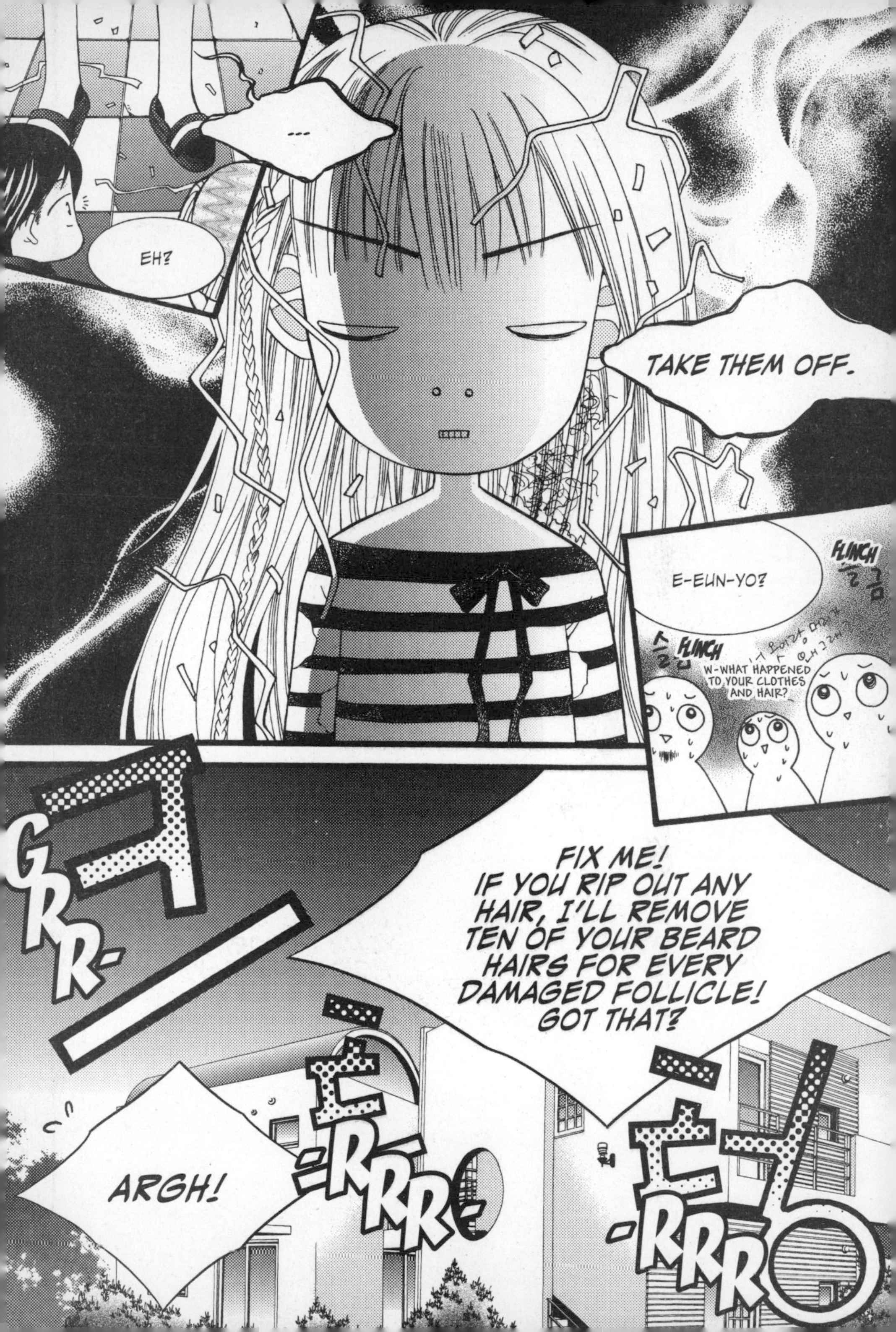
...
EH?
TAKE THEM OFF.
E-EUN-YO?
FLINCH
FLINCH
W-WHAT HAPPENED TO YOUR CLOTHES AND HAIR?
GRR-
ARGH!
FIX ME! IF YOU RIP OUT ANY HAIR, I'LL REMOVE TEN OF YOUR BEARD HAIRS FOR EVERY DAMAGED FOLLICLE! GOT THAT?
-RRRR-
-RRRO

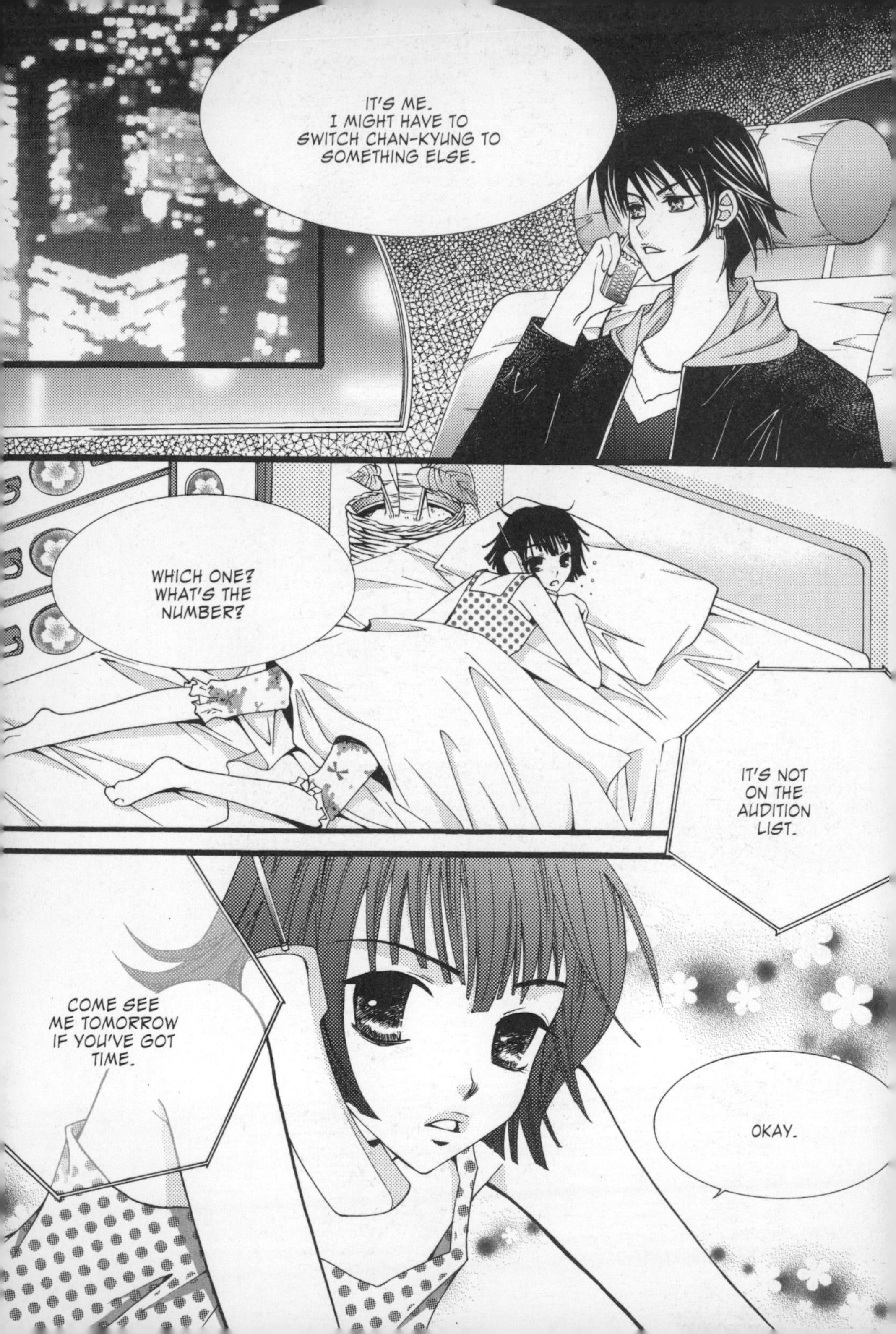
IT'S ME. I MIGHT HAVE TO SWITCH CHAN-KYUNG TO SOMETHING ELSE.
WHICH ONE? WHAT'S THE NUMBER?
IT'S NOT ON THE AUDITION LIST.
COME SEE ME TOMORROW IF YOU'VE GOT TIME.
OKAY.

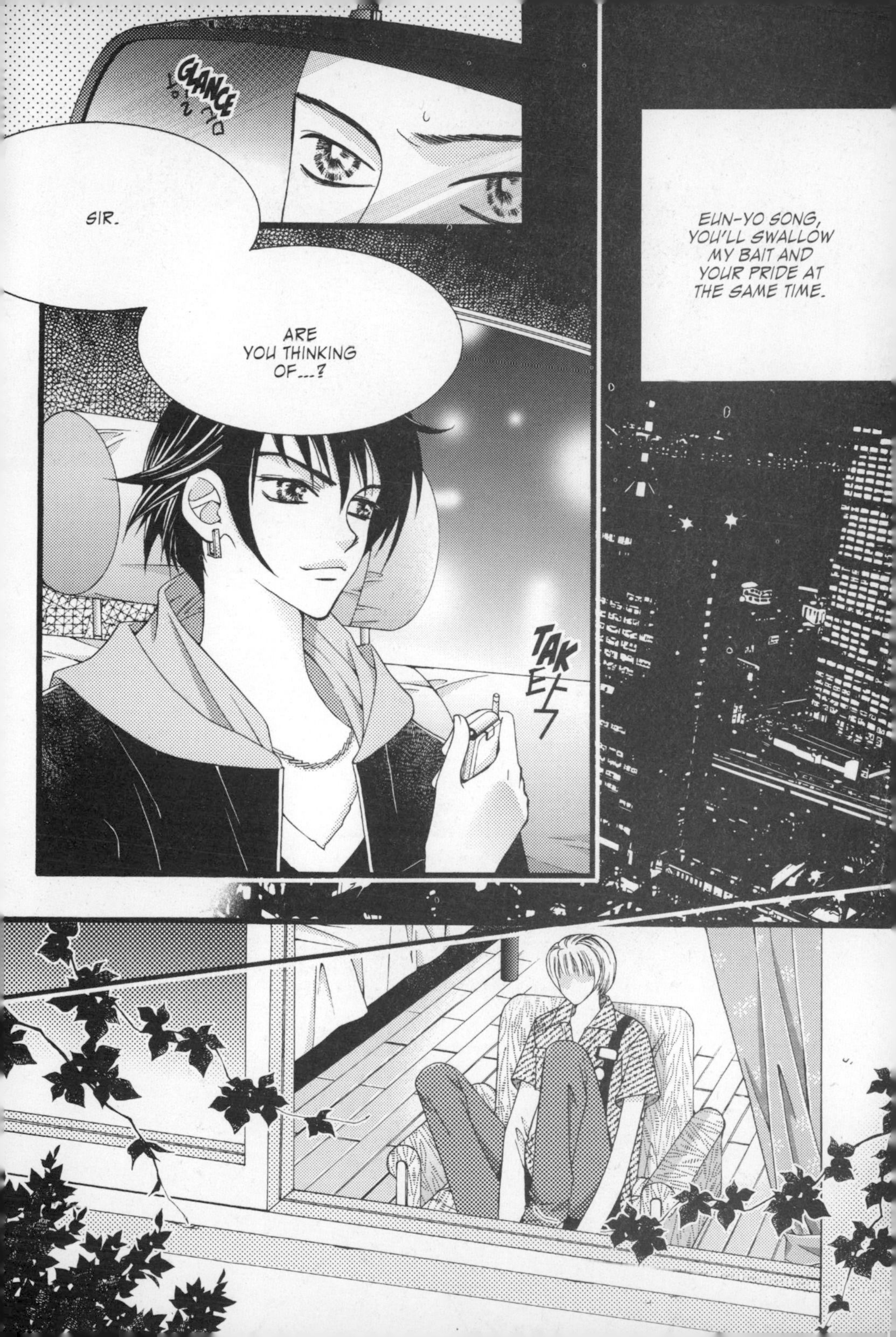
GLANCE
SIR.
ARE YOU THINKING OF...?
EUN-YO SONG, YOU'LL SWALLOW MY BAIT AND YOUR PRIDE AT THE SAME TIME.
TAK

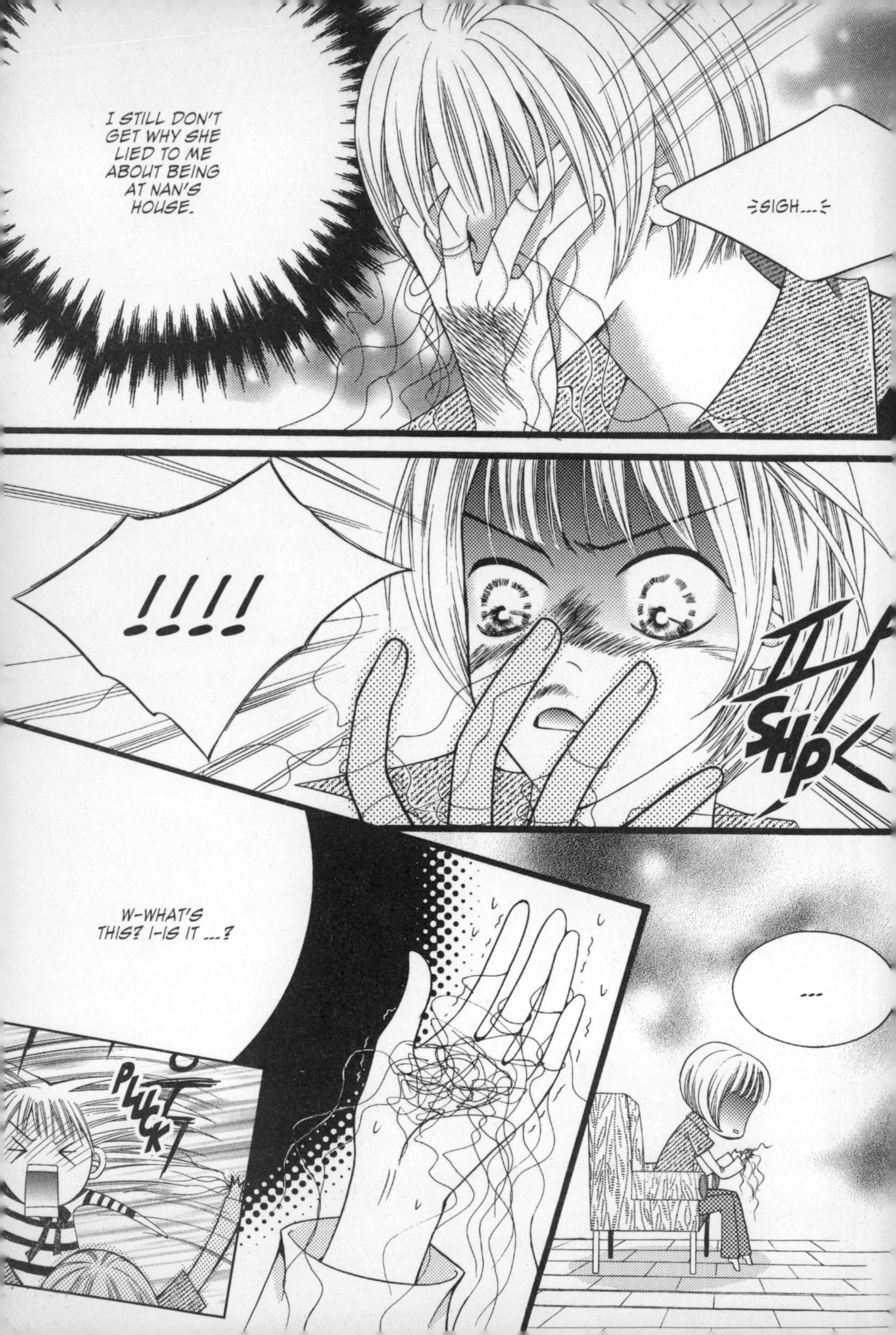
I STILL DON'T GET WHY SHE LIED TO ME ABOUT BEING AT NAN'S HOUSE.
≡SIGH...≡
!!!!
SHP
W-WHAT'S THIS? I-IS IT ...?
PLUCK
...

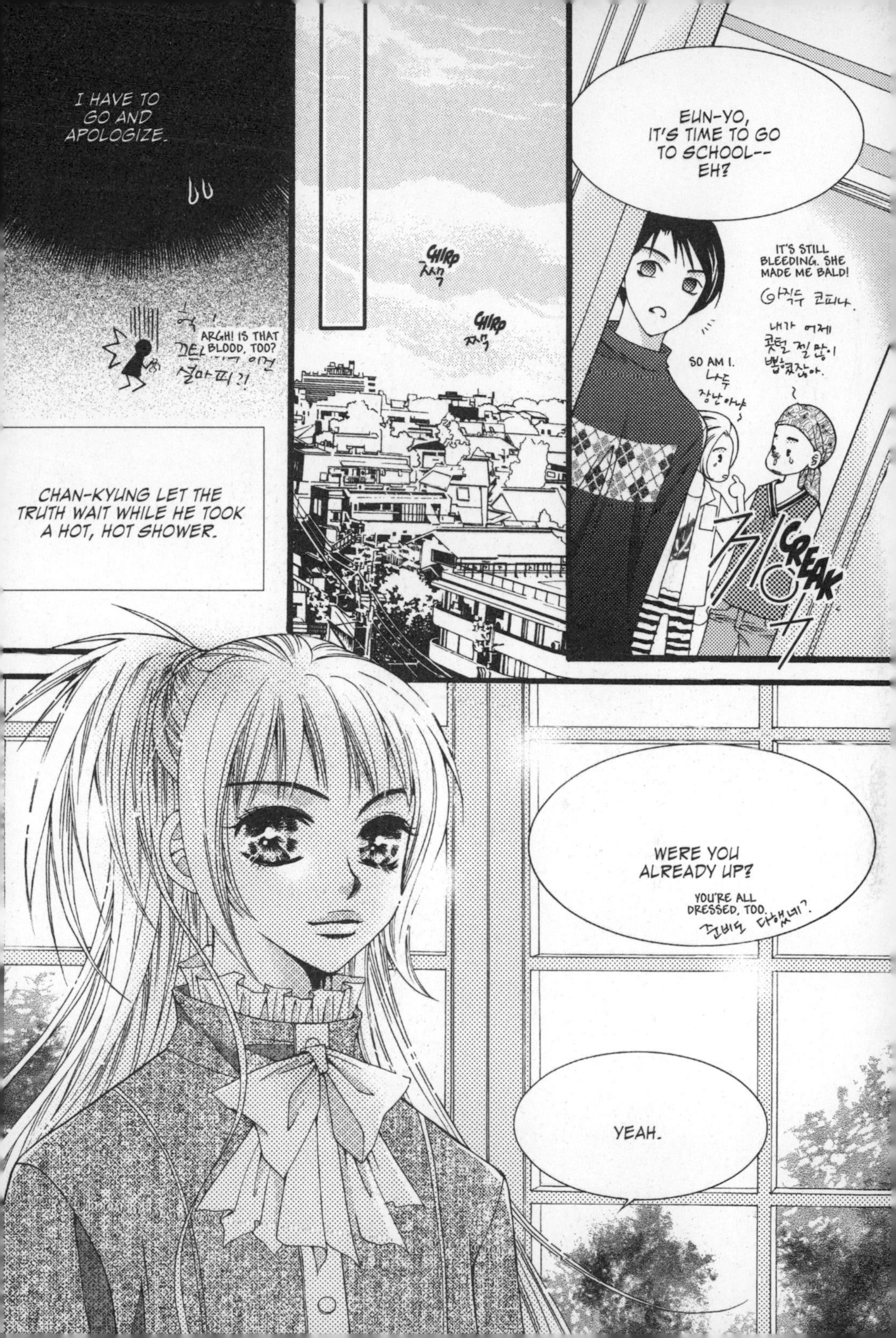
I HAVE TO GO AND APOLOGIZE.
ARGH! IS THAT BLOOD, TOO?
CHAN-KYUNG LET THE TRUTH WAIT WHILE HE TOOK A HOT, HOT SHOWER.
CHIRP
CHIRP
EUN-YO, IT'S TIME TO GO TO SCHOOL-- EH?
IT'S STILL BLEEDING. SHE MADE ME BALD!
아직두 코피나.
SO AM I.
나두 장난 아냐
CREAK
WERE YOU ALREADY UP?
YOU'RE ALL DRESSED, TOO.
준비도 다했네?
YEAH.

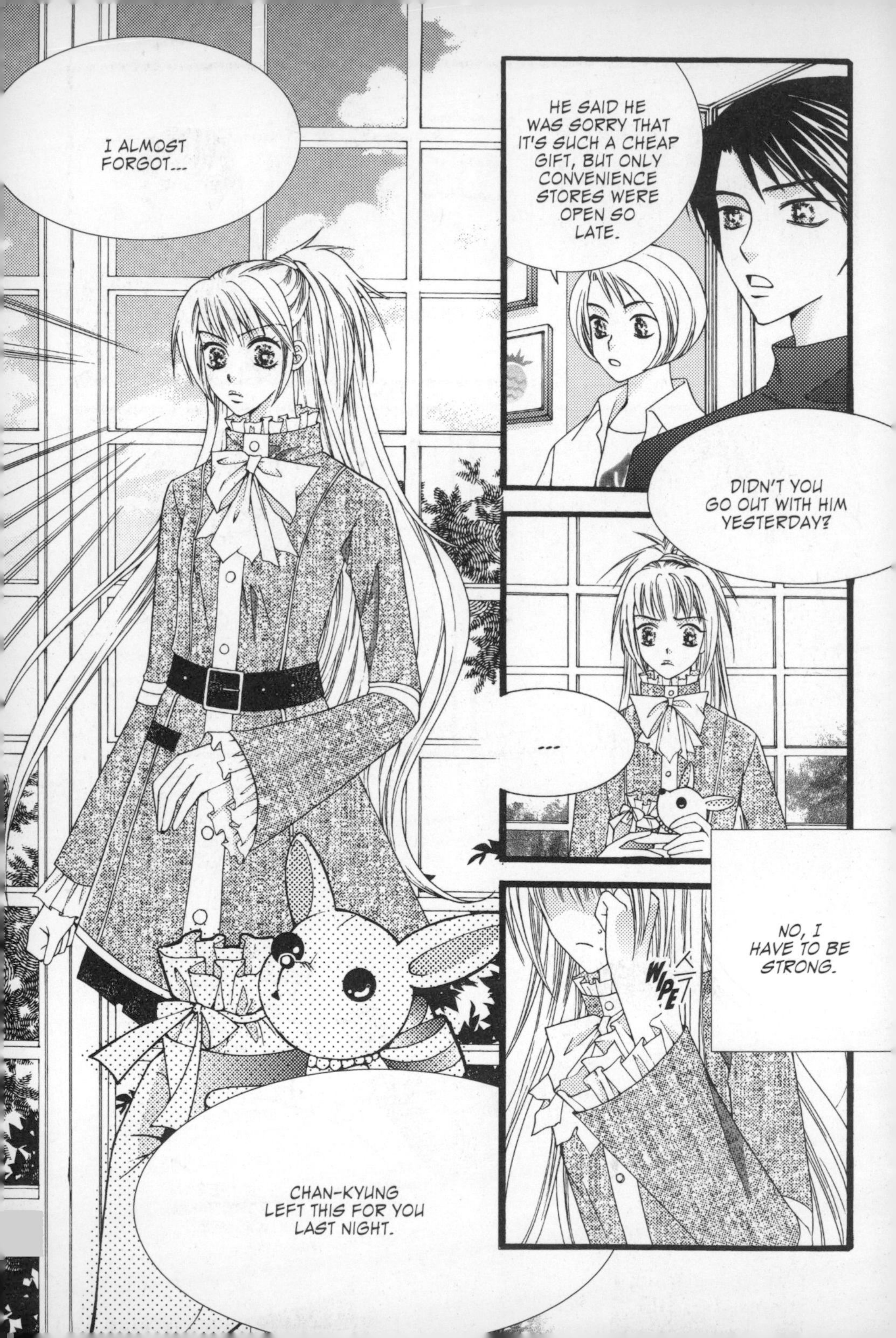
I ALMOST FORGOT...
CHAN-KYUNG LEFT THIS FOR YOU LAST NIGHT.
HE SAID HE WAS SORRY THAT IT'S SUCH A CHEAP GIFT, BUT ONLY CONVENIENCE STORES WERE OPEN SO LATE.
DIDN'T YOU GO OUT WITH HIM YESTERDAY?
...
WIPE
NO, I HAVE TO BE STRONG.

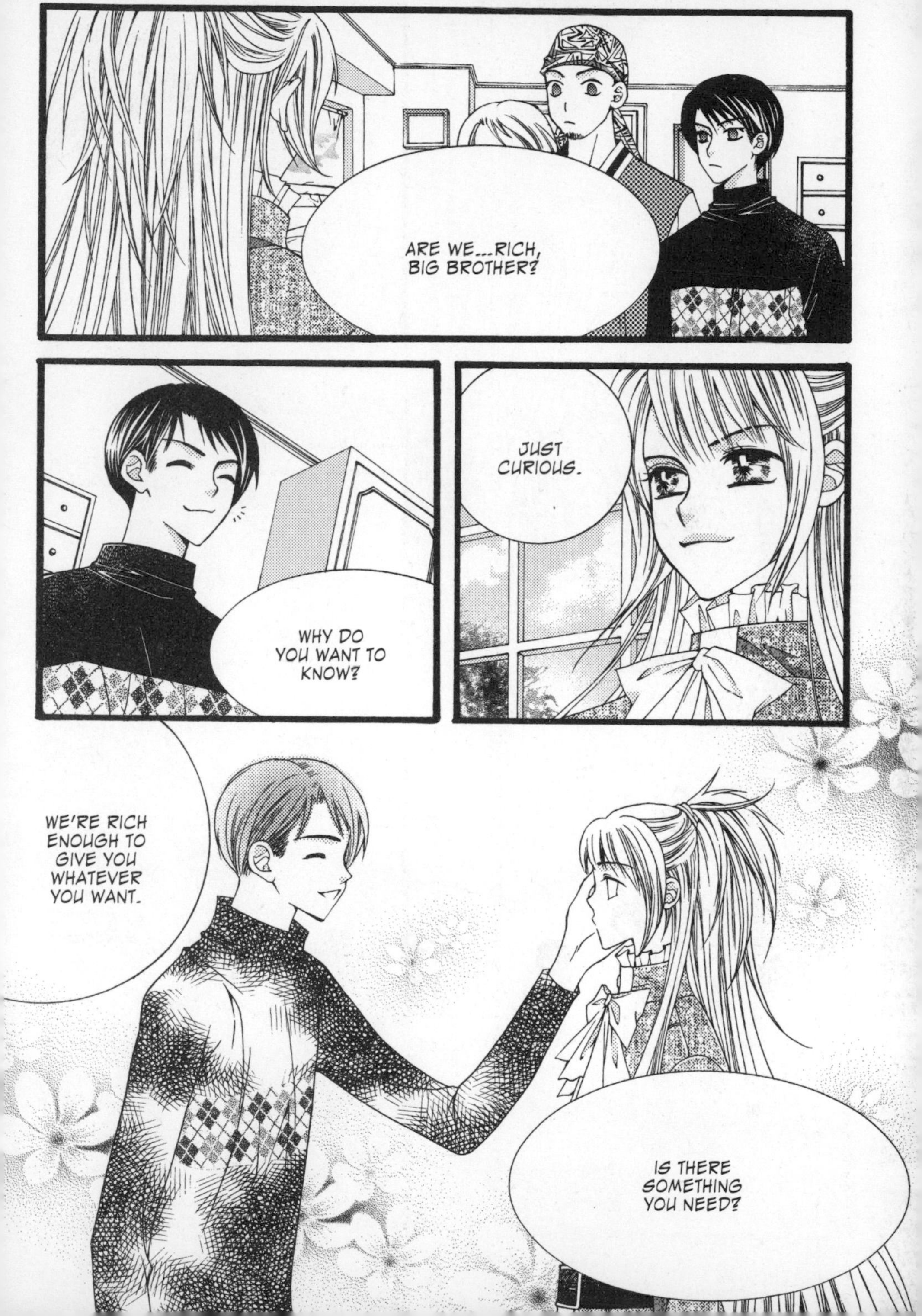
ARE WE...RICH, BIG BROTHER?
WHY DO YOU WANT TO KNOW?
JUST CURIOUS.
WE'RE RICH ENOUGH TO GIVE YOU WHATEVER YOU WANT.
IS THERE SOMETHING YOU NEED?

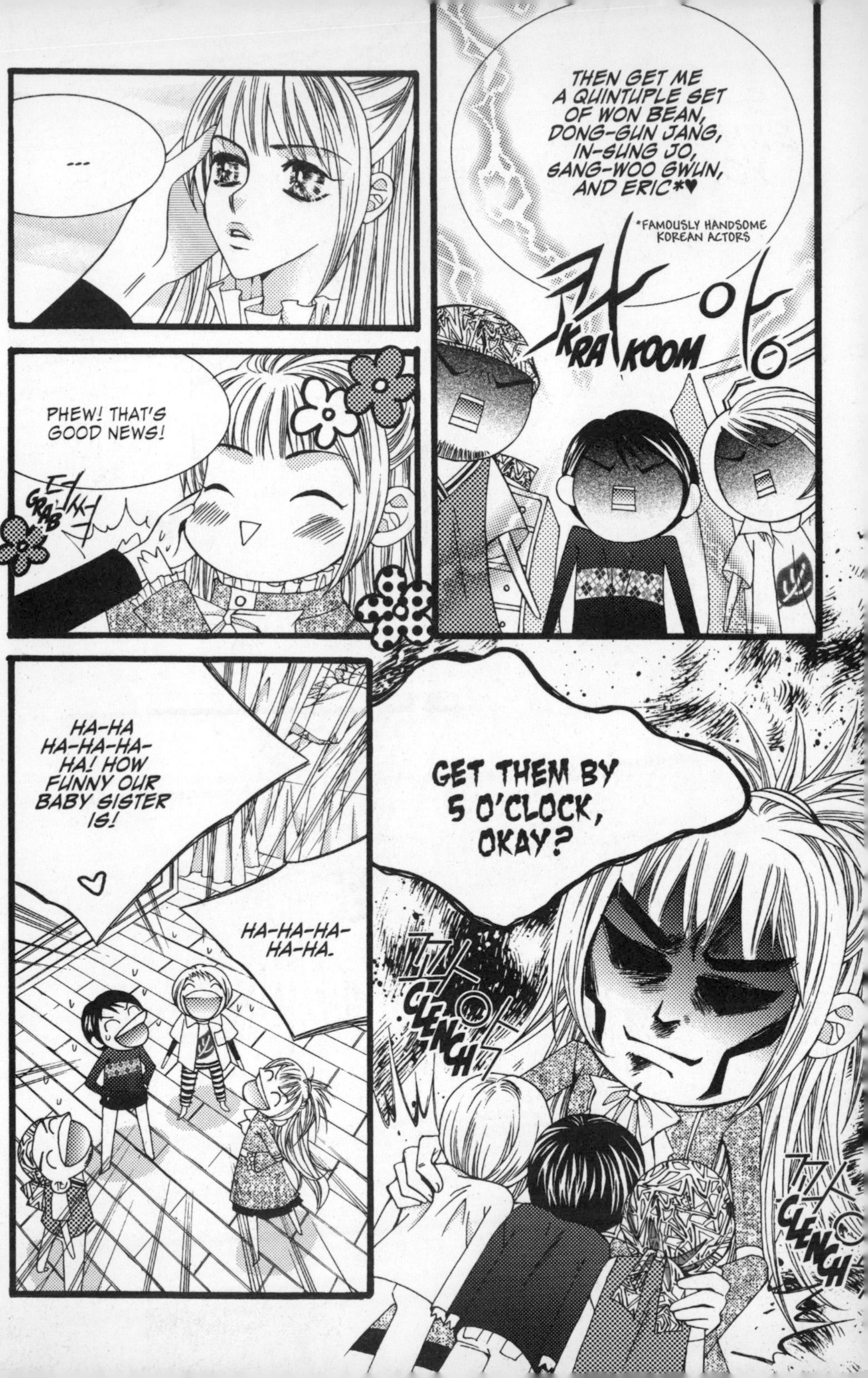
...
PHEW! THAT'S GOOD NEWS!
GRAB
THEN GET ME A QUINTUPLE SET OF WON BEAN, DONG-GUN JANG, IN-SUNG JO, SANG-WOO GWUN, AND ERIC*♥
*FAMOUSLY HANDSOME KOREAN ACTORS
KRA KOOM
HA-HA HA-HA-HA-HA! HOW FUNNY OUR BABY SISTER IS!
♡
HA-HA-HA-HA-HA.
GET THEM BY 5 O'CLOCK, OKAY?
CLENCH
CLENCH

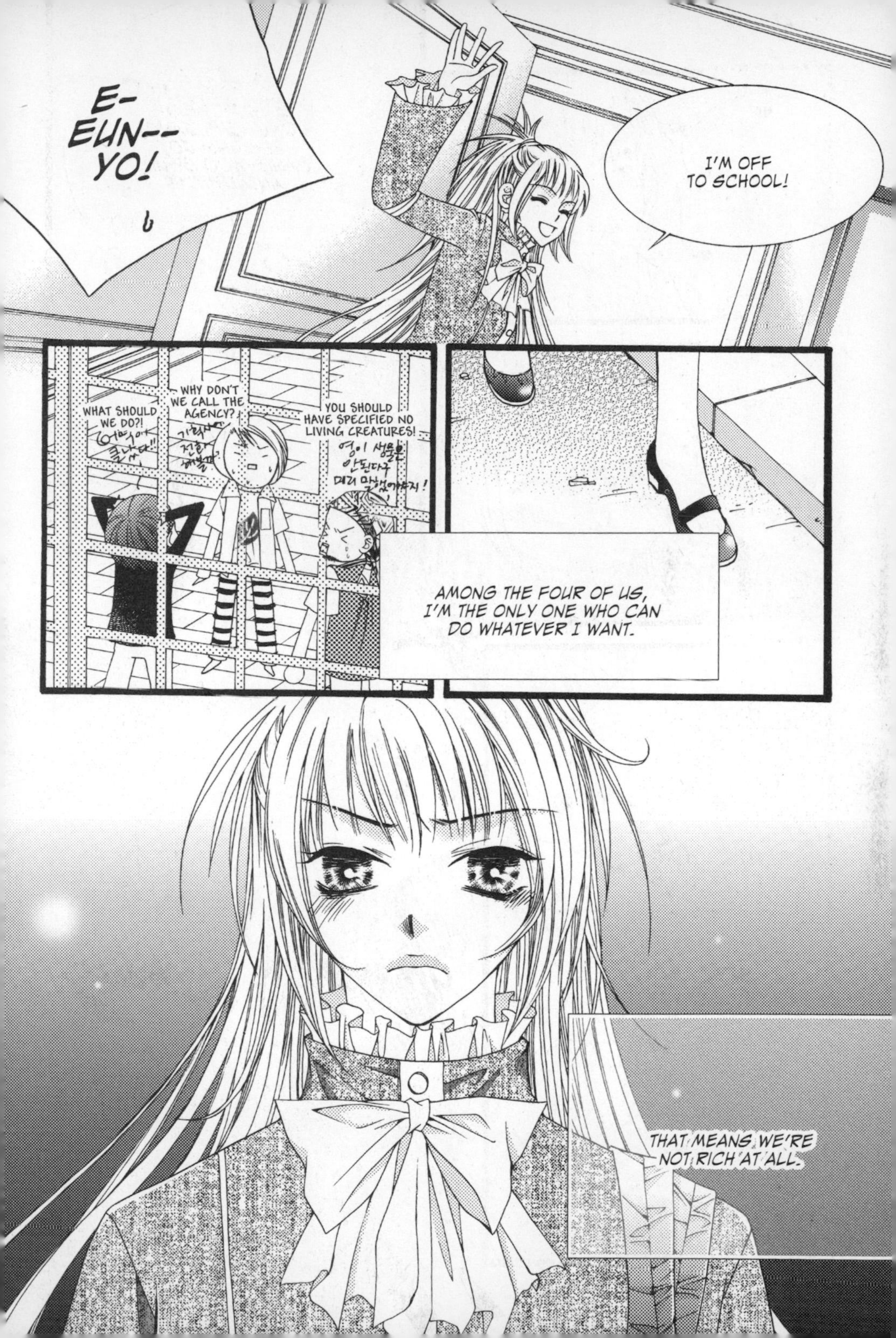
E-EUN--YO!
I'M OFF TO SCHOOL!
WHAT SHOULD WE DO?!
WHY DON'T WE CALL THE AGENCY?
YOU SHOULD HAVE SPECIFIED NO LIVING CREATURES!
AMONG THE FOUR OF US, I'M THE ONLY ONE WHO CAN DO WHATEVER I WANT.
THAT MEANS WE'RE NOT RICH AT ALL.

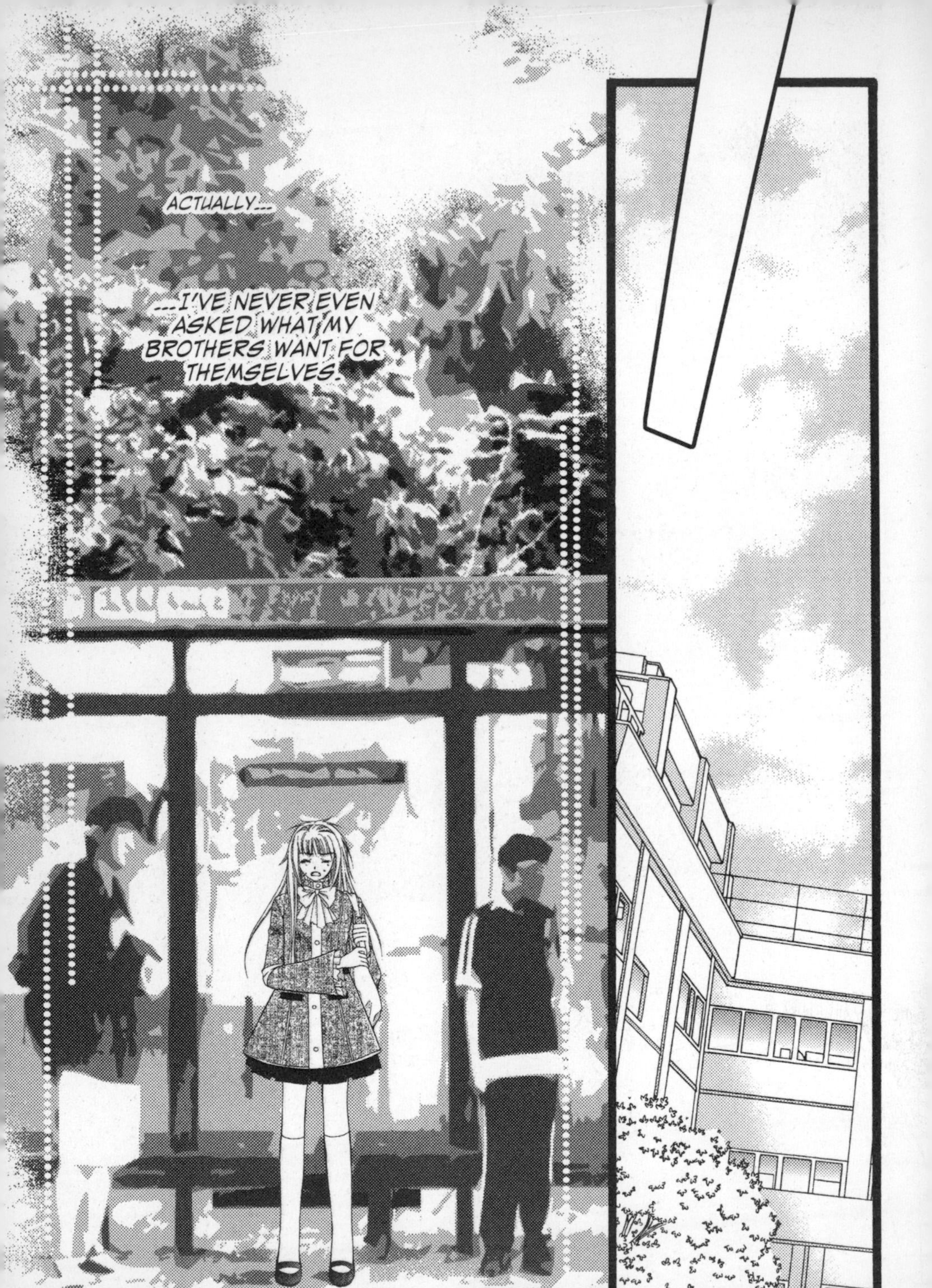
ACTUALLY...
...I'VE NEVER EVEN ASKED WHAT MY BROTHERS WANT FOR THEMSELVES.

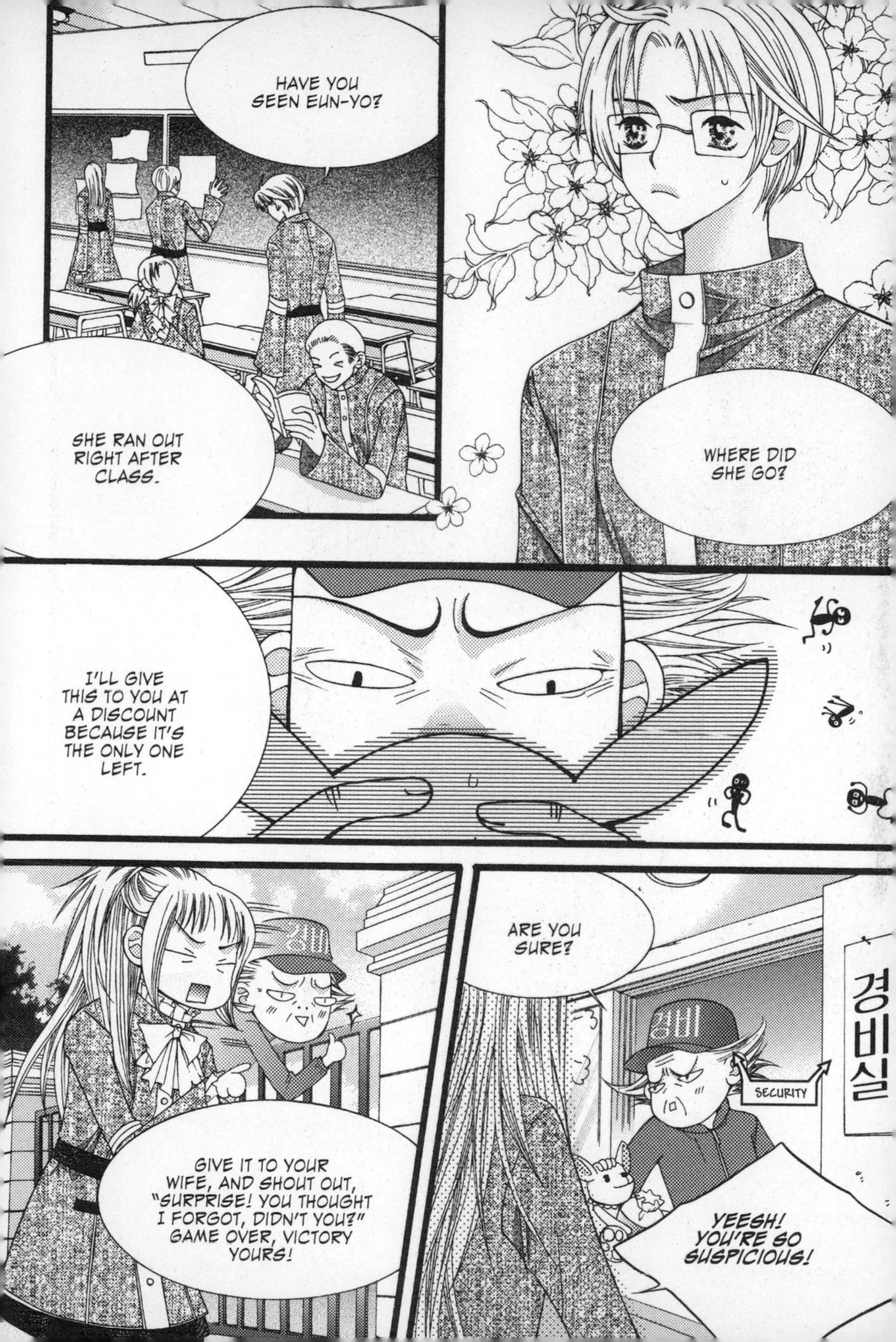
HAVE YOU SEEN EUN-YO?
SHE RAN OUT RIGHT AFTER CLASS.
WHERE DID SHE GO?
I'LL GIVE THIS TO YOU AT A DISCOUNT BECAUSE IT'S THE ONLY ONE LEFT.
경비
GIVE IT TO YOUR WIFE, AND SHOUT OUT, "SURPRISE! YOU THOUGHT I FORGOT, DIDN'T YOU?" GAME OVER, VICTORY YOURS!
ARE YOU SURE?
경비
경비실
SECURITY
YEESH! YOU'RE SO SUSPICIOUS!

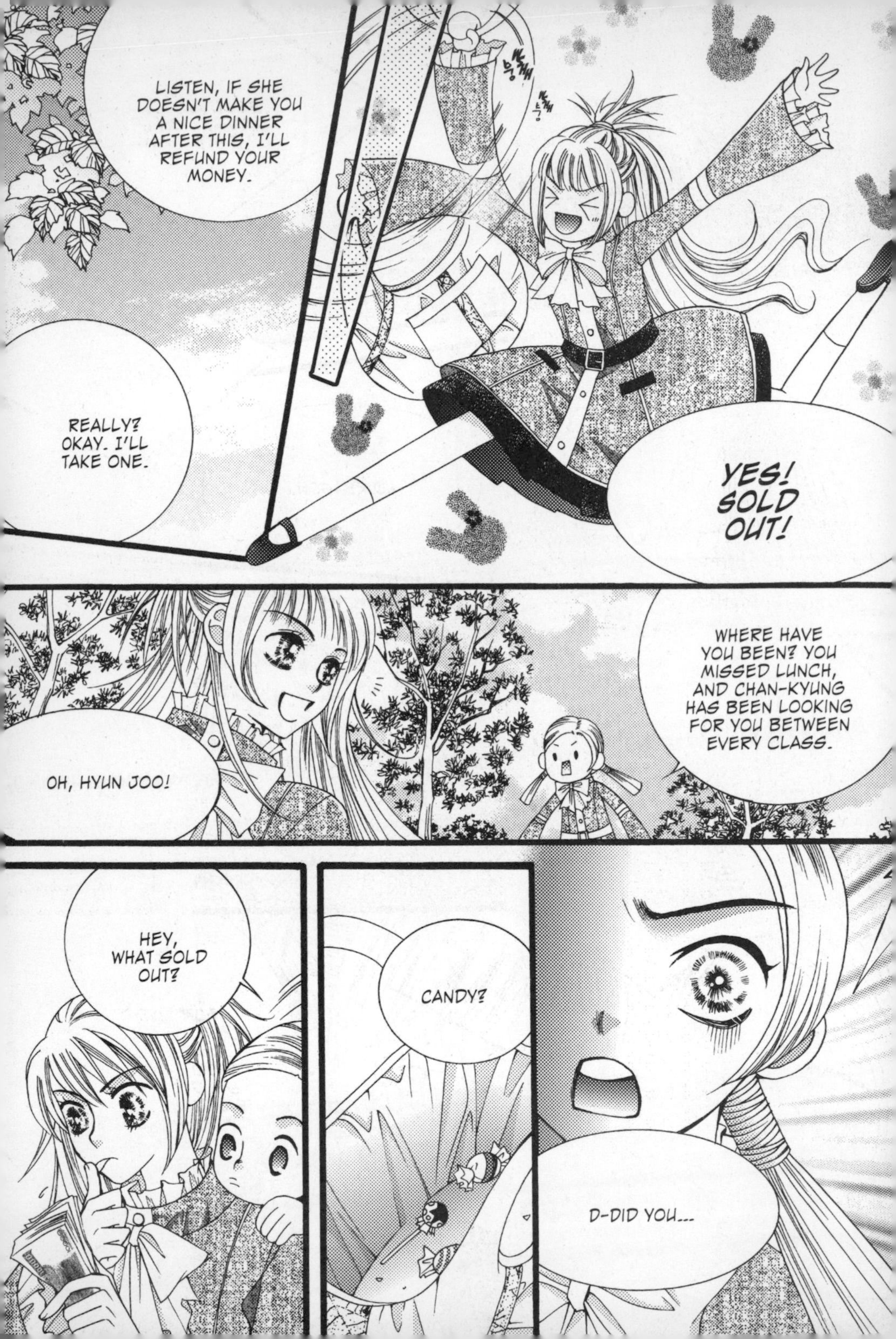

LISTEN, IF SHE DOESN'T MAKE YOU A NICE DINNER AFTER THIS, I'LL REFUND YOUR MONEY.
REALLY? OKAY. I'LL TAKE ONE.
YES! SOLD OUT!
OH, HYUN JOO!
WHERE HAVE YOU BEEN? YOU MISSED LUNCH, AND CHAN-KYUNG HAS BEEN LOOKING FOR YOU BETWEEN EVERY CLASS.
HEY, WHAT SOLD OUT?
CANDY?
D-DID YOU...

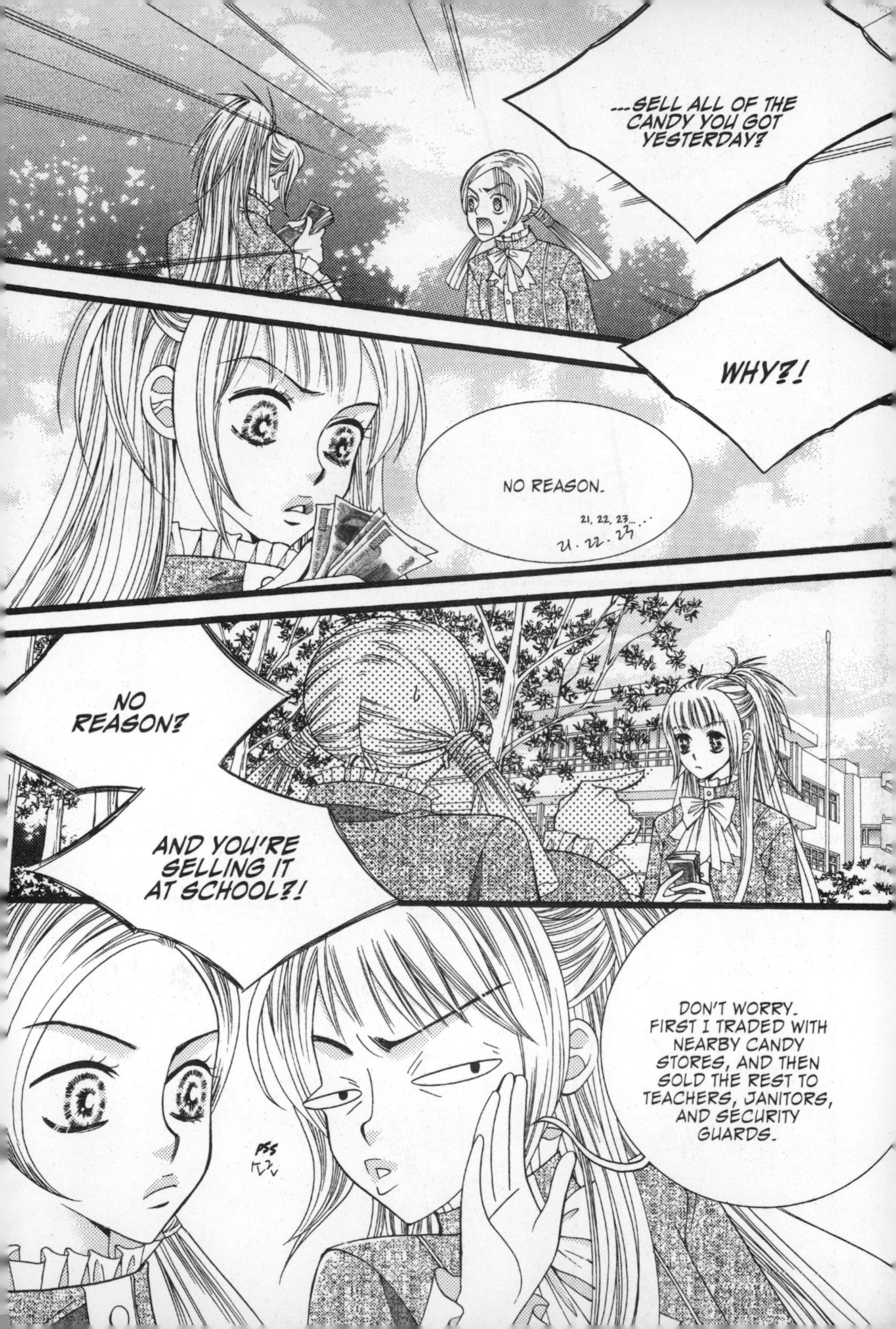
...SELL ALL OF THE CANDY YOU GOT YESTERDAY?
WHY?!
NO REASON.
21, 22, 23...
NO REASON?
AND YOU'RE SELLING IT AT SCHOOL?!
PSS
DON'T WORRY. FIRST I TRADED WITH NEARBY CANDY STORES, AND THEN SOLD THE REST TO TEACHERS, JANITORS, AND SECURITY GUARDS.

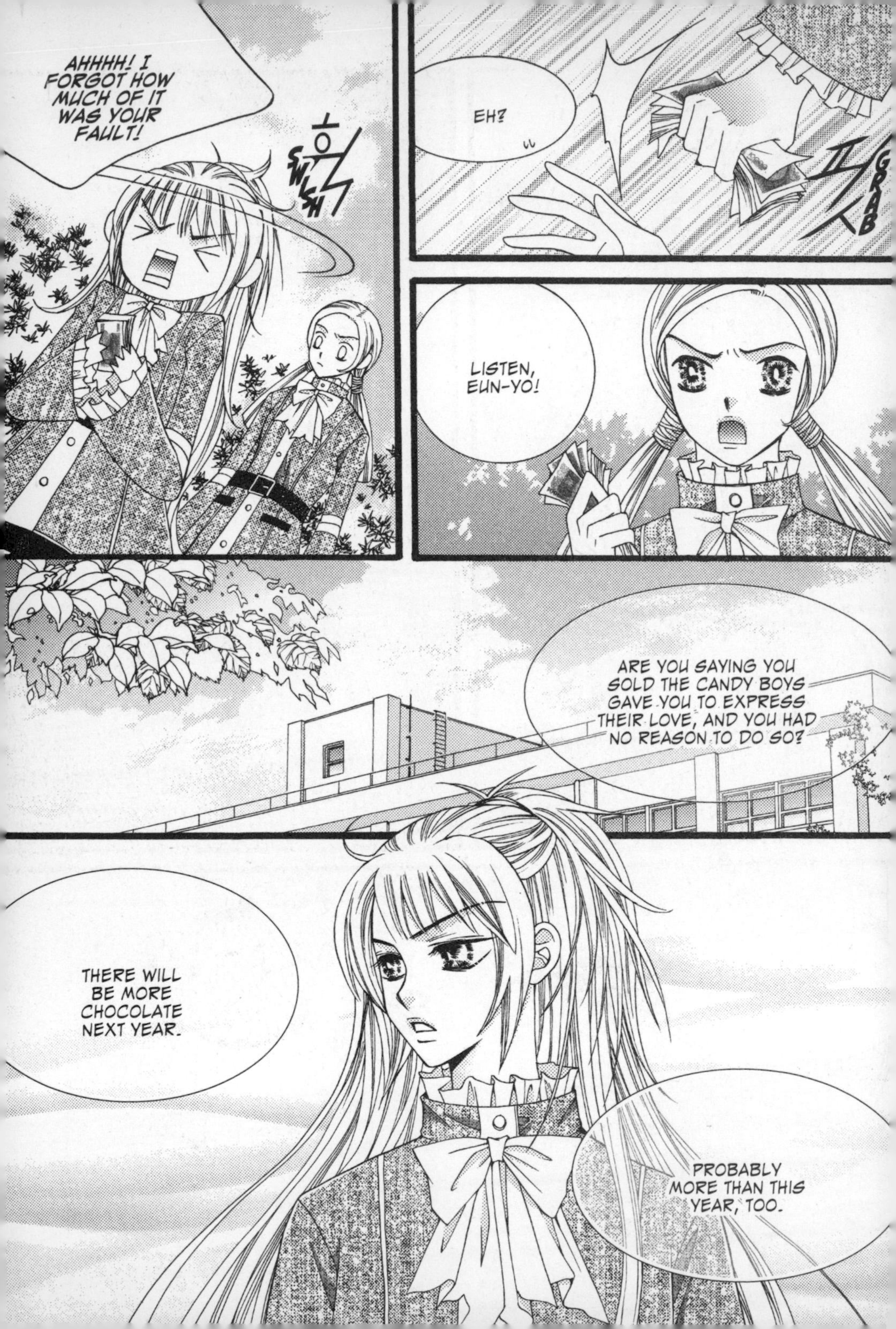
AHHHH! I FORGOT HOW MUCH OF IT WAS YOUR FAULT!
SWISH
EH?
GRAB
LISTEN, EUN-YO!
ARE YOU SAYING YOU SOLD THE CANDY BOYS GAVE YOU TO EXPRESS THEIR LOVE, AND YOU HAD NO REASON TO DO SO?
THERE WILL BE MORE CHOCOLATE NEXT YEAR.
PROBABLY MORE THAN THIS YEAR, TOO.

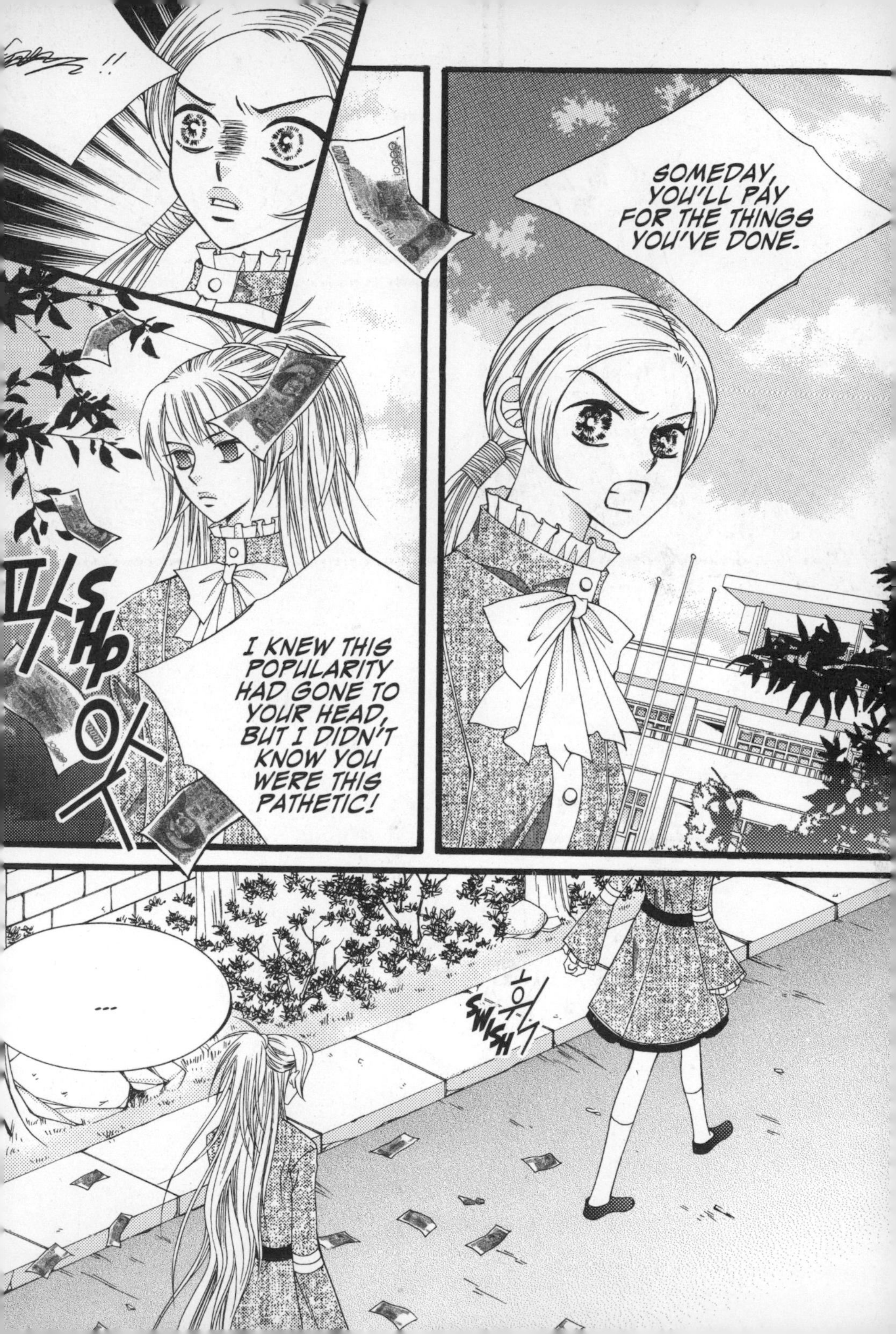
SHP
I KNEW THIS POPULARITY HAD GONE TO YOUR HEAD, BUT I DIDN'T KNOW YOU WERE THIS PATHETIC!
SOMEDAY, YOU'LL PAY FOR THE THINGS YOU'VE DONE.
...
SWISH

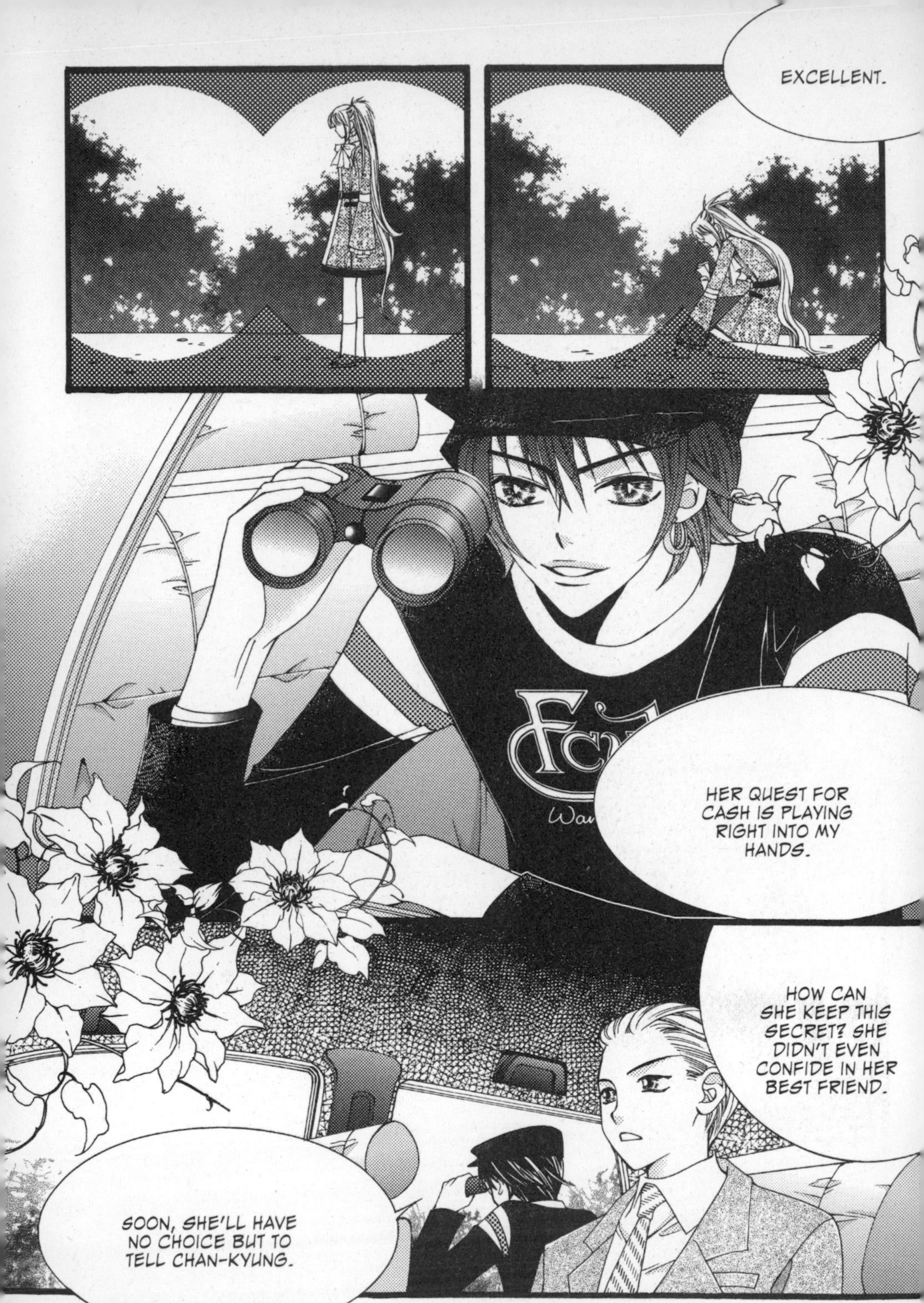
EXCELLENT.
HER QUEST FOR CASH IS PLAYING RIGHT INTO MY HANDS.
HOW CAN SHE KEEP THIS SECRET? SHE DIDN'T EVEN CONFIDE IN HER BEST FRIEND.
SOON, SHE'LL HAVE NO CHOICE BUT TO TELL CHAN-KYUNG.

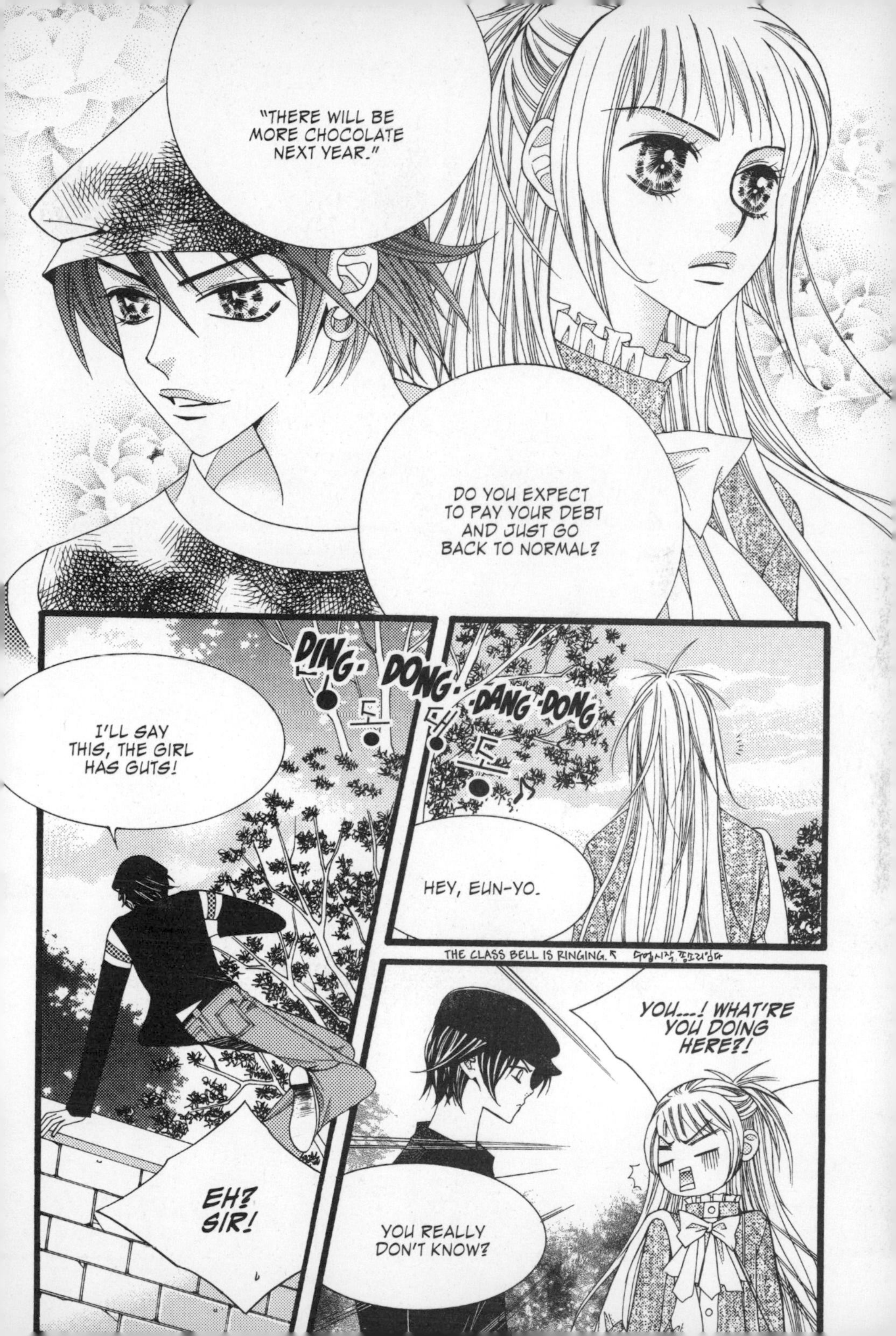
"THERE WILL BE MORE CHOCOLATE NEXT YEAR."
DO YOU EXPECT TO PAY YOUR DEBT AND JUST GO BACK TO NORMAL?
I'LL SAY THIS, THE GIRL HAS GUTS!
EH? SIR!
DING-DONG-DANG-DONG
HEY, EUN-YO.
THE CLASS BELL IS RINGING. ↖ 수업시작.종소리임다
YOU...! WHAT'RE YOU DOING HERE?!
YOU REALLY DON'T KNOW?

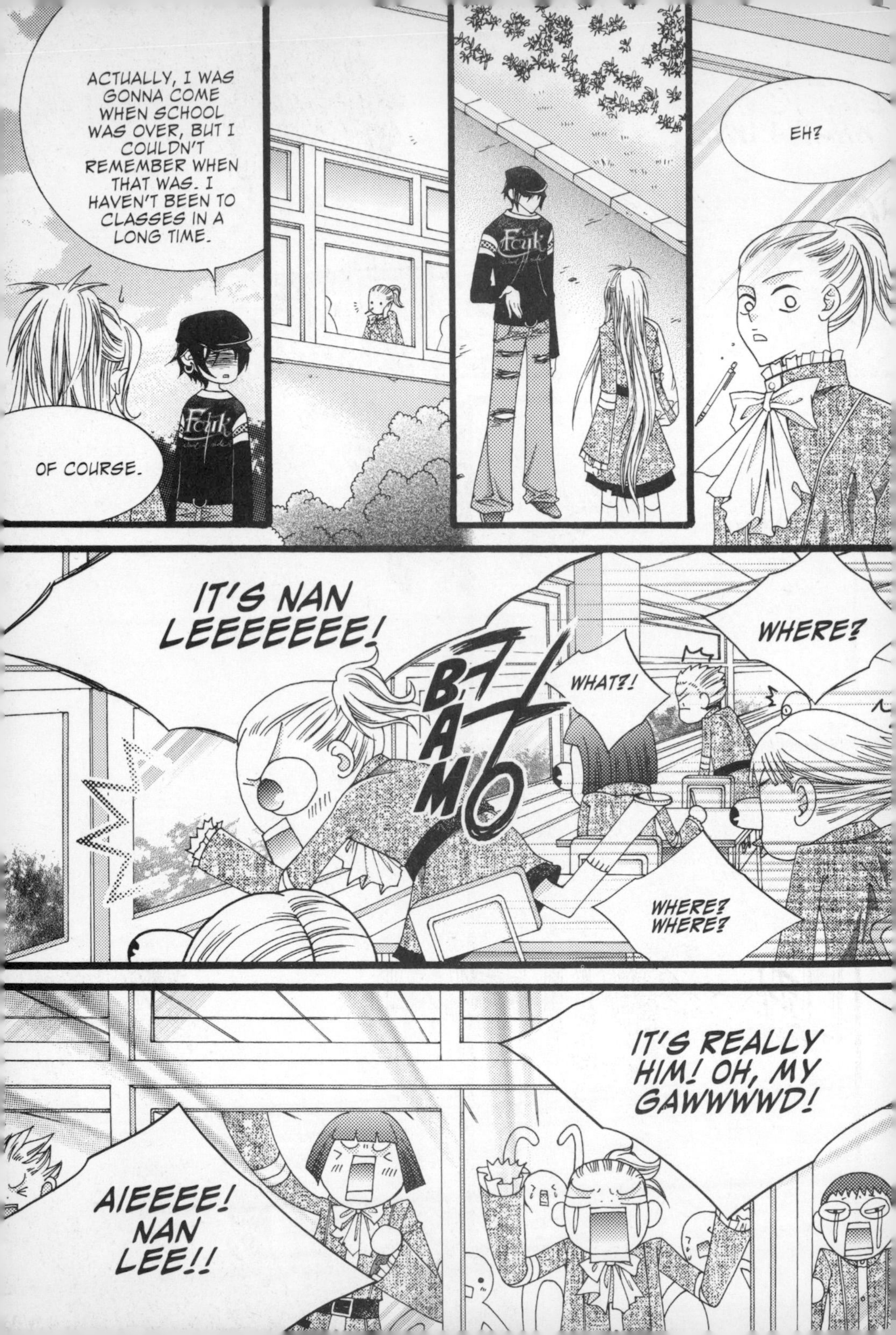
ACTUALLY, I WAS GONNA COME WHEN SCHOOL WAS OVER, BUT I COULDN'T REMEMBER WHEN THAT WAS. I HAVEN'T BEEN TO CLASSES IN A LONG TIME.
OF COURSE.
EH?
IT'S NAN LEEEEEEEE!
BAM
WHAT?!
WHERE?
WHERE? WHERE?
IT'S REALLY HIM! OH, MY GAWWWWD!
AIEEEE! NAN LEE!!

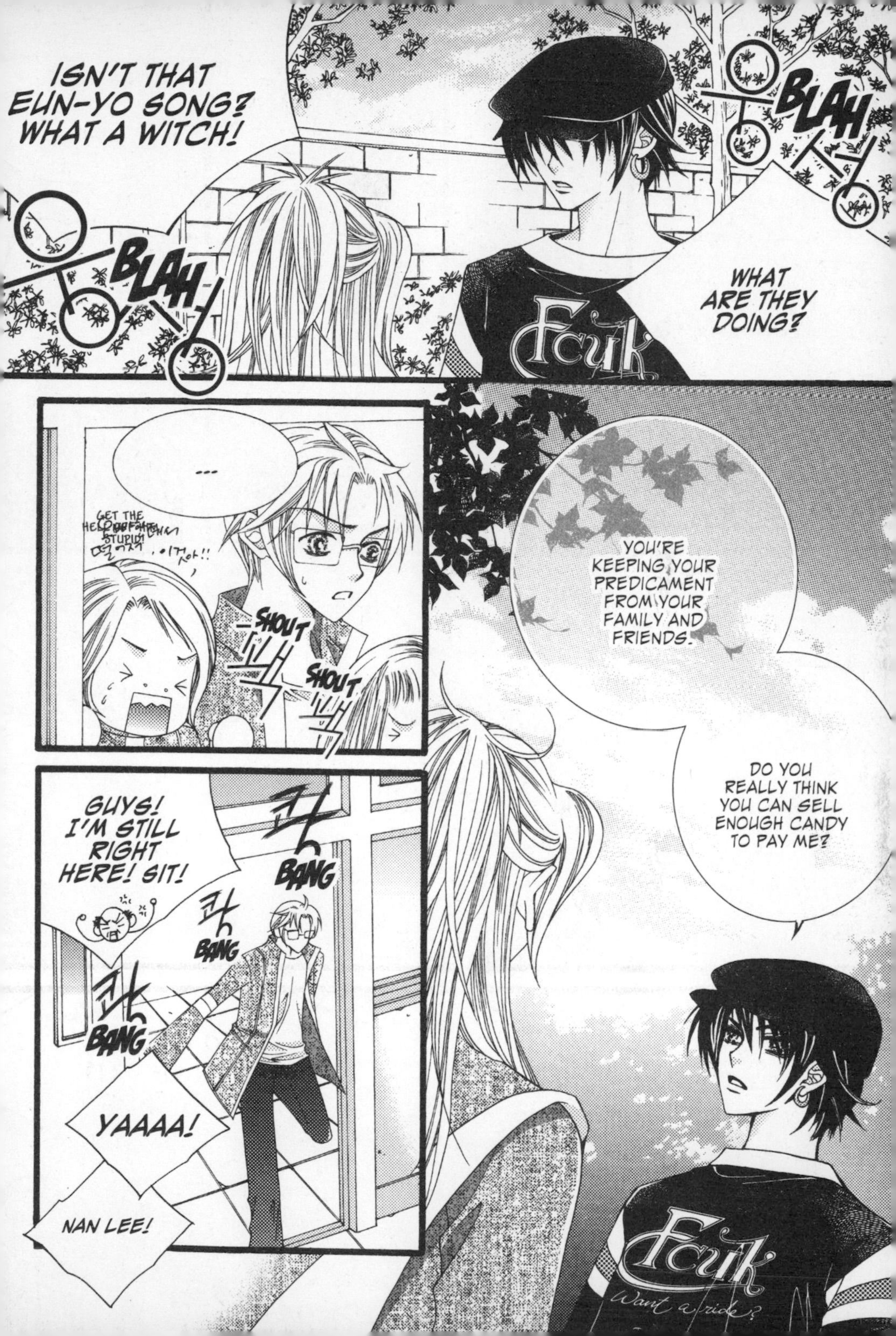
ISN'T THAT EUN-YO SONG? WHAT A WITCH!
BLAH
BLAH
WHAT ARE THEY DOING?
FCUK
...
GET THE
STUPID!
SHOUT
SHOUT
GUYS! I'M STILL RIGHT HERE! SIT!
BANG
BANG
BANG
YAAAA!
NAN LEE!
YOU'RE KEEPING YOUR PREDICAMENT FROM YOUR FAMILY AND FRIENDS.
DO YOU REALLY THINK YOU CAN SELL ENOUGH CANDY TO PAY ME?
FCUK
Want a ride?

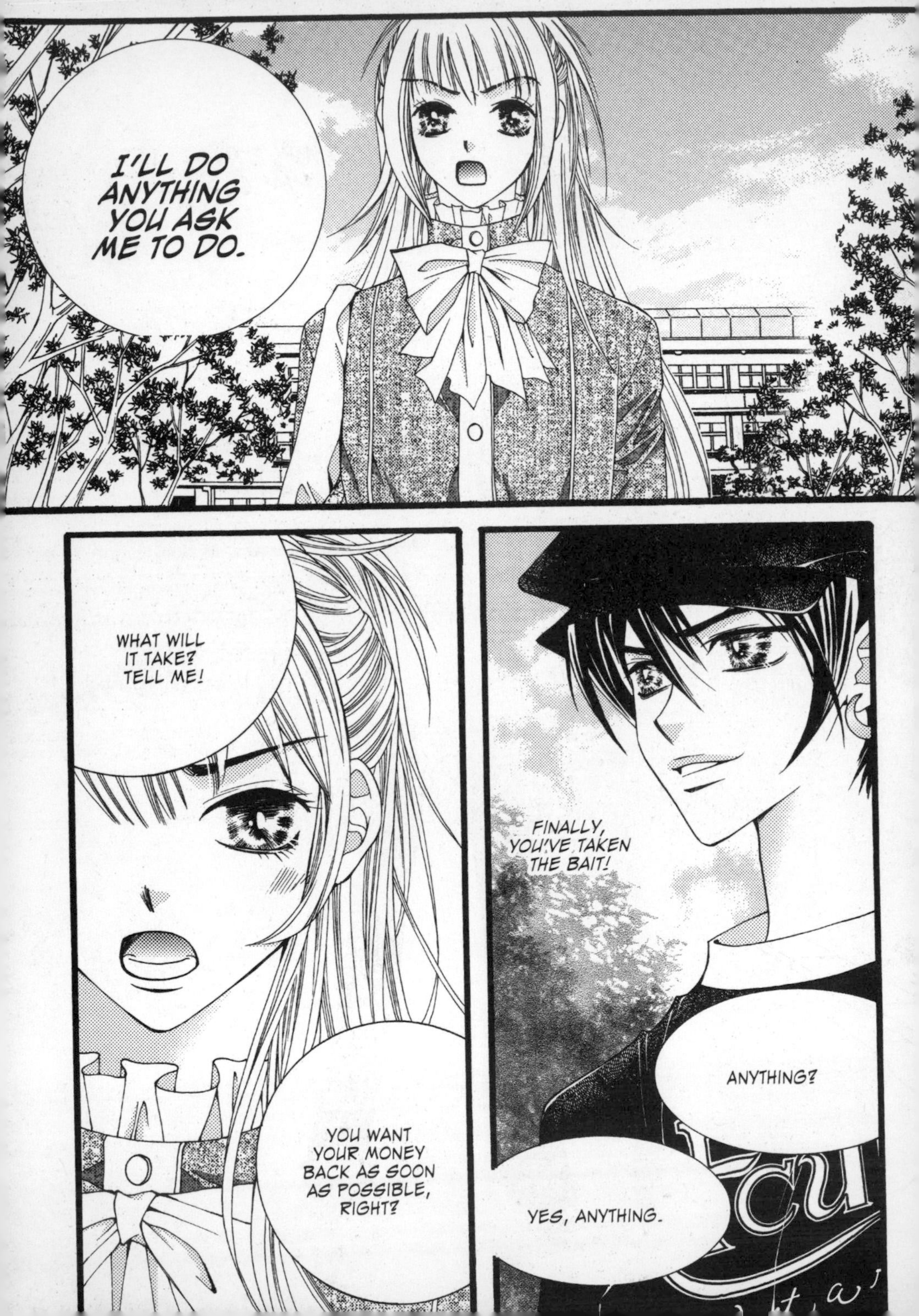
I'LL DO ANYTHING YOU ASK ME TO DO.
WHAT WILL IT TAKE? TELL ME!
YOU WANT YOUR MONEY BACK AS SOON AS POSSIBLE, RIGHT?
FINALLY, YOU'VE TAKEN THE BAIT!
ANYTHING?
YES, ANYTHING.

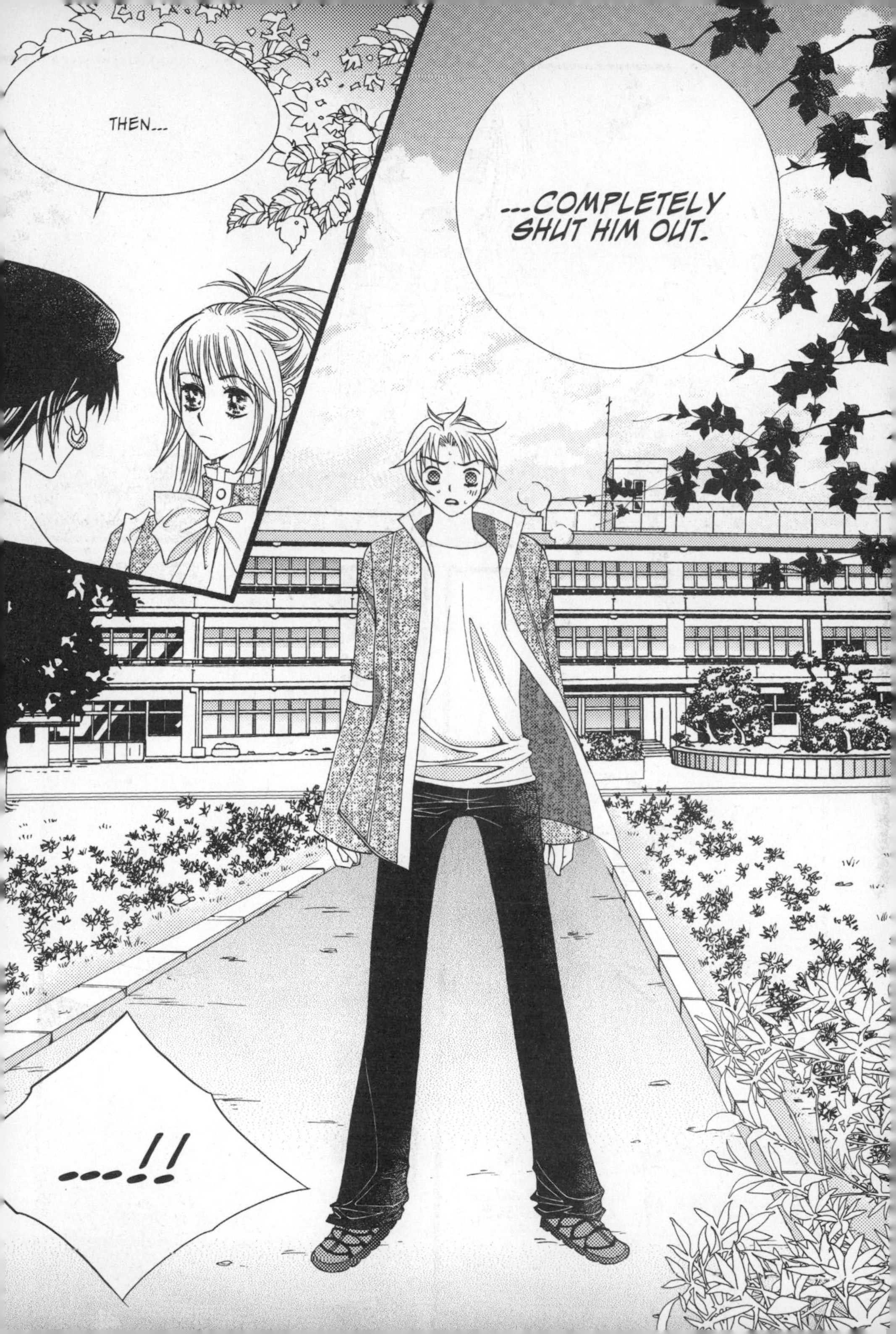
THEN...
...COMPLETELY SHUT HIM OUT.
...!!

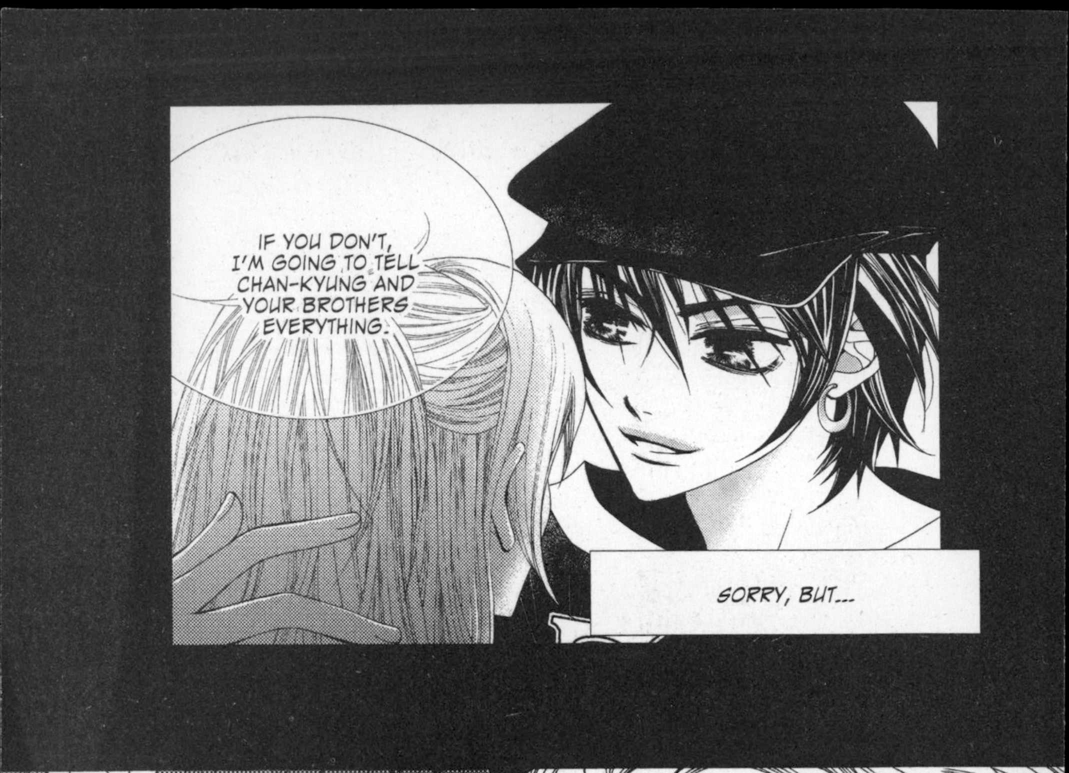
IF YOU DON'T, I'M GOING TO TELL CHAN-KYUNG AND YOUR BROTHERS EVERYTHING.
SORRY, BUT...

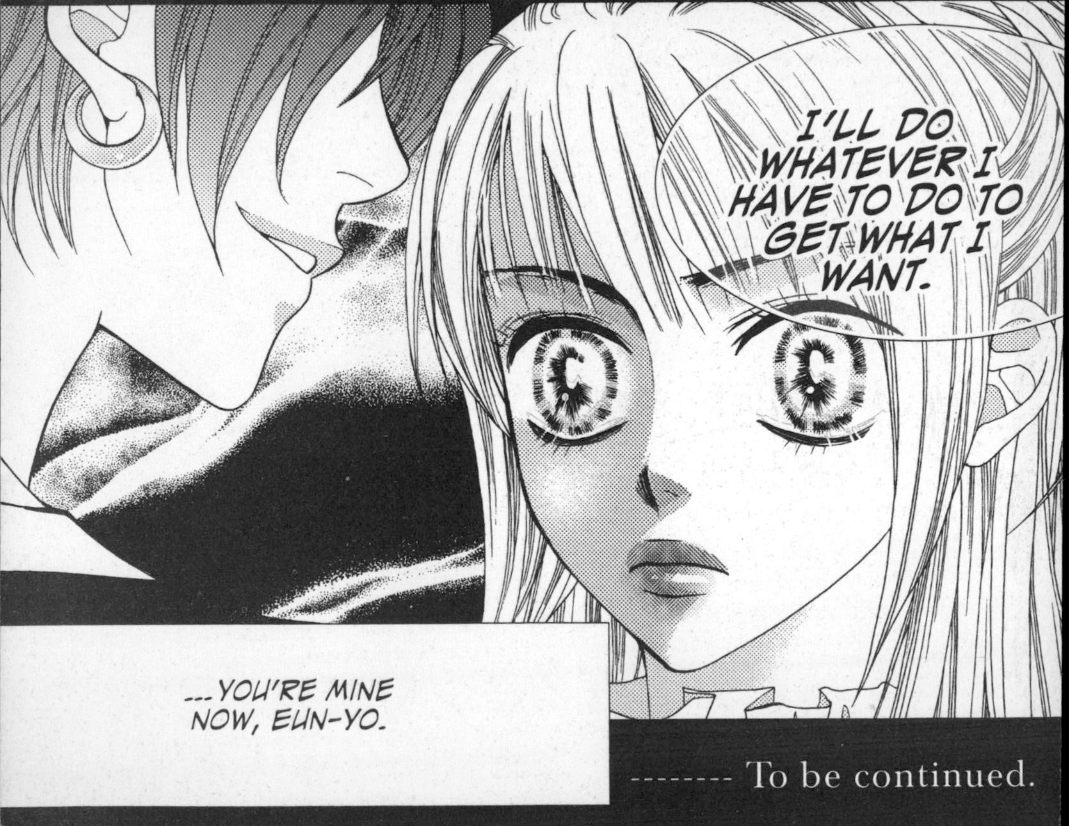
I'LL DO WHATEVER I HAVE TO DO TO GET WHAT I WANT.
...YOU'RE MINE NOW, EUN-YO.

-------- To be continued.

NEXT ISSUE!

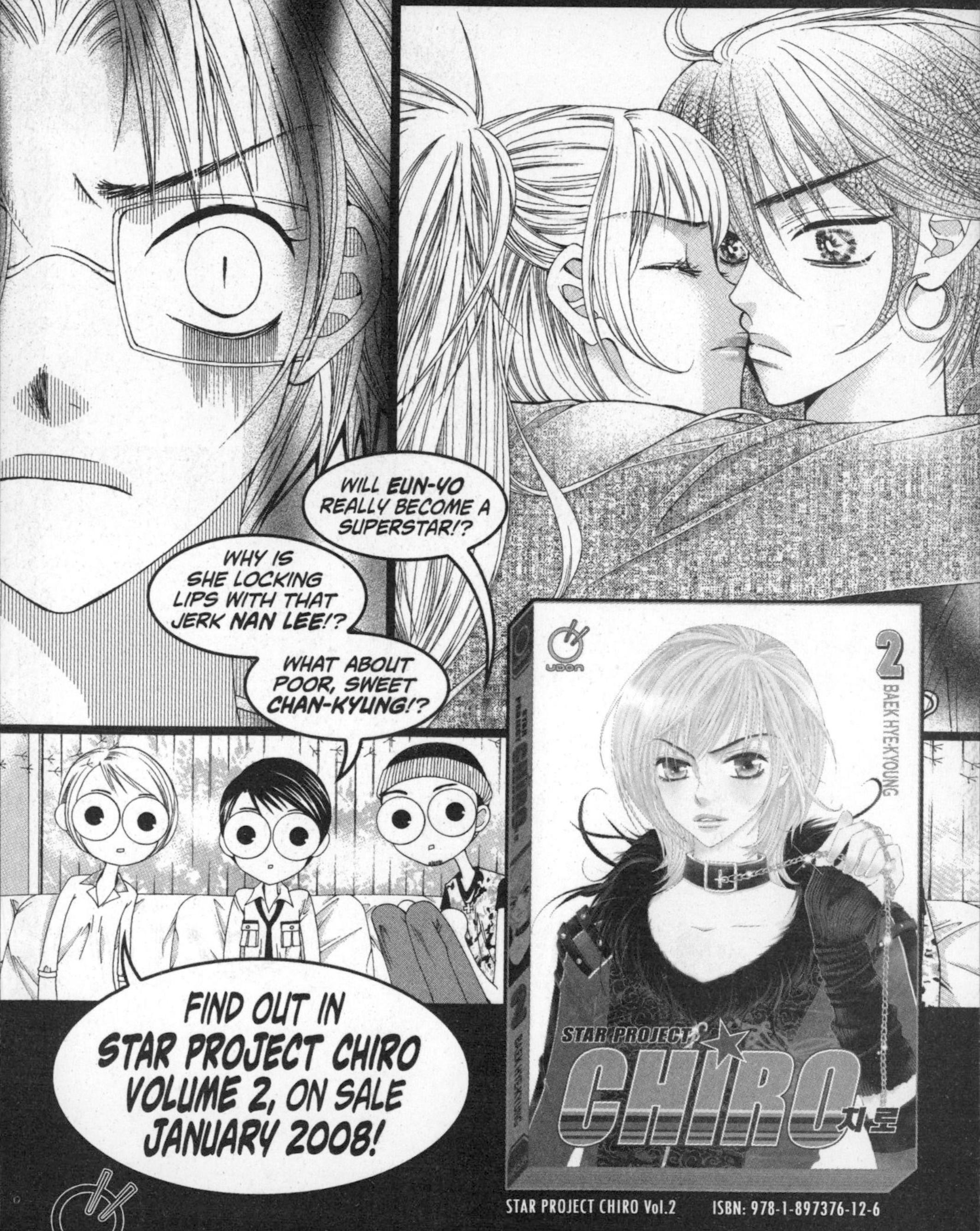

WILL EUN-YO REALLY BECOME A SUPERSTAR!?
WHY IS SHE LOCKING LIPS WITH THAT JERK NAN LEE!?
WHAT ABOUT POOR, SWEET CHAN-KYUNG!?
FIND OUT IN STAR PROJECT CHIRO VOLUME 2, ON SALE JANUARY 2008!
2
BAEK HYE-KYOUNG
STAR PROJECT CHIRO

STAR PROJECT CHIRO Vol.2 ISBN: 978-1-897376-12-6

WWW.KOREANMANHWA.COM

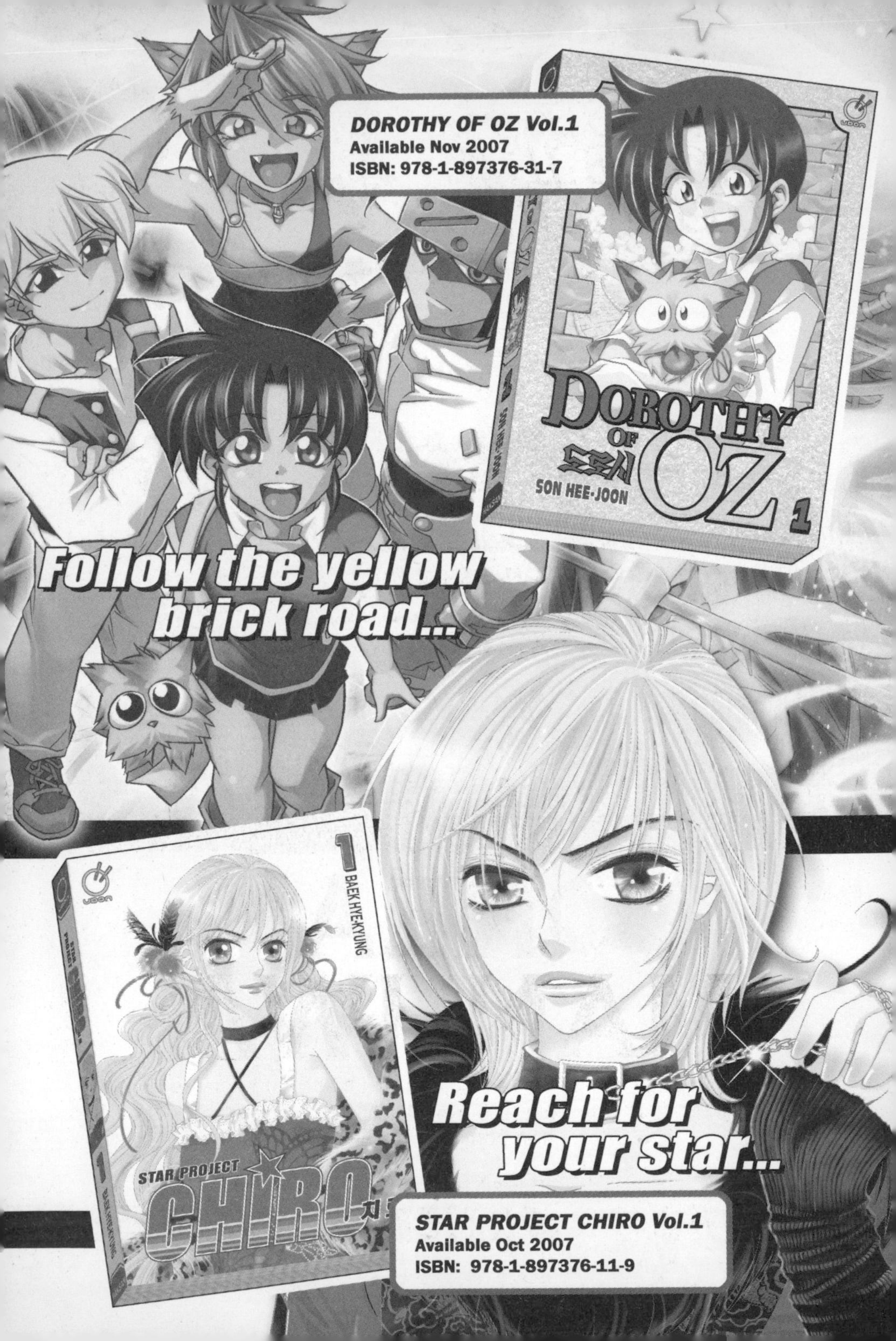

DOROTHY OF OZ Vol.1
Available Nov 2007
ISBN: 978-1-897376-31-7
DOROTHY OF OZ
SON HEE-JOON
1
Follow the yellow brick road...
1
BAEK HYE-KYUNG
STAR PROJECT CHIRO
Reach for your star...
STAR PROJECT CHIRO Vol.1
Available Oct 2007
ISBN: 978-1-897376-11-9

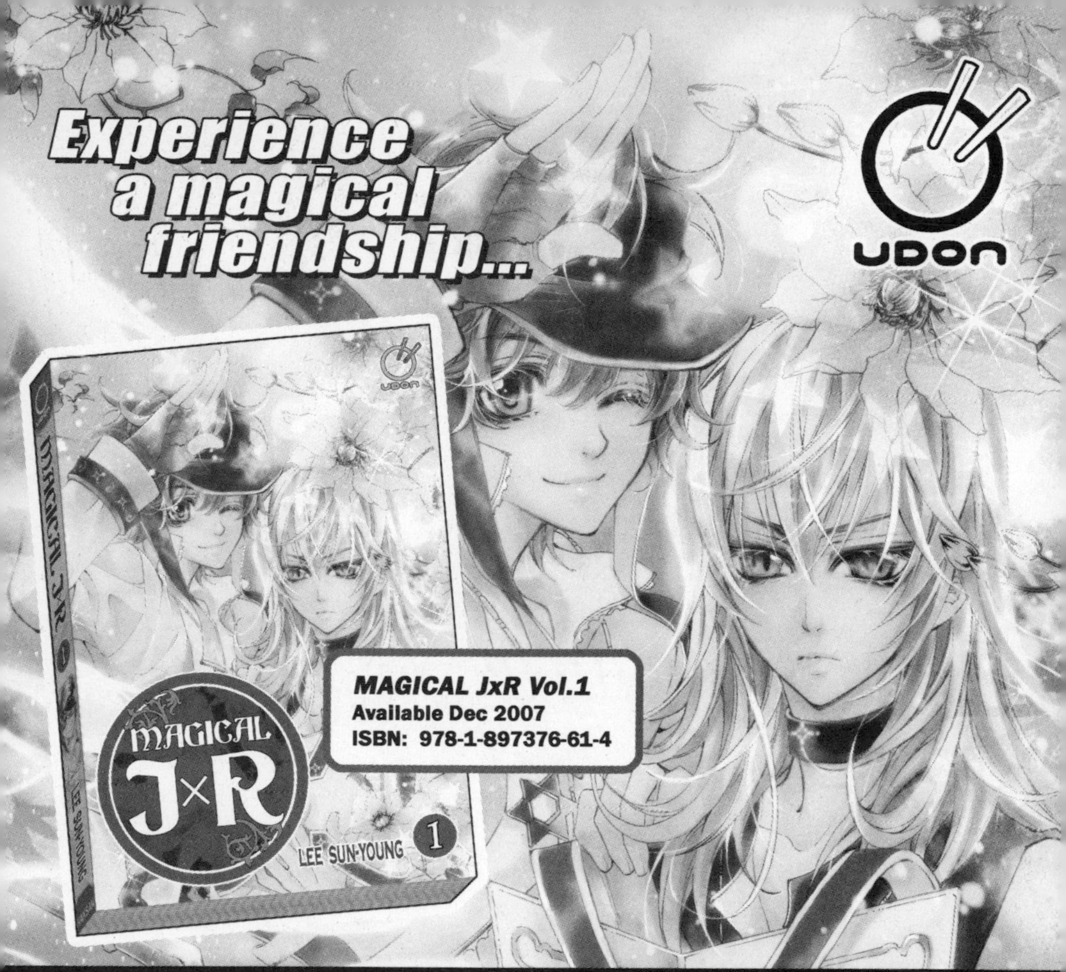
Experience a magical friendship...
UDON
MAGICAL JxR
LEE SUN-YOUNG
1
MAGICAL JxR Vol.1
Available Dec 2007
ISBN: 978-1-897376-61-4

STAR PROJECT CHIRO Volume 1

Story and Art : Baek Hye-Kyoung

English Translations : Ji-Eun Park
English Adaptations : Jamie S. Rich

Editorial Consultant: J. Torres
Coordinating Editor: Hye-Young Im

Lettering : Marshall Dillon with Terri Delgado

Cover & Graphic Design :
Erik Ko with Matt Moylan

English Logo : Alex Chung

STAR PROJECT CHIRO #1
©2007 BAEK HYE-KYOUNG.
All Rights Reserved. First published in Korea by
Haksan Publishing Co., Ltd. This translation rights
arranged with Haksan Publishing Co., Ltd. through
Shinwon Agency Co. in Korea.

English launguage version produced and published by UDON Entertainment Corp.
P.O. Box 32662, P.O. Village Gate, Richmond Hill, Ontario, L4X 0A2, Canada.
www.udonentertainment.com
First Printing: September 2007   ISBN-13:978-1-897376-51-5   ISBN-10:1-897376-51-0
Printed in Canada

STAR PROJECT CHIRO 치로

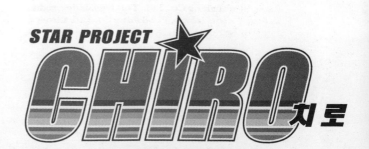

...... CONTINUED FROM THE BACK COVER:

HEY, WHAT GIVES...!!
BANK OF MEOW
ONE
FISH
MEW-MEW

STAR PROJECT CHIRO 치로

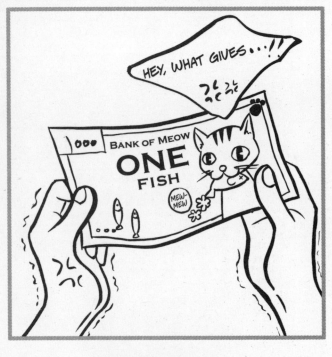

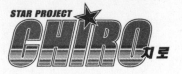